Pig in the Middle

by the same author

BITTER ORANGE (*Hutchinson*)

DESMOND HAMILL

Pig in the Middle
The Army in
Northern Ireland
1969 – 1984

Methuen London

First published in Great Britain 1985
by Methuen London Ltd
11 New Fetter Lane, London EC4P 4EE
Reprinted 1985
Copyright © Desmond Hamill 1985
Photoset in 11 point Times by 𝍖 Tek-Art, Croydon, Surrey
Printed in Great Britain by
Richard Clay (The Chaucer Press) Ltd,
Bungay, Suffolk

British Library Cataloguing in Publication Data

Hamill, Desmond
   Pig in the Middle : the army in Northern
   Ireland 1969–1984.
   1. Northern Ireland — History — 1969-
   2. Northern Ireland — History, Military
   I. Title
   941.60824   DA990.U46

   ISBN 0 413 50800 5

For Brigid, Sean and Sara

Contents

	List of Illustrations	ix
	Preface	xi
PROLOGUE	12 - 14 August 1969: Londonderry	1
PHASE ONE	August 1969 - April 1970: The honeymoon	8
PHASE TWO	April 1970 - August 1971: It starts to get rough	33
PHASE THREE	September 1971 - February 1972: The Army forces the pace	68
PHASE FOUR	February 1972 - July 1972: A can of worms	95
PHASE FIVE	July 1972 - May 1974: A shooting war won – a political battle lost	118
PHASE SIX	May 1974 - April 1976: The uneasy stirrings of 'police primacy'	159
PHASE SEVEN	May 1976 - February 1978: The police take a high-risk profile	191

PHASE EIGHT   March 1978 - August 1979:   224
               The Provisionals strike back –
               the Army wants control

PHASE NINE   September 1979 - August 1984:   251
               The Army steadies itself –
               the withdrawal continues

               Postscript   283
               Maps   284
               Bibliography   287
               Glossary   291
               Index   302

List of Illustrations

PLATES

between pages 84 and 85
1   **a** B Specials are pulled out as troops come in.
     b Soldiers shelter behind a Pig.
2   A patrol moves cautiously along William Street.
3   **a** Abuse in the Bogside July 1971.
     b Women stage an anti-internment demonstration.
4   A policeman frees two Catholic girls.
5   A quiet moment during a Catholic protest march in Belfast.
6   One soldier watches for bricks and bottles, the other watches
     for a sniper.
7   **a** and **b** An afternoon in William Street, Londonderry.
8   **a** and **b** A soldier endures stoning.

between pages 212 and 213
9   Soldiers deal with a riot in Londonderry.
10   **a** and **b** An injured officer is rescued by his men.
11   Police and army casualties are evacuated from the border area.
12   **a** and **b** IRA gunmen display their weapons, 1979 and 1980.
13   Girls scream abuse at soldiers.
14   An anonymous bomb disposal expert walks alone to defuse a
     fire bomb.
15   A bomb disposal expert defuses a bomb planted in a petrol
     tanker.
16   Sean Downes is fatally injured by a baton round during
     disturbances in Belfast.

CARTOONS
by Cummings *page 9*; by Mahood *page 30*; by Rowel Friers *page
32*; by Martyn Turner *page 48*; by Mac *page 67*; by Rowel Friers
page 83; by David Langdon *page 119*; by Ivor *page 163*; by Cummings
page 170; by Mahood *page 196*; by Martyn Turner *page 225*; by
Rowel Friers *page 268*.

MAPS
Northern Ireland *page 284*; Belfast *page 285*; Londonderry *page 286*.

Acknowledgements and thanks for permission to reproduce photographs are due to Clive Limpkin for plates 1a, 1b, 2, 5, 6, 7a, 7b, 8a and 8b; to the *Daily Mail* for plates 9, 11, 14, 15 and 16 (by Alan Lewis); to the Press Association for plates 3a and 3b; and to Pacemaker for plates 4, 10a, 10b, 12a, 12b and 13.

The cartoons on pages 30, 119, and 196 are reproduced by kind permission of *Punch*; and the cartoons on pages 9 and 170 are reproduced by kind permission of the *Daily Express*.

The cartoon by Martyn Turner on page 48 first appeared in *Fortnight Magazine* and that on page 225 in the *Irish Times*.

The cartoon by Rowel Friers on page 83 first appeared in the *Belfast Telegraph* and that on page 268 in the *Irish Times*.

The maps were drawn by Neil Hyslop.

Preface

What I set out to do with this book was to show how the Army itself saw and understood its role in Northern Ireland since 1969. By 'the Army' I mean the military forces from all arms who came from the United Kingdom as a whole, rather than the province itself, to operate 'in aid of the civil power'. To do this, I examined contemporary papers and documents and contacted a wide range of people who were connected with military matters in Northern Ireland. Some refused to talk, some were reluctant, but most decided that it would be worth trying to put their view, provided it was on a non-attributable basis. That is why so many of the quotations and points of view are unsourced. By remaining anonymous, however, those I talked to, and soldiers in particular, felt they were able to talk more freely, and their stories are the basis of this book.

There are, of course, some areas and subjects which have been left out — either deliberately, or through lack of knowledge. But then *Pig in the Middle* does not pretend to be an exhaustive account of this period, but rather one which, by introducing for the first time an 'Army view', makes the period more intelligible.

Desmond Hamill   Windlesham August 1984

Prologue

Londonderry
12–14 August 1969

The marching season was under way. All day long the massed lines of 15,000 Protestant Apprentice Boys had marched through the city. Bowler-hatted, umbrella-armed, their dark suits slashed with the brightness of the Purple Sash, they swung along with impeccable discipline to the music of flute, pipe and accordian bands and the stirring words of 'The Sash' and 'Derry's Walls'. Many of the onlookers were dressed for the occasion, the men in their Sunday-best suits and with their wives on their arms, commemorating the deeds of their predecessors who, in 1689, stormed the gates in the face of King James II's invading army.

Towards the end of the celebrations the Protestant crowds came out on to the ramparts of the ancient city of Londonderry where the towering walls brushed against the edge of the Catholic Bogside. Here they stood and gazed down at the Bogsiders below. A few pennies were tossed down. It was a traditionally arrogant gesture, and those below knew quite well what it meant. The smouldering antagonism of years burst into flames as they answered back. Stones, bricks and even marbles fired from catapults came soaring up towards the Protestant watchers.

A more recent memory also angered the Bogsiders: while their traditional marches had been banned, those of the Protestants had not. Four months previously they had defied this ban. Then, in preparation for the expected arrival of the Royal Ulster Constabulary (RUC), they had started to barricade the approaches to the Bogside. At midnight they had yet to finish this work. As Bernadette Devlin, newly-elected Westminster Member of

Parliament for Mid-Ulster, recalled:

Suddenly a boy yelled, 'My God! They're coming!' Everyone stopped dead. It was one of the most horrific sights I have seen. High above us the city wall was lined with a great mass of silent people. Slowly the mass started to move, down through the walls, into the two roads not yet barricaded, and when the two battalions of police met, they joined forces and started to stomp towards us, beating their shields with their batons and howling dreadfully in the manner of savages trying to intimidate their foes. Before this everybody just fled.

Now, on this August afternoon, the Bogsiders were better prepared for the arrival of the RUC as the violence increased and spread. Barricades were already in position, built of planks, paving stones, furniture, scaffolding and anything else that was to hand. The police moved between the Catholic and Protestant factions and for a while endured the shower of missiles. Then they charged, rattling their batons on their riot shields, in order to clear a space immediately below the city walls. Some Protestant bystanders joined in the retaliation to the Catholic missiles. A police armoured car was set on fire. The two sides were not only in place but ready for battle.

A tall building dominates Rossville Street, the entrance to the Bogside. Above it floated the Irish tricolour and the Starry Plough, the flag of James Connolly's citizen army of 1916, and here, on the rooftop, open-air petrol bomb factories were set up. They were kept supplied by children, who also threw the petrol bombs down on to the police below every time they tried to pass. Other than by shooting them off the rooftop, there was no way that the police could get rid of them. As darkness fell and the battle raged on into the night, the sky was lit by burning buildings. Bernadette Devlin roamed the barricades, breaking up paving stones and encouraging the defenders. From radios came Republican music and exhortations to 'Keep the murderers out. Don't weaken now. Make every stone and petrol bomb count.'

On the other side of the barricades, along the shifting front line, 5 platoon of the RUC Reserve from Mountpottinger Police Station in Belfast was on duty. There was a head constable with four sergeants, nineteen constables and four special constables. That they had been brought so far was a measure of how stretched the police resources had become. With the rest of the police they were in the thick of it. In police headquarters senior officers listened anxiously to the crackle of messages being passed between units.

> *Black One to Sierra:* I fancy the position now is that if we withdraw and go back down William Street here, the crowd will come out of Abbey Street and also the top of the street and turn round and follow us down and stone us again at the end of Rossville Street — which would be a worse position as far as we are concerned. Over.
>
> *Sierra to Black One:* The object was to try and regroup and do something about the crowd in Rossville Street and we can't hold too long a front unless we get some more men in there on foot. Over.
>
> *Green Two:* We are getting it fierce tight here but we'll have to win this war.
>
> *Black Five:* We're on fire! Tight at the corner of William Street and she's not making much shape at the barrier. We've had four goes at it but we haven't got through yet. They are right on top of us but we are keeping at it and ready to go in. If we break the barrier we are home and dry.

Standing in the shadows, two officers watched the fighting: Graham Shillington, deputy inspector general of the RUC, and Lieutenant-Colonel W.A.E. Todd, commanding officer of the Prince of Wales Own Regiment, one of the province's three garrison battalions. Todd was not in uniform, but if the military were called in it would be his men who would move out on to the street. Shillington had decided that the situation was so grave that he had come from Belfast to make a personal assessment on the spot. In the light of burning buildings he could make out a crowd of some four hundred people exchanging stones and missiles with another crowd about half the size. In between, to his dismay, he could see some very tired policemen trying to hold them apart. He knew most had been on their feet since eight o'clock that morning. They had been told to bring sandwiches and flasks of tea, but there had been no substantial food all day and it was clear that they could not go on much longer. The radio waves were still crackling with streams of messages.

> *Green Two to Sierra:* Come on! Send all available armour to the junction of Rossville Street and let's have a go if we break through here. Over.
>
> *Sierra to Green One:* Watch! There are some trenches dug on those roads. There's a manhole cover lifted. Watch! Tell the barricade breakers to watch these points. Over.
>
> . . .let's have all support in Lecky Road and let's finish them off. Come on!
>
> *Green One:* You are on fire! Consolidate. Consolidate what you have there. Don't go any further than Fox's Corner. . .Can we have more

support immediately and we will hold this place? Over.
. . .can we get more foot people in there? Over.
. . .come on armour! Come on armour!

Both Shillington and Todd were thinking about using tear gas (CS gas), a choking, smarting gas which would incapacitate the rioters by flooding their eyes with tears. Todd had already issued some of his own supplies, and more from the ordnance depot, to the police.

'What are your feelings?' the policeman asked the soldier, for he was not expert in its use. 'What do you think of the wind and weather conditions?'

The soldier looked up into the darkness and felt the wind. 'Very suitable,' he replied.

The policeman nodded. It was up to him to take the decision, but he first had to get clearance from the Northern Ireland Home Affairs Minister at Stormont. As he was doing this at Victoria Barracks, the radio messages were still coming in.

Green One to Black Five: Armour right! Get in front of me. We'll smash the barrier out in Abbey Street. Any Land Rovers still available in Green unit follow me in. We'll smash it out first and then nip out quick and then we'll have another sortie if we get away with it. Over.
Two to One: This is Little Diamond, the barrier, just for your information. Over.
Green One to Green Two: I know bloody fine where it is but I'm not going to stick me head in a noose. We go in, smash up and get out toute bloody suite. Out.

At 2 a.m. the tear gas was fired. As it happened, the wind was not very suitable, but the police did notice that the gas deterred rioters and that they withdrew slightly. With buildings blazing around them, the police advanced to hold a new front. They realised they could stay there only by using more CS gas, but very few of them had been issued with respirators, and as the wind gusted the gas back towards them they began to choke. In fact, most of the respirators were brand new and still in boxes with cardboard packing stuffed between the vents. Shillington watched all this as he walked along the city wall from which the pennies had been thrown the day before. He had a good view down into the Bogside and he could just make out the crowds milling around. Then an hour later, in the early summer dawn, he saw stones and bottles start to rain down once again on his weary men and realised that now the Army would have to be called in to help. Back at the police headquarters other reports – patchy and not very clear – were beginning to come in from other disturbances round the province.

As the day lightened, some of the weary and battered policemen in the city could see, across the River Foyle, Army vehicles moving into the grounds of the shore base Sea Eagle. It was a precautionary measure. In the Bogside a reporter for *The Times*, John Clare, climbed up the high building in Rossville Street.

> It was a ten-storey block lined by about forty teenagers, many girls. I counted eighteen milk crates, each containing twenty bottles half-full of petrol and with a piece of rag rammed down the neck. Girls aged 14 or 15 toiled up the stairs carrying crates of stones and bottles. After ten minutes I could hardly see with the tears running out of my eyes. In the courtyard behind the flats young people leant against the walls, weeping and choking. In a corner small boys aged 8 or 9 decanted petrol from a tin drum into milk bottles. As I made my way back to the police lines a fire-bomb burst four feet away. A policeman turned to me bitterly and said: 'That's what you call police brutality!' From the roof someone shouted: 'We are the people.'

During the day the Bogside remained in a state of siege and there was an attack on Rosemount police station, which was set on fire. A local civil rights leader and recently elected local MP for Stormont, John Hume, managed to arrange a truce whereby the RUC would agree to stop using tear gas if the rioters withdrew. The RUC also agreed not to force the barricades. More sectarian rioting broke out later that evening, however, and Catholic crowds found themselves being baton-charged by the police. Broadcasting that evening, the Northern Ireland Prime Minister, Major James Chichester-Clark, announced that he had recalled the Northern Ireland Parliament and that the B Specials (part-time policemen) would be used 'to the full, not for riot or crowd control but to relieve the regular police.' The following day, 8,500 B Specials were called up and ordered to report immediately for duty. The violence was continuing on into the third day.

Near the city walls 5 platoon, RUC Reserve, was still on duty. Tear gas swirled round them and they were constantly under attack. From time to time, when they had to move, two Humber vehicles gave them cover, but to hold any new position they had to use tear gas cartridges and grenades. As dusk had fallen the previous evening, they had had to withdraw a short distance, and by morning the rioters had regained their old positions in William Street and Little St James's Street. When Shillington did his rounds, he found his men almost overrun. Such was the pace of events that he was having difficulty in keeping up with exactly what was going on but he was certain of one thing: the number of policemen he had was totally inadequate for what was happening. He passed this message on to the Inspector General, Anthony Peacocke, in Belfast.

Peacocke was also a worried man. Reports were coming into his police headquarters at Knock of trouble breaking out all over the place. Barricades were being set up in the Falls Road in Belfast; in Coalisland a mob hurled petrol bombs into the police station; in Newry lorries and cars were being overturned and Catholic vigilantes were reported directing the traffic; there were clashes in Lurgan and Strabane; in Armagh the police station was under siege for half an hour, in Dungiven the station was attacked with stones and petrol bombs and a steady stream of women and children were reported crossing the border into the South.

Lack of policemen was not the only matter which worried Peacocke. He had in mind the legal requirements of the Government of Ireland Act — that all civil power should be deployed before the Army could be called in. Two weeks earlier, when the commissioner of police for Belfast had suggested that the time had indeed come — then — for the Army to be called in, he had found his political masters in the Goverment — totally dominated by the Protestant Unionist Party — not at all keen on the idea. They had been told quite clearly by Westminster that such a request would bring into question the whole position of the Stormont Goverment of Northern Ireland. This was something the Unionists wanted to avoid at all costs.

At midday, however, Peacocke decided that whatever the political restrictions or consequences, his men could not hold out any longer without help. He called for a meeting of the Security Committee and told them that control would be lost in Londonderry within a matter of minutes. The Army had already been warned, and at 4.45 p.m. Peacocke signed the official request for the Army to come to the aid of the civil power. In Stormont, Republican Labour MP Gerry Fitt — who was also an MP at Westminster — had just told the House that the Government of Northern Ireland no longer had any relevance in the affairs of the Irish people. All the Opposition members except one had already walked out when the Home Affairs Minister, Robert

Porter, rose to announce that troops had been deployed in Londonderry. In a quiet voice he said that the step had been taken with the full approval of the Governments of the United Kingdom and of Northern Ireland. In Westminster, the Home Secretary, James Callaghan, told Westminster MPs:

The General Officer Commanding Northern Ireland [the GOC] has been instructed to take all necessary steps, acting impartially between citizen and citizen, to restore law and order. Troops will be withdrawn as soon as this is accomplished. This is a limited operation and during it the troops will remain in direct and exclusive control of the GOC, who will continue to be responsible to the United Kingdom Government . . . The Ireland Act of 1949 affirms that neither Northern Ireland nor any part of it will in any event cease to be part of the United Kingdom without the consent of the Parliament of Northern Ireland, and the United Kingdom reaffirms the pledges previously given that this will remain the position so long as the people of Northern Ireland wish.

Phase One

The honeymoon
August 1969–April 1970

Ten miles from Belfast along the fast M1 motorway lies the small but busy town of Lisburn, the birthplace of the Irish linen industry. There is some light industry in the town, and on the rivers and lakes nearby some good coarse fishing. Conspicuous in the middle of the market square is a vigorous statue of General Nicholson, with pistol and sword, leading the attack on Delhi in 1857 in which he was killed at the age of 35.

Not far from the dashing general is Thiepval Barracks, headquarters of the Army in Northern Ireland, where the generals nowadays are rather older and face more complex problems — if only since 1969. Before that time the senior Army post — that of General Officer Commanding Northern Ireland — was traditionally one in which a general who enjoyed country pursuits could round off a good career. For here he could shoot, fish, hunt, play golf or follow any other of the country sports as well as engage in a busy social round. On the purely military side, all he had to do was to look after a brigade.

Newly installed in this pleasant post was Lieutenant-General Sir Ian Freeland. A trim, athletic-looking officer, he had once commanded an Irish regiment, the Royal Inniskilling Fusiliers. Irish history, however, had never been part of the syllabus for staff officers, and the roots of Irish problems lie tangled deep in the complexities of the past. It was not part of a modern officer's brief to know that Ireland had never been properly colonised or subjugated after the victories of Elizabeth I; that when James I had organised the plantation of Ulster in 1610 the Scots had already been

'Begorrah, I'll knock the living daylights out of that
other Christian to prove what a good Christian I am.'

coming across for centuries to settle in Antrim and Down. Mostly
from the lowlands, the Scots were thrifty, hard-working and dour;
they were also steeped in the stern doctrines of Calvinist teaching.
In the wild and wooded country all round them were the dispossessed
Catholics who staged an unexpected uprising in 1641 to try to regain
their land. Half a century later a Catholic king, James II, tried to do
this for them, but he was overthrown by revolution and chose to fight
his last battles at the River Boyne and at Aughrim. His defeat here

assured the Protestants that their lands would be safe — at least for the time being — but the battles confirmed for ever their fears of Catholic aspirations. Nor were the soldiers to know that the Byzantine twists and turns of Irish history meant that the Catholic Republicans who now faced them came in a line from Belfast Presbyterians who had originally sought their independence from Britain. For in 1791 it was they who had asked Wolfe Tone — one of Ireland's great fighters for freedom from England — to spend a few days in the city 'in order to assist in framing the first club of United Irishmen'.

Confrontation between Catholic and Protestant had been a way of life for decades and there was nothing new about sectarian riots in Belfast. As Andrew Boyd recalled in his book, *Holy War in Belfast:*

> On Sunday morning, 17 August, the streets around Millfield, the Pound, Shankill Road and Falls Road were in a state of utter desolation . . . everywhere pavements torn up. In some streets barricades had been erected and shops boarded up against attack. In every street which bordered on the Catholic and Protestant districts, pickets of armed police and soldiers stood guard.

That riot took place in 1872, and the inquiry which followed confirmed allegations of police partiality towards Protestants as well as unjustified aggression against Catholics.

When Westminster finally passed the Government of Ireland Act 1920, Ireland became politically divided for the first time, with the Irish Free State in the South and Ulster, in the North, remaining part of the United Kingdom. In the North this was the beginning of years of Unionist rule, for the province had been granted its own parliament — Stormont. Not only did this set the province apart from the rest of the United Kingdom, but it meant that there would be no control from the Central Government at Westminster over Northern Ireland affairs.

This did not bring an end to the troubles, for a reorganised Irish Republican Army — the IRA — began the fight to get the British out of the North and bring it into the Free State to form a thirty-two-county Ireland. It was Lord Brookeborough who first determined after the Easter Rising of 1916 in Dublin that such a thing would never happen in the North. He decided that a force was needed, properly equipped with weapons, to defend its own local areas. So the police auxiliaries, known as 'B Specials', came into being, first around Brookeborough itself — his country seat and family home — and then spreading out across the six counties of the North. They were to prove an obstacle for many an IRA operation, and Brookeborough and his men regarded most, if not all, Catholics as potential traitors.

It was no wonder, then, that the B Specials were much admired by the Protestants and that so many of them joined. But then, as in the late 1960s, they were largely an untrained, local 'vigilante' force although in uniform and with official sanction. They were hated and loathed by the Catholics, and Tim Pat Coogan, in his book *The IRA,* recounts incidents from a period in the early 1920s which probably explains why.

There was in Belfast at that time a group of ex-servicemen, police and B Specials who became known as the 'Murder Gang'. At night they would move into Catholic areas, in stockinged feet and with blackened faces, terrifying the locals as they loomed out of the dark to shoot down individuals or throw grenades into houses.

A custom known as the 'murder yell' sprang up. Anyone seeing a member of the gang gave a long-drawn-out, high-pitched, keening yell of 'M-u-r-derr-eh' which was taken up by the entire district. Colonel Roger McCorley told me that this sound, with the banging of dustbin lids, pots and pans, was the most eerie he had ever heard. On hearing it, McCorley and his IRA patrols would hasten to the spot, guiding each other with red-tinted flashlights. When the shooting stopped and the invaders were driven off, the keening died away. The flashlights would be switched to green for 'all clear'. The memory of those terrible days survives today in a street ballad:

> Oh, she got up and rattled her bin,
> For the Specials were a-coming in,
> Tiddy-fal-la, Tiddy-fal-la.
> Oh, she got up and rattled her bin,
> For the Specials were a-coming in,
> Tiddy-fal-la, Tiddy-fal-la.

So in 1969 it was on this powder-keg of Irish history that Sir Ian Freeland sat, and from the start he had felt there was something wrong. Despite the evident trouble, he noticed an air of complacency both in the Unionist Government at Stormont and in the Royal

Ulster Constabulary. The Inspector General, Anthony Peacocke, was an urbane, silver-haired gentleman who had spent nearly forty years working his way up through the ranks. He assured Freeland that the Protestants would not cause trouble, 'because they never did'. A British civil servant was heard to remark caustically that those taking part in Apprentice Boys' marches were not apprentices and certainly not boys! Sometimes, however, in the after-dinner cigar smoke in the houses of great men, Freeland would be told that things were getting a bit 'out of hand' and that something should be done. In the cold light of day he would look at his orders to find that the Army was to be called out only in the gravest of emergencies; by tradition it was always the police who dealt with trouble.

By the spring of 1969 his small garrison of some 2,500 men was already bolstering an equally small police force. After a series of bomb explosions half his men were guarding public buildings and installations. An additional problem, which was to affect the Army for a long time, was that Northern Ireland matters not dealt with by Stormont — such as defence and foreign affairs — were still dealt with in London by an official of Principal level. It was a bizarre situation when the Permanent Under-Secretary and Secretary to the Northern Ireland Cabinet had to consult with the Home Office — sometimes in the small hours of the morning. This senior official would have to consult a principal whose other duties included responsibility for collecting dog licences throughout the United Kingdom. On one occasion when an Army officer telephoned him at a weekend he received a 'very shirty' reply. 'Look here!' he was told, 'I've been a civil servant for thirty years and I've never been asked to come out on a Sunday.' The officer replied that it was time he got used to it because the whole place was going up in smoke.

So it was that at 4 p.m. on 14 August 1969 the Chief of Staff, Brigadier Dyball, was called to a meeting of Cabinet ministers in the Prime Minister's office at Parliament Buildings. Dyball gave the impression of being relaxed and in control. He was not in full uniform but was wearing a khaki sweater with an open neck shirt with the red tabs of a brigadier. (This confident informality was not lost on the Inspector General of Police who next day, for the first time, appeared at another meeting of ministers not dressed in his full uniform but also wearing a sweater — blue with leather elbow patches.) Dyball received the request for military assistance and said quietly, 'OK! You want them in — I'll call them in.' He left behind a Cabinet showing marked signs of relief though one observer thought this relief a little misplaced. 'It was thought that if we now had the police, the B Specials and the Army totally committed, then we could beat the Micks,' he said. 'The trouble was there were two levels of thinking at that time because the Army was not there to beat the Micks. There was an enormous chasm of understanding between the Stormont and Westminster Governments.'

Just fifteen minutes later the troops were on the move — eighty men of the Prince of Wales Own Regiment who were ordered to Waterloo Place in Londonderry. They arrived to find a slight smell of tear gas in the air, pungent and catching at their throats. Some B Specials still stood around with white handkerchiefs across their faces, batons in their hands. The soldiers put a barrier across the street and three minutes later the police withdrew through it, leaving the soldiers now in the front line.

It was a hot, humid evening and for a few moments nothing happened. Then a crowd came round the corner, stopping suddenly at the sight of the soldiers. The people shouted and brandished sticks and cheered when a grey-haired man pushed his way to the front as a spokesman. He was Eddie McAteer, who had been a Nationalist MP and once published a blueprint for civil disobedience called 'Irish Action'. During the civil rights campaign, however, he had frequently urged moderation. He said he was glad to see the soldiers on the scene, and that what he wanted most was to get the general temperature lowered. It would be better for the police to get right out of sight because the crowd was still excited and a little unsure of what was going on. Eamon McCann wrote:

> The police pulled out quite suddenly and the troops, armed with machine guns, stood in a line across the mouth of William Street. Their appearance was clear proof we had won the battle, that the RUC was beaten. That was welcomed. But there was confusion as to what the proper attitude to the soldiers might be. It was not in our history to make British soldiers welcome . . . . Bernadette Devlin, her voice croaking, urged, 'Don't make them welcome. They have not come here to help us,' and went on a bit about British Imperialism, Cyprus and Aden. It did not go down very well. The RUC was beaten; the soldiers had not attempted to encroach on the area. They had deployed themselves around the edges. And anyway, everyone was exhausted, clothes torn and faces begrimed, their eyes burning from tear gas. It was victory enough for the time being.

The local dairy counted the cost of the three-day battle — 43,000 milk bottles. One milkman remembered a note he found on a doorstep which had read, 'No milk today please but leave me 200 bottles.' In William Street Major Hanson looked round and checked his men. Everyone was in position, the first Peace Line had been established, and for the moment it seemed very easy to be a military unit called out 'in aid of the civil power'.

Across the province real terror was gripping many Protestants as they watched events in Londonderry. In Belfast the police were tense and edgy, angry at what was happening to their colleagues. Terror then spread to the Catholics as rumours came in that the dreaded B Specials were in action and the stories grew more lurid by the minute. Barricades went up, and petrol bombs began to fly through the air.

In Plymouth, Devon, the 3rd Battalion the Light Infantry were on United Kingdom standby and ready to move at twelve hours' notice. Late that Thursday night a call came through to them warning that they might be on the move. 'Don't take this for gospel,' the caller said. 'But be ready to go.' Closer to the action but still not involved, two officers in civilian clothes watched from Hastings Street police station, Belfast, as the violence grew. The station had been under virtual siege for days, the focal point of many an attack, and outside the officers could see where barrage after barrage of stones and petrol bombs had landed. The senior of the two officers commanded a battalion and was responsible for internal security in the city. However, he had only just over five hundred men. As midnight approached they both walked along the street until, standing in the darkness by traffic lights smashed by rioters, a policeman advised them to go no further. By now policemen were themselves travelling when they could in semi-armoured vehicles because a Special Branch report had warned that isolated policemen were liable to be shot. Some police were in the Shorlands, armed with Browning 0.30 medium machine guns. These had a range of two and a half miles, fired six to eight rounds a second and could in fact be fired only in bursts. It was not a suitable weapon for internal security duties in a heavily built-up city, and its deployment was a measure of the desperation felt by the police.

That night the Protestants went on the rampage and six people were shot dead as whole streets were burned to the ground. One nine-year-old boy was shot dead in his own home as fire from the Shorlands raked across the city. A soldier home from leave was killed by a stray shot, while allegedly making petrol bombs in an attempt to stem the Protestant attacks. A mile away across the city a police station in Donegall Pass reported coming under fire. This was an illustration of the danger and confusion being caused by the Shorlands, for in fact it had been hit by stray rounds from the Browning machine guns which must have come right over the roof of Divis Flats. Dawn revealed scenes of absolute devastation in Catholic areas, where one hundred and fifty houses had been destroyed and another three hundred damaged. In the early grey light people gathered wearily behind their barricades, some now ten feet high and strengthened with anything to hand — trees, telegraph poles and some sixty Corporation buses.

It was not until midday on Friday 15 August that the decision was finally taken to use troops in Belfast. The brigade commander, Brigadier Hudson, found the police commissioner, Harold Wolseley, staying in his office, a very tired man with his wife bringing him his meals. The policeman had been worried since the beginning of the month but nothing had been done about his suggestion to deploy the Army. There had been only one liaison meeting — a study day at Ballykinlar, an Army training camp on the County Down coast. Even then there had been only a general discussion. No plans had been made and certainly no maps had been produced. No one else there had ever thought that Belfast would give trouble and the policeman had not been in a position to say, 'Send me an Army officer and I will show him round.' So the Army knew nothing of the rigid sectarian geography of the city with its myriad little side streets wandering haphazardly through sensitive Catholic and Protestant areas. The idea had always been that if the Army were out on the ground, the civil power would always be there to guide it.

Hudson moved to the assistant commissioner's office and asked Sam Bradley where his men might best be placed. Bradley showed him the map and suggested that his troops should establish a Peace Line between the Catholic Falls and the Protestant Shankill. He called it the Orange-Green line. It was well known but to his surprise the Army officer had never heard of it. He took a deep breath and started to explain the complexities, warning at the same time that there was a real danger of Protestant rioters coming in and burning down more houses. At this stage there was no question that the Army would be in charge of one area and the police another; the idea was that they should work together.

That final commitment of the Army to the streets of Belfast was greeted by the Cabinet at Stormont with resignation. A Cabinet minister described the feeling there as almost one of political bankruptcy. The Cabinet, the Government and the Unionist view was that in the old days — the 1920s — when the Army had to come in and deal with 'this menace', there was no nonsense and it did what it was told. Now, however, the Army was acting under Westminster, which was running the show. The Army was not taking orders from the Unionist Government and if that Government at Stormont rebelled seriously against this situation then it would, in effect, be making a Unilateral Declaration of Independence along the lines that Ian Smith's white Government in Rhodesia had done. That was always the Unionist dilemma.

The man who led this Government was Prime Minister Major James Chichester-Clark. He had resigned from the O'Neil administration earlier in the year, giving as his reason the timing of the 'one man one vote' reform, although he said he was not against the principle of this reform. He had then been elected Prime Minister. He was a big man and did not lack physical courage, but the winds of change fanning the fires of violence across the province were much too strong for him to control. He tried his best, ordering an amnesty for those convicted of or charged with political offences since the previous October. One of those released was the Rev. Ian Paisley, the leader of the Free Presbyterian Church, who had taken to local politics with a line in booming oratory and a fanatical opposition to what he thought were modern trends towards Rome. These strong feelings were held equally firmly by many Protestants, and Chichester-Clark found himself on a number of occasions facing very hostile meeting of Unionist extremists in rural areas, where he had been physically assaulted at least twice. He would still insist on driving home each night despite the dangers but when, as now, the troubles were really bad he would stay in his small flat at Stormont Castle to monitor the situation. Here he would be found in the mornings, a rather lonely figure sitting in shirt sleeves and red braces, having breakfast and reading the overnight reports of violence around the province. It was not an easy time for him.

Still no extra troops had arrived in the province and the three garrison battalions were finding themselves over-stretched in dealing with violence that had spread from one side to the other. In Belfast the 2nd Battalion the Queen's Regiment and the Royal Regiment of

Wales received orders to move out and place themselves between the warring factions. The commanding officers felt that there was a *de facto* sectarian boundary running along the line of Divis Street and the Falls Road. To the south was the Catholic area and to the north the Protestant area. They planned to move through the Protestant areas to that line where they would establish themselves and literally keep the two sides apart.

So in the late afternoon the 2nd Battalion the Queen's Regiment started to move into the city, through the barricades and past the burning houses and vehicles. A huge pall of smoke rose from a burning mill and many houses were empty. One officer thought it all looked rather like a Second World War newsreel. All around was the shambles produced by the fighting and the soldiers had little idea of what was happening. The aim of the operation was to restore peace and therefore there was no question of forcing entry where one was formally refused. They stood in their combat gear and, despite their being a sight traditionally hated above all others by Republicans, housewives came on to the streets with trays of food and tea. Small crowds gathered round the control posts, friendly and curious. In the Shankill the police were still out in force but the soldiers knew this was a Protestant area where the local inhabitants would chat to 'their' police.

Now the Royal Regiment of Wales was also on to the streets, with orders to shoot only as a last resort. At Clonard monastery the CO, Lieutenant-Colonel Napier, found a crowd of about thirty frightened people and some priests who seemed concerned with protecting the monastery and the surrounding area. He went to the top of the monastery and looked out over Cupar Street and Kashmir Road and saw parts of Bombay street ablaze.

That night there was another pitched battle between Catholics and Protestants and the police. Despite this, morale was reported high in the Catholic areas. Barricades round the Falls and Ardoyne kept out both the police and the Army; keeping out the Protestant gangs was another matter. A local MP, Paddy Devlin, recalled that a large number of houses were destroyed that night. 'Bombay Street was attacked that night and the police would not come out. The police were paralysed. There was no defence for the Catholic people. I sought weapons from Dublin but I got nothing. There were no arms in Dublin.'

It now appeared to many Catholics that the Army, out at last on the streets of the city, had just stood by and watched the Protestants pillage and burn. The truth was that there were not enough troops to do anything else and most of those who were there had little idea of what was going on. Even so there was no doubt in some minds that the side the Army had come to support was the Catholic side. The frightening reality of that night can perhaps best be summed up in the words of a song which Protestant extremists wrote to commemorate the event.

> On the 15th of August we took a little trip,
> Up along Bombay Street and burned out all the shit,
> We took a little petrol and we took a little gun,
> And we fought the bloody Fenians till we had them on the run.

It was not until the Saturday afternoon that the 3rd Light Infantry arrived on the streets. As they moved through the barricades towards the Crumlin Road they noticed that all the barricades had a good supply of petrol bombs, each with a wick in the top ready to be lit. They were met by the Rev. Ian Paisley who called out, in his booming voice, 'Thank goodness you have come. Welcome!' The CO, Lieutenant-Colonel Ballendon, had been warned that people were liable to claim that the troops were on their particular side, and had given orders to his men to behave as neutrally as possible. For five minutes his men stood in the Crumlin Road, peering all round and up to the rooftops of the houses and mills, searching for snipers. Then, remembering their orders to look neutral, they moved into the middle of the road and stood facing both ways. Flames were still creeping round a corner pub, and here the soldiers stood barely a yard apart.

A police officer arrived, unarmed and visibly upset at what was happening. He pointed to a street and told the officer, 'That is one of the streets I must walk down with you. We must let the people see we are working together.' There were double-decker buses all over the place, most of them in barricades. Some had bullet-holes neatly spaced out as if from a burst of machine-gun fire. People poured out to tell them tales of horror — they were frightened that the Protestants would attack again, and even more frightened that the B Specials might be sent in. At Tennant Street police station the soldiers were horrified to see Land Rovers with huge, jagged holes that must have been made with weapons like crowbars. They watched the police coming in off duty, dropping with fatigue as they stored their shields — chipped, bashed and bent.

That night, despite the three battalions now deployed, the rampaging went on. The Protestants stormed in, hurling more petrol bombs. A small Army patrol came up on one of these gangs, but their orders were very strict: 'Do not fire unless life is threatened.' They dropped back and asked for reinforcements. When a full company arrived it was too late; Conway Street and Norfolk Street were ablaze from end to end. One young officer who went behind a Protestant barricade was shocked to find policemen there as well. Petrol bombers would creep forward, ignoring orders through Army loudhailers to get back or be gassed. A little light would twinkle through the darkness to land with a crash of glass and a 'woosh' of flame. Then the tear gas would be fired. Despite fighting all round, the soldiers stuck to their orders to use minimum force. Even when one soldier was slightly injured by gunfire that night, not a single Army round was fired. Instead, the men strengthened their positions behind the barbed-wire knife-rest barriers and, where they could, lay wrapped in ponchos and tucked into doorways or along the edge of the street trying to rest.

After the first twenty-four hours the Army found the mood of the people changing and hardening. In the Catholic areas men manning the barricades were polite but made it quite clear that what they called 'the Committee' did not want the Army around. This 'Committee' included Catholic priests, and it maintained that there was peace, law and order in these areas, and therefore the Army was superfluous. In the Protestant areas there were no committees and the soldiers chatted to people on the barricades as a matter of policy. It was now obvious to the police that in the Catholic 'No Go' areas — where paramilitary groups, rather than the forces of law and order, were in control — the Army was acting on its own. Whatever the legal theory, the soldiers were no longer acting 'in aid of the civil power' but in certain areas acting in place of that civil power. Public announcements did nothing to clarify the matter. A Government spokesman said it was 'entirely a matter for the GOC Northern Ireland', while an Army spokesman countered with, 'We are in aid of the civil power and it is at the request of the civil power that we take action.'

At the weekend the Northern Ireland Prime Minister, Major Chichester-Clark, stated once again his belief that the real cause for disorder flowed from extreme Republican elements and 'others determined to overthrow the state'. When his Minister for Home Affairs tried to get confirmation for these views from the police, he received a cuttingly-bitter reply from a Special Branch officer.

> It would be absurd to say that the present situation has been brought about solely by the machinations of the Movement. What has happened in fact is that the IRA/Republican Movement has been infiltrating and manipulating the Civil Rights Organisation with great energy. The speed of success of the latter in producing the present condition in the streets has caught the IRA largely unprepared in the military sense . . . . Reliable sources report a shortage of arms. Their command structure behind the barricades in the city is weak and lacks cohesion due to our swoop and detention of a number of their top men.

In Britain, a confidential Scotland Yard memorandum backed up these observations.

> The Northern Ireland Civil Rights Association is at first a genuinely broad-based organisation. It includes all shades of anti-Unionist opinion from those on the extreme left such as the revolutionary People's Democracy — to Republicans of all varieties. This is the principal organisation involved. The IRA — the military arm of the Republican Movement — is not organised or equipped to play a significant independent role within this body. However, members are encouraged to join and take an active role as individuals. Indeed a member of the IRA council is on the Executive of the Civil Rights Association and many others have taken part in demonstrations without identifying themselves by tricolours and banners.

By the weekend 10 people had died: 1,600 had been injured; 170 homes had been destroyed: 16 factories had been gutted by fire and the total cost of the damage was estimated at around £8 million. Up at Stormont a civil servant who had been watching the week's events with a somewhat jaundiced eye felt that the Army had been badly briefed, badly instructed and had little idea of what it was doing. He pointed out that it had, in some instances, put its troops in entirely the wrong places because it had acted on information from the police. However the troops had, at last, actually been deployed. He said:

> You won't believe this, but in fact Westminster made it quite clear to us that not only did we have to commit the whole of the RUC and find

ourselves failing but we had to commit the B Specials as well and find ourselves failing. Can you imagine! The most discredited force in the whole of our modern history and we had to commit them before Westminster would agree to commit the Army.

With the Army committed, the GOC came into public view for the first time to spell out that his soldiers were under military control and that there was no question of the police giving them orders. He did not pretend the job would be easy. He knew his men might become targets for mob hatred and violence from both sides if the political problems were not solved quickly. 'The honeymoon period between troops and local people is likely to be short lived,' he forecast. 'Indeed, it is probably at its height right now.'

For someone who looked beyond the immediate day-to-day events there seemed already to be a fundamental flaw in the new policy. There was no co-ordinated civil/military approach to deal with a problem which rose from basic political, economic and social conditions. 'Pre-planning!' snorted a senior Army commander derisively. 'You must remember that the Government's policy was to have the Army out only in the very worst situation. The Stormont Government and the RUC did not want us in. That is a very important ground rule to remember in all this.'

In 1689 a decision had been taken to raise a 'Standing Army to Deal with the Problem of Ireland'. Now, nearly 300 years later, soldiers were still dealing with it, although in only a small part of the original country. What few people realised at this time was just how long these soldiers would be required to stay. That first weekend of rioting in which ten people died was a foretaste of the bitter, sectarian rioting which was to punctuate the affairs of the province for years to come. It also showed how ill-prepared the Army was to deal with such violence within the United Kingdom, bound as it was by its laws. The Army's experience had always been in colonial situations where the rules were simple, the chain of command direct and the objective clear. Just what were the soldiers supposed to be doing as they moved in some confusion through the streets of Belfast and Londonderry? Were they really acting 'in aid of the civil power' to restore order? Were they fighting a guerilla war? Were they, as some supposed, caught now in a bizarre and deadly game of 'pig in the middle' between more than just two opposing factions? Some saw these possibilities as separate and distinct; others as all inextricably mixed.

The failure to come to a meeting of minds on this was to lead within two years to such actions as the Lower Falls curfew, internment, interrogation in depth, a mounting casualty list and the total alienation of the Catholic population, to say nothing of the embitterment of the Protestants. For the time being, however, it was all a short-term affair.

From the Army point of view the IRA — soon to be split into Official and Provisional branches — had three distinct advantages. First, the British Government had been showing over the years a marked tendency to withdraw from territories after long-term terrorist activity. (In fact Britain had just pulled out of Aden.) Second, there was the example of the Americans pulling out of Vietnam. Third, there was the gathering force of the civil rights movement round the world.

The British, and some other colonial powers, had been seen to follow a pattern. At the start of terrorist activity there were always strong denials that the Government would give way to violence. After violence had continued for a while it would be decided that the asset was not worth preserving and the colonial government would pack up and go. On this basis the Provisionals were to build their strategy. They decided first that they would kill thirty-six British soldiers (the same number as had been killed in Aden), and later raised this figure to eighty. They believed that this would force the British to negotiate.

The Army was aware, however; that it, too, possessed some advantages. One was that the troops were providing protection for the Catholics against sectarian violence and acting as a buffer between them and the police. Another was that the Catholics' main target was the Protestant-dominated Stormont Government. In due course Army Headquarters staff at Lisburn discovered how the Provisionals were to try to overcome this. They would mobilise the Catholics in a 'smash Stormont' campaign, linking it with similar aims of bona-fide politicians which would help to blur the sharp image of their violence. They would make certain that British soldiers would once again be seen as the traditional enemy.

Within a very short time the Army found itself the target for abuse. *Citizen Press*, the broadsheet of the Northern Ireland Civil Rights Association reported:

On Thursday, the homes of two Catholic British Army ex-servicemen in

Derry were raided . . . the raid was certainly the precursor of more to follow and it has also been confirmed what many of us thought all along — that the peace-keeping role of the military is a political disguise to enable the unionist clique to round up and terrorise its political opponents and those who bravely defended their homes and their lives from the attacks of the RUC and the B Specials.

Free Citizen, the broadsheet of the People's Democracy, declared:

Army justice on the Shankill Road appears to have been decidedly rough and ready. Proceedings in the magistrates court are described as 'hilariously irregular' by at least one lawyer involved. Major Hitchcock has a rough and ready guide for justice. 'Anyone smelling of CS gas is being arrested because he has no business to be in the area where it was fired.'

At a different level, a Cabinet member of the Stormont Government, Brian Faulkner, complained that the Army had stabilised and formalised the 'liberated' areas set up by rioters and this allowed the IRA to build up into a 'closely-knit and powerfully-armed subversive force.'

Instead of moving in to support the civil power they dug in as a sort of peace-keeping force on the fringe of the barricaded areas and tacitly accepted the right of various Republicans and known IRA men to rule and speak for these areas. . . . The desire to approach this situation cautiously can be fully appreciated, but it was a grave misjudgement of the kind of men with whom the Army was dealing.

The barricades on both sides were a source of considerable pain to the Army. Some were 'talked' down but the suspicions of decades which had led to their being built would not disappear overnight. No one was yet ready to accept Army guarantees of safety but Westminster was reluctant to use brute force and bulldozers because of a fear of large-scale and bloody rioting. So the soldiers continued, wearily, to hold the line between the factions, using their physical presence and their traditional reservoir of patience and good humour.

Some young soldiers arrived to be confused by their training. What they had actually been trained in was the formal drill of the 'box formation' — to receive bricks and stones. Trained in the 'shoot one round at that big black bugger in the red turban' style and they had all practised it on Long Kesh airfield. All the old drill. Dannert wire . . . unfold the banners . . . bring out the camera . . . get the magistrate to read the Riot Act and say 'move now!' Then the cameraman and baton men would go forward and lay a line of white tape across the road and unfurl the banner which read ·HALT OR WE WILL OPEN FIRE'. 'Very impressive!' recalled a young officer disarmingly. 'The first time we did it the order was written in Arabic.' But when they arrived in Ulster they were confused by having to blacken their faces and crawl around with weapons, against an enemy they could not identify.

The Stormont Government was still very twitchy about the 'No Go' areas, and constantly pressed the GOC to do something about them, particularly in Londonderry, as one observer recalled:

Freeland was pressed very hard by the Cabinet to occupy the Bogside. Now he sat there with that Death's Head smile of his and said to them 'Look! If you ask me whether I can take the Bogside as a military exercise — yes I can. In three hours. I can take it over and totally command it.' Now I always thought of Freeland as one of the least mentally-agile soldiers I ever met but at that point he added, 'Three hours to take over and about three years to get out again. Is that what you want?' And the whole Cabinet sat back in stunned silence.

One evening, however, Chichester-Clark appeared on television and to the horror of most Army officers announced that the barricades in Belfast must come down. They knew this spelt much trouble, and they quickly called a planning conference. The GOC made it quite clear that while the Prime Minister had pre-empted him, enough was enough. He would re-take the initiative and put up his own barricades — except that his would be known as the Peace Line. It would be a continuous wall of corrugated iron sheeting ten feet high, which would zig-zag its way between the Protestant Shankill and the Catholic Falls. It would follow the exact boundaries even if this meant cutting streets in two.

There were objections on the ground. No one wanted their barricades removed before anyone else's, and there had to be a certain amount of face-saving allowed. 'Get yon mad major out of here!', shouted one irate youth. 'Then we will wait until the men come home and we'll take them down ourselves.' The tactful major concerned withdrew and started work on the Peace Line instead. With pneumatic drills and bolt pistols the soldiers hammered steel stakes into the tarmac road to hold the wall and slung coils of barbed wire between them. At Westminster, it seemed to the Home Secretary James Callaghan that the GOC had shown great wisdom at this time:

> It was his restrained tactics which in the end proved successful. I should add that he got very little help or understanding from the Belfast City Council, who were supposed to help him determine the route of the Peace Line. His comments on the quality and level of ability of the councillors and administrators were absolutely sulphurous. And I expect he was right.

The soldier on the ground was constantly on the go and if he got three hours' sleep a day he was lucky. Always on standby he slept with his boots on and his weapon strapped to his wrist. Often he cat-napped in doorways, under bridges or in flimsy shelters by the barricades. One unit took over the public baths in the Falls Road and the soldiers slept in the changing cubicles, more often than not with icy water trickling down their necks. Others moved into schools and the Grenadier Guards, fresh from Chelsea Barracks, took over a burned-out mill. It was an unpleasant job which many were beginning to dislike, as journalist Mary Holland noted:

> It would take just one drunk to take a swipe at a soldier for the streets to fill with menacing-looking troops on one side of the barricades and a jittery, angry crowd on the other. In Belfast they have to suffer abuse from a people particularly eloquent in obscenity. They have been stoned and have had broken bottles thrown at them. A sympathetic and sensible NCO from Durham told me he had never known his men so edgy. He was anxious what their reaction would be if, say, a British soldier was shot by a sniper.

One distinct disadvantage under which the Army operated was that despite the 'brave' efforts of the Special Branch they were really on their own, especially in the Republican 'No Go' areas. They were not trained to act as police, and trying to set up any sort of intelligence system in the glare of the world's press was not easy. Neither did they react easily to the changing winds of political expediency. They were the blunt instrument of government, according to one Stormont official. They had been told, 'There is a problem. Solve it!' However, the army was not built to act in a political role. 'It is built to act as the mailed fist of a failed government,' he commented. 'At the very least the Army should have had firm political control, but it did not.' Although Sir Ian Freeland repeatedly asked for a statement of aims and a policy for the security forces, he was never given one. He was made Director of Operations, which allowed him to take the chair at Army/police meetings, but he had no other powers. A senior officer said:

> Politicians and the media often referred to our having 'softly-softly' or 'go in hard' instructions. No instructions of that sort ever arrived! We worked on our own, knowing damn well that if things went successfully all would be well and if they did not we would carry the can. The one firm guideline we had was the law — until we tried to get the lawyers to interpret it!

There were of course channels for control, and despite brave remarks from Freeland about his own authority, he was controlled politically. However, this control was divided, first between Westminster and Stormont and further in London between the Ministry of Defence and the Home Office. The only possible advantage to accrue from the confusion over how to conduct a counter-insurgency campaign was that at Westminster a bipartisan approach was established between the main parties. The Army viewed this approach as a sensible decision not to allow divided domestic opinion to lower morale in the way that had 'broken' the Americans in Vietnam. On the whole, however, officers would have preferred either strong control or none at all to the hesitant direction they were getting. They based their arguments about no political control on the theory that in times of insurrection they had a common-law duty to suppress it; in other words, when they found a situation in which the Queen's writ no longer ran, they had a duty to restore the Queen's Government with whatever degree of force was necessary. It followed from this that they were not bound by orders from political superiors either to do something or not to do something. It was accepted, however, that this was a grey area which had never been tested in the courts. So in practice there was political control, whether it was decisive or not. An Army lawyer put it like this:

> Whatever the theory, in practice the GOC is controlled by his political

masters. Now this, incidentally, is perhaps the most important facet of an unrecognised change in the responsibilities of the Army which have been brought about by modern communications. In India between the wars the Army commander of a district, maybe as junior as a major, could declare martial law without asking anyone's authority. He just had to tell someone. Nowadays, with the speed of modern communication, no officer would ever be given that responsibility. Now the control is centralised and a lot of these happy, laughing things about 'what powers have the Army got?' are no longer relevant . . . because the Army would never be allowed to use them.

It was a messy situation all round, and as the weeks went by two developments were to erode yet further the morale of both the police and the Protestant community. These developments came against a background of growing violence and verbal abuse. The Rev. Ian Paisley, like a prophet of doom from the Old Testament, told a rally that the presence of the troops was the biggest confidence trick ever played on Ulster because the soldiers themselves had told him they were there to 'keep the Catholics happy'. William Craig, another stern-faced Protestant politician, got a standing ovation when he criticised the decision to give the Army control of security. He called for the dismantling of the Peace Line and for joint Army/police patrols. 'I hope as you go from this hall tonight to every part of Northern Ireland,' he told 2000 members of the Ulster Loyalist Association, 'you will carry a spark that will ignite a great flame of purposeful propaganda.'

As fear and intimidation spread, the soldiers dealt with worsening riots. In one fracas at the bottom of the Shankill Road, 41 people were arrested, but only after 700 gas cartridges and grenades had been fired and 48 soldiers and 54 policemen injured. Seven hundred Royal Marine Commandos were flown into the province as Lord Cameron issued his report into the causes and nature of the violence and civil disturbances. He found a failure of leadership on all sides and that the Stormont Government had been 'hidebound' and 'complacent'. There had been 'serious breaches of discipline and acts of violence by the RUC during the civil rights campaign' and 'subversive elements' had used the civil rights platform to stir up trouble in the streets. Moreover the B Specials, in Lord Cameron's view, were a 'partisan paramilitary force recruited exclusively from Protestants'.

The Protestants seethed with anger. Everything they stood for was being criticised and whittled away. With an amazing ignorance of local conditions, the report was published on a Friday, when weekly pay packets were handed out and the men would head towards the pubs for the weekend. It recommended the disbandment of the B Specials and their replacement by a part-time unit to be called the Ulster Defence Regiment (UDR) under the direct military control of the GOC. The Protestants were rocked back. By the time they came out of the pubs on Saturday evening they were spoiling for a fight. Those in the Shankill set off down the road towards the Catholic Unity Flats, which had often come under attack in the past.

With a huge Union Jack waving before them and encouraged by the reverberating boom of a great Lambeg drum, they surged forward. At the bottom of the road and in front of Unity Flats, 'their' police were drawn up to receive them. Behind the police, in a wide arc, stood soldiers in riot gear. There was little light, and what there was filled the street with dark shadows. The mob swept up towards the thin police line. There was hand-to-hand fighting, but the line held. When the shooting started two policemen fell to the ground. One, Constable Arbuckle, was already dying.

The police withdrew and a company of Light Infantry moved through to deal with the Protestant mob. The opposition to them was rough, and so were they. They punched their way up the street under fire to reappear dragging rioters — sometimes by the hair, sometimes by the feet with their heads bumping along on the ground behind. Soldiers emerged out of the gloom with bloodied faces, or with ears slashed open. One rioter was hurled into a Land Rover with such force that he hit the roof before slumping to the floor. Sir Ian Freeland commented later: 'We gave them a bloody nose.' A police surgeon was to describe the injuries as the worst he had ever seen after a riot — and he made this comment two years later. Three men were killed that night and over sixty injured — more than half with gunshot wounds. It took the soldiers the rest of the weekend to fight their way to the top of the Shankill Road.

It was quite clear that the decision to disband the B Specials had been taken in London on the basis of Lord Hunt's recommendations, and without any reference to the Stormont Government, which was seen as a 'backward, reactionary force' which had to be pushed to one side. At Lisburn, a senior officer voiced his displeasure.

John Hunt was wrong. It was no good him coming here and complaining,

'You've got chaps out in the villages hitting Catholics over the head.' That was how the B Specials have solved it the first time and it was madness to disband them out of hand and condemn them just to placate the Catholics. That's where they were wrong. Nothing was going to placate the Catholics except union with Ireland. Throwing things like that to the Catholics was just a bloody waste of time. All it did was depress the majority who felt they were being sold down the river. It also deprived the police of some very useful elements of intelligence and control.

More shocks were in store for the Protestants, for on top of all this came the appointment of Sir Arthur Young, as the new police chief, specially hand-picked by James Callaghan — and he was an Englishman! Few people were happy either with his coming or his performance. He infuriated Unionist politicians by walking down the Falls Road arm in arm with Jimmy Sullivan, who was later found to be heavily involved in the IRA. He worried the police when he issued a Force Order which said, in effect, that the RUC would become a non-aggressive, non-retaliatory civilian force with no riot role. Senior policemen felt that this led to a very unwholesome attitude, with junior police officers being far too ready to defer to the Army. Young's appointment also amazed some Army officers who had seen him in action elsewhere. 'It was quite inexcusable,' said one. 'His record was known and it was totally predictable that he wouldn't listen to the RUC. He made the same mistake in Malaya and Kenya.' Another officer described him as being all things to all men, who would say, 'Yes, of course we must work together — and be tough.' What the Army felt, however, was that when it came to any sort of crunch he had always disappeared or given contrary orders. 'He had no understanding of the need to be firm and by currying favour with the Catholics he was disloyal to his own men.'

As the year drew to a close, the situation eased a little. The taunting of soldiers on duty dropped off. Invitations to Christmas celebrations poured in, sporting events were organised with local youngsters, and in one area of central Belfast a soldier talked of the locals as 'the nicest, friendliest, most hospitable and sometimes most maddening people in the world.' After one hundred days of operations, the Army was now well into a 'hearts and minds' campaign. *The Times* reported:

More than 200 of Londonderry's more energetic youngsters, aged from eight to sixteen, were playing volleyball and football or boxing, leaping vaulting horses and scaling walls at the naval base HMS Sea Eagle this afternoon. Lance Corporal John Pounder of the 2nd Battalion the Light Infantry was climbing in the Black Mountains with a party of youths from the centre of Belfast; Private Maurice Osborne, of the 2nd Battalion The Queen's Regiment, was doing a little house decorating for an elderly widow and a party of Grenadier Guardsmen were preparing to go on a meals-on-wheels operation to housebound old people in Londonderry.

'. . . C Company will cover you up Divis Street, you will have a tank escort through the Falls Road area and B Division will mount guard while you have Christmas dinner with the McMurray family.'

By Northern Ireland standards the last few months of the year were quiet. Military Police went out on patrols and the people accepted them. As some barricades in Belfast tumbled down the politicians emerged, blinking in the sunlight. There was talk of reform. The Catholic population, however, viewed this with some cynicism for the Unionists were still in power and any reforms would take years to implement.

There was to be another development, as 1969 passed into 1970, which was to have considerable bearing on the campaign the Army was to fight over the next decade and more — the split in the IRA. Since the 1950s, the IRA had been inclined to lean more towards political rather than violent action to achieve its aims of driving the

British out of the North. Over the years, the Republicans had steadfastly maintained that there should be no recognition of the established political institutions North or South, and they had unwaveringly followed a policy of abstention. Now, in December 1969, the Army council, the effective day-to-day executive body of the IRA, voted by three to one to give at least token recognition to the three parliaments of Westminster, Dublin and Stormont; and when Sinn Fein — the political wing of the IRA — held its annual conference in January 1970 a motion was put to this effect. There was, however, a group which felt humiliated by the failure of the IRA to defend Catholics in the North the previous August and which was strongly opposed to such a move. They fought hard against it but then, sensing defeat, walked out and in due course formed the Provisional IRA, claiming to be the true inheritors of the IRA traditions of 1916. They were to become better known as the Provos — or in security force circles as PIRA — and became the main enemy of the established forces of law and order.

Lisburn was well aware that the Army could not stay 'neutral' forever. Its methods were potentially too rough, and it would only be a matter of time before the Catholics had their worst fears confirmed: that it was not themselves who were being protected, but the Unionist Government. That time came in the spring of 1970, when the marching season arrived again. Some Lodges of the Orange Order, the largest Government organisation in Northern Ireland, with between 80,000 and 100,000 members, planned a parade into the Catholic areas of New Barnsley. A local nationalist politician tried to get it stopped, because he had heard that the Provisional IRA was — for the first time — planning to interfere with such a parade. He failed.

The authorities let them march into New Barnsley, where the Provos had the crowds built up waiting for them. Then the Army came in, and the old people living there were slaughtered with the gas everywhere. We got through to the military to change their tactics and they brought in more men with their faces blackened, hammering on their shields, arresting every male in sight although it was only twenty or so hoods throwing stones. They whacked through the doors, banging them down with their feet, to get at them.

From behind the barricades, which had been left intact to make political discussions more favourable, the Provisionals had planned well. Their policy of alienating the Catholics from the Army by forcing soldiers to react vigorously in Catholic areas was succeeding. The scale of rioting became such that the GOC was forced to act. In April he appeared on television saying firmly that the Army could not stay on the streets for ever, and that people must try to settle their own differences. He also announced much tougher retaliatory policies warning that in future petrol bombers were 'liable to be shot'. The Provisionals retaliated by saying that they would shoot soldiers, if Irishmen were shot. The Protestant Ulster Volunteer Force — an extreme and illegal, paramilitary unit — quickly joined in, offering to shoot a Catholic in return for every soldier shot by the IRA. *The Times* quoted a Belfast citizen saying: 'Anyone who isn't confused here doesn't really understand what is going on.' For Lieutenant-General Sir Ian Freeland and all his men, the honeymoon was over.

PIRA orchestrated escalation!

Phase Two

It starts to get rough
April 1970—August 1971

Over the years, in many colonial situations, the Army had developed a counter-insurgency doctrine which demanded close political cooperation between the civil administrations, the police and the military. This 'meeting of minds' had worked to great effect in the rural areas of Oman, Borneo, Malaya and, particularly, Kenya. Here, the Army had been able to harry and destroy rebellious gangs with military efficiency. The task was found to be much more difficult when these gangs moved into urban areas such as Aden, Nicosia, Ismailia and Jerusalem. In these towns and cities soldiers found themselves fighting an enemy in plain clothes, indistinguishable from the local population and under the gaze of an interested and often adversely critical world press. In these conditions it was absolutely essential that the 'meeting of minds' was total and complete.

When the Army found itself involved in a counter-insurgency campaign in Northern Ireland — despite the official theory of being 'in aid of the civil power' — it also found there was no 'meeting of minds' about anything. There were in fact two objectives, as the Army saw it. One was to defeat the terrorists, the other was to create a political structure which would be acceptable and allow the province to be governed normally. These two objectives were not always compatible, and indeed at times the interests of one would override those of the other. There was no well-defined objective to which the Army could work steadily and logically.

The Army approach in mid-1970 was to keep general violence as low as possible while taking out the gunman and the bomber. It was a slow process for it had to get these terrorists into court and prison without upsetting the Catholic population to the extent that they would refuse to discuss political change. At the same time they had the uneasy feeling that the politicians might 'screw it by giving in.' Soldiers were fond of pointing out that when Harold Wilson's Labour Government had set a time-table for withdrawal from Aden, this had ensured defeat for the policies for which the Army had been fighting. The effect of the American experience in Vietnam was also considerable. This seemed to underline to the more thoughtful officers that the possession and unlimited use of fire-power, far from solving a difficult situation, had merely made it worse. This realisation also helped to short-circuit what would otherwise have been stronger calls by some officers for 'freer rein'.

With the Government trying to introduce reforms there was a reluctance to allow the security forces to act too strongly. Those adversely critical of this — and these were not only extreme Unionists — complained that riots were being contained but not effectively quelled; that 'No Go' areas were being allowed to remain; and that a serious disrespect for the rule of law was being allowed to take root.

At Lisburn there was now a feeling that things were going badly because, since 1969, the authorities had consistently 'got it wrong', having dismantled the security apparatus, which was designed to control subversive organisations, before they had completed the political concessions, which were designed to stop people wanting to be subversive. The classical way to deal with the situation would have been to say to Stormont, 'Here are the troops, deal with the trouble.' In other words, the troops would thump the trouble-makers, restore order and then hand control back. There was no doubt in the Army mind that this would have worked — but only on a short-term basis. What the authorities tried to do, most laudably, was remove the causes of grievance which were partly political and partly related to security (in that the police were so one-sided). What the Army would like them to have done, however, was to have made the necessary political changes, put the B Specials under control of the Army and at the same time increase their ability to control subversive organisations in less obvious political ways. They should not have disarmed the police, which left the Army as the only force to keep law and order; they should have gone flat out to build up intelligence — something that was not done satisfactorily for years. The kernel of the argument was that by letting up on the security side the authorities had enabled the IRA to build themselves into a much stronger force.

A general election in June brought in a Conservative government and Reginald Maudling as Home Secretary. He was considered 'brilliant if a little lazy'. His apparent lack of urgency infuriated some senior Army officers as it did Bernadette Devlin who, exasperated during a debate in the House of Commons, darted across the Chamber to pull his hair and slap his face. Maudling's attitude rather hid the change of emphasis that came with the new Government. Whereas Callaghan and the Labour party were inclined to be cautious, Maudling and the Conservatives were inclined to give the Army its head — although only up to a point. Protestants in Northern Ireland hoped that Maudling would produce the firm smack of a Tory government maintaining law and order, though Maudling himself said he wanted to get away from this phrase and use 'freedom under the law' instead.

The pressure on that freedom grew. At the end of June an Orange parade passed close to the raw edge of the ghetto divide in the Ardoyne and a gun battle started. Three Protestants were killed. On the other side of the city Protestants attacked the Short Strand, with mobs trying to petrol-bomb a Catholic church. The Army refused to move, saying it did not have enough men. Instead, it sealed off the bridges leading from the area to the city centre, which effectively cut off 6,000 Catholics and left them surrounded by 60,000 Protestants. Six people died that weekend in Belfast and there was also rioting — though no shooting — in Londonderry. Forty soldiers were injured and nearly 90 people arrested for various offences. The GOC announced that anyone carrying a firearm was liable to be shot.

Protests began to mount that the Army was not prepared to defend Catholics against Protestant attacks, and that as the Army was attacking the Provisional IRA in the Catholic areas the soldiers were in fact siding with the Protestants. However, similar protests came from the other side as well. *The Investigator,* a short-lived broadsheet described as 'the official voice of Grovefield Loyalist Centre, Willowfield', declared:

ARMY ATTACK ORANGEMEN
The Army attack on Orangemen after the Brethren were ambushed by Republican thugs on the Springfield Road is typical of their anti-loyalist actions since their arrival in our land. The Army has allowed gunmen to shoot down people and then defended the Republican scum when the

Protestants endeavoured to fight back. The favourite weapons used by the Republican mob on the defenceless Orangemen were potatoes filled with razor-blades.

The new Home Secretary came across, visited the scenes of rioting and met the soldiers. At Stormont the Unionists told him that they were dissatisfied with both the GOC, Sir Ian Freeland, and the Chief Constable, Sir Arthur Young. At Lisburn officers held their counsel but privately some were constrained to voice unease — about the Home Secretary.

Reggie Maudling had no idea. He would never go out. We would get people to meet him and he would wander round and say things like 'Are you going to Ascot?' He was hopeless talking to community leaders on the streets. After his first visit here he sat in my office with his head in his hands and said, 'Oh, these bloody people! How are you going to deal with them?' Well, I said, 'Secretary of State, we are not going to deal with them. It's you — your lot who have to deal with them. We have got to have a policy.' But we never did have a policy. That was the problem.

During this period the overall position was made worse by the wholesale movement of very frightened people. In Belfast some 30,000–40,000 people left their homes because of intimidation and went to areas among their co-religionists where they could feel safe. It was the largest movement of a civil population since the Second World War. Such was the bitterness that the last act of many, before they left in lorries piled high with possessions, was to set fire to the house and slam the front door. The old buffer zones of mixed-religion areas disappeared, the ghettos shrank in on themselves, their boundaries becoming more sharply defined. They became places where terrorists could operate, stifling what opposition there might be with threats of knee-capping, tar-and-feathering and, for the more serious crimes, a 'head job' — a hood over the head and a bullet through it.

Then one day in July information arrived at Springfield Road police station about a cache of arms at 24 Balkan Street in the Lower Falls area of the city. It confirmed information received the previous day, and backed up some long-term intelligence. So there was little hesitation at Lisburn in ordering a search. Sixteen minutes after being tasked, a joint Army/police unit had turned up fifteen pistols, one rifle, a Schmeisser sub-machine gun and a quantity of explosives and ammunition. They also turned up a veritable hornet's nest of protest, which rapidly got out of hand. The small patrol became the target for a growing crowd. CS gas was fired to clear the area. Barricades started to go up and soon soldiers were reporting that grenades were being thrown at them. In one incident five of them were wounded. The crowd shifted and reformed, more gas was fired and as other units moved in they reported coming under fire from petrol and gelignite bombs. A taxi-driver said he had seen a man armed with a sub-machine gun heading for the area and the Army received a report saying the IRA intended to give battle that night.

At 10 p.m., with the rioting going full blast, the GOC imposed what he described later as 'a movement restriction on the civilian population of that area for the sake of their own safety and the safety of the soldiers.' Permission for a curfew, he explained, would have taken too long, which was not an underestimation, as it would certainly have been illegal. A helicopter hovered overhead, ordering people to get inside or be arrested. That night, in a massive house to house search, the troops came under fire and they returned it. Five civilians were killed, one being run over by an armoured car, and 15 soldiers and 60 civilians were injured. The Army search produced a haul which was proudly presented to the press; 52 pistols, 35 rifles, 6 automatic weapons, 14 shotguns, 100 home-made bombs, a grenade, 250lbs of explosives, some 21,000 rounds of ammunition and 8 two-way radio sets.

Sir Ian Freeland himself took the decision to impose the 'curfew'. Although he had been under pressure to take a harder line, he did not consult any Stormont Government minister. A highly-placed official there thought that, had he done so, 'even those die-hard Unionists might have baulked at the idea.' As it was, they exulted in the outcome and the Information Minister, Captain Brooke, son of Lord Brookeborough, took the press in an open lorry on a triumphant tour round the deserted streets of a cowed Lower Falls. From this time on, soldiers coming to the province were told:

> The casualties thought to have been incurred by the IRA were three killed. However, they may have incurred more casualties; unknown through being spirited away by Republican sympathisers to the South or elsewhere. That the IRA suffered a severe defeat, there can be no doubt, and it could well force a change in their tactics for the future.

There is some doubt as to the accuracy of that assessment, and local Catholics were extremely angry, particularly because the Army had not appreciated that the Lower Falls was run, not by the Provisional IRA, but by the Official IRA — a significant difference. They felt that the Army had been determined to impose its will on the Lower Falls and that when Provisionals from outside came in and started firing, this merely confirmed what the Army wanted to think. In Whitehall there was a cooler reaction, which probably showed how little anyone had thought of the long-term implications. It was not felt that there had been any conscious decision to 'out do' the Labour Government. As one senior minister put it:

> Reggie was running it. Not a good way of doing things. The Home Secretary has quite enough to do without running Northern Ireland in that sort of situation. And he wasn't the most . . . uh . . . dynamic of people. Nicest of men but not the most dynamic. I think we felt this would die down . . . that if we showed enough resolution and force they would pack up. Shows how wrong you can be!

The Lower Falls 'curfew' attracted comment and adverse criticism from many different quarters which only went to show how difficult it was for the Army to do anything that was generally acceptable. One young Army officer thought it had been a clumsy mistake. Catholics in West Belfast and Londonderry had told him it had been deliberately ordered by Downing Street as an example of what could be expected from a Conservative government. 'It is the perception of events which creates reality,' he observed. 'This is more true in Northern Ireland than other places where people can discuss things rationally.'

Fortnight, which described itself as an 'independent review for Northern Ireland', took up the case of the 'curfew' and allegations of Army brutality which, it argued, needed a detailed answer. Otherwise, it suggested, the 'rival mythologies' which lay underneath so much of the trouble would only be reinforced. The Army should go out of its way to remove any legitimate doubts and to re-establish what respect it could among the people of the Lower Falls. On the broader issue it argued that there was a grave danger of the Army's being 'lured into the quagmire of Ulster politics.' One danger signal was the reluctance of the Army and its supporters 'to consider the possibility that it may in any way have been at fault.'

The Lower Falls 'curfew' was in military terms a success. A forceful challenge to the state had been met with a forceful answer and total military domination. In political terms it was a disaster, not only alienating a whole community but building up within it an even more active resentment against authority.

That some regiments had 'behaved excellently while others were less than reasonable', as a local Catholic put it rather kindly in the circumstances, was neither here nor there. What the imposition of this 'curfew' showed was not only a panic reaction and a paucity of ideas but also that no one had yet grasped a fundamental fact — that an insurgency campaign is a battle for people's minds. From now on there would be a significant change in relations between the Catholic community and the Army; a change from sullen acceptance to open hostility. Efforts to maintain contact with local leaders would now be met with indifference and a shrugged 'What's the use?' Recruits poured in to join the Provisional IRA.

A year after the military had been called in there still seemed to be some odd ideas of what the soldiers should be doing. In September 1970 the GOC, Sir Ian Freeland, held a combined Army/police study day. He announced that political direction had been given for the RUC to assume complete responsibility for law and order, including dealing with riots. The Army, he said, would then only be called in under exceptional circumstances when the police could not cope. For while the Army's task was to support the police, 'this support would not be available in unlimited numbers for an unlimited length of time.' The Chief Constable agreed that the time had come for the police to take a step forward in this direction. He explained that numbers were a crucial factor in achieving this and proposed that the size of the police Special Patrol Group should not only be doubled but strengthened by getting an equivalent number of unarmed soldiers posted to it. One officer who sat through it all observed:

It was a very odd study day. This idea was being put across as a joint policy but it was pretty clear that Freeland and Young were scarcely on speaking terms. I mean when either answered a question they would do it in a most uncomplimentary way to each other — not abusive but very cutting. I listened very carefully to this idea of getting the troops out so soon. I must say it did seem a slightly optimistic view of the situation.

Another officer, coming into the mess at lunch halfway through the day, muttered, 'All this shows is that the Army hates the RUC and the RUC hates the Army!'

It was high time to take at least part of this uneasy situation by the scruff of the neck. The MOD decided to ease the command situation by appointing a Commander Land Forces to deal with the day to day operations and leave the GOC to deal with the political side. The first CLF to be appointed was the 'ebullient' Major-General Anthony Farrar-Hockley, who had fought in the Korean War as adjutant of the Gloucestershire Regiment and been taken prisoner by the North Koreans. He soon made his presence felt and by November was announcing that the Army faced 'a long haul ahead and was nearer to the threshold of harder operation.' This was the first time a senior officer had admitted that the Army might be facing a prolonged terror campaign by the Provisional IRA. It was the sort of acknowledgement many Protestants welcomed, for the Provisionals had by now become more active, killing some policemen in a series of bomb explosions as well as losing some of their own men in premature explosions. They 'had begun a bombing campaign,' wrote Michael Farrell of the People's Democracy (a radical, left-wing group), but they weren't prepared to acknowledge it because they weren't ready for an all-out confrontation with the Army.'

On the ground there was a distinct change in attitude to the soldiers, which was noticed in the Lower Falls by a local Catholic priest, Canon Murphy. As far as he was concerned, the people were shattered by what had happened since the Lower Falls 'curfew' and considered the Army had burned all the bridges so carefully built between them and the people. Following the lead of their parents, the children had become more anti-Army, stoning soldiers when they could. Again, as so often, much depended on the local unit. A local priest recalled:

Unfortunately, while some regiments behaved excellently, others didn't. There was a fair amount of . . . not brutality, but extreme inconvenience . . . unnecessary obstruction. At some houses I went to the man would say, 'The military were very efficient, proper gentlemen, they didn't even wake the baby and I offered them a cup of tea.' Others would say, 'They were real bastards. One put his foot through the television and smashed it.' This was in the autumn when the Provos were regrouping and getting ready and it all stemmed from that Lower Falls curfew.

Observing the growing discontent, a *Sunday Times* journalist, Eric Jacobs, wrote:

> I find it hard any longer to believe anything that anyone says that has been done to him by anybody else unless I have seen it with my own eyes. Attitudes are so deeply ingrained that people will expect those they class as enemies to behave like enemies — and then they would expect to be believed when they tell you about it.

As the Unionist Government at Stormont proposed political reforms which were neither quick-acting nor accepted by the Catholics, the Army made another effort at its 'hearts and minds' campaign. Up towards Ballymurphy the Royal Anglians started a disco in the Henry Taggart Memorial Hall. Soon lurid tales were making the rounds and the disco was closed. The local girls, however, continued to go there to watch film shows. There were more lurid tales . . . and there was more trouble.

Just what were newly arrived soldiers to make of all this? If they read an official document, 'Some Facts about Northern Ireland', they would learn that the central thread running through the disturbances of the past fifty years was the refusal of Republicans and a large number of Catholics to accept the partition of Ireland. In turn this had produced fear and mistrust amongst the Protestants, who regarded the Catholics as a subversive force permanently in their midst. The Protestants would have to be assured that they would not be united with the South against their wishes, and the Catholics would have to 'lose their romantic hopes of reunification by force with the Republic'. What was more, the inhabitants of Ulster had to understand that it was the United Kingdom which sustained them financially and that 'the latter is becoming disenchanted with seeing investment frittered away through everlasting strife.'

In September a new commander, Brigadier Frank Kitson, was appointed to 39 Brigade in Belfast. He came with experience in Kenya, Cyprus, Malaysia and Oman and straight from a year's Defence Fellowship study, which had resulted in a book on counter-insurgency called *Low Intensity Operations*. Kitson had a sharp and restless mind. He was firmly convinced that a counter-insurgency campaign needed close civil/military coordination to be successful, and he constantly badgered Lisburn to move in this direction and appoint local civil administrators. He argued that political and legal restraints made it impossible to destroy all the subversive organisations and that there must be a coordinated policy of de-escalation of violence and of atttrition. He felt that always facing up to street activity was not necessarily a good idea: one riot would breed another, and if there were a casualty the funeral would produce another incident. He put forward the view that there were occasions when soldiers should act and others when they should not.

Lisburn was not overly impressed. It was felt that Kitson's ideas were 'fallacious and even tendentious' and ran counter to the general policy of Army withdrawal. The first task was to stop the rioting. It was no good, argued one officer, calling for a civil administrator like a District Commissioner in the colonies. It was thought more important to sort out the military administration because while there were two brigades in Belfast, there was none in the country. The second Belfast brigade headquarters staff was sent back to England, much to the fury of some local politicians and indeed some Army officers, and Kitson was left to run the whole city. The other proposal made at this time was that there should be brigade headquarters for Belfast, Londonderry and 'the country' — which would cover the border areas of south Armagh — each with an integrated police headquarters under an assistant chief constable with full powers including the running of the local Special Branch. The brigade structure was to come in time — the full police cooperation was not.

Now, with local government creaking badly, and broken down altogether in some places, Brigadier Kitson made a further plea for better civil/military coordination, particularly in the field of community relations. However, there were other areas as well. Kitson was concerned that if there were to be civil development then Lisburn should consider tactical security requirements at the same time. He was also concerned about evictions in sensitive areas like New Barnsley. Again, close coordination would ease this problem. He also wanted a civil representative at lower levels: someone who knew how to cut through bureaucratic red tape and get things done — things like mending leaking roofs, restoring smashed pavements, sorting out arrears of rent and electricity payments. He did, in fact, get a 'Mr Fixit' to work at Belfast City level but had no one further down the line. One CO remarked pertinently, and prophetically: 'It is worth considering that if the security forces do not set up a committee so that local people can express their views, the terrorists may decide to do this.'

Kitson's theories were to have an effect on Army counter-insurgency policy in the years to come, although in some Army quarters they were seen as 'merely bringing together everything anyone knew on the subject'. He also became a controversial figure for his views expressed in *Low Intensity Operations*. In this book he argued that in a democratic country it was the duty of soldiers to wage war in any of its forms — just as it was the duty of people to elect representatives who would wage war only when necessary. Soldiers themselves should have faith in the moral rectitude of their Government because often it was not possible for them to know enough of the facts to make personal judgements. However, if they thought their country wrong, they should cease to support it and take the consequences. 'Moral issues can only be related to the circumstances of a particular case,' he wrote 'and then they must be faced by soldiers and civilians alike on moral grounds.'

Kitson has since become the best-known soldier in the British Army; but it was one central idea which quickly made him the *bête noire* of the Left. This was that the Army should be geared towards and ready to face popular movements long before they took the shape of subversion or an uprising. His critics claimed that he had been sent to Northern Ireland especially to try out all his counter-terrorist theories. A French-Breton journalist for the French daily *Libération*, Roger Faligot, who is described by his publisher as 'one of France's leading specialists on modern Irish history', became excited enough to write: 'A man has declared war on Europe; a free Europe; a special war. A man distinguished by his rich military experience; his political outlook on warfare; and his militaristic conception of politics.' He claimed that Kitson had been offered Ireland as a 'testing-ground' for his theories. These were based on the principle that the Army was of growing importance in any counter-insurgency operation and that an integrated politico-military apparatus 'offers a systematic surveillance of men and ideas, the infiltration and manipulation of political groupings, the trades-union movement, the media, the social services, and ultimately the paralysis and the neutralisation of potential dissidents and opponents.'

Faligot advanced the claim that counter-insurgency experts meeting in Lisburn had come up with a policy of isolating the IRA within the nationalist community; combining a policy of repression from the front within the framework of Direct Rule and a programme of housing and employment reforms with equal opportunity for both communities. According to Faligot, Kitson dissociated himself from this. He felt rather that the IRA should be split; a fake peace movement should be initiated; Republican cadres should be arrested on a selective basis; gangs should be infiltrated and manipulated; there should be a campaign of assassination to terrorise the population', and there should be a massive psychological war to discredit the IRA. Most of these, Faligot claimed, seemed 'too extraordinary and ambitious', and the more traditional method of Direct Rule was imposed on the province instead.

Senior Army officers and politicians dismissed the idea that Kitson had been sent to the province expressly to try out his ideas, 'even though this belief was held by many wild Irishmen'. He was, as one pointed out, still only a brigadier. In Northern Ireland soldiers were working 'in the dark' and it was felt by a number of senior officers that Kitson contributed more than most to new ideas. It was also accepted as slightly unfortunate that his book had come out while he was there and pursuing 'a fairly punchy line' on the streets. He was a 'live wire' taking advantage of his experience, and some of his ideas undoubtedly upset the more conventional sections of the Army. One officer under whom he served said:

> Frank is a very clear-minded person. He is completely without prejudice. He looks at each situation in the coldest, hardest and most unsentimental way. He analyses it with great incisiveness and then makes a clear, detailed plan of what to do. But he is very sensitive to all the various influences at work. He is a hard man but a religious man. He was a very good choice. Few other people would have brought Belfast under control at that time in the way he did.

The year 1971 opened with four days of vicious rioting in Ballymurphy: grenades and petrol bombs were thrown; buses were hijacked and set alight. The Army and police carried out widespread house searches under showers of missiles that now included steel ball-bearings, darts fired from catapults, and bolts from crossbows. A few days later, at the request of the Army, shopkeepers withdrew crossbows from sale. One rather embittered RUC officer commented, 'The worst thing the British Government had ever done was to bring in the Army. The IRA now has a classic, slow-moving target on their streets—the British Army of Occupation.'

A young officer who spent most of his time on these streets

wondered to what extent the actual presence of soldiers was a catalyst to a mob. If people were going to smash windows in the Diamond in Derry, should the Army let them get on with it and then mend the windows — or should soldiers intervene, with the danger of an even bigger fracas or a full scale riot? For many of the young commanders at the 'sharp end', this was one of their biggest problems for they had to consider to what extent it was all a 'come on'.

Despite the rioting, the Army was engaged in secret talks with IRA leaders, or 'community spokesmen', as they were called then. These came to an end in February when the CLF, Major-General Farrar-Hockley, named five men who he said were involved — Frank Card, Billy McKee, Leo Martin, Liam and Kevin Hannaway. He did this because Lisburn had good intelligence that the murder of soldiers was being planned and he wanted the public to know that the Provisionals were deeply involved in the disturbances. He also wanted to let the Provisionals know that the Army had identified its leadership. The Provisionals went ahead with their plans, hitting five soldiers in one ambush and hitting another three with snipers. Then they shot dead Gunner Curtis, aged 20, of the 94th Locating Regiment, Royal Artillery. He was the first soldier to be killed since the Army had come in 'in aid of the civil power'. The Ulster Prime Minister, Major Chichester-Clark, immediately announced: 'Northern Ireland is at war with the Provisional IRA,' and demanded more troops. He did not get them.

However, both the RUC and the Army were about to get new commanders. First, Sir Arthur Young left. This worried some Catholics, who felt it would mean the restoration of the old link between their police and the Unionists. Many senior Army officers, though, were pleased. They felt he had disarmed the police and tried to turn them into a new-style force with no fibre to stiffen their resolve and improve their morale and performance. 'What's more,' said one, 'Young and his directives stripped away what credit the police had so that nobody listened to them any more, or did what they said.' So Sir Arthur, or 'Mr Softly, Softly' as many Unionists called him, left and was replaced by a local policeman, Sir Graham Shillington.

The GOC, Sir Ian Freeland, also left. His replacement, Lieutenant-General Erskine-Crum, had a heart attack, and an Artillery officer, Lieutenant-General Harry Tuzo arrived. He had been told by the Chief of the General Staff (CGS), General Sir

Geoffrey Baker, 'Fasten your seat belt; you are going to Northern Ireland', to what Tuzo felt was a strange, semi-political job where military efficiency had to be combined with diplomacy and the ability to reconcile different points of view.

Nowhere were these qualities needed more than at the regular Monday meetings of the Joint Security Committee, held regularly since 1969, when the GOC had been designated Director of Operations. While it was presided over by the Prime Minister of Northern Ireland, the GOC would brief him directly, and was therefore its key member. The meetings would also be attended by Cabinet ministers, the Chief Constable, and other security and specialist officers as and when necessary. It was the Committee which made the political decisions concerning security. The operational decisions were made at a regular meeting on Thursday, at Lisburn, which was chaired by the GOC himself, and attended by the Chief Constable.

At the very first Joint Security Committee meeting Tuzo attended, he received the firm impression that the Stormont Government did not think the Army was being tough enough. However, he made it quite clear from the start that his brief was to try to keep the legally-constituted Government in power, but that this did not mean clobbering the Catholics. 'The Cabinet got very twitchy with him after that,' said a senior civil servant. 'He was the first intellectual soldier they had ever met. He was much too bright for them . . . and much too bright for this place!'

Tuzo's first impressions had been that everyone was far too anxiously trying to be kind. He quickly made it clear to his staff that he thought there was nothing to be gained by 'pussy-footing around', and in an assessment he wrote ten days after he arrived he stated that the Army should be 'even-handed, resolute and tough'. He also said that the Army should plan ahead on a three-year basis, which would allow him to start doing things about mundane matters like accommodation. He was well aware that his men were 'absolutely pigging it'.

In March 1971 the campaign took an ugly turn when three young off-duty soldiers were murdered. They were Highland Fusiliers: two of them were brothers aged 17 and 18, the other was 23. Inexperienced, they had been picked up in a city pub, probably on the pretext of being taken to a party. On a dark, lonely lane above the city at Ligoniel, they got out of a car to relieve themselves and were each shot in the back of the head. These murders seemed to shock everyone. The Official IRA claimed their units had not been involved. So too did the Provisionals, although Michael Farrell, in his book *The Orange State,* claimed that one of their units had carried out the murders as 'reprisals for Army repression in the Ardoyne'.

In Dublin the Irish Prime Minister, Jack Lynch, condemned the murders, calling the assassins 'enemies of the Irish people'. Two days later the Defence Secretary, Lord Carrington, said that no more soldiers under eighteen would be allowed to serve in Northern Ireland, and within a week 170 had been replaced.

When the next soldier, Corporal William Bankier of the Royal Green Jackets, was shot dead, the Protestant *Newsletter* ran a headline: 'Another night of terror in Belfast'. A prominent Unionist suggested to some senior Army officers that the Army should have taken hostages and shot them in reprisal. One officer recalled that in Palestine the Government had agreed to form a special assassination squad to deal with terrorists. 'They only shot one, a fellow called Israel Rubivitz,' he said. 'Then the Government renegaded on the deal. In Cyprus we still had such people around but they weren't allowed to do anything. We certainly have no one like that in this place.'

There were more mundane problems. One Army commander got fed up when he found that it usually took four soldiers to hold down one struggling figure, 'even if the fellow was the most black-hearted terrorist'. So the soldiers were instructed in Aikido, which meant that one soldier could deal with one person. Another officer used to get very cross at restrictions laid down for the use of baton rounds, or 'rubber bullets' as they were more commonly known as.

> It used to madden me to read that it should not be fired in any circumstances where it could hurt anybody. My view was that if it didn't hurt anybody, what was the point in letting it go? The aim *was* to give people a whacking great thump! I mean the people against whom it was fired were presumably wrong-doers . . . but our legal people would say it was the general public at large and they weren't sure if we should fire them at all!

There were also legal problems, particulary when soldiers were arresting someone. They would be expected to use the correct legal terms even in the hurly-burly of confrontation. Getting it wrong

and this, men, is the "Yellow Card"... which is translated into English as "Carte Blanche"....

sometimes involved the Government in paying huge sums in compensation. Despite the provisions of the Special Powers Act, soldiers did not at this time have the legal authority to stop people in the street and hold them, nor had they the power to set up vehicle checks, or to break up a meeting.

There were problems the other way round as well. Every soldier was under a military obligation to obey orders if they were legal. Section 3 of the Criminal Law Act 1967 allowed a soldier — or anyone for that matter — to use reasonable force in the prevention of crime. The problem was that if a soldier exceeded this he could be charged and tried in a criminal court. After the first petrol bomber had been shot dead in the act of throwing a bomb, it was decided to issue soldiers with precise instructions. These came in the form of the Yellow Card which he carried with him. It was argued that the Yellow Card was for the soldier's protection. The idea was to draw the top line of what he could do well below the top line of what the law said he could do. This meant he could exceed the instructions without necessarily breaking the law, and if he did not exceed them he would certainly be all right. Even this produced some dissension within the Army's legal department itself. One Army lawyer said:

> To have to justify any violent act a soldier might have to take by use of Section 3 of the Criminal Law Act 1967 is ludicrous! The whole basis of Section 3 is that you are talking about a private citizen, in a situation where he needs to use force to defend himself or someone else — or to stop crime generally. Now this did not even *begin* to meet the situation where the state, as a matter of state policy, decided to use one of the state's arms — the Army — to preserve and maintain law and order. This was never satisfactorily resolved and we drew attention to it time and time again.

Another Army lawyer put it this way:

> Now this is a hell of a situation into which you put an eighteen-year-old! But the fact of the matter is that you can't use your troops unless you subject them to the law. The moment you start doing anything else you are producing military anarchy. You must have some regime otherwise it would just be a case of bang, bang, bang — hooray, hooray let's go out and shoot people.

The Yellow Card was, for soldiers on the ground, a cumbersome set of instructions, as it prevented the opening of fire except in closely-defined circumstances. It was difficult, as one soldier pointed out, to see your friends blown up around you, pick up the bits, put them in a plastic bag and then go on and read the Yellow Card. The general feeling was that if a soldier really stuck to the rules, he would not be doing his job properly.

As more soldiers were killed, Chichester-Clark flew to London on 18 March to ask for more troops, more arrests, a total curfew in Catholic areas, saturation raids and searches and a much bigger role for the UDR. These demands were rejected and he came back virtually empty-handed, prepared to resign. The British Prime Minister, Edward Heath, asked him at least to wait until Lord Carrington went over the next day. There was no real chance, however, that the Defence Secretary could save him.

While he was seen as a 'very straight up and down man' in London, Chichester-Clark was also considered to be 'making a hash' of the situation. He and his Cabinet were not held in very high regard by the Army. A staff officer recalled:

> The prime ministers of Northern Ireland always had one great complaint, and that was that they did not control the security forces. Just as bloody well they didn't! My God! They once complained about lack of co-operation and we went to see them. They produced a list of six requests. The first was 'two extra men on road blocks'. They had no broad political ideas. They just wanted to smash the Catholics.

One incident illustrates the problem. Carrington and Tuzo had been at a Cabinet meeting to discuss the background to the serious rioting on the Antrim Road. The Cabinet, however, had merely complained that the soldiers were too slow to catch the rioters. 'Why don't you put them in gymshoes, so that they can run faster?' said Captain William Long, MP, expressing the considered view of the Cabinet of the Northern Ireland Government to the Secretary of State for Defence. It was a revealing remark to some of those present, for it showed that the Cabinet had no conception of the real, overall problem; that all they were concerned about were tactics on the ground. Carrington's face showed stunned disbelief at this proposal, but there was not a flicker from Tuzo. He had heard all this many times before. He just gave the classic, diplomatic answer, 'We'll think about it'. It was, in fact, a sensible tactic and many regiments did put their fastest runners in track suits and gymshoes so that they could catch up with rioters.

So it was that Lord Carrington, Sir Geoffrey Baker and General Tuzo came once again to the big cabinet office with its huge bay window looking out over the lawns to the greenhouses and stables. The Army officers and the Unionist politicians sat around the long table to discuss the crisis. Above them, over the fireplace, hung a large and fading oil painting. It was an Arcadian idyll with shepherds and peasants reclining in the sunset. It was an emotional meeting. Lord Carrington was 'very charming' but said quite firmly that while the Army could not continue to pour in resources to mount 'punitive expeditions', it would maintain whatever level was needed to keep the peace.

It was not enough to save Chichester-Clark; and indeed the Army feeling was that, while it was sad to see him go, it had to happen. In his place came Brian Faulkner, a 'hard, wee man' who was seen as a good negotiator. He was the politician who had been waiting impatiently in the wings for this moment but he was unpopular with the Catholics for his 'hard line' views and with some Protestants because he was trade, not gentry. To the Army, Faulkner was a man nurtured in the hothouse of Stormont, where everyone had been playing general post in the Cabinet for twenty years. His advantage was that at least he had been in all departments, and was 'light on his feet', which was to his credit. He was seen as a professional, and if a counter-insurgency campaign had to have a mixture of political and economic measures, then he was the better man to tie it up. On the other hand, there was a strong feeling that he had all the cards stacked against him and that the damage had been done.

Coordination was needed, particularly in the field of intelligence. 'The RUC was a shambles,' one officer said bluntly. 'They had always kept to themselves, they had no contact with London, they had no expertise.' That very month the Director of Intelligence at Lisburn, a civilian, had received a detailed assessment which pointed out the tremendous problems faced by the intelligence organisation of a country sliding from a peaceful situation into one of subversion and insurgency. Many new intelligence targets were appearing and more information was needed. It did not, however, necessarily have to be of the same high quality as that obtained in normal peacetime conditions because it was to be used to form the basis of operations. One of the main problems, however, was that Special Branch officers were being prevented, as a matter of policy, from providing information and intimate support to Army commanders on the ground. Success or failure now depended very much on unofficial contact on the ground at Divisional level. Quick and adequate information at that level was vital; it was no use waiting for it to come from top government levels. It would, the Director was told, be a simple matter to solve. All it needed was a word from Special Branch headquarters to change the policy, for the policemen on the ground, with very few exceptions, would be happy to oblige.

The assessment did not achieve what was wanted, however, and control remained centralised. Army commanders could only theorise as to why this policy was coming down from Stormont. One said:

> Stormont was in a very difficult position because it was officially responsible for law and order, but as the police had been disarmed it had to rely on the Army. However, the Army did not come under them but under the MOD and the Westminster Government. Now, if you had total control of the information at the top you could pass it across and pressure the Army to do things it might otherwise not do. The pressure would be on the lines of 'Well, our informers are terribly hard to get and if you don't use the information when we get it, it discourages them.' The advantage to Stormont was that it could present itself — particularly to its hard-line supporters — as doing something. The disadvantage to us was that we knew for a fact that if the Army did act, there would be a riot and we would have to react to that, producing the sort of punch-up Stormont needed to show it was maintaining law and order. No one ever said this — I'm sure such a Machiavellian thought never crossed anyone's mind. But it was one of the biggest problems we had in trying to pursue a coherent policy. I used to find myself with riots on my hands when I didn't want them — several times. I would say 'I don't give a damn about recovering five rifles. They aren't important compared to the fuss . . .', but they would then produce all this sob-stuff about informers.

The Army now started to build up the intelligence system and poured in huge sums of money, men and effort. It would be a long time, however, before the full effects were to be appreciated. In the meantime, some hard planning had to be done. The CLF, Major General Farrar-Hockley, reasoned that the Provisionals would now have to go for a bombing campaign or they would be finished. There were a number of options to counter this. One was a curfew, but it would be difficult to enforce. There was also the danger of shooting the wrong people, like children running messages for their parents, or doctors out on call. So the idea of internment came back into favour; it would at least have the advantage of removing the Provisional leaders and gunmen from the community. But an Army intelligence officer who went to police headquarters to liaise with Special Branch was horrified by what he found. 'When we saw their list of names,' said one, 'they were so old, so bloody out-of-date, it was pathetic! And this from people who had been talking about internment . . . saying we *must* have internment: demanding it every time someone got shot.'

Faulkner was soon to show how tough he wanted to be. At the end of May he announced:

> At this moment any soldier seeing a person with a weapon or acting suspiciously may fire to warn or with effect, depending on the circumstances, without waiting for orders from anyone . . . this is a firm warning to the whole of the Ulster community as to what can happen at this time.

So the temperature rose as the Provisionals also pushed forward with their policy of turning the Catholics against the Army. A priest remarked:

> It's terrible to see some of the kids the Provos recruit. You know, the really good kids. But there's nothing much more exciting the Church can offer them than holding a gun, or firing it, is there? I mean the place has just gone wild! They even go to gun lectures once a week. No one stands up to the Provos; they don't want their sons beaten up. I remember one man who wouldn't give up his car. They put his arms against a wall and broke them with hurley sticks. He thought it better than having his knees shot off.

Neither the Army nor Brian Faulkner was really happy about the idea of internment, but Faulkner was coming under increasing pressure from his Cabinet to have it introduced. In May 1971 it was decided that some planning would have to be started in case the decision to go ahead was taken. A former secretary in the Ministry of Home Affairs, William Stout, in whom Faulkner had great confidence, was recalled from retirement to head a small security unit. Stout had the advantage of having been around during the internment operations of the late 1950s. A great deal of planning had to be done in terms of accommodation and staffing should internment become a reality. For this reason arrangements were made on a contingency basis to extend and improve the accommodation at Long Kesh — which was in any case occupied by some troops — and the cover story was that it was simply an extension for the arrival of more troops. The cover was nearly blown by a reporter who happened to fly overhead and then asked Stormont what was happening. He did not push very hard, and the cover story held. So, with great reluctance in some quarters and unseemly pushing in others, internment and all it meant edged nearer.

In June General Tuzo appeared on BBC television. He said that while a permanent solution could not be found by military means, the Army could maintain an ascendancy over the IRA which would allow the politicians to find one. Early in July there was more rioting in Belfast and in Londonderry. In the early hours of the fourth morning of the rioting in Londonderry, a man from the Creggan estate, Seamus Cusack, was shot by the Army, and died in Letterkenny Hospital across the border. In the mourning and the rioting which followed another man, Desmond Beattie, was shot by the Army. The police said he was about to throw a nail-bomb at the time. There was uproar, but the Home Secretary refused to sanction an inquiry, despite threats by the Social Democratic Labour Party (SDLP) to walk out of the Stormont Parliament — which in the end they did. The SDLP had been formed the year before by absorbing most of the supporters of the old nationalist Party, the national Democratic Party and the Republican Labour Party. It was the party which spoke for the majority of Catholics in Northern Ireland, and the walkout was a blow to political process. Unionist politicians, however, sided with the Army, their feelings most probably voiced by the Home Affairs Minister, John Taylor, who said:

> I would defend without hesitation the action taken by the Army authorities in Derry against subversives during the past week or so when it was necessary in the end to actually shoot to kill. I feel it may be necessary to shoot even more in the forthcoming weeks in Northern Ireland.

Lisburn was not impressed. The marching season was coming up again and there were enough problems around without their being increased by strong words. The CGS, General Sir Michael Carver, who had replaced General Baker, came over to see Sir Harry Tuzo (who had just been knighted in the Queen's birthday honours list). One reason for his visit was to see how the GOC could be helped. Another was to see what could be done to help the Westminster Government by keeping Northern Ireland quiet during the crucial run-up to the October vote on Britain's entry to the Common Market — while at the same time not antagonising the Irish Prime Minister, Jack Lynch.

The GOC told Carver that Stormont was pushing for a tougher security policy. Pressed to produce a military reaction to this demand, Sir Harry said everything possible was being done in a straightforward, military way; only the unconventional could be new, and all that was left was the Double Act, which was to ban all marches — in particular the Protestant ones about to take place — and to introduce internment. Sir Michael Carver said he did not feel that this was a good idea, and in fact it was the last thing he wanted; Sir Harry agreed with him. Then they discussed the building of the Long Kesh prison and agreed that this should be completed as quickly as possible.

There were ten explosions the next day along the route to be taken by a Protestant procession, though the march itself went ahead in reasonable order, and at a subsequent press conference the GOC and the chief constable were inclined to congratulate themselves rather than the reverse. The Provisionals then stepped up the pressure. A soldier was shot dead and a Provisional unit, wearing white medical coats, rescued a wounded IRA man from the Royal Victoria Hospital in Belfast. Next they blew up and completely wiped out the *Daily Mirror*'s ultra-modern printing plant, worth £2 million. By the end of the first six months 55 people had died and some 600 had been treated in hospital for injuries. Brian Faulkner argued that if these figures were translated into United Kingdom terms they would mean 2,000 dead and 22,000 injured — something Westminster would not be able to ignore.

Trying to avoid the introduction of internment, the GOC now put forward the idea of an arrest operation of one hundred suspects. His idea was both to collect information and to show the Provisionals that 'the hairs on their head were numbered'. This would take place after the Apprentice Boys' march in Londonderry on 12 August. On the ground, some officers were absolutely appalled at the thought. This 'dummy run' could only act as a warning to the Provisionals, who, if and when internment was introduced, would very sensibly have disappeared. One commander, knowing that the Commander Land Force was to change very soon, extracted a promise that there would be no hasty decision. He hoped then to persuade the incoming CLF that it was not a good idea. In a discussion of the problem with the MOD in London on 18 July by secure telephone, the arrest operation was agreed in principle; it was also agreed not to ban the march but to get the route changed to make it less provocative and easier to guard. The next day the Army chiefs met the Defence Secretary in London and put the plan to him. While they were doing so there was a call from Faulkner to Lord Carrington. Faulkner said he was now under enormous pressure, particularly from Ian Paisley, to bring in internment. To relieve him it was decided to bring forward the arrest operation to 23 July.

It was not a great success. Only twenty people were prosecuted as a result, a few arms were found and the Catholics were once again infuriated. Violence increased and so did pressure to ban the Londonderry march. Paisley insisted it went forward and by now Faulkner was making it clear that, if it were banned, internment would have to be the *quid pro quo*.

On 29 July Tuzo gave a long interview to the *Belfast Telegraph* in which he described internment as 'a distasteful weapon . . . but it could obviously have an important effect if employed at exactly the right moment in the right framework.' It was not, however, the right thing to do at the moment and would create other problems. In its 'Viewpoint' column the paper commented:

> . . . the underlying message is that life will be harder for the terrorists in the weeks and months to come. It is easy to say this 'tougher line' policy should have been enforced long ago. But the Army is dependent largely on its intelligence system, and it is only since the IRA campaign intensified in June that the breaks have been coming its way. . . . The appeal to the Apprentice Boys to call off their march in Derry will doubtless be ignored, although who can quarrel with the general's view that an agreement to stand down for a year would greatly enhance their reputation. Once again the soldiers will play the role of the 'men in the middle', diverting their energies from the all-important anti-terrorist drive.

On 3 August the Northern Ireland Committee of the Cabinet met in London and what had been agreed between the MOD and Lisburn was passed on. In Belfast, this decision not to ban the march or introduce internment increased the pressure on Faulkner from all sides. In turn he tried very hard to get both the GOC and the CGS to agree that the worsening security situation required internment. Neither officer would agree to this. They were determined not to be used as political tools, although one officer said: 'We felt we couldn't go on forever letting these fellows who were causing all the trouble go scot-free.'

The next day Faulkner informed Tuzo that he was under enormous pressure from both Catholics and Protestants to ban the Londonderry march in order to avoid bloodshed. Tuzo passed this on to London saying that he could not morally resist the request but adding that he was still not recommending either a ban or internment. The following morning the CGS, Sir Michael Carver, flew happily off to Cardiff to open a military tattoo. He had hardly arrived when he had a message to say that Faulkner was insisting on both a ban and internment. From Cardiff and Belfast people headed for London to discuss the matter. They all met at the airport, and the Army officers travelled into town alone so that Tuzo could brief Carver. He said it was his opinion that if Faulkner did not get what he wanted he would fall from power. Both officers admired Faulkner as a shrewd politician. They knew that if he did fall, someone from even further to the right in the political spectrum would take over, and they were sure that Faulkner would play this card for all he was worth.

There was a long meeting at 10 Downing Street. The Army commanders were called in for a short period to give their assessment of the situation. Before Heath and Faulkner went into conclave together Sir Harry said firmly that he felt that the disadvantages of internment outweighed the advantages. The Cabinet had before it a number of options ranging from picking up thirty suspects to going for as extensive a pick-up as possible, which meant over 500. There were differences at Lisburn over which option to take. The senior commanders had not seen one single list containing all the names because no such list existed, and they were inclined to go for the smaller figure. The names, however, had been collected by the RUC, whose recommendation was to go for the full number. In due course Faulkner's demands were agreed. Operation Demetrius, the code name of internment, would be started at 4 a.m. on Tuesday 10 August and, most importantly, it was decided by the Cabinet to go for the full list of names. It was also decided that all processions would be banned for at least six months.

Now the main concern was to move as fast as possible. The new CLF, Major-General Robert Ford, had arrived only three days previously and had had to take a great deal of advice and information at face value. No pre-planning had been done other than a most cursory look at Special Branch lists. The various lists of suspects from intelligence sources now contained 520 names. Ford was faced with planning a huge operation in a very short space of time. That evening he attended a series of meetings where the names were gone over again and again. There was constant argument over whether X or Y should be included or whether indeed some suspects were north of the border or south. The Army knew that the lists were doubtful, but also knew that they had nothing better to go on. The alienation of the police now meant that the Army's knowledge of the Catholic areas was very limited, and what they had was not always being passed on. The Army knew that there would be mistakes but their orders were quite clear: internment was not to be selective, but as wide as possible. It was an invitation to disaster, but Faulkner — and Westminster — had succumbed to extreme Unionist pressure. The next morning Major-General Ford sent his recommendations to the GOC as 'jointly agreed' between himself, the Deputy Chief Constable, the Head of Special Branch and the Director of Army Intelligence. Once that had happened there was no chance that anyone at a higher level would question the lists.

It was, however, considered impossible to carry out a simultaneous arrest of this number with the existing number of troops. There were fourteen major units in Northern Ireland and it was impossible to increase this before the evening of Monday 9 August, when one unit would arrive, to be followed by another on Tuesday and the best part of an armoured reconnaissance regiment on Tuesday and Wednesday. The CLF was also very worried about security for the operation. Quite a few people in Whitehall and Stormont were aware of the plan for 4 a.m. Tuesday. He decided to implement a cover plan showing that the additional forces were needed in Londonderry to deal with the Apprentice Boys' march on Wednesday — for which in fact the troops had originally been ordered — and to put out indications at various levels that the Army was just not ready for internment (and indeed that an internment plea made by Faulkner had been rejected by Stormont and

Westminster). This story was spread through various sources from Army headquarters. It was also decided to make a plan within a plan, because the CLF was sure that the Tuesday date would be leaked. It was therefore decided to make the arrests on Monday, starting at 4.30 a.m., without the assistance of any uniformed police. This time was chosen because the hooligans were regularly on the streets until 3 a.m. During the next hour, up to 4 a.m., they would go to their homes, all over the province, dead tired. 4.30 a.m. was the only time the Army could expect to find them in bed. So tight was security that in Stormont only Brian Faulkner knew of the changed plan, and in Whitehall only the CGS, the Defence Secretary, the Home Secretary and the Prime Minister.

With no extra troops and no uniformed police, the Army was going to be stretched to the limit. Using everyone, and doing without a reserve, it was possible to go for only 450 arrests. So the lists were pruned. As part of the cover plan the normal intensity of operations also had to be kept up, Brian Faulkner even going away for the weekend. The Army staff were not told that Operation Demetrius was to be on Monday, and planning went on right through the weekend for the reinforcement of Londonderry. All the staff 'worked like mad' because they thought the Londonderry operation was actually going to take place. So, the Army felt, complete surprise would be achieved.

On Saturday 7 August there was an incident just outside Springfield Road police station which showed how easily a fatal mistake could be made, and how easy it was for such a mistake to be swallowed up and lost in more momentous events. In the morning rush hour, with traffic nose to tail, a car backfired. In the car were two men from south Armagh with cement on their boots, on their way to a sub-contracting job in the city. In the car behind was another man who was with them. When the car backfired, the sentry at the police station — a paratrooper — ran into the street, dropped to one knee and put a shot through the rear window of the car and the driver's head. The passenger was grabbed by other soldiers, taken inside and beaten up. An hour later the third man was still wandering up and down the road outside, shocked, and mumbling an incoherent story which did not match the Army's story of being fired at. The man who was beaten up was later released to the Mater Hospital where, despite extensive bruising to his face, he refused to say any more about the matter. No firearms were found and indeed nor was any trace of firearms. No charges were made against the men and nothing was found to connect them with any subversive or terrorist organisation. The incident was another example of the increasing violence. Between 4 and 8 August at least 144 shots were fired at military personnel in twenty-two separate incidents. At that time it was an enormous number.

In the early hours on Monday 9 August, as the internment swoops got under way at 4 a.m., the Springfield road incident was forgotten. Thousands of troops across the province began a major house-to-house search, and as they did so the women came out to bang dustbin lids and blow whistles, the traditional warning. Acting under the Special Powers Act, the Stormont Government authorised the arrest of 450 people.

The arrests were carried out entirely by soldiers, but in each arrest unit there was a Special Branch officer who identified the suspects. Then, after formal re-arrest at a police station, they were passed on to the three holding centres at Magilligan, Girdwood and Ballykinlar.

The poor quality of the intelligence assessments soon became apparent. Soldiers arrived to arrest men who had been in the campaigns in the 1940s and 1950s: there was another suspect aged 77 who had first been jailed in 1929; another was blind and yet another, in Armagh, was found to have been dead for four years. Stormont MP Paddy Devlin reckoned the Army got the wrong men because they and the police had not been behind the barricades and did not know the new leaders who had emerged recently. A company commander in Londonderry found that his men had few of the right names and addresses. Often the man they wanted lived next door to the house they tried. He felt that it stirred up enormous antagonism. 'I think that in common with a lot of other people,' he said 'we were emotionally opposed to internment. We just didn't think it would do an awful lot of good.' Then tales of brutality, which were to haunt the security forces for years, started to emerge. Michael Farrell of People's Democracy, one of those arrested, reported:

> Almost everyone had been beaten up. Many had been blindfolded and terrified by being thrown out of a moving helicopter which they were told was high in the air but in fact was only a few inches off the ground. More had been forced to run the gauntlet barefoot between lines of troops with batons and across barbed-wire and glass-strewn ground.

Three hundred and forty-six men were arrested — 70 per cent of those on the lists. The operation was considered a tactical success, and by and large it was over by 7.30 a.m. After forty-eight hours 79 men were released and the rest placed either in Crumlin jail, Belfast, or on the *Maidstone,* which had been brought in as a prison-ship and moored in Belfast Lough.

The 'dummy run' in July might well have warned the IRA, but the Army still felt that their special cover plan had fooled them. Intelligence sources said later that the IRA had not expected it. The Army do not believe that they would have lifted 346 if the IRA had expected it (even though some of those should not have been arrested at all). An officer explained that a number of the top men had got away, but this was only to be expected. The impression was that down at the 'working level' most of those wanted had been arrested.

On Monday the Northern Ireland Prime Minister, Brian Faulkner, said that the aim had been to 'smash the IRA'. He went on to explain that he had taken this step solely to protect life and property. 'We are, quite simply, at war with the terrorist,' he said, 'and in a state of war many sacrifices have to be made, and made in a cooperative and understanding spirit.'

What was happening on the streets of Belfast and throughout the province was, however, happening in a spirit far removed from 'cooperative and understanding'. Violence was breaking out on a scale unequalled since 1969. In widespread shooting thirteen people died, including a priest, Father Mullen, who was administering the last rites to a man mortally wounded in Ballymurphy. Hundreds of homes were destroyed by fire and Catholic refugees started to trek across the border to camps set up by the Irish Army.

At Stormont Castle the Cabinet met, stunned by the orgy of death and violence sweeping the province and which by the end of the month was to produce a death toll of 35 — compared with just 4 the previous month. The speed and virulence of the reaction from a large section of the Catholic population — particularly the young — surprised the Army. However, some officers felt that the planned terrorist incidents which had been taking place were now really cut back; that the tempo of IRA operations had been halted. They showed a brave face in public, saying a major defeat had been inflicted on the IRA with soldiers killing between 20 and 30 gunmen. While this press conference was going on, Paddy Kennedy, a Stormont MP, was holding another, introducing Joe Cahill as the leader of the Provisional IRA. Cahill claimed that his organisation was still intact — only 30 had been lifted because they had received a warning and had gone — and they had had only 2 killed. He admitted supplies were running low and appealed to the Republic for help. General Sir Harry Tuzo recalled, some time later:

> That period has been awfully misrepresented. My recollection is clear. It was a perfectly ordinary progression, with consultation with everyone — and ultimately a decision, very finely balanced, was very, very carefully thought out to do one thing: to intern some four-hundred-odd people against whom there appeared to be a case. On the matter of intelligence there was no question but that we, as Johnny-come-lately, had to rely on the intelligence net that existed. It was a police net and it takes years to build up. Internment was not an instantaneous success and the error was perhaps that we were too undiscriminating . . . that was where we slipped up!

Beyond doubt the real error lay once again in the inability to realise that an insurgency campaign is a war for people's minds. Internment was totally one-sided. No Protestants were arrested, and it was certainly not because every Protestant hand was clean from terrorism. It was resentment over this, and over what the Catholics saw as the casual brutality of the soldiers, that fuelled the orgy of destruction and pushed the communities even further into their bitter enclaves.

The day after internment 45 Commando Group Royal Marines came across as a reinforcement unit. They immediately noticed a tense and hostile atmosphere as they operated in small units with other regiments. In the Bogside they were involved in a 'long and arduous' barricade-clearing operation where they and others came under heavy sniper fire. Obstructed by one crowd, mainly children, they agreed to withdraw for a while when Stormont MP John Hume assured them that he could get the crowd to disperse. When over an hour later the crowd was still there, larger and more menacing, they decided to remove it forcibly with water cannon. Missiles and rubber bullets were exchanged, and in the end John Hume and fellow MP Ivan Cooper were arrested and charged. As they were allegedly taking part in a peaceful demonstration they were, in the eyes of the commandos, 'excellent material for the Republican anti-military propaganda machine'. What the marines did not realise was that they were breaking the law, and when in due course this came to be challenged it was to cause a monumental upheaval in the corridors of Whitehall as the legal experts rushed through legislation to cover soldiers who acted in this way.

Then 45 Commando went into print in the regimental magazine: an officer publicly criticised the political direction of the campaign. It was the first time a serving officer had done so and the magazine's editor got a sharp rebuke from the Under-Secretary for the Navy. The editor was largely unrepentant. His view was that the criticism was slight and anyway reflected the feelings on the ground. The 'offending' article had opened and closed with paragraphs which summed up this feeling quite bluntly:

The British Army, as the instrument of internment, has become the object of Catholic animosity. Since that day the street battles, countless explosions, migrations from mixed areas and cold-blooded killings have done little to reassure us that internment would, by the removal of the gunner, provide a return to a semblance of law and order, a basis for a political solution to Ulster's problems. Ironically it appears to have produced the opposite effect; the two factions of the IRA, previously engaged in a struggle for supremacy, have called a temporary truce, the Catholic population of Northern Ireland is now even more alienated and hope that Catholics and Protestants could live in harmony is even more remote. . . .

Fortunately 45's stay in this depressing and unhappy country is a short one. The recent shootings of British soldiers during the past weeks and the continuing explosions make it evident that internment was quite inefficacious. It has, in fact, increased terrorist activity, perhaps boosted IRA recruitment, polarised further the Catholic and Protestant communities and reduced the ranks of the much needed Catholic moderates. In a worsening situation it is difficult to imagine a solution.

While the senior officers were saying that the operation had been a success, some of the commanders on the ground were furious. Their argument was that what the Army had been trying to do all along was to separate the two IRA wings from the support of the Catholic population. The policy in Belfast in particular was one of de-escalation and attrition. It was based on avoiding incidents which drove the population into supporting the IRA either because they thought of them as their defenders, or because they thought the Army so awful that they would back the IRA instead. Attrition would get the IRA off the backs of the people. The brigade commander was not greatly bothered what the IRA did to the Government; at that time the plight of the Government was not considered desperate. The biggest problem was the Protestant community, which would not stand for de-escalation because it meant, for example, stopping Protestants marching through areas they had always marched through because now the marches might cause riots. So this policy was very unpopular with the Protestants, and much of the day-to-day work of the soldiers involved trying to sell them the idea and to control them from reacting violently to it. This had been the basis of tactics right through until internment.

Shortly afterwards there was a meeting of officers from all over the province to discuss the situation. One officer recalled how Brigadier Kitson had got to his feet and harangued his astonished colleagues with a withering indictment of the whole operation. 'I think he was jolly nearly sacked for what he said,' the officer remarked. 'He told them that it had been done in the wrong way, at the wrong time and for the wrong reasons. Didn't seem to go down terribly well!'

The soldiers' objections to internment — the brigadier was not the only person to feel strongly about it — were based on a number of reasons. In essence they felt that because it was the biggest boost that could be given to the Protestant community, it should have been used to compensate them for something big being given to the Catholics in order to persuade them to support the IRA rather less. For instance, Stormont was what Catholics seemed to hate more than anything, and to have done away with it and introduced Direct Rule at that stage would have been a good boost for them. 'We should have done both these things at the same time,' an officer complained. 'In other words, when we would have gained politically as well as militarily.'

Another complaint was that too many people had been arrested. It caused the maximum furore, and the Army simply did not have the practical means to handle such large numbers of internees. Those arrested were kept centrally and not interrogated by the military. 'Not very sensible,' observed an officer, 'We couldn't ask them the questions we wanted to, and some were interrogated by very dubious methods that caused a maximum fuss later for very little return — whatever anyone says.'

It was also the wrong time for the operation. The Army felt that it should have been done in March, but they were not ready, and in

August the intelligence still proved to be insufficient. The ideal arrangement would have been to get the public relations side, the civil side and the intelligence organisation all ready, as well as the arrangements for handling those arrested, and then, if it really was necessary to arrest people, to do so in small numbers.

Lisburn might have felt that they had got the Provisionals off the backs of the people, but the sting came back in the mounting casualty lists. August was the first month in which there were 100 bomb explosions. Looking at it more broadly, in the four months before, the fatalities had been 4 soldiers killed, no policemen and 4 civilians. In the four months after Operation Demetrius, 30 soldiers, 11 policemen and 73 civilians were killed. Moreover, the Army was now able to pick up Provisional suspects and get them interned, very often on nothing more than suspicion. As a result they also picked up many innocent people. By mid-December over 1,500 people had been arrested by the Army and nearly 1,000 released. The Provisionals, desperate to turn the Catholic community against the security forces, were able to exploit the lax safeguards of the internment process — if indeed there were any safeguards — and ensure that even more innocent people were arrested.

As if to compound the mistakes, the system of interrogation left a great deal to be desired, particularly the type which came to be known as 'interrogation in depth'. No one below the rank of the CLF knew that a small number of men had been pre-selected for this interrogation.

Soon the accusations of torture began to flow in. It was said that the Army and police had physically ill-treated and tortured men who had been arrested and detained during the internment swoops. The allegations ranged from prisoners being forced to run barefoot over broken glass to their being subjected to a series of sensory deprivation techniques.

Lisburn decided that this was largely propaganda, every bit as dangerous as the shooting war and often just as successful. It was being run, Lisburn felt, on the basis that if enough mud was thrown around, some of it would stick. One officer explained that the 'details' about alleged atrocities had appeared so quickly that no one could have got hold of them in the time available. He thought the technique 'very polished'. On 19 August 1971 the Chief of Staff, Brigadier Marston Tickell, held a two-hour press conference. At the end he still felt he could not answer the question of who was winning the propaganda war — the Army or the IRA. He admitted, though, that the Army was concerned about the allegations and wanted them cleared up as soon as possible.

The torture allegations caused such a furore that the Government was forced to institute another enquiry, chaired by the Ombudsman, Sir Edmund Compton. Amongst his findings published in November 1971, was one showing that eleven men had been interrogated 'in depth', and that, while they had not suffered physical brutality, five of the techniques used constituted physical ill-treatment. These were: posture on the wall; hooding; noise; deprivation of sleep; and a diet of bread and water.

Many people thought that Compton's report was unsatisfactory, for two main reasons. First, it did not answer the central question of what was or was not justified in an emergency, and neither did it discuss who was responsible for the interrogation — the Army, the RUC, Special Branch or British Intelligence. Second, it produced what for some people was a very odd definition of brutality. 'We consider that brutality is an inhuman or savage form of cruelty, and that cruelty implies a disposition to inflict suffering, coupled with an indifference to, or pleasure in, the victim's pain. We do not think that happened here.'

The uproar over interrogation surprised and irritated many soldiers. The rules under which these techniques of interrogation took place had been operating for some time, the Joint Services Intelligence School at Maresfield having developed them from experiences arising out of the Korean War. Soldiers such as the former CLF, Major-General Anthony Farrar-Hockley, had been subjected to the techniques by the Chinese and the North Koreans. As a result it had been decided to train soldiers how to resist them, particularly those in the Special Air Service Regiment, and Royal Air Force flying crews who were liable to be caught behind enemy lines. The techniques had been used in Aden, where they had caused a stir and given rise to allegations of torture. There had been an enquiry and the rules governing their use had been revised when Dennis Healey was Defence Secretary.

The techniques came to be used in Northern Ireland when the CGS, General Sir Geoffrey Baker, decided that the RUC did not know how to interrogate properly. The Director of Intelligence, Dick White, was sent across, and it was agreed that the RUC did need training. It was decided that Army Intelligence would give the training, but would not take part in the actual interrogations. Few senior officers knew the details of what was going on. 'I blame myself for not asking,' said one, 'but you know the way these intelligence people work — it's all supposed to be so frightfully hush hush that you don't really like to ask.' Others had let it by on the basis that the system had worked before so it might as well be tried again now that the situation was really bad. One officer said rather irritably:

Naturally one worries — after all, one is inflicting pain and discomfort and indignity on other human beings, but the facts are that first, the interrogators in Northern Ireland were not Army but Special Branch officers, and second, that society has got to find a way of protecting itself . . . and it can only do so if it has good information. If you have a close-knit society which doesn't give information then you've got to find ways of getting it. Now the softies of the world complain — but there is an awful lot of double talk about it. If there is to be discomfort and horror inflicted on a few, is this not preferred to the danger and horror being inflicted on perhaps a million people? So internment and this very, very small scale interrogation was set in train and both were eventually talked out — because the world has become a more talkative place than it was when we used these techniques in colonial situations.

'In future don't shoot till you FEEL the thump of their bullets'

Phase Three

The Army forces the pace
September 1971—February 1972

By the autumn of 1971, policy was in a real muddle. For a start, there were two governments trying to respond to the old demands for reform while dealing with a real guerilla war. Two years before, when the soldiers had first marched on to the streets, the unrest had come from a desire for political reform and the IRA had been a dry husk of an organisation. Now, the civil rights protestors had been replaced in the front line by the fighting men of the Provisionals, whose declared aim was the overthrow of the state.

Internment had exposed the raw bitterness of the communities and driven them more into the isolated enclaves in which the gunman could reign supreme. Not only did the Provisionals deal out their own forms of 'justice' — ranging from tarring-and-feathering to knee-capping and murder — but they also collected protection money, allocated houses on Housing Executive estates, ran the publicly-provided sports and social centres, and licensed the fleets of black taxis which had replaced the Corporation buses burned on the barricades.

The security organisation in Belfast was improved but still imperfect, as the CGS was told when he came over on a visit that autumn. The extra weapon of internment was one of major importance but it had only weakened the IRA and made them less capable of fighting. The Catholic population was still waiting for intimidation to ease up, and an increasingly impatient Protestant population could no longer be kept in check by the promise of internment. Much now depended, the CGS was told, on preventing Protestant action by persuading them that the security forces were being successful against the IRA. Equally, a great deal depended on persuading the Catholics to turn against the IRA and political extremists. The RUC had collapsed in many areas and the Army had two main missions: to rout out the IRA and improve general security, and to keep Protestants from gathering at key points. There was a small advance too, on the intelligence side, achieved by a decision in principle to allow Special Branch officers to talk directly to Army officers at Divisional level. 'The drawback to that little advance,' one officer remarked ruefully, 'was that there was no organisation to back it.' Lisburn still felt that internment was a weapon feared by many and that if the word 'snowball' could be applied at all, then it could certainly be applied to all the extra intelligence pouring in. In setting about strengthening the intelligence set-up, men from the Special Air Service (SAS) were brought in on an individual basis. There had been regular requests from the Army commanders, including the CLF, for them to come in and operate as SAS units. These requests, however eloquently couched, were always turned down flat. 'The Government was always scared that it would be the start of the slippery slope,' explained an intelligence officer. 'They failed to realise that the SAS like everyone else had to operate within the law.' But if the SAS were not allowed into the province in force, they helped individually to train the new undercover teams which were beginning to operate — the Military Reconnaissance Force units. There were also a special section made up of a number of IRA activists and a deserter from the Army, who had been apprehended and then persuaded to work for the Army in this role. The group was known as 'Freds' and lived in one half of a semi-detached house in Holywood while their 'minders' lived in the other half.

Overall, the intelligence scene was gloomy. The lessons learned in Kenya, Aden, Malaysia and even in the campaign in Ireland between 1919 and 1922 had been forgotten or ignored. There was no coordination between the various services such as M15, M16, the RUC, the Army and other smaller units which had been set up. Moreover at this stage some personnel were simply not up to the job, and one senior intelligence officer from M15 was removed from Belfast at the request of the Army. The differing rivalries and loyalties did nothing to help the situation. Both M16 and the RUC, for instance, would mark papers to ensure the other did not have access to them. Many units had direct access to senior commanders at Lisburn over the heads of field commanders. But while they were worrying about intelligence, trouble was brewing behind the barricades of Londonderry, which, unlike those in Belfast, had been allowed to stand.

A short time after internment Sir Harry Tuzo visited Londonderry to meet some 'notable' Catholics. Later he said that it was probably the most stupid thing he did during his whole tour in the province. He travelled there with the British Government representative, Howard Smith. As one member of the party remembered it, they were confronted by these 'notables' — sometimes known as the 'Committee of Twenty' — in a hotel just outside the city and treated to a diatribe on just how awful the Army was and how badly it was behaving. The GOC listened, and offered to stop military operations for a whole month if they could deliver peace. Everyone was delighted, thinking peace was about to break out. 'Of course they didn't deliver,' shrugged a staff officer. 'They just went on home and carried on as before. Harry did it to call their bluff. He was bored with their "holier than thou" attitude . . . but he did think of it as a sincere effort to improve the situation.'

Londonderry was right up in the north-west, on the border with the south, far away from Belfast and to some senior officers it felt like the end of the line. They sensed that in Belfast and Stormont there was a pressure-group with what they called the 'let Derry burn' attitude: that whatever happened it was Stormont's policy to sort out Belfast first. So it was that when the new brigade commander arrived in Londonderry in October he was expected to come with three extra battalions — enough military force to sort out the areas behind the barricades, soon to become known as the 'No Go' areas; however, he arrived on his own as these three battalions had all been diverted to the capital city.

This attitude was critical, because while it existed the force levels would not be increased sufficiently to deal with the problem in the city. To the military this was one which had arisen long before they came on the scene. It was a problem made up of high unemployment, a matriarchal society and the religious 'mix' of the community. This 'mix' was the exact opposite to that in the rest of the province, being 70 per cent Catholic and 30 per cent Protestant. Unemployment reached up to 20 per cent for men, which left more of them with nothing to do than the women, who could at least find work in the shirt factories. In many cases, of course, this made them the main bread-winners. 'Dad stayed behind and loafed,' observed an Army officer, 'because there was bugger-all left for him to do.'

Out of this problem arose what the Army called the YDH — the Young Derry Hooligan. These youngsters were the main threat to law and order — at least up to 4 July 1971, when gunmen first appeared on the streets to pose a new and sinister threat. In the eyes of the local Army commander, this hooligan element was a decisive factor in the planning of operations which led up to and included Bloody Sunday on 30 January 1972. As late as the autumn of 1971 the CO of an infantry battalion in the city gave this appreciation:

The hooligans are tough, unemployed youths, aged between 11 and 23, who are beyond parental control. They are the product of the ghetto environment. They are not necessarily politically motivated but they are wholly anti-authority in attitude and their activities have been channelled into violence in support of Nationalist and Republican causes against the forces of law and order under the control of the Government in power. They now number some 500 with a hard core of about 250. They thrive on violence, including in their ranks many of the petty criminals and thugs of the city. They are described by the People's Democracy as 'Brave Fighters in the Republican Cause' and looked upon as 'innocent stonethrowers' by the majority of the population in the Bogside and the Creggan. They are organised into gangs and have developed sophisticated tactics of brick, iron, petrol bomb, gelignite bomb and stone throwing. They operate sometimes on their own but most recently under cover of snipers. They specialise in attacks on the security forces, in destruction and arson, in hijacking vehicles and intimidation. In the Bogside their overt offensive activities are confined to the fringe of the Creggan Road — Little Diamond — William Street — City Walls — Bishop Street Without — Letterkenny Road. Outside the Bogside they support covert hit-and-run tactics.

Nearly every day some of the hooligan element deploy on to William Street and endeavour to extend their activities into the commercial centre of the city. Only once have they been successful, in October 1970, after which it was decided to take the battle into the Bogside by deploying the military forward of William Street on to the '42 Line' whenever the hooligan element threatened violence. Since July 1971 this forward deployment has not been automatic because the threat of the gunmen within the Bogside has demanded more caution than previously and because of restrictions placed on military commanders.

The CO pointed out that with the low force levels the most the Army could do about the hooligans was to deploy a few snatch squads. However, because the Army had 'never physically occupied the Bogside or the Creggan', the hooligan had an advantage — he could always slip back into the cover of his ghetto. The CO concluded his appreciation quite bluntly:

> Each military plan since October 1969 has included the requirement to arrest members of the hooligan element, and each military operation to affect arrests, either by snatch squad or company strength scoop operations, has invaded the Bogside.

Up to July, when the gunmen came out, the Army reckoned that it had operated a policy of restraint and containment within the city. After that date, however, it would enter the 'hostile areas of the Bogside and the Creggan' for specific tasks, although even then soldiers felt that they were operating in such a restrained manner that it was not possible for them to restore law and order as they should. In the opinion of some local commanders this policy made it very difficult to deal with the gunmen, and it also encouraged the IRA to increase their influence on the people. Moreover, it discouraged the community from submitting to the authority of the Government and providing information to the security forces because the soldiers were not there all the time. Neither did the policy offer relief to those in the Bogside and the Creggan who actually disapproved of the IRA, the hooligans and the conditions of semi-siege.

In view of all this it was decided to abandon the idea of leaving the 'Committee of Twenty' to keep the peace. So, during the late summer and autumn, the Army increased the pressure, by sending in bigger patrols and, on five occasions, full battalions of some 300 to 400 men. However, even this did not seem to achieve the required results. 'We sort of steamed through these areas in a broad phalanx,' said one company commander, 'letting off hundreds of tear gas cartridges and grenades . . . doing nothing, really, but irritate people.'

The troops in Londonderry began to find themselves being 'sucked in' where they did not want to be. They were forced to use their weapons. If they sent in a small patrol to deal with a gunman it could quickly be surrounded and beaten up by a hostile crowd. If a bigger force went in, the troops found themselves using their Internal Security weapons — such as CS gas and rubber bullets — at an even earlier stage than normal. This inevitably turned the Catholic community against the Army and towards the IRA as their defenders. Then, growing anger and resentment brought about massive civil rights disobedience.

In a rather vain attempt to show that the Creggan and Bogside were not 'No Go' areas, the Army occupied a factory at Bligh's Lane in between to guard a little police post. Each day a solitary policeman would be escorted in and would sit in his office, drinking tea, until it was time to go off duty. He was guarded by a full company of soldiers, and he never put foot outside.

The situation in Londonderry was unpleasant, but it was still only simmering. It was Belfast which was ablaze and where the Army concentrated its forces. The conditions were still, even after two years, very new and strange to a great many soldiers and the lessons had to be learned the hard way. A company commander who was tasked to move a tarmac machine blocking the Falls Road decided that the best way would be to throw a cordon sanitaire round it and do what he wanted in the middle. His men carried out his instructions to the letter and in the process were slated, petrol-bombed and stoned. The ordinary soldiers were now being tested in a way for which they had never been trained.

The result of this incident was that pressure increased, and so did the shooting. It was decided that the only thing to do was to go out and patrol constantly to show people who was running the place. On this occasion there was a gun battle which lasted for some five hours during the night but the company did stamp their presence on the area and it cooled down.

It was not a campaign, however, where company commanders could always lead from the front. Where they could do so, many tried to get as close to the 'sharp end' as possible. One made it his golden rule that he went on patrol every single night unless there was a particular reason not to. He felt that it was very important to identify with his riflemen and the dangers they faced, and that he should not just command from his Ops Room.

On patrol I had my leading scout, myself and a radio operator on one side of the street. On the other would be the leading scout, the patrol commander and so on back down the street with the rest of the men. I would be under command of the corporal although we'd worked out that if I wanted to do something particular — like have a look at some derelict house — then I could overrule him. But the important thing was that if we got into a gun battle, then it was his section and he must command it. So I would then get out of his way. In battle my job was commanding a company, not fighting in a forward section. I couldn't afford to get caught in that initial fire fight. But then neither did I like going back to the rear when it happened. That hurt.

New techniques of patrolling were being evolved all the time. One was designed for five parallel streets with the company commander in the centre and platoons on the streets to his right and left. This gave the commander a considerable degree of control and flexibility and allowed the more senior company officers to get a feel of the ground and the conditions. Some units would arrive with little or no specialist training (although in time this was to change and everyone would go through a very elaborate course). They would find that their area was the home of the gunman and the sniper and that in consequence tactics were far more military than police. To be stationary in an open area was to invite a bullet, and the mental approach to operations was governed by rifle, beret and blackened face rather than baton, helmet and shield. On battalion was amused to recall that in one early operation in Divis Flats an IRA gunman almost advanced the well-known ambitions of nearly every member of the battalion by shooting into a small alcove which contained two majors and three company sergeant-majors.

Living conditions were grim. No one got much sleep; there was a constant round of work with mobile patrols, foot patrols, base duties and one section was always kitted-up at immediate minus — ready to move instantly, another section at two to three minutes' notice. There was also the administrative work of the company to get through, operations to organise and intelligence to be studied.

One company lived in a huge attic at the top of Albert Street Mill. Each platoon had one enormous room full of three-tier bunks. 'It was cramped and sweaty. I don't think we ever got more than two or three hours' sleep at a time.' There was one further room with a few partitions — for the company Ops Room, officers' sleeping-quarters, sergeants' sleeping-quarters and the company store. Each time it rained, the water poured in. The company quartermaster slept in a room on the floor below. He got the roof fixed when the company commander threatened to bore holes in the floor so that the rain water would pour straight through on to his bed. The company commander had a small room to himself. It was about 8 feet by 10, with his bed and a small bedside locker. He even had a small window although it was sandbagged because an IRA gunman fired at it from time to time. On the other side of a sort of partition almost up to the ceiling was the intelligence room 'with all the usual mug shots of suspected villains' round the walls. Here there was a rack for his rifle and flack-jacket. His leading scout and radio operator also had their kit in there so that they could grab it quickly when they had to move fast. Crammed into the room were a couple of tatty old armchairs where the odd guest could sit and chat.

Most units lived a life of total involvement, each bound up in its own little concrete jungle. Soldiers read papers and switched on the television news and saw what was going on in other people's back yards. But on the whole each was convinced that his area was the kernel of the whole province. The British soldier has always been a rather phlegmatic type and to him this sort of thing was simply part of the job. To walk round the Falls Road was much the same as walking round Moss Side in Manchester or Mile End in London; they even crouched and took cover in familiar settings, like the doorways of Marks and Spencer's or Boots. But to some, particularly young officers out for the first time, it could be a cultural shock. One platoon commander said:

> I don't think that the men felt the same sense of shame or intrusion which I felt when going into someone else's home. I could never come to terms with bursting in at four in the morning . . . screaming children! . . . women! . . . It was absolutely hateful and I loathed it. I remember the very first time. In those days we didn't knock but went straight through the door. I can't remember the details but I can remember a sense of revulsion – of almost physical sickness. Not because of the dirt and squalor. It was an emotional reaction to invading someone else's house . . . seeing adults and kids, bleary-eyed and scruffy and dirty . . . and then there was no one we wanted in that house! Ninety-nine times out of a hundred there never was!

There were also frightening moments – frightening because of the responsibility of giving orders. One company commander was told that an Official IRA meeting was to take place in a certain house. He had to raid it. He quickly realised that an ordinary foot patrol would be seen a mile away and the alarm would be given. Much the same would happen to a mobile patrol. He decided to use a civilian car with four soldiers wearing anoraks over their Army sweaters and with their berets stuffed in their pockets. Two minutes after they went in the rest of the company would deploy to make sure that they got out again. The major recalled:

> I thought that we'd be in for a rough ride. Everyone else was busy getting ready but I'd given my orders and had nothing else to do. I was absolutely terrified! I went along to a particularly marvellous officer of mine and asked him if he was happy about it all because as the biggest, strongest and bravest man in the company he was going through that door first. Well, he said, 'No, not a bit. I'm absolutely terrified!' and I said, 'Thank God! So am I.' As it happened the operation came to nothing. There was no one there.

It was not only gunmen with whom the soldiers had to deal. Women, too, could be a major problem. In most areas their early warning system for the approach of any stranger meant a general stand-to with the banging of dustbin lids and the blowing of whistles. Hundreds of women could gather very fast and become a dangerous menace to a small patrol. Putting out larger patrols, however, meant putting them out less often. To combat this, one unit decided to overstretch the other side. It sent out five two-vehicle patrols at the same time, one going to the very centre of the Falls and the other to the four corners. As soon as there was a general stand-to they had orders to withdraaw. Two hours later they repeated the performance and went on doing so for the next two days.

Towards the end of the two days some patrols found the stand-to scouts asleep and would shake them by the shoulder saying, 'You should be banging your dustbin lids and blowing your whistles, we are back,' and they would say 'Oh, yes!' and start doing so. This went on until a message through the local priest persuaded the women to stop coming out each time a patrol went by, and slowly the area cooled down. Of course the soldiers also got caught in 'public relations ambushes' – the sort of 'come-on' calls which would lead them blundering into old ladies or invalids in wheelchairs.

The Provisionals were striking back at what targets they could and most of them were in the soft under-belly of the province – commerce, industry and the people themselves. Until internment that year 34 people had died, including 11 soldiers and 4 policemen. In the second half of the year that figure was to soar to 135, including

32 soldiers, 5 members of the UDR and 7 policemen.

To someone like Michael Farrell of the People's Democracy it seemed that the Army was meeting the Provisionals with 'tougher and tougher methods of repression.' Roads were being blown up on the border and the number of internees was steadily increasing. Stormont, he felt, 'backed the Army's physical repression' by two positive measures. The first was to authorise the deduction of rates and rent arrears directly from social security benefits and from wages. The second was to suspend local councils where the majority of councillors refused to attend because of internment.

Indeed, the Army was behaving in a much more robust fashion. There were widespread house searches and a much more intense surveillance of people, with heavy domination of certain areas. It was a 'repressive period', as a senior police officer recalled later; although it fell far short of the demands of the Protestant majority for such measures as the death penalty, compulsory identity cards, curfews and seek-and-destroy missions. It was also made to seem more repressive than it was because it followed a low profile period, and because the Army still failed to see much difference between Catholics and the Provisionals. The effect was to encourage a flood of recruits to the Provisionals and to alienate the Catholic people from authority. In provoking this reaction the Provisionals had, of course, achieved one of their major aims, and as time went by the authorities came to admit that 'the introduction of internment must be regarded as counter-productive.' This 'repressive phase' was, according to one senior police officer, to continue for another five years until the RUC started to take back responsibility for security from the Army.

In November the Army claimed again that the IRA was being beaten; in the following two days there were thirty bomb attacks and the death toll went up. Then the Army announced that it had evidence that the Provisionals were using dum-dum bullets and a new internment camp was opened at Long Kesh, with Wessex helicopters delivering some 219 detainees. Brian Faulkner talked about the Army having to use 'harder tactics' because 'to some extent time is running out for Northern Ireland.' Brigadier W.F.K. Thompson was to write later in *Brassey's Annual*:

This determination [of Faulkner's], combined with the increasing flow of intelligence as a result of internment, enabled the Army to wage a most successful operation against the IRA who, despite the continuing upsurge of violence were, the Army believed, showing signs of a breakdown by the end of the year. A large part of the original IRA officers in Belfast had been lifted or had taken refuge in the Republic. Mr Joe Cahill, of the Provisionals, admitted they were running short of guns and ammunition, and appreciations of the situation written at this time by the Official IRA said they could not stand the loss of men and equipment much longer.

On the streets attitudes were hardening. A Catholic priest recalled being at the bottom of Cook Street with a crowd of about fifty young boys. He likened them to the boys in *Lord of the Flies*.

> You know that book, he asked, where the boys become cannibals? Well these ones had also gone wild – absolutely wild! They set fire to a building and then the fire brigade comes along and the next thing these kids do is to start stoning the soldiers. For why? Because the soldiers sent for the fire brigade for to put out the fire. They went on starting fires and the fire brigade kept coming back – five or six times. Eventually I had to resort to a big stick, lifting it and saying 'Move on up that street or I'll kill youse,' . . . you know . . . then they started running. But the parents don't give a damn.

While Lisburn thought that the Provisionals were being beaten, they also noted that the IRA had shifted its bombing and sniping operation into high gear. As they saw it, the Provisionals were now trying to make Northern Ireland 'ungovernable' and turn it into a liability in the eyes of the rest of the United Kingdom – to sicken the British into withdrawal. The Provisionals were aiming to bring down the Stormont Government – indeed not just the Government but the whole edifice of Stormont itself. One way of achieving this was by violence, with which they were able to continue because a great deal of the adverse criticism it might have generated was being softened. The reason for this was that bringing down Stormont was also the quite legitimate political aim of the SDLP. Although they would try to do so constitutionally, in the heat of the struggle this difference was sometimes overlooked. This violence was backed by a predominant theme of hatred, which did not go unnoticed by one officer at Lisburn, Brigadier Maurice Tugwell, who wrote:

> Northern Ireland's politicans were portrayed as racist fascists, the RUC

composed of sadistic bullies, Protestants were, to a man or woman, bigots and British troops, who so recently had been welcomed as fair-minded saviours, were now blackened as oppressors, torturers and murderers. Since it was the latter who posed the principal obstacle to IRA attacks, they took the brunt of the hatred. Brutality allegations formed the main component of the attacks, and front spokesmen of impeccable moral credentials carried allegations to audiences who would never have read *An Phoblacht* or believed a word of an identified IRA spokesman. The Provisionals drilled their supporters in Catholic areas on their role whenever a shooting incident ended in the death of an IRA volunteer. The man's weapon was to be spirited away and the victim cleaned of forensic evidence indicating he had handled a gun. 'Eye witnesses' would be briefed and presented to journalists. Evidence was never to vary: the dead man would be described as unarmed and innocent of any offence. The soldier's action would be condemned as murder. One journalist [Tony Geraghty of the *Sunday Times*] who experienced this procedure said: 'I speak as someone of Irish extraction on both sides, yet even I am surprised on occasions at the instant and expert mendacity to which journalists and no doubt other interested parties such as the police and the security forces are treated in episodes of this sort.

The Army still had not got its own public relations act together, and journalists were still being kept back from the action, despite remarks over a year earlier after the Lower Falls 'curfew'. At that time officers had been told at a study day: 'It is important that the press should have access at all times to observe the military operations. We made a mistake in excluding them from the Lower Falls for their own safety. If the press wish to run the risk of covering such stories, this is a matter for them to decide and in the long run it is likely to be to our advantage.'

Everyone was becoming embroiled in the violence, not least the ambulance service which was constantly being used, and not only for civilian casualties. They would get caught in riots and fire-fights like everyone else. 'Did you ever stand at a wall and hear "crack" and "thump" as the bullet hit the bricks above you – and not think of survival?' one ambulanceman asked before he went back to the depot one evening to wait for the next call. The calls were colour coded: 'Red' meant there had been an explosion; 'Red Two' meant an unexploded bomb; 'Green' was used for a riot; and 'Blue' for somebody shot.

Before long they got a 'Blue' call. As they drove up the Whiterock Road all they could hear was the bang and clatter of automatics and rifles. As one man said, 'There wasn't a sinner about!' They got through to their control, who told them that the gunfire was heavy, that they should not get involved but the wounded man was a soldier and in a bad way. Throwing caution to the winds, they raced forward to find a patrol and were told that the wounded soldier was in the middle of a field. To get to him they had to crawl through a series of back gardens, dragging their medical gear with them. The soldiers gave them covering fire as they dashed from one position to another and eventually reached their man. He had been shot in the chest and they treated him right there 'with the bullets going zip, zip, zip in the grass all round us.' But suddenly the soldiers giving them covering fire ran out of ammunition.

The two of them lay with the wounded soldier on a stretcher, and the officer with them called for reinforcements which came in the shape of two Scout cars with Browning machine-guns. As these opened up they ran for it, taking cover with another patrol and calling up another ambulance because they could not reach theirs. As they got the soldier into the ambulance, he died. The shooting was still going on and yet another soldier was hit in the same field. They went through a repeat performance and then had to wait for an hour before they could get out of the area. 'Is there anything you want?' enquired an officer, enormously impressed. 'Yes sir,' replied one of them. 'If I could just have a change of trousers waiting for me.'

The intensity of operations was very great, particularly for the commanders. They might sleep perhaps from 4 a.m. to 8 a.m., and that was it. They were constantly on patrol, organising the next patrol, de-briefing the last one, or screening someone. Soldiers could get very tired and make mistakes. In four months they would get out for one four-day Rest and Recreation (R and R).

The four-month tour was a time period which produced endless arguments. The advantages were that soldiers did not get stale, that they were not away from their NATO commitments for too long and, most important, that they were not away from their wives and families for too long. However, both operationally and from the intelligence point of view it was far from favourable. Most batallions felt that they were not fully effective until they had been there a month, and it would be almost halfway through their tour before their intelligence became effective. The four-month tour was also responsible, in some ways, for soldiers not realising that they were fighting a long drawn-out campaign.

Again, many soldiers found themselves arriving for these four-month tours with little training for the particular job they faced. One recalled that his unit had been waiting to go to Cyprus for a United Nations tour when they were diverted. Another recalled that they always thought it would be a short-term matter – that they looked back to the 1950s when there had been a lot of violence which had been contained by the police. But one young officer said:

> I think we were aware of the political dimensions. And it is only fair to point out that we as officers – and most of the men as they understood it – were anti-Stormont, anti-Orange Order and very probably anti-Protestant as well! We had a feeling there was injustice over housing, jobs, education and even justice. I think we certainly felt that we were on the side of the Catholics . . . there was a huge amount of sympathy for them. That lasted a long time and it was probably the ham-fistedness of the Army as much as the politicians that put paid to that.

One local Republican politican who might have been expected to denounce the Army felt that it was a miracle that the soldiers, many aged only 18 or 19, had not behaved 'worse than they did'. They lived in dirty quarters and went on patrol to come back, eat, sleep and go out again. 'Everyone spitting at them and swearing at them and calling them English bastards and all that!' he said. 'Everybody did it. Not just the odd ones. They stood up to it very well!'

In December, Lisburn was again being pressed to get civil representatives appointed to work at ground level between the Army and police. It was pointed out that places like Ballymacarret in East Belfast had been virtually cleared of the IRA, but the military was inexperienced in dealing with Government departments and this had produced a vacuum. If it was not filled with a civil representative the area would go 'hard' once again. No representative was appointed and in a matter of six weeks a weak but nevertheless resurrected IRA had filled that vacuum. It was exactly what the brigade commander had meant when he talked of 'lost opportunities' after internment.

On the night of 4 December 1971, McGurk's bar was blown up by a Protestant unit in Belfast. The nearest unit was the Royal Regiment of Fusiliers, and the bang was so loud that soldiers in the headquarters thought at first that they themselves were under attack. However, one company, whose commander, Major Snow, was to be fatally wounded later that evening, went at once to the scene of the explosion. People were already clambering over the wreckage. Ambulances and fire-engines started to arrive, and soon steam was rising from the smouldering ruin as firemen played the hoses on the rubble. Another company commander took over the rescue operation and soon there was a human chain moving the rubble, brick by brick. Other soldiers searched for trapped people. Mechanical diggers got to work and the crowd grew; it became more difficult to keep them back. By 10 p.m. there were eighty soldiers working on the site surrounded by officials of the Gas and Electricity Boards, priests, politicians, pressmen and a crowd of some 400 onlookers.

At the same time a Protestant crowd gathered in North Queen street, moved to Duncairn Gardens, closer to the disaster, and began to jeer at the Catholics. Soon a crowd of Catholics had formed and the two groups started shouting at each other. It was obvious that trouble was brewing, and Major Snow went to sort it out. He drove between the crowds and persuaded them to go home. As he stood in a doorway doing this a gunman opened up from New Lodge and he was fatally wounded. Hearing about the shooting, an ambulance roared and revved across the rubble to get him. As the medical team tumbled out, the locals shouted to them that there was a gunman in the area. No one took any notice. 'We had our job to do,' said a medical orderly. 'That was most important. One of our officers had been hit.' The men got him on to a stretcher and into a 'pig' – an armoured car. At that stage no one thought he was going to die.

The crowds continued to mill about and the soldiers tried to disperse them. They came under fire from pistols, shotguns and rifles. On one occasion when they returned fire they saw a man fall and dragged away by the crowd. In another incident a crowd moved back to leave a gunman alone in the street; after he had fired they surged round him and then back again, taking him with them. By midnight it was confirmed that at least eight people had died in the explosion at McGurk's Bar, and nail bombs were being thrown. The news also came through that at a community centre disco at Newington 400 people were trapped.

The shooting and rioting continued while rescue workers scrabbled through the broken building. At 2 a.m. the Fusiliers

Ireland United

launched a big search operation in the New Lodge district, arrested two IRA suspects and found a revolver and a shotgun. By the morning the death toll at the pub had reached 15, with 8 injured. In the rioting 7 people had been wounded by gunfire — 3 soldiers, 3 policemen and 1 civilian.

This sort of increased violence helped to focus political attention once again on Northern Ireland; political attention which after internment had been diverted because of the Common Market negotiations on Britain's entry to the EEC. It seemed to Lisburn not only that the IRA were in disarray but also that the Protestants did not realise this. Would not this moment be an ideal 'window of opportunity', which could be used to introduce Direct Rule? If it were done now it could be done without much fuss, it would stun all sides and it would be an established fact before there could be a lot of speculation about it. After all, it was something which had been discussed within the MOD, with senior civil servants in Northern Ireland and with politicians in London. At this stage the Army was very aware of a lack of long-term political direction. It had a lot of soldiers in Northern Ireland, it was taking casualties and it was imposing some sort of military rule. It felt quite clear that there was no military solution to the problem and therefore the solution had to be political — but it wanted to know what this was. The Army also wanted to know what it — as the military force — was actually doing in Northern Ireland, and pressed hard for political direction. At the MOD there appeared to be no alternative to Direct Rule. It seemed to be a logical step to centralise control of the police, the Army and political development. It remained only to decide when this should be done. Such a decision, however, would require the full attention of the politicians, and particularly the Prime Minister. This was not forthcoming, yet.

By the end of 1971, 43 soldiers had been killed. The Army announced that while some 17,400 rounds had been fired at them and 1531 nail-bombs thrown at them, they had recovered 605 firearms, including 26 machine guns, 243 rifles and 105 hand grenades. It had also been the year that the Home Secretary, Reginald Maudling, had produced a memorable phrase when he talked of 'achieving an acceptable level of violence'. A close colleague explained later what he thought this really meant:

> I think that arose from the realisation that one man with a rifle or bomb, in one night, could either shoot a lot of people or do a lot of damage. Whatever you did you couldn't eliminate every single person. However, if the authorities got the level of violence down to the point where very few people were doing it, that was acceptable. I would have thought that the Army, on the whole, did go along with this definition because they realised that there was no way — unless it was all called off — that you could actually guarantee that there was going to be no violence.

At the end of the year the *Belfast Telegraph* said in an editorial for New Year's Day: 'If it is true that the darkest hour precedes the dawn, then Northern Ireland may hope for streaks of light in the sky in 1972. At times the year just past could hardly have seemed worse. The turning point must come soon. . . . ' The year 1972, however, was to prove the most violent of all: a year unmatched for the sheer scale of death and destruction. It opened bleakly enough. After four days, troops in the Clonard in Belfast came under fire but were unable to return it because schoolchildren came out into the streets. Some days later a soldier was killed by a mine near Keady which had been detonated from across the border. Then a 200lb bomb — the largest so far — was found in a milk churn and safely defused.

As tension increased, the focus of attention was to switch from Belfast to Londonderry, where a very different problem existed.

1a B Specials – one with a handkerchief round his face to lessen the effect of CS gas – are pulled out as the first troops move in. August 1969, Londonderry.

1b Soldiers shelter behind a Pig – the one-ton Humber APC, watched from an aptly-named bar by the manager.

2 A patrol moves cautiously along William Street. Two locals watch curiously as others are body-searched: the patrol commander with the tear-gas gun decides on the next move into the Bogside. 1970.

3a Abuse in the Bogside after soldiers shot two men. July 1971.

3b All in the line of duty, as women stage an
anti-internment demonstration outside a military post in Londonderry.

4 A policeman frees two Catholic girls
accused and punished by the IRA for being informers.

5 A quiet moment during a
Catholic protest march in Belfast. 1973.

6 One soldier watches for bricks and bottles,
the other watches for a sniper
and both listen to endless verbal abuse.

An afternoon in William Street, Londonderry.
7a An old man barely makes it to the pub in front of the soldiers.
7b A youngster vents his fury on a Ferret rushing by at speed.

8a and **8b** To advance incites, to retreat encourages.
To stand and endure means that it can go on for hours.

Lisburn felt that while it could dominate Belfast, it could not dominate Londonderry. There were, of course, differences of opinion over this but the policy was that the Army had to work in cooperation with the local people, which was why the 'No Go' areas had been allowed to stay. Plans made in the autumn to put in three battalions to 're-take' the Bogside and Creggan had been subsequently dropped because this number would not be enough to cope with the increasing sophistication of IRA attacks. These were now made by groups of at least ten, who very carefully worked out how they got the weapon, used it and got rid of it, and how they planned the escape route, the cover-up operation and the distraction. To deal with this the Army would have to saturate the area with more troops than was politically acceptable at the time.

By the end of 1971 it had been decided that the policy of company and battalion strength operations in the Bogside and Creggan were, as one soldier put it, 'causing the most frightful fuss!' It was not just the Young Derry Hooligan who was being hit by rubber bullets and choked by CS gas, it was happening to everyone in the area. So there was another change in approach; an Army brief written on 17 January 1972 stated that 'the policy in Londonderry is to play the Creggan and the Bogside in the lowest possible key compatible with the general security situation. Taking into account the morale of the troops, it is the intention to keep Londonderry out of the headlines. There has been an established pattern of violent opposition to operations carried out there.' This casts interesting light on Army policy in view of what was to happen in the city at the end of the month.

All marches had been banned since 9 August 1971, but on Christmas Day 1971 some thousand people marched in Belfast in defiance of the ban, and were stopped only by large numbers of soldiers and policemen. More illegal marches were held in rapid succession, and the Northern Ireland Civil Rights Association (NICRA) announced that it would hold a big march in Londonderry at the end of January, which would be addressed by Lord Brockway and other Members of Parliament. Ironically, the Catholics had been asking for a ban on marches, because they were fed up with Protestant marches. Now, however, the Army watched as the organisers prepared to issue a defiant challenge to the Stormont Government that it was not capable of enforcing such a ban. This did not go unnoticed at Stormont, and it was made clear that the ban would be enforced.

On 24 January, Chief Superintendent Frank Lagan met the brigade commander, Brigadier Pat MacLellan, to discuss the whole range of eventualities which might now arise. Memories of this meeting differ. Lagan said that he felt that the march should be allowed out of the Catholic Bogside and into the centre of the city — a Protestant area. If necessary people could be photographed, and arrested later. He felt that to stop it would only produce a spate of other troublesome marches. He stated later that 'the brigadier was in agreement with me on this.' MacLellan disputes this, saying that he made clear his view that the march should be contained within the Bogside. After all, the main aim of the march was to demonstrate that the Stormont ban could not be effectively imposed in Londonderry, and that subsequent arrests of people in the Bogside and Creggan would be virtually impossible. That evening he signalled the CLF with this information. The next morning the two men spoke on the telephone. MacLellan said the Bogside and Creggan should be cordoned by blocks, and that these should be covered by riflemen because of the danger of snipers. He would need two, if not three, extra battalions.

The next day MacLellan flew to Lisburn to discuss the Operational Order, in which he forecast the threat as coming from three main points. First, it was a deliberate attempt to defy the marching ban which would result in a direct confrontation with the security forces. Second, the IRA would take advantage of the event to fire at the security forces and to bomb shopping and commercial premises in the city. Third, hooligan reaction to the Army was expected in the form of stones, bottles and nail bombing, the arson of private premises and vehicles, and a high degree of violence. On the matters of hooligans the order was quite specific:

> Although NICRA claims that this march is a non-violent protest, the organisers will have no control over the hooligans who will ensure that violence is inevitable. The deployment of troops is to take account of this situation. An arrest force is to be held centrally behind the check points, and launched in a scoop-up operation to arrest as many hooligans and rioters as possible.

Initially, the Army intended to deal with any illegal march 'in as

low a key as possible and for as long as possible.' No action was to
be taken against it until either an attempt had been made to breach
the blocking points, or there was violence against the security forces
in the form of stone, bottle and nail bombing. In the section dealing
with the dispersal of the marches, the order was quite clear. 'If the
Creggan march takes place entirely within the containment area of
the Bogside and Creggan it will be permitted to go unchallenged.'

Despite this, Lagan was very disturbed at the way in which the
Army planned to contain the march. He knew that some officers
were suspicious of him, thinking him too sympathetic towards the
Catholic community. But the fact was that he had earned himself
considerable respect among the Catholics. He had a community 'feel'
for Londonderry, but to some Army officers it was sinister. In the
event, all Lagan's appeals to allow the march to go ahead to the city
centre, with ringleaders being identified so that they could be
arrested later, were brushed aside.

Major-General Ford picked 1 Parachute Regiment as the arrest
unit for a number of reasons. First, of the other two battalions which
could be used one had been in the province for only four days, and
the other for about a fortnight; whereas the paratroopers had been
around for some eighteen months and were very experienced.
Another reason was that 1 Para had been specially trained and
encouraged to be tough by the Belfast brigade commander so that
he could use them as a 'stabilising influence' when things got rough.
When they appeared on the streets of Belfast, people tended to
disappear. 'One platoon of 1 Para,' said an officer, 'could do what
one company of any other battalion could do in Belfast. We hoped
that their reputation had spread to Londonderry.' Other officers
were less than enthusiastic about them and felt that their tactics were
totally counter-productive. The previous Saturday they had shown
every desire to be as robust as possible during a rather violent clash
with demonstrators at Magilligan internment camp nearby. 'I think
it was wrong to choose them for a very tricky operation where tight
control was essential,' commented one senior commander. 'Frank
Kitson would disagree — he thought they were very good in Belfast.
But you have to take what is available, and anyway, we were
expecting trouble on the barricade, not during the arrest operation.'

At this stage there was a great deal of pressure from Stormont to
take tough action against the hooligans. General Ford agreed with
this policy; he felt that the timing was critical. The damage they

caused was increasing — around £4 million worth by now — and local Catholics were complaining that shops were being looted. Indeed, at a meeting with the Strand Road Traders' Association, Ford had been told in no uncertain terms that the Army was failing to protect the local shopkeepers. He was asked to intensify patrolling and he had agreed. So it was decided that the climate of opinion would support the view that the Young Derry Hooligans should be taught a lesson. It was expected that there would be some 450 of them, and that to have any effect at least 40 should be arrested. It was planned to have magistrates ready so that those arrested could appear in court first thing on Monday morning. This was not stressed in the Operational Order but stated verbally. However, it was stressed that one thing which should not happen was for 1 Para to take on the march itself. The marchers and the hooligans would have to be well separated before any action was to be taken. The last thing the Army commanders wanted to do was to scoop up old ladies and peaceful marchers. A staff officer from Londonderry said:

> We had for months being trying to arrest hooligans. If there was a suitable opportunity that Sunday to scoop up some at the barriers then it had the approval of both the brigade commander and the chief superintendent of police. Mind you, we had no idea that General Ford was determined to arrest as many as possible. The whole idea was to have a peaceful day — certainly not to launch 1 Para to bring back one hundred courses. It was totally against our policy to do anything that could be seen locally, or worldwide, as provocative. We were trying to have a unilateral position in parliament — to keep the States, France and other Catholic countries happy. I find it extraordinary that anyone should try and think we were using 1 Para to hit the Catholics hard. It was the one thing we were trying not to do!

At brigade headquarters in Londonderry there was little doubt about the threat of gunmen. In the previous fortnight there had been 80 confirmed shooting incidents in which 319 rounds had been fired at soldiers and police and 84 nail bombs had been thrown. Two soldiers had been killed and two wounded, which, an officer pointed out, did not say much for the shooting skills of the IRA. Moreover, on 29 January an intelligence report had been received at Lisburn which said 'the IRA are determined to produce a major confrontation by one means or another during the march.'

Even so, there was still no plan or any intention to 'flush out the IRA'. The Army had learned by now that it was no use mounting an operation into territory like that unless it had very good intelligence: it would be a waste of their time.

On Sunday 30 January the marchers assembled on the Creggan estate. It was a fine, sunny afternoon and they were in high spirits. At first there were only a few hundred, but as the soldiers watched from their positions high on Derry's walls, and from the barriers they had set up around its base, they saw the numbers swell to between two and five thousand. The crowd did not move in any sort of military formation; rather it swarmed along, spread right across the road, led by a lorry with a large Civil Rights banner on it. It was a good-humoured crowd, with women and children among it. As the column came towards William Street, the most critical point where the Army had a barrier and was expecting trouble, the hooligans took up positions at the front of the march. The march leaders turned away from confrontation with the Army — a decision which had been taken before the march started. Not everyone agreed with it. There were jeers and catcalls. The hooligans at the front, in particular, refused to turn aside and the crowd pressed them from behind, right up to soldiers of the Royal Green Jackets who blocked the road. They stood firm, and as the main body of the march turned away the pressure eased. This also meant that the press of people round the barrier thinned out and as it did so, the missiles began to fly through the air.

By now General Ford was on the ground with a company of 1 Para and in touch with brigade headquarters on a secure radio link. The brigade commander had decided to stay at his headquarters across the river where he could be in touch by radio with what was going on. Up above hovered a helicopter — his 'eyes' — which he was using to give him an accurate report of what was happening on the ground. As the hooligans stormed the barriers he waited, determined that the arrest unit would not go in until the hooligans had separated from the march. Chief Superintendent Lagan was in the brigadier's office just across the passage from the Operations Room. He knew that there was a plan to launch an arrest operation, but knew no details other than that 1 Para would do it, and he still questioned the wisdom of this. MacLellan, too, was apprehensive. He knew very well that there was a feeling amongst officers from Belfast that the Catholic hooligans should be given 'a good hiding'; he also realised that in a

Protestant-dominated city such action would attract greater support. However, Londonderry, with its Catholic majority, was a very different problem. It needed some subtlety and sensitivity, and he did not see why this should automatically be equated with softness. It was also very difficult for a brigadier to have a major-general around on such an occasion, especially a forceful one 'determined' to have a success. There was probably some truth in the old adage that 'one over one is never the right chain of command on active operations'.

So these three men waited, and the first move came from 1 Para. Just before 4 p.m. a Para officer came through in the brigade net and asked for permission to send in the arrest unit. MacLellan turned down the request on the basis that the marchers and rioters had yet to separate, and then went to see Lagan. 'The Paras want to go in,' he told him. 'For Heaven's sake!' Lagan retorted, 'hold them until we're satisfied that the marchers and rioters are well dispersed.' The brigadier said nothing and went back to the Ops Room, where his brigade major was also in touch with General Ford on a secure wireless net which was not being logged. The general, out with the forward troops, felt that being on the ground gave him the right 'feel' for the operation, although he accepted that the brigadier, with his helicopter, had a better overall picture. However, he himself now came through and spoke to the brigade major, making it very clear that the time had come to 'get a move on and send in the Paras'. The brigade major passed on the message, telling MacLellan, 'The general has been on and says this is the time to go in.' Again MacLellan said 'no', because the rioters and the marchers had not yet separated. A few minutes passed, and then came word from the helicopter that the separation had finally taken place, and MacLellan gave the order to move.

Once he had done this, he came back to where Lagan was waiting. He knew that the policeman was unhappy that his advice had not been taken. 'I'm sorry,' MacLellan said, 'but the Paras have gone in.' He did not mean this as an expression of regret that something had happened beyond his control, but rather to soften the news for an already disappointed policeman. Lagan's immediate understanding, however, was that the Paras had gone in on someone else's instructions — not on the orders of the brigadier. But MacLellan was at this stage satisfied that the hooligans and marchers had separated. He had given the order himself, and the paratroopers had gone in with some encouraging words from General Ford.

From this moment on versions of what happened differ drastically. The soldiers say that as they were moving in to arrest the hooligans they came under fire, and this fire was returned. Indeed, there had already been a report of one shot being fired at soldiers a little earlier, and another of a nail bomb being thrown. In the following fracas — or massacre, according to local people — the paratroopers fired 108 rounds, killing 13 people, 7 of them aged under 19 years old, and injuring another 13, including 1 woman.

People in Londonderry, the civil rights marchers, and NICRA leaders, all said that during the shooting the Army was not fired at. Local priests protested that those shot were unarmed, that many were running away from the troops when they were hit, that the Army failed to stop firing when white handkerchiefs were waved, and that the priests themselves were prevented from assisting the wounded and dying. The uproar reverberated across Ireland and round the world. In one small Army headquarters further along the border there were at first cheers when news came in that three had been killed. When the numbers increased to nine, and there still had been no reports of any security force deaths, an officer warned his men: 'I wouldn't cheer so loudly. There is something very wrong here.'

The operation, on what came to be known as 'Bloody Sunday', quietened Londonderry down for a long time, but did little for the Army's image — whatever reasons it gave for opening fire. It was, by all accounts, a complete disaster. One senior officer said later that it had been wrong to use the paratroopers, whatever their reputation in Belfast, considering that the previous week, at a demonstration in Magilligan, they had 'shown themselves to be a bit out of control.' If there had been a choice he would have chosen either the Royal Marines, whom he considered steadier in a situation where very tight control was needed. Another officer explained that if the same thing had happened in Belfast, no innocent people would have been killed; 1 Para's reputation would have meant that they would all have gone to ground. Moreover, people in Londonderry were not used to shooting and they had remained on their feet. 'It was a local success,' an officer said rather ruefully, 'in that hooligan damage during the next month was just about nil. But that was a very small reward for thirteen dead and the tremendous impact it had everywhere.'

Later, an offical enquiry under Lord Widgery was to find that while the Army had been fired on first, some of the return fire 'had bordered on the reckless.' He also found that none of the killed or wounded was ever proved to have been shot while handling firearms or bombs. The Army was particularly upset about this. In private, officers pointed out that Chief Superintendent Lagan had been so shaken by the day's events that he had not been around immediately afterwards to make certain that the police forensic experts got to work straight away. 'That would have stopped sympathisers from getting the victim's clothes and bodies scrubbed clean,' said an Army officer bitterly. 'No wonder there was no evidence of explosives!'

The fact of the matter, however, was that after hearing the reports of the shootings. Lagan went back to his office at Victoria police station where he stayed in contact with his senior officers for the rest of the evening. The police routine had already been started to deal with the aftermath of the incident, and Lagan ensured that this was continued. He stayed there until 1.30 a.m. on Monday morning, when he went home, and was back at his desk at 9 a.m. During the whole of this day he was in close contact with his officers to make sure that they had all the back-up and advice that they might need in what he knew was a very difficult situation. Whenever he left the office, his deputy was given clear instructions as to how he could be contacted. Shocked by the tragedies of the previous day, Lagan was nevertheless keenly aware that as the senior police officer in the area, he had to act in a firm and responsible manner, giving leadership, guidance and directives when and where they were necessary.

So it was that the police scenes-of-crime officers, trained by the forensic science department, moved in quickly to take swabs from the bodies of those who had been killed. There was then a delay before the clothing could be removed, because the three pathologists, who were to carry out the post mortem examinations, needed to examine this before it was taken off. The swabs, together with all the clothing, were then delivered to the Forensic Science Laboratory in Belfast on the morning of Wednesday 2 February, which was not considered an unduly long delay because of the numbers involved.

In Belfast, the forensic scientists had by now 'cleared the decks' for the rush of work they were expecting. The only test they could make at that time was one using a chemical — sodium rhodizonate — which would show the presence of lead as a purple stain. The greater amount of lead, the stronger the colour. Realising that this was a relatively unsophisticated test, they contacted the Home Office Central Research Establishment at Aldermaston. Here, scientists had available an American system of neutron activation analysis, which would also show the presence of antimony, mercury and barium — all present in gun-shot discharges — as well as lead. However, this was a long and involved procedure, and to test evidence from all thirteen bodies would have taken several months. With Lord Widgery's Tribunal of Enquiry due to sit in a month, there was no time for this. So in Belfast the simple chemical test was used.

These showed a completely negative response in only five cases. All the other bodies, and the clothing, showed a positive response. Indeed, some showed a very large concentration of lead, the amounts in the clothing matching that on the bodies. The crucial issue was the interpretation of where these lead deposits had come from. It was pointed out that someone hit by a bullet, or by fragments of a bullet, would show a very positive response to a lead test. A similar result could be obtained by contamination from another source, either from someone standing close by firing a weapon, or, even more important, by coming into contact with someone who had fired a weapon. In the context of Bloody Sunday this was a critical factor, as it would of course include soldiers who had handled bodies, and wounded people, on the way to the hospital.

At the official inquest into the shooting, the Londonderry coroner, Hubert O'Neill, was scathing.

It strikes me that the Army ran amok that day and shot without thinking. They were shooting innocent people. These people may have been taking part in a parade that was banned, but I don't think that justifies the firing of live rounds indiscriminately. I say it without reservation — it was sheer, unadulterated murder.

An Army officer was equally blunt:

The Paras are trained to react fast and go in hard. That day they were expecting to have to fight their way in. It was very tense. In those street conditions it is very difficult to tell where a round has come from. Once one was fired, that section, quite frankly, lost control. For goodness' sake, you could hear their CO bellowing at them to cease firing, and only to fire aimed shots at actual targets!

In Dublin, anger also came to the surface as 20,000 people marched through the city in protest. When they reached the British Embassy they petrol-bombed it and burned it right through. The

Irish Government then declared a national day of mourning for the thirteen dead.

The theories about that day's events covered the whole spectrum from those who thought that Westminster and Stormont had ordered the killing of as many Catholics as possible to 'teach them a lesson', to some who thought it may have been inspired by Russia's KGB. A number of Army officers felt that there had been over-reaction on the part of the paratroopers, but none of them could credit that there had been a deliberate attempt to 'kill as many Catholics' as possible. They pointed out that this would have meant senior officers, staff and regimental officers and some 500 soldiers all conspiring together to 'murder men of military age' in front of some 3,000 people and half the world's press. To them this did not make sense, because from the beginning no one had tried to hide anything. They pointed to a significant paragraph in the brigade operational orders for that day under the heading of 'PR'. It read:

> Unit PROs should make every effort to collect and conduct press and television men around deployment areas, in order that newsmen will subsequently give a balanced report to their readers and viewers of the proceedings.

Now the pressure was to mount for Direct Rule as the Army began to realise the sort of problem which it faced with more than one master. Sensitive action would be treated as weakness, strong action as brutality. The attempt to allow the Catholics to run their own affairs had led to the establishment of the 'No Go' areas. On the one hand these had allowed the IRA to recruit and train; on the other their existence had infuriated the Protestants. Lack of 'action' against the Protestants had led to a charge of bias against Catholics. While the Army was involved in a real fight against the Provisionals, there was always the background threat of Protestant violence being unleashed against them. It was time to sort out this mess.

A can of worms

February 1972–July 1972

The Provisionals kept up a steady stream of bombings and killings following Bloody Sunday. They felt that in some ways they were close to getting rid of the Stormont Government once and for all; and their morale was further boosted by an escape from a prison-ship, the *Maidstone*. One night seven Provisionals jumped overboard into Belfast Lough and swam an icy 300 yards to the shore. They managed to keep clear of the Army and police, and later held a jubilant press conference.

The Official IRA decided to boost its own image as well and planned an operation which it felt would have an impact in the wake of Bloody Sunday. Its target was the headquarters mess of the Parachute Regiment at Aldershot, in England. A bomb was planted to cause maximum damage and duly went off on 22 February. No Parachute Regiment officers were killed, but five cleaning ladies, a Catholic chaplain and a gardener were blown to bits. Despite this, the Official IRA proudly announced in Dublin that 'our intelligence reports indicate that at least twelve officers were killed.' Even when it became quite clear that all the dead were non-combatants, the Officials branded this as 'a general signal by reactionary and hypocritical politicians to attack the Republican movement and condemn the action.'

That month two Catholic priests, Father Faul of Dungannon and Father Murray of Armagh, claimed that since internment, 2 per cent of the adult Catholic male population of the province had been arrested and held incommunicado. Four hundred of these men, they said, had been 'brutually treated and tortured'. They produced a booklet including a mass of statements from men claiming that they had been beaten up and, in sixteen cases, medical evidence to back these claims. They stated: 'We feel compelled to apportion the major share of blame to officers of the British Army and senior officers of the RUC who must have known what was going on even if they did not always participate. We find these officers devoid of honour and guilty of inhumane conduct.' The booklet also printed part of a letter purporting to have been sent by the GOC, Sir Harry Tuzo, to a Bellaghey housewife.

> You sent me this list of tortures compiled by Father Faul. I must now tell you that these are basically untrue. We have investigated in detail every case he had put to us and I regret to say that in most cases the complainants have refused to substantiate their allegations when questioned by investigators. Indeed they have refused to cooperate in any way. This can only lead a reasonable person to conclude that these people are more interested in propaganda than in eliciting the truth.

February also saw the fiftieth soldier killed in Northern Ireland while giving aid to the civil power, and the embarrassing realisation that most of the acts carried out by soldiers were illegal. The problem was that both the police and the Army were acting under the Special Powers Act of 1926, which gave wide-ranging powers to the Stormont Government to deal with unrest. However, an earlier Act – the Government of Ireland Act of 1920 –imposed certain limitations on what Stormont could do. One was that it could not give legal powers to the Army. This was tested in court by John Hume, MP, and others who were charged on 18 August 1971 with failing to disperse when ordered to do so by an Army officer under the relevant section of the Special Powers Act. When Hume was duly convicted in the magistrate's court, he appealed on a single point of law – that the powers given to the Army under the Special Powers Act were unconstitutional. In the Belfast High Court, the Lord Chief Justice of Northern Ireland, Sir Robert Lowry, upheld the appeal and quashed the conviction.

So it was that within hours of this ruling the lights burned late at Westminster as an embarrassed Central Government rushed through a one-clause act to legalise the actions of its soldiers. The Home Secretary, Reginald Maudling, emphasised the need for speech, and explained that the particular regulation which had been challenged in the courts was one which allowed a commissioned officer to disperse a crowd.

> But it appears that the court's judgement would equally affect other regulations including, for example, the power to stop and search people and vehicles suspected of carrying explosives . . . it is also necessary to ensure that members of the Armed Forces would not be liable to any legal proceedings based on this technical point in respect of the exercise of power since 1969. . . .The side effect of the bill will be to declare that the law, so far as the powers of the Armed Forces are concerned is, and always has been, what it has hitherto been believed to be.

To some, it looked like a successful effort to indemnify what the soldiers had been doing. An official, however, explained that because the Special Powers Act was an enactment by Stormont, there had been doubt as to whether it could confer powers on the Army. 'The 1972 Act *declared* that it could do so. So the Army's actions had been legal all along – the Act did not "legalise" them, much less "indemnify" the soldiers.'

Lord Hailsham, in the House of Lords, said he thought that events would probably overtake the bill 'which is less important than some people have thought.' The meaning of this was not immediately obvious, but in fact the Government was beginning to see the dangers of having joint control of any sort over the security forces. Sensitive political issues could be introduced by a subordinate Parliament creating powers in respect of the Army, when in fact the real power lay with the Parliament at Westminster. It was, in fact, the first sign that Westminster was thinking of taking over complete control of security matters – including the police: a step which almost inevitably would mean the imposition of Direct Rule.

Although Parliament had passed this law quickly to regularise the position of the troops in Northern Ireland, in all other respects the Army was operating under common law. This meant there was no dispensation for the military in their activities. In fact, at this time they had fewer powers than even a constable, and as they patrolled through streets and across the open country where they were attacked by bullets and bombs, some soldiers felt that they were being unduly restricted. Some complaints – notably from regimental officers – trickled up to Lisburn, with the added sting that senior staff officers were not fighting hard enough on these matters. On hearing of this, a senior official observed:

> What is not understood properly is the reluctance of the British Parliament to give powers to the military. That has been the traditional stand for hundreds of years. I agree that soldiers are legally restricted, and that was why we issued the Yellow Card. It is a very well phrased document, and it restricts the soldier in order to protect him. One of the phrases being bandied about now is 'Duty Target'. Well, you know if a soldier in his wry way calls himself a 'Duty Target', it is really a quite justifiable way of looking at his role. You see, one of the critical factors in the campaign is that a soldier can only react – never act: he can't shoot first unless his life, or a colleague's life, is being threatened.

The feeling at Lisburn was that what the politicians were trying to do was to achieve dramatic results without upsetting any apple-carts; that they really wanted some alchemy which the Army could use to squash terrorists without making inroads into basic liberties and the sort of areas which would be prejudical to votes. Some felt that this was only to be expected; others that the politicians had squandered the time gained for them by the Army, which had then been left 'holding the can'. Another view was that the British Government had chosen the wrong ground on which to meet the Provisional IRA. By acting in support of the civil power – Stormont – it was supporting a provincial government which was not trusted by a large proportion of the population. This exposed it to criticism of partial support for the Protestant majority and suppression of the Catholic minority; which meant in turn that there was no fully-mobilised support for its counter-insurgency campaign.

What the Army was beginning to realise was that it had been left an absolute can of worms. The internment operation, which should have been an effective measure, failed, because all it amounted to was 'picking up all the people the local copper didn't like'. Whatever it did now was against this background of a badly-bungled operation. Its position was very complicated, and the Army was no longer sure exactly which way it should go – towards aiding the civil power or replacing it. The Army accepted that the police had taken a battering, not only from the people but from the Government as well, having being castigated right, left and centre, and having had their B Specials removed; it accepted, too, that morale was down.

The difficulty was that, while there were some fine characters in the force, most police leaders had, by and large, given up. Often the Army found them only too happy to hand over responsibility, particularly when they were faced with situations beyond their experience.

On to this stage now lumbered the ominous figure of William Craig, who had been sacked as Minister of Home Affairs in December 1968, because he had publicly challenged the Cabinet's contention that the British Government had powers to intervene in Northern Ireland affairs under the Government of Northern Ireland Act. He had also accused Westminster of applying financial 'blackmail' to force Stormont to agree to reforms. Craig now called on the memory of the 1912 Covenant, which had been signed in blood, and which had pledged the northern Protestants to fight against Home Rule for Ireland. His onslaught was directed at any political initiative which might 'weaken' the Protestant position. He announced the formation of Vanguard, an umbrella organisation for Protestant factions, and he called for a rally, at which he arrived with a motorcycle escort and inspected rows and rows of bowler-hatted and beribboned men. 'We are determined,' he told them, 'to preserve our British tradition and way of life. And God help those who get in our way!'

The following day he was interviewed on RTE, Irish television, and he talked about a situation in which loyalists might be led to take violence against their enemies. 'Would this mean killing all Catholics in Belfast?' he was asked. 'It might not go as far as that,' Craig replied. 'But it could go as far as killing.'

Despite the gathering clouds, soldiers were still 'milling around, not quite knowing what they were on about'. A company commander explained it like this:

> We were looking for a particular Provo and we had a cordon round this estate. Suddenly someone broke cover and started up the hill. I expected my men to challenge and shoot. I heard the challenge but no shot. The man being challenged disappeared. The section commander explained that while the man had been carrying something, he could not see if it was a weapon, and so he had not fired. Now, two years later that man would have been challenged twice and then shot. As it happens I knew him, and knew he committed murders later on. We weren't thinking

along the right lines then, or he wouldn't have got away.

Another commander explained how one of his men had been blown up on the border. They had just moved down there and were covering a Sapper operation. The soldier lay down in what he thought was a good firing position. It was. It had been used before by marines and noticed by the Provisionals. This soldier lay down on five or six charges of explosives; his foot was not found until five weeks later.

Some border commanders felt that they were odds on to a loser trying to keep the border shut. They suffered every tactical disadvantage and were 'like lambs being brought to the slaughter, putting our heads over the chopping block of the border. Was it really necessary?' One commander suggested an artificial border some two thousand metres in, which would force the opposition to come forward into an area where they could be handled. There would be a minimum number of soldiers forward and a strong reserve which would keep the Provisionals guessing. 'What the Provisionals really like,' he said, 'are soldiers in bases. Moreover I believe closing the border ignores the human factor. The people from Keady and southwards look to Monaghan for their social nights out, their whist drives and tombola and their shopping. When we blow up the roads they use we are straight away seen as the British aggressors.' The proposals were rejected on the grounds that this would be abandoning part of the United Kingdom to terrorists.

Next there was to be a series of bombings which would stretch the ability of Faulkner's Government to breaking point, as Westminster became more and more irritated with his failure to control the security situation. All bomb blasts are appalling, but when one goes off in a crowded restaurant in the middle of a busy shopping Saturday, it seems somehow even more dreadful. So it was when a bomb was planted on 4 March 1972 in the Abercorn restaurant in the middle of Belfast. At 4.30 p.m. it was as packed as it could be. That was when the bomb exploded.

A bomb blast in a confined space is devastating. First the shock wave spreads out, faster than the speed of sound. Some heavy objects deflect the waves, but other solid material is changed instantly into gas, creating an enormous increase in volume and pressure. People in the way can have their limbs torn off, and in the millisecond which follows the energy waves go into their mouths and upwards, taking away the tops of their skulls and other parts of the body so that sometimes all that is left is the spine, held together by the vertebrae. The shock wave, travelling at some 13,000 miles per hour, pulverises the floor immediately below the explosion. It slows down quickly, but more damage is done by the blast wave which follows at half the speed. This has the pressure of pent-up gas behind it and it can also tear off limbs, perforate eardrums and smash up furniture, the pieces of which in turn become deadly weapons. For a few seconds a fireball goes with it, singeing hair and removing eyebrows and eyelashes. Then the blast wave bounces off the walls, reinforcing the original explosion and very probably brings down the roof on the people below.

That was what happened in the restaurant that afternoon. Two women were killed and 130 others injured – some of them quite appallingly. Two sisters out shopping for a wedding dress were caught in the blast. Both lost both their legs, one her right arm as well. From the 7 people most badly injured there were 16 limbs either totally missing or hanging on by a shred of flesh. 'For days afterwards all you smell is burnt hair and flesh,' said one doctor who worked through that night. 'You bath, you do anything to get rid of it but you can't. You get used to ghastly smells in hospitals – but you never get used to this one.'

The Provisional IRA denied planting the bomb, and blamed Protestant extremists. They pointed a finger at the Woodvale Defence Association, who angrily denied it. This Association was a local Protestant paramilitary unit which had recently complained, in a newsletter, that the management of the Abercorn Restaurant had refused to play 'God save the Queen!' after its evening entertainment programmes. But there was no doubt whatsoever in the minds of Army intelligence and the police that the people responsible were members of a 'cowboy' unit of the Provisional IRA.

On 10 March the Provisionals declared a seventy-two-hour cease-fire. Three of their men had blown themselves up and three had been injured the day before in a house in the Falls Road area of Belfast. In Dublin they listed three conditions for the truce to continue: the withdrawal of the Army, the abolition of Stormont and the release of all political prisoners. Westminster did not reply, and soon the conflict was raging again. Bombs went off all over the place. Six people, including 2 policemen, were killed in Lower Donegall Street by a no-warning bomb. The next day 26 people were injured in Londonderry, then 20 shops were damaged in Enniskillen.

Unknown to Faulkner, the prospect of Direct Rule from Westminster was hardening all the time, particularly since Bloody Sunday. Edward Heath's attitude was that he would not go on carrying the can for decisions made in Stormont: that if his Government were going to get into trouble, he would want to be responsible for that trouble. He was thinking now of removing the responsibility for law and order from Faulkner and hoped Faulkner would agree to this idea. In the middle of March, William Whitelaw, Lord President of the Council and Leader of the House of Commons, said that he did not think that the full extent of the heavy financial burden was fully realised. He suggested that the people of Northern Ireland did their best to relieve this burden, 'even at some cost to your own ambitions and desires.' There were flurries of speculation in the press about a Westminster package which would include a government based on proportional representation, the ending of internment and the transfer of all security matters to London. Faulkner was worried about this, and his Unionists began to mutter about a 'sell out' to the Republicans. On 15 March Faulkner was asked if he would go over to London in a week's time to discuss the situation. He now began to look desperately round for military proposals to put to London which would assure Heath that the problem could be solved by strong security policies.

The day before he flew to London, Faulkner asked the CLF, Major-General Ford, to lunch with him. It was a strange meeting and Ford was at first puzzled by it: they lunched quite alone, even without waiters in the room, and helped themselves to food from the sideboard. During the meal, however, the purpose of this lunch *à deux* became clearer as Faulkner pressed Ford for ideas. He wanted to know how the Army might 'improve' the security situation with a tougher policy; if this were not possible within the political constraints of the moment, what might the Army do if these constraints were lifted? Ford explained patiently that even if political constraints were lifted the Army could do little more than it was already doing because it still had to operate within the law. Faulkner gave no clue as to what proposals he might put to Heath, but Ford was convinced that Faulkner had no inkling of the sweeping changes with which Heath was going to face him.

So Brian Faulkner and his deputy, Senator John Andrews, flew to London for a meeting in Downing Street with senior Government ministers. Such was the gravity of the situation that the CGS was stopped at the very last minute from taking off for America and he, with the GOC, Sir Harry Tuzo, was also there. During a series of meetings over nine hours Faulkner was told quite bluntly that Westminster was taking over all security matters. These included: the RUC, the RUC Reserve, all executive responsibility for law and order, control of the courts, responsibility for the administration of law and justice and the power to create new penal laws and offences. It amounted to leaving Stormont as a rubber stamp for Westminster decisions. This was too much for Faulkner, and he said he would resign. He went back to Belfast, briefed his colleagues and returned to London to say that they would all resign. So it was that William Whitelaw came to Belfast as the first Secretary of State for Northern Ireland.

The Army welcomed Direct Rule wholeheartedly. They felt that this would give them the long-term and broad-based political direction which had been lacking from the Stormont Government. Previously the GOC had been in an 'impossible position'. He took his military orders from London but overall security instructions from Faulkner. 'He had a logical, legal mind,' said an officer who served under him. 'He also had the ability to see the overall picture. But everything being put forward by Faulkner was put in a way that was unacceptable to both sides. Tuzo was a very liberal man and he must have found this intolerable.'

Direct Rule was a big surprise to the Unionists, who had never accepted something that the Army had been trying to get across to them for some time: that there was no purely military solution. Nor had they realised that if Direct Rule came, it would have been forced by local events – not as an independent action on the part of Westminster. But Direct Rule was to bring its problems for the Army. With the removal of Stormont, the main 'obstacle' to Catholic advancement, the way seemed clear for a fresh round of political initiatives. Once again the change of course was abrupt as the Army adopted a low profile and watched, helplessly, as its hard-earned military success was washed away and the Catholic areas, as one officer commented bitterly, 'were handed back to the Provisionals on a plate.'

The immediate effect of the new policy of Direct Rule was that street patrols were reduced, which meant that the soldiers picked up less of the odd bits and pieces of information which helped to build up basic background to an area and the people who lived in it. The practice of 'hot pursuit' was stopped. Soldiers could no longer tear after a suspected terrorist, chasing him down streets and through gardens and houses; which, of course, meant less pressure on terrorists. With the easing of pressure the 'No Go' areas began to build up again as rival mini-states. New recruits who joined the IRA were unknown to the security forces. All this, according to Lisburn, immediately endangered three years of careful work building up intelligence centres linked 'to the community. Other aspects of the policy came in: with the phasing out of internment, released internees went back to join and strengthen the ranks of the Provisional IRA and other terrorist organisations; covert operations were also affected and as basic intelligence dried up, these operations became more hazardous and some were blown.

Another problem was that of interrogation techniques. Following the Compton report into allegations of brutality during the internment operation of August 1971, another committee was set up, headed by Lord Parker and including John Boyd-Carpenter and Lord Gardiner, to report on the methods used in interrogating detainees. The committee was particularly concerned with the five 'interrogation in depth' techniques, described by the Compton report as constituting physical ill-treatment but not brutality. They issued their report in March 1972.

Lord Parker and John Boyd-Carpenter held that the methods were justifiable in exceptional circumstances subject to certain safeguards. Lord Gardiner, however, did not believe that such measures were morally justifiable, whether in peacetime or even in war against a ruthless enemy. The Prime Minister, Edward Heath, then took the decision that these techniques would not be used again. As far as the Army was concerned these interrogation techniques had had a mixed success. According to some officers they had indeed brought in information; but against that were set the bad public image they presented and the question of whether such methods were really applicable in Northern Ireland. This decision was seen as a political setback for the security forces and a propaganda victory for the IRA.

There was by now a widespread public view that interrogation consisted of close, hostile and brutal questioning with the sole object of extracting immediate information – if necessary by force. This impression meant the old bogeyman of brainwashing continued to rear its ugly head. In the view of some officers this was an unfortunate development; they were also concerned that the lack of adequate pre-planning had led to some units having to operate on a shoestring and in appalling conditions. A former senior psychologist in POW Intelligence, Cyril Cunningham, commented: 'They have been flung prisoners like so many bones to a pack of hungry dogs and ordered to crunch them and make them yield something of substance. It thus creates a situation calculated to drive experienced and otherwise humane interrogators into becoming brutal rogues out of sheer frustration.'

It was clear to the expert interrogator that brutal and hostile behaviour was by and large unproductive. It was essential to create an 'intelligence environment' and it was when this broke down – or as in the case of Northern Ireland did not exist – that spontaneous verbal interrogation took place. David Chatres, writing about intelligence and psychological warfare operations in Northern Ireland, commented:

> The hallmark of the expert interrogator is the ability to manipulate the prisoner's social situation, to manoeuvre the victim into a position of stress, tension or even ostracism so as to increase pressure and stimulate conversation. The Chinese communists used such group dynamics with devastating effect in Korea and it was in response to this that the British Army developed its techniques.

Another result of the policy of banning these techniques was that intelligence sources dried up: they became too frightened because they thought that the Army was backing down. As one officer put it, 'The moment you show weakness intelligence starts to dry up.' At this stage, however, the Army had begun to spend more time and money on the intelligence operation, introducing new, sophisticated methods. But still it did not trust Special Branch enough to tell them, and invariably this increased tension between the two forces.

The casualties rose during this initial period of Direct Rule. In one month 28 soldiers were killed and over 100 wounded. There was little doubt that the political decision not to do much was having considerable effect on Army morale. Whitelaw had taken a very simple view when he took over. He had said to the Army that it should play everything very carefully until he understood what was happening, and then he wanted to move to a political solution. The need for this may well have been understood in the higher reaches of Lisburn, but on the ground it resulted in very difficult conditions.

Commanding officers complained that close control of troops on the ground was against a background of immediate crisis, rather than a general security policy. 'There were endless detectives on high and low profiles,' said one CO. 'Directives on whom you could arrest and whom you could not arrest . . . ad hoc control, depending on rows in Parliament or the papers. There were people in court cases one was not allowed to touch . . . then suddenly one was allowed to arrest them. You know – one bad bombing and you'd be allowed to arrest everybody.'

Another officer remembered going to an 'extraordinary' lecture at Lisburn during the summer. Briefing officers spoke about the 'mass of moderate opinion about to be mobilised,' and 'the great white snowball of peace' that was rolling out of Londonderry. 'It wasn't as simple as that!' he snorted, 'You only had to see a few streetfuls of either side beating hell out of each other to realise that! There just weren't these great hordes waiting for white snowballs of peace to roll over them. I went back down to the Springfield Road police station after that lecture and the bullets were fairly whistling round my head.' Just before this, another officer had been told to destroy all his intelligence on Catholic gunmen and take down their mug shots round the office walls because this 'betrayed the wrong attitude.' One senior minister commented that it was the nearest thing he ever remembered to officers actually getting disagreeable about Government policy.

The CLF, Major-General Ford, was very apprehensive about this policy. He could see the whole country developing steadily into an area of lawlessness; there was the problem of the Protestant extremists becoming increasingly frustrated at what they considered to be a very wishy-washy security policy, and of what action they might take; the morale of the troops, particularly that of the officers, was also worrying him. He collected all the commanding officers together and gave them a pep talk. They complained that the low profile restrictions were causing casualties and felt that the policy had nothing to do with their jobs. They were told that they had to pull themselves together and get on with it, improve their techniques and become more sophisticated in their reaction to incidents which were often the 'come-on' type leading to ambushes.

The Army commanders took these matters up with Whitelaw, whom they saw regularly. They could not actually tell him what he should be doing – however much they wanted to – because he, ultimately, gave the orders. So they told him that while they understood the political requirements for the low profile policy it was making their job much more difficult; in particular they pressed on him that the IRA was taking advantage of the lack of military activity to build a more secure basis for itself. The answer from the politicians was that the Catholic population would not let the IRA do this; but the Army officers could see it happening all round them. They were convinced that the Army had a better understanding of what was going on and they rated the Government as being politically naive. As far as they were concerned, the London politicians just did not understand that the IRA was determined to continue with its overall policy to force them out, and that this could be done in a number of different ways, as Morris Fraser, a child psychiatrist, found in Belfast when he talked to youngsters barely in their teens:

> The boy in the green anorak took my pencil and drew two parallel lines on the back of an envelope.
> 'That's the street, right?'
> He added a neat row of dots outside each line, then a rectangle in the middle.
> 'These are the lamposts, and that's the Army Land Rover coming up the street. You tie your cheese wire between two of the lamp-posts about six feet up. There's always a soldier standing in the back of the jeep; even with searchlights, he can't see the wire in the dark. It's just at the right height to catch his throat. Then, when the jeep stops, we can come out and throw stones.'
> His friend, two years older, disagreed.
> 'Only kids throw stones. What we do is fill our pockets with them and carry hurley sticks. If you put a stone on the ground and swing a stick as hard as you can, you can hit a soldier below his shield and cripple him. We once cut a squad of thirty-six down to six in ten minutes like that.'
> The third boy supported him.
> 'Then,' he said, 'we come in with petrol bombs. If a soldier lowers his shield to protect himself against the stones, you can lob a bomb over the top and get him that way.'

On Thursday 22 June 1972 the Irish Republican Publicity Bureau in Dublin issued a statement saying that the Provisionals would suspend their operations as from the following Monday, provided that there was a public reciprocal response from 'the armed forces of the British Crown'. At Westminster Whitelaw replied that as the purpose of the

Army was to keep the peace, it would of course reciprocate if the IRA ceased its operations. In Belfast, Faulkner commented that the offer from the IRA came 379 lives, 1,682 explosions and 7,258 injuries too late.

That day there were a number of gun battles in Belfast, and five people were injured. As the Monday deadline drew closer, so the Provisionals increased their attacks. Three soldiers were killed by a mine on the Glenshane Pass; Army posts in Belfast came under attack, and there were other incidents round the province. Just before the deadline a policeman and two soldiers were killed.

It was a cease-fire which Westminster thought important. In fact, in order to make it easier for discussions to be held, Whitelaw himself signed a pass for a prominent Catholic politician which stated that he was an MP and that 'he and his passengers' should be allowed to pass freely. It was also a fragile cease-fire. During it a gun battle with the Army was described by the Provisionals as a 'freelance' operation and they promised to punish those involved. However, it probably saved the lives of two officers in plain-clothes who walked into the Bogside early one morning for a bet, after a heavy drinking session. They spent the day there being questioned by the IRA before being allowed to walk back to their barracks. Only two months before, Ranger Best, of the Royal Irish Rangers, had not been so lucky. Home on leave from his unit, he had been picked up by the Official IRA, tried by a kangaroo court, sentenced, tortured and shot.

The Protestants were uneasy about the 'truce' which had started on Tuesday 27 June. The next thing they started putting up their own permanent barricades in parts of Belfast to replace the temporary ones which had been going up. Then the Ulster Defence Association (UDA) decided to become involved. The UDA was the coordinating body for a whole variety of Protestant vigilante groups and was the largest Protestant paramilitary organisation in the province. By Friday there were road gangs in masks and anoraks breaking up the road surfaces with mechanical drills at street corners around the Shankill and driving stakes and girders into the roads. Then the UDA decided to seal off a corner of the Woodvale area where a number of little streets, at the southern end, run into the Springfield Road, which is a Catholic area. About fifty Catholic families lived here, and the Army said that they would not tolerate barricades there. The UDA was now in effect settling into permanent 'No Go' areas. On the afternoon of Monday 3 July the battalion commander in the area was told by the UDA that 2,000 Protestant families were insisting on living inside barricades, and soldiers began to move in to stop another convoy of Protestants arriving with road drills and other such equipment.

But then, in light rain, the masked and in some cases armed men of the UDA began to arrive and de-bus around Ainsworth Avenue. They poured in, filling the streets, those in the front ranks carrying shields similar to those used by the Army. In an hour and a half there were some 8,000 of them massed to out-face the Army. A subaltern spoke to them first, but clearly the situation was way beyond him. The commanding officer then arrived, followed by the brigade commander as the seriousness of the situation became apparent. The soldiers were heavily outnumbered, even with reinforcements. In the early evening Brigadier Boswell rang the CLF to tell him that his men were still heavily outnumbered and that intelligence had reached him that there was a truck at the rear of the UDA ranks full of arms and ammunition, with the crew geared up to issue them when they got the order. The brigadier told the CLF quite clearly that if these thousands of men advanced his soldiers would be overwhelmed unless they were allowed to fire.

As the tension mounted, a small convoy of army vehicles drew up. It was four hours since the first UDA men had gathered and now the CLF, Major General Robert Ford himself, arrived. It was raining, and reporters and television crews with lights were clustered round. The Army officers conferred briefly and it was decided to talk to the UDA inside. With the brigadier, his own ADC and one military policeman Ford, was led into one of the small terraced houses. A number of masked men were already in there, including the four UDA leaders. At that time the Army officers could not be certain of their identity, although they had a pretty shrewd idea which later turned out to be correct.

It was a tense meeting, which lasted for some three hours. Before arriving, Ford had received authority from the Secretary of State that if the soldiers were going to be overrun, and there was no other way to stop the UDA, then they should open fire. It was now his task to persuade the UDA leaders that the Army meant to do this. It took a long time to convince them, but as they talked, the Army officers got the impression that the UDA men somehow wanted to prevent an all-out confrontation with the Army. They had already gained considerable propaganda points by the fact that the CLF himself had been seen to arrive to talk with them. Would that be enough? Each half-hour of talking helped the overall aim of reducing tension and eventually, in that small, hot and very crowded room, the UDA and the Army came to an agreement: Army patrols and barricades would sit on the interface, with a small number of UDA men being allowed to remain on the Protestant side. All the others were to disperse.

So the vast bulk of the UDA then marched off down the Shankill, singing and shouting that they had won a great victory. During the night those allowed to stay behind formed their own patrols which moved along with the soldiers and so gave the impression these were really joint Army/UDA patrols. It was another propaganda victory for the Protestant extremists.

A violent clash with the Protestants at this stage would have put the Army in an unenviable and probably impossible position. It had been averted, but the threat still remained in the background, and while it did the paramilitary and terrorist units turned their frustration to random sectarian killings. They came now on an almost tit-for-tat basis. In one incident two Protestants were found dead beside their burned-out car; in the boot was the body of a Catholic who had been shot earlier. Brian Faulkner wrote:

> They were telling the Government that if it thought peace could be bought cheaply by a deal with the IRA, they would be buying more trouble from another source. That such a message should be conveyed in such a grisly way was a symbol of how politics had become devalued in Northern Ireland.

The cease-fire lasted only thirteen days, but while it was on, Whitelaw had the top Provisional leaders flown secretly to London for 'peace talks' which were held in the Chelsea flat of one of his junior ministers. Nothing came of this, the Provisionals being unable to grasp the significance of the amount of ground they had gained by actually getting invited to London for talks with senior ministers.

The cease-fire itself ended in a messy incident in the mainly Catholic housing estate of Lenadoon, on the fringe of Andersonstown. Houses left vacant by Protestants had been re-allocated to Catholics. The Army tried very hard to keep the peace, even to the extent of offering money to re-house some of the Protestants. There seemed, however, to be a total block between all parties. The Catholics insisted that they should move into the empty houses and as they tried to do so, the Protestant UDA objected and the Army stopped the Catholics. Two days later the Catholics tried again, after giving the Army a 4 p.m. deadline to let them in. The crowds were big and trouble broke out, with those on the Catholic side shouting abuse across the barriers at the Army. As the whole situation began to get out of control, more soldiers moved into the front line. When the Catholics, who were being organised here by the Provisional IRA, moved up a furniture van, the Army rammed it. Shooting started, some reports suggesting that the Officials opened fire first to make sure that the Provisionals really did become involved in breaking the cease-fire. Whatever actually happened, it did not take long for the Provisional IRA to announce, through Dublin, that the cease-fire was off. The Army was convinced that the incident had been a set-up by the Provisionals to give them an excuse to resume their operations.

As violence spread that weekend ten people were killed in Belfast including a priest, Father Fitzpatrick of Ballymurphy, and a 13-year-old girl. In London, Whitelaw announced he had been having talks with IRA leaders in the Chelsea flat of the Northern Ireland Minister of State, Paul Channon. Protestant opinion was outraged, with Faulkner saying that 'these talks were the logical conclusion of the policy of appeasement which Direct Rule has initiated. But they represented pragmatism gone mad.'

The Provisionals hit back hard. On 13 July 3 soldiers were shot dead in Belfast and within a week 6 more had died, bringing the total number of soldiers killed in Northern Ireland since the military came to the aid of the civil power in 1969 to 100.

Then came the bombing blitz. The Army said that warnings were inadequate or too late; the Provisionals said that the Army deliberately ignored them. Friday 21 July started with the discovery of a 21-year-old Catholic shot dead in a Belfast street. Then in Londonderry three large car bombs exploded in the heavily-guarded city centre, causing much damage but no injuries. There were explosions in other parts of the province and the Dublin-Belfast express train was derailed. In Belfast the Provisionals planted twenty-two bombs within a one-mile radius of the city centre. In a period of less than one hour, after lunch, with the streets full of shoppers, they all went off, one by one.

For much of the afternoon the city centre was reduced to panic. No one knew where the next bomb would explode. Men and women wept openly, hugging each other in terror in the main streets where they stood for safety as the dull bangs went off all round and the columns of smoke rose into the afternoon sky. Thousands tried to get out, causing traffic jams and more chaos. People crowded into the Oxford Street bus station waiting-room as a warning came through of a bomb planted on nearby Albert Bridge. As a Land Rover of Welsh Guardsmen arrived a car bomb exploded by them. Two were killed instantly and the blast ripped on through the waiting-room, killing another four and scattering pieces of bodies across the road.

The Provisionals said that they had given adequate warning; the police pointed out that they received an average of fifty hoax calls each day and it would be impossible to check them all in time. 'There is a black sin in the face of Irish Republicanism today that will never be erased,' said an editorial in the *Sunday Independent* in Dublin. 'Murder now lies at the feet of the Irish nation and there is no gainsaying that fact.'

That night the politicians and the security chiefs met at Stormont. It had been a long, black day and it was now midnight. Whitelaw was shocked at what had happened and now the senior officers in Northern Ireland were to tell him that the operation to get rid of the 'No Go' areas – which had long been planned – should go ahead. Whitelaw had been resisting this; it had been a strong point of disagreement between his office and Lisburn. In April, in a BBC radio interview, he had said that he would not sanction any military invasion of the Bogside or Creggan. The discussion went round and round, but now Whitelaw did not need much persuading. The CGS, Sir Michael Carver, had already labelled the day 'Bloody Friday' before anyone could think of anything else. He wanted this name to stick in people's minds. So at 1 a.m., Whitelaw, with his head in his hands, said there must never be another Bloody Friday. The 'No Go' areas must be reoccupied, governed properly and if necessary dominated by the Army. The most secret plan for Operation Motorman, as it was to be called, would, he promised, be put to the Cabinet for approval immediately.

Since Direct Rule the military had been specifically instructed not to enter the 'No Go' areas because their presence might be seen as an inflammatory gesture and upset the cease-fire. This gamble on the terrorist movement honouring a cease-fire and talking constructive politics had not only failed but proved to be militarily expensive – as

Lisburn had constantly been trying to point out to the Secretary of State. Whereas in March it was thought that the Provisionals had around 500 gunmen, now the figure was put at nearer 1,500. The contempt that they were able to display towards the security forces had also boosted their recruiting – as had the release of detainees. Their arms and ammunition were stocked up; at the beginning of the year a 150lb bomb was a rarity – now it was commonplace. The constant testing of the political temperature during military operations had led to mistakes and the drying-up of intelligence – the life-blood of a counter-insurgency campaign. On the political side the Army felt that by talking to the Provisional leaders, however good the motives, Whitelaw had cut the ground from under the feet of the SDLP and convinced most Protestants that they were being sold down the river. It had been difficult for the Army to operate in that atmosphere.

Bloody Friday was the catalyst which allowed the Army to get back to the old status quo, in which they were around all the time, patrolling and running the show. It allowed the Army to say 'I told you so' to the politicians and to insist that Operation Motorman was run as the Army wanted it run.

Officers came over from the MOD to be briefed. This was done personally by Sir Harry Tuzo who explained his rationale to them so that they would not think that it was just another unreasonable request from Northern Ireland. 'In broadest terms he told us that he wanted to saturate the place with troops to clear out certain nests of vipers.' The visiting officers were stunned by the size of the operation, which would need twenty-seven battalions and an additional brigade headquarters. It would be the biggest military operation for the Army since Suez, and they wondered where they would find all the soldiers. One officer recalled that the bayonet strength in the province was really much smaller than, say, the 9,000 policemen who had been on duty for a day's demonstration in Grosvenor Square in 1968. However, they went back to examine all the possibilities, well aware that Northern Ireland was 'full of bear traps' and that the whole thing could turn into the most appalling public relations exercise.

It was felt by Lisburn that Londonderry might be the most difficult part of the operation. They did not know that Operation Motorman was very nearly not needed at all. About this time three officials of the Northern Ireland Office (NIO) drove up to a house in the

Bogside where a number of 'community groups' were represented at a meeting. There were tea and whiskey and a couple of hours of discussion aimed at persuading the Derry people to take down the barricades themselves. It was clear that the people at the meeting were anxious to find a way of removing these rat-infested structures which were not only unhealthy but dangerous to children in other ways. By the time the meeting ended it was agreed that the 'community workers' whom the NIO officials assumed were Provisional and Official IRA present in their 'socially conscious' role, would persuade the people of the Bogside to take down voluntarily their barricades. Unfortunately, as so often with carefully laid plans in Northern Ireland, it all came to nothing. Late one night a call was received to say that serious disagreement had arisen over the whole issue and everyone was back to square one. The officials shrugged their shoulders philosophically and the planning for Motorman went ahead.

London wanted to do it cautiously, with infantry pushing in slowly on foot. The CLF thought that very dangerous. Intelligence from the Bogside and Creggan was just about non-existent and there was no way of knowing if the IRA would fight. His plan was to move quickly with about one hundred Armoured Personnel Carriers (APCs) going in simultaneously. At that stage Lisburn did not know that Whitelaw was to go on radio and television and virtually announce what was happening, giving the gunmen the chance to slip away.

The RAF flew a reconnaissance flight over the city with special equipment which could detect newly-turned earth. This was discerned in places and the presumption had to be made that some of the barricades had been mined. To deal with this, and with the fact that some were concreted into the roads, it was decided to bring four specialist tanks across from Germany to deal with them. These tanks were commonly known as AVREs (Armoured Vehicle Royal Engineer) and had been designed to deal with concrete pill-boxes in the Atlantic wall back in 1944. They had a great blade on the front and a wide, stubby barrel which fired a projectile that looked rather like a dustbin. The thought of these rambling along the streets of Londonderry, covered with camouflage sacking and bringing memories of the Czech and Hungarian uprisings, alarmed those Army officers and politicians who were planning the operation. So the AVREs were brought on a long, very secret route, with top-level consultation at every stage of their journey. They would be seen only at the very last minute and then removed as fast as possible.

Major-General Ford, as operational commander, went across to Stormont to brief the Cabinet sub-committee concerned with Northern Ireland. There in the old cabinet room were Heath, Whitelaw, Carrington and Tuzo, as well as the CGS, Sir Michael Carver. They listened attentively as Ford presented them with a detailed plan for the operation. When he had finished Heath questioned him about the expected number of casualties. Ford's immediate reaction was to say that because the Army had no reliable intelligence assessment of the likely IRA reaction, it was impossible to say. Heath pressed him. 'Would there be 1,000?' he asked.

'Certainly not!' the general replied, slightly startled.

'Well then, are there going to be 100 casualties?'

Ford considered this figure, working out that 100 people, from both sides, could very well end up in hospital with as many as ten or fifteen dead. It was still four days before the operation and anything might happen.

'Yes, Prime Minister,' he agreed at last, 'there might be as many as 100 casualties.'

Heath thought for a few moments and then turned to the others. 'I think that up to 100 casualties is politically acceptable,' he told them, 'although I hope it will be many less.' They all nodded and Heath turned back to General Ford. 'The operation is on,' he told him.

The logistical side of the operation was enormous. Seven of the extra battalions had come in that weekend, along with their support units. They arrived over a thirty-six-hour period, in huge, C130 transport planes which landed at Aldergrove airport every five minutes. Riot gear for such a huge number of troops was also a headache – it just was not available. In the end extra helmets and shields and other gear were found in Hong Kong and flown across on a special VC10 flight and back again afterwards.

The aim of this operation was very clear: it was to establish a continuing presence in all hard areas to dominate both IRA and Protestant extremists. This would neutralise their ability to influence events until a political settlement had been achieved. The military wanted to make it clear that the operation was neither punitive nor repressive, and was not merely to restore law and order. Rather they wanted to be seen as a 'liberating force designed to remove the IRA and Protestant extremists from the backs of the people'. They wanted to recreate peaceful conditions in the various enclaves so that further political progress could be made.

In Londonderry, the AVREs finally arrived by sea on the last leg of their long journey the night before the operation. Unfortunately someone had forgotten about the tide, which was out. There was much waiting, cursing and swearing before the tanks could be brought ashore, but they were in position at H-Hour early the next morning. General Ford, happy about the operation in Belfast, was still a little worried about Londonderry – Bloody Sunday was still on everyone's minds. So he had gone to the start line near William Street. Twenty-six companies had surrounded the Bogside and Creggan and were to go in together.

The first tank rumbled off to deal with the first barricade. It demolished that successfully and then, to the general's surprise, trundled straight on up the road instead of turning immediately left to deal with the second barricade which had to be demolished before the convoy of troops could get through. It did not seem a good omen so early in the operation. The general raced after the tank, halted it by simply standing in front of it and then climbed up on top. It was, of course, completely closed down as it was expecting to hit mines planted in the barricades. As he scrambled up to the turret, the commander's hatch opened rather cautiously. 'You fool!' the general shouted above the noise of the engine and the radios. 'You've gone the wrong way! Turn round and follow me!'

The only way for the tank to do this was to back into someone's front garden, which was not going to do much for public relations, but there was nothing else for it. The general clung on, crouched behind the turret as the tank turned and went through the next barricade which was also thought to be mined. As it happened, it was not. Further up the street the tank pulled to one side, not knowing where to go next, and the general jumped off. Already bunched up behind them was the long convoy of APCs, Saracens, Humbers and other vehicles, some brought back off the scrap heaps because the modern APCs were tracked vehicles and Lisburn again wanted to avoid the impression of Russian tanks in Czechoslovakia. The leading vehicle stopped. Frustrated, the general hammered on it but it too was closed down as he went on down the line, unable to get any sense out of anyone, until he found the company commander. The major informed him that the leading APC was lost. 'I'll tell you the way to go,' the general said briskly. He had been stationed in the province in quieter times and knew this area well. 'Follow me!' Once again he set off and from this moment the operation went as planned.

Probably the most important aspect of the operation was that the lesson of internment had not been wasted, and the soldiers moved into the Protestant areas as well. In some areas the Protestants, not wanting to be outdone by the Catholics, had conveniently erected some flimsy barricades for the Paras to knock down, for interestingly it was this regiment which had been earmarked to deal with the Protestants. This time there was to be no chance of accusations of bias. All over the province, Catholics and Protestants alike woke up to find the Army all round them, occupying schools, football grounds, halls and blocks of flats. Whatever the reasoning behind Whitelaw's broadcast, certainly one result was that a number of terrorists had slipped across the border to Buncrana in County Donegal. Resistance was very light and to some soldiers it seemed that the people were quite pleased to have the barricades down at last. Two men shot dead in Londonderry were the only casualties, far less than had been expected or feared.

There was a prize awarded that day in the *Bogside News* for the biggest and best barricade. It went to one in which a bulldozer tank had sunk its blade – and had had to leave it there.

Phase Five
A shooting war won — a political battle lost
July 1972–May 1974

There were now 22,000 troops in Northern Ireland: the largest number since Partition in the 1920s. The Provisionals, however, showed no sign of weakening. They were stronger, better equipped and more experienced and the Army knew less about them than ever before. They had succeeded so far in getting Stormont suspended; in getting a British Secretary of State to talk to them in London; and in getting Dublin and London to talk to each other about Northern Ireland. They were planting bombs in heavily-guarded city centres — devastating the centre of Londonderry — and were now killing soldiers at a faster rate than ever before.

This, however, was to change over the next year and a half as the Army gained more knowledge of the enemy it was fighting and an ascendancy over him. In this 'second honeymoon period' Westminster was to carry the political initiatives forward step by step, and the only thing that stopped the Provisional IRA from filling the political vacuum was its own political ineptitude. First, the Army had to gather itself, sort out what it was doing and to establish control.

A commanding officer who took his battalion to Belfast just after Motorman, felt, after he had been there for some time, that the training had been wrong. His men had been trained to be reactive, to patrol and to shoot, which he began to think had little relevance to the outcome of an urban guerilla campaign. He put forward an argument based on the Army's shooting 28 people a year, of whom 4 were innocent. 'Now,' he said, 'if by some staggering improbability our shooting was improved by 25 per cent — and by God the rounds used to whistle down those ranges! — what would we have done?

'Reminds me. Should have included a tableau showing the military superseding the civil power during an industrial emergency.'

Shot 35 people of whom 5 were innocent, and what conceivable difference would that have made to the campaign?' He was concerned that training in intelligence gathering was minimal and, even more important, that there was no training in the arts of a policeman. It was much more effective, he thought, to be able to collect evidence, assemble it and prove a case in court, than to kill people. Killing just antagonised everyone, whereas if someone had a fair trial and got 'done', there was never much fuss.

Another battalion which took over two square miles of the Upper Falls 'which was no longer British' was amazed at the sheer level of shooting. In the first three weeks it had a man hit each day and 2,500 rounds fired at it as well as petrol and nail bombs. It quickly established a new pattern of patrolling, with patrols working in tandem to cover each other and moving very fast, knowing it was extremely difficult to spot a gunman in a built-up area. What the men hoped to do was to threaten the sniper or bomber with their sudden, unexpected presence so that he would be much more cautious in what he did. After six weeks the officers congratulated themselves on how the area had quietened down and they decided to check the logs. Activity, they found, had dropped to six shooting incidents a day in their two square miles. Then they realised just what an extraordinarily high level of violence there was around.

Views changed with people, patches and regiments, even though they might be side by side. A company commander there at the same time said he never thought of soldiers as policemen. They lived in an unruly jungle and it was the law of the jungle which worked. If there was a bank robbery in his patch he would react, but he would not do anything about a car with an out-of-date tax disc — other than take note of it and check to see if it matched the number plate of the car.

Soldiers who had already done tours were now coming back and were finding a difference. Previously, for instance, they had 'detention without trial' which meant that they could lay their hands on any suspect and have him detained without much of a case — if any at all. 'I didn't think about the moral aspects of that,' said one. 'I was much too busy. Mind you, I thought about it afterwards!' By the end of 1972 there was a system of Interim Custody Orders, which had to be examined and signed by the Secretary of State. Everything was much more structured and officers would now have to make a reasonable case against anyone before having him locked away. Some officers, though, particularly the younger ones, were still not very happy with the system. All it required, explained one, was for him or some other officer to go and stand behind a curtain and say that the Army believed that the accused was involved in such and such and the commissioner would say 'Right, inside!' Officers would go backwards and forwards between their stations and Long Kesh to attend hearings, and some even flew from England.

Some soldiers tried very hard to keep their fingers on the pulse of their patches, particularly when they had the IRA 'on the run'. One company commander was not happy about the civil representatives; he felt that they had no standing with the local people. At this time he had his eye on someone living in his patch who seemed to be an influential figure and on the fringes of the IRA. He wanted this man to be accepted by the authorities as the *de facto* leader because he felt that he could deal with him. He knew that without getting the Church behind the idea it would never get off the ground. He went along to the local priest and explained that the IRA was no longer a force in the area, but that unless an effective leader was produced, the IRA would undoubtedly return. The priest was not impressed, even after some hours of talking.

It really got quite heated. I fell into all the old Pooh-traps which I shouldn't have done . . . discussing religion and education. I got so angry that I advised him to grow a beard. I told him that every morning he would be looking into the mirror at the face of a man who had failed to take this chance and had therefore condemned his flock to years of brutality and murder. At least the beard would hide the face of someone who was as good as condoning murder.

Another commanding officer found himself becoming more of a civil governor than a military commander. He saw the interaction between the civilian field and security and how the two could not be separated. He found that he was always being approached to 'get things done': small things, like paying for damages in searches, maybe only amounting to £10, but causing a great deal of aggravation. On one occasion he became involved in discussion with a local firm, an iron foundry, with the personnel manager and shop stewards. He was trying to persuade them that when the shifts changed and the men went home, they should walk down the middle of the road.

At that time there was one dreadful man there who wore particularly big, heavy boots. They were all Protestants, of course, and they would tramp through the Catholic areas on their way home. Well, the Catholics often used to sit outside their doorsteps in their slippers and this fellow — yes — would stamp on their toes with his hob-nailed boots and there would be the most frightful scene. We had to try and get this fellow's workmates to persuade him not to do this!

For some three years now the Army had, to a large extent, been 'milling about' without any very clear and specific aim, and certainly with little knowledge of the people it was fighting. This was beginning to change. Kitson's policy of making every company commander identify and pursue the terrorist structure in his own area pushed each company into becoming a low level intelligence unit. It also pushed those companies into developing a real understanding of the terrorist and the local people. This policy was continued by his successor and eventually it spread to Londonderry and the rest of the province.

In the spring of 1972, training teams for soldiers going to Northern Ireland (NITATs) were set up in England and Germany. They were designed to be as professional as possible and a curious episode in the Army's campaign in the province is connected with them.

Early in 1972, a young scientific officer in the MOD, who also happened to be a trooper in the Territorial Army, was on an exercise in Germany. He was in a specialist 'stay behind' party behind two West German brigades, and he considered the whole exercise was farcical. Knowing full well that his role in a real war would be to operate behind the enemy lines, he suddenly thought, 'My God! if we were behind the Russian lines right now, what the hell would we actually do?' The main source of information at that time was a manual on the Russians, which had in it such 'vital' information as details of a Russian general's full-dress uniform. So, when he arrived back from the exercise, he sat down and wrote a note to his training officer. He pointed out that for their role, a soldier on the ground needed to know what the Russians were like, how they mounted their sentries, how they searched for enemy 'stay behind' parties, and what sort of training their behind-the-lines technical troops went through. In short, he said he needed to know how the enemy would appear to him, and the other way round.

This approach gained some support, and then he happened to meet one of the NITAT commanders, and persuaded him of the need for similar information in Northern Ireland. So, in the late spring of 1972 he was asked to go to Northern Ireland to carry out such research there. By all accounts he was a very difficult young man, and because, as a civilian, he was not subject to military discipline, he was able to say what he liked. Few professional soldiers enjoyed the experience of being told where they were going wrong by a civilian scientist, and by his own admission he was often appallingly rude and tactless, and antagonised a great many people.

He was not given access to any highly-classified information, and was, at the most, only able to spend a week patrolling with any one unit. So he found that he had to gather the bulk of his information from the soldiers themselves, usually when they had returned to England or Germany. What he did discover was that, while soldiers very often had a clear insight into the enemy, their information was very 'bitty'; what he had to do was collect it and present it. He was well aware that his preconceptions might shape what eventually came out, and so he developed a method to counteract this. He started with a list of topics and talked to everyone about them: training, re-supply, bombings, shootings and so on. He would separate this information, filing it under the appropriate heading, and very often under more than one heading. Then, after studying that material, he would restructure this large file with a new set of headings, so that he was not trapped by any preconceived ideas on what was important, and then he would write his report. The reports he produced did not contain any startling information; what they did do was attempt, for the first time, to present complete, coherent pictures of the enemy on which Army training, tactics and strategy could be based.

The first research was into the Provisional IRA in the major urban centres. It showed that the Provisional gunmen were usually unemployed, working-class Catholics, some of whom would probably have been ordinary criminals if it were not for the movement; this was not altogether surprising because the Catholic areas had very high levels of unemployment. They were mostly young, under 23, and those who survived did so because they became 'street-wise' and cunning. However, as the leaders were picked up so the volunteers became even younger. The greatest single factor in their joining the Provisional IRA was a family connection.

Most of them were known to the security forces, but unless they came under pressure from the security forces, the pattern of their days changed very little, and they had a tendency to live a life as near to normal as possible. When they came under pressure from the Army they would change their habits. For instance, they would avoid sleeping at home when arrests were being made. But as soon as that pressure eased, they would switch back again to their normal living habits. A typical example would be a young volunteer who would get up around 11 a.m., have breakfast/lunch around mid-day, and then go off to the pubs, clubs or the bookie. This was a time for generally strolling and hanging around. He would have his tea between 5 and 6 p.m. and spend the rest of the evening drinking, lounging about, and talking of women and horses and relating accounts, often exaggerated, of his exploits. Surprisingly little time, if any, would be spent in serious discussion of IRA business or operations. These gunmen would often wait for the schools to come out before they did anything serious, because then they could use the schoolchildren as 'dicks', or lookouts. They bothered little with their weapons, and the average gunman was unable to strip down the weapon he used, or even deal with a jam; the real experts at this were the women who carried weapons from the hides to the firing positions — they could strip them down in seconds. But with these thumb-nail sketches came a warning to soldiers of the danger of characterising the enemy; there were others, described separately, who were not like this, and they would be the real killers.

The Provisionals' main strategy at this time was to show Westminster that the province was ungovernable. Their organisation was loose, with companies based largely on close-knit areas and directed if at all by a battalion and brigade structure. In all this they differed noticeably from other terrorist organisations, such as the Protestant Ulster Volunteer Force, EOKA in Cyprus and the Vietcong in Vietnam. Their operations were crude and simple, and their success stemmed mainly from a natural flair for urban terrorism, the support of friends, relatives and sympathisers in their own areas, and the mistakes of the security forces.

The local Provisional intelligence officer was supposed to cover a wide range of matters from the Army and the police, through the Protestant paramilitary organisations, to commercial and political intelligence. In practice he concentrated on just two aspects — targets and security. Security was mainly tied up with looking for informers and a lot of time was spent reading the de-briefs that each man was expected to write up immediately after he had been screened by the security forces. From this the Provisionals could find out quite a lot about the areas in which the Army was interested and for whom they were looking. The rule was that a Provisional would not be in too much trouble if he talked to the Army, provided he told his intelligence officer straight away what he had said.

The scientist dug into all other relevant aspects of the Provisional IRA and its members including those detailed in documents captured by the Army. These showed that the Provisionals put little thought into anything other than the obvious matters of a shoot. Most of their best brains were locked up within Long Kesh. What the Provisionals needed most from people was silence and this they were quite prepared to get by intimidation and killing. Fear and mistrust of the Army also helped in this, and they put a lot of effort into turning people against the Army. One way was to start rumours; people under stress are always vulnerable to these and the rumours gained enormously in the telling. Many of them were based on stories of Army brutality, so that any strong action by the Army helped the Provisionals' campaign.

One thing this scientist discovered was the soldier's frequent inability — or lack of inclination — to appreciate the real depths of feelings in both communities: the Protestant fear that the rising

Catholic birthrate would rob him of all he had earned; and the Catholic fear not only of the Protestants, but of the Army and the Provisional gunmen as well. In the Catholic and Protestant ghettos people lived all the time in fear of armed men: the Army who might stop them in the streets or search their houses at all hours of the day and night; the UVF; or the Provisionals. Against this sort of thing they were helpless, and they never knew when it might occur. The intimidation they faced would usually be out of sight; an unguarded remark of misunderstanding could lead to a beating or even death. The soldier, on the other hand, was at least able to retreat to his company headquarters at intervals and, after four months, get out and return home.

Consequently, the scientist decided to take time to research the local people in the main Catholic areas. As he has since said,

> If I had asked anyone at Lisburn if I could do this, or even told them, they would have gone beserk! So I didn't tell them. I just gathered the necessary information at the same time as I gathered information for other papers. I suppose that when it came out each thought that someone else had authorised it. In fact I think it was the most important paper I produced.

What he tried to do with this information was to paint a comprehensive picture of the people and their life-style — as they would affect the soldiers, and as the soldiers would affect them. He wanted the soldiers to realise that in these communities they would meet individuals, and not generalities. The only way soldiers could come to understand the local people was by spending time with them — in their homes. He argued that it was not true to say that the Irish could not listen to reason because frequently the 'logical, reasonable argument' used by an Englishman was a set of irrelevant platitudes to an Irishman because it did not take into account the basic factors and fears of his life. Once a soldier understood these basic factors then 'their actions, words, thoughts and feelings are as understandable and predictable as are those of any other people'.

He said that it was the women of the family who had the strength of character, who held things together and bore the brunt of the problems. Even so, the mothers had little concept of the right or wrong way to bring up a family — it was just something that they did. The smaller families tended to keep their houses neat and clean, but the larger ones did not; if two such homes existed side by side, neither would resent or find anything wrong in what the other was doing. The men were independent, and had little responsibility within the family other than 'give the kids a clip if they interfered with him'.

The street was the main community, and in some places half the people would have the same surname and would be the dominant force. There were many family feuds and squabbles but ranks always closed when an outside influence loomed. These communities were tight and insular, and their reaction to outsiders was one of indifference and ignorance. World events meant nothing to them, only the Pope and the USA provoking a mild interest, but they seriously expected the whole world to be 'up-tight' about what was going on in Northern Ireland. Basically they were not great respecters of persons and what respect there was, was fickle. Politicians were too remote and were heroes one day and traitors the next. But people who could get things done did have respect accorded to them, and this included Army officers and NCOs; 'There is always a great cry for "the major", the highest rank they can expect direct access to.'

He reported that complete Catholic families tended to fall into three main categories: those who supported the Provisionals, those who supported the Officials, and those who were uninvolved. It was rarer for just one member to belong to an organisation, or to a different organisation, and where this happened it tended to cause considerable friction in the family. These affiliations affected not just their politics and friends, but also the pubs and clubs they frequented. There was, however, a significant difference between Belfast and Londonderry: in Londonderry most families seemed to have some members employed and some unemployed whereas in Belfast entire families either worked or did not. It was not so much a financial state as a state of mind after generations of high unemployment. 'It affects the family's whole attitude to life. However, surprisingly, the people themselves don't see much distinction between those who work and those who don't.'

Separate research on the Protestant side looked first at the Ulster Defence Association, a mass organisation with a hard core. At the end of 1971, when many Protestants thought that there was a real chance of Westminster 'selling them out' to the Republicans, a number of Protestant vigilante groups had come together under the umbrella organisation of the UDA. After Direct Rule, when

Catholic 'No Go' areas became widespread, the UDA began large-scale demonstrations and created their own 'No Go' areas in response. After Motorman and the disappearance of the 'No Go' areas, the UDA kept going because it felt that it might be needed again, and because the mass organisation, filled with many troublemakers and criminals, was a useful cover under which the hard core could operate. The UDA had two almost completely separate sets of people: the hard core and the rest. The comparatively innocent majority were likely to have jobs, turned up for a few meetings and sometimes stood guard outside the pubs or clubs where the hard core met. This latter group tended to be unemployed — and when not out on 'business' were to be found in the clubs or pubs.

This hard core was composed of men of real physical strength, great character and often considerable charisma. They stayed in power by the use of violence, force of personality and the loyalty of their followers. The scientist's research warned officers to be careful in dealing with them because 'it is quite possible the UDA leaders may have the stronger personality.' The leaders often tended to be ex-Territorials or regular soldiers, hard, ruthless and shrewd but very often likeable; they were adept at wheeling and dealing and had a remarkable flair for understanding what 'makes people tick'. With the merciless form of selection of the UDA, those who ended up at the top were very often of a high calibre. But their hard men required action, and for the leaders to remain at the top they had to provide it. So in many ways the UDA needed contact with the Army much more than the other way round. It was always anxious to be considered as a 'third force', and usually only allowed those with the rank of 'major' and above to talk to Army officers. They would attack the Army only in order to show everyone that they were a force to be reckoned with, or if they got really angry because some Army operation had stung them.

The Ulster Volunteer Force, which was illegal, was a dedicated, hard core organisation. Members tended to be older than those in the UDA — around 30 — and often more motivated. They did not get involved in petty crime and their operations were usually well thought out. They had two aims: to carry out terrorist operations against Catholics, and to be prepared for large-scale operations if there was a civil war. Written into their initiation oath was a clause which said that they would not take up arms against the security forces.

Over and above these were a number of smaller Protestant extremist organisations that sprang up from time to time — such as Tara, the Red Hand Commandoes, and the Ulster Freedom Fighters. Most were small splinter groups which were tolerated by the UDA. In particular, the paper concluded that the UDA, as a legal organisation, found them useful for taking the blame for atrocities committed by groups under its 'umbrella'.

It was these organisations which were now to be involved in the wave of terrible sectarian killings that was sweeping the province. Protestant violence had been a feature of the troubles since 1969 when police had stood by and watched a mob attack a People's Democracy march at Burntollet. It became more widespread later that year, in August, when they had rampaged through Belfast. This was how the Protestant backlash was to be felt; for in this year there were to be over 300 civilian deaths, 122 classified as assassinations; 40 Protestants and 81 Catholics. Two journalists who made a special study of this backlash, Martin Dillon and Denis Lehane, came to the conclusion that the bulk of these murders had been carried out by Protestant assassination squads. In *Political Murder in Northern Ireland* they wrote:

> The anger, the bitterness of a people who felt their only crime had been loyalty, was translated into the most ruthless and dedicated campaign of civilian killing that has been seen in Western Europe since the Second World War. The Protestant backlash had been a long time coming but when it finally came it made its presence felt with a vengeance only the righteous can inflict.

They went on to say that of the 200 deaths they investigated, only two could categorically be laid at the door of the Army and then only because the Army had admitted responsibility. These were the killings of Patrick McVeigh on 12 May 1972, and Daniel Rooney on 27 September the same year. Of the eight killings they were unable to attribute to anyone, they said none was likely to have been committed by the Army. The Army was, of course, being accused by some people of carrying out a policy of terror assassination. The favourite culprit was the SAS, which in 1972 was not operating in the province. The journalists pointed out that the Army was by far the best trained and equipped fighting force in Ulster and went on:

If it intended a massive campaign of sectarian assassination — for whatever reason — it could surely manage more than the handful we see here. Indeed, if it chose so to act, then the total of two hundred dead would pale into insignificance besides the hundreds or thousands the Army could kill. And it has to be asked, what possible motive could the Army have for such a campaign? No individual or group has yet produced a satisfactory answer to that question.

In the weeks of that summer of 1972 the main task of soldiers stationed in the Protestant areas of East Belfast was to monitor the massive marches which were being organised and to keep the two sides away from each other. The area had been taken over separately from West Belfast by 24 Brigade.

These Protestant areas had their own, particular atmosphere. Apart from the personal danger to soldiers, the commanders in East Belfast were more frightened that 10,000-15,000 Protestants marching in the centre of the area would produce a bloodbath than that the IRA would ever produce one. Protestant mobs were, they felt, always much more unpleasant.

There was an argument that soldiers were 'in cahoots' with the Protestants' paramilitary units, because most of the violence was coming from the Catholics and because the soldiers did not want to fight on two fronts. Some commanders could see how readily this line of thinking had developed. East Belfast, for example, was a huge area, and night patrols used to meet groups of people who were not in a proscribed organisation walking about the streets as vigilantes and there was no law that allowed the soldiers to stop them. These vigilante groups were strongly disliked. It was felt that there was no very serious danger other than the general danger everyone faced, and that there was no need for them to perform in this way whatsoever. One officer remarked that they gave the impression of being big bullies, out looking for trouble. 'It just savoured to me, right through, of nasty, Nazi bully-boys. The whole smell of the place was like that.'

Sometimes the organisers of marches would try to trick the soldiers by changing routes at the last minute and then disappearing so that they could not be found. In fact they never got across the river and into the main Catholic housing areas, nor did they march into Ballymacarrett on their own side of the river. So the soldiers felt that they had probably achieved what they had been sent to do.

The view of the man at the 'sharp end' is usually rather different from that of the man taking a broad view from the high ground. One observer at the MOD did feel that the Army had been very dubious about opening up on Protestant paramilitaries because of the possibility of a 'second front'. He felt that this view had remained for too long. It meant that these areas were being left to the police and it was some time before they became active and confident enough to deal effectively with 'some of the real viciousness' that was going on.

Meanwhile Whitelaw was trying to get a political initiative going. In September there was a conference of 'moderate' Catholics and 'moderate' Unionists at Darlington, in England. The SDLP declined to attend because internment had not ended. Paisley announced that he would not go with his party, the Democratic Unionist Party, because there had been no inquiry into a shooting in the Shankill Road when the Army had shot some civilians. William Craig, of Vanguard, (a large pressure-group that grew from the Unionist party split) curtly turned down an invitation from Faulkner to attend as an adviser. The conference was not altogether satisfactory but it got the ball rolling. It was followed by a Green Paper — a discussion paper — in which the Government put forward some ideas. One was that there should be no change in the status of Northern Ireland without the consent of the majority. Another was that the Catholic minority must have a part in executive power sharing. All this, the paper suggested, must be part of a package acceptable to the Dublin Government. What the Westminster Government was trying to do, of course, was bring the 'moderates' together and so outflank the 'extremists'. With this done, the Army felt that at last some political control was beginning to assert itself and that things were now on the move.

But internment was still a ban to political progress, whatever the Army might feel about its value in the fight against terrorism. However, with intimidation rife and court convictions therefore doubtful there was a dilemma to be resolved, and Whitelaw asked one of the law lords, Lord Diplock, to look into it. So, towards the end of the year Lord Diplock came across, travelled around, saw a great deal, and spoke to many people. At one stage he even insisted on watching at a riot. He wanted to find out exactly what sort of difficulties the soldiers were facing as they tried to control the violence, and during it, to arrest people. Soldiers were not trained as policemen and often it seemed merely a technicality — like the use of the wrong words — which allowed a 'known' terrorist to escape justice. Some quite large sums of compensation had been paid to people who said that they had been arrested unlawfully, and Diplock considered it totally unreasonable for a soldier on the ground to expect to know the legal justification for every arrest.

Diplock proposed two major changes. The first was the 'no jury' court for cases involving terrorist offences to be heard before a single judge, one reason given for this being that witnesses were being intimidated. In putting forward this proposal Diplock succinctly outlined the dilemma that was faced. 'Unless the state can secure their safety, then it would be unreasonable to expect them to testify voluntarily, and morally wrong to compel them to do so.'

The other major change brought in the 'soldier's arrest'. In future, all a soldier has to say was, 'I am a member of Her Majesty's Forces. I am arresting you.' This was not limited to terrorist offences — a parking offence would be enough. The arresting soldier, however, had to have grounds for suspecting an offence. Very slowly a system that had never been designed to deal with terrorism was being adapted.

So, in the New Year, the Emergency Provisions Act 1973 was brought in, based on Lord Diplock's proposals, which went some way towards easing the legal complications under which the soldiers and the courts worked. Not all politicians would accept that easing the system was desirable, indeed the main representatives of the Catholics, the SDLP, had withdrawn from the system until such time as internment was ended. Without political progress, however, terrorism could not be defeated. To use Diplock's own phrase, 'the dilemma is complete', and until it was resolved the Army would have to press on.

A secondary schoolboy in Belfast recalled:

On Monday 12 February, it started to snow. It had snowed all night and in the morning it had settled on the roofs and trees and cars. At morning break we had a snowball fight with the prefects and the masters. We rolled Big Ted, the woodwork master, in the snow. Every day there is a running battle between us and the Protestant school across the road. The police escort the Protestants and the Army escort us down the road. But that day I saw a very strange thing. Catholics and Protestants, police and soldiers, were all snowballing each other happily. But I don't think I'll see anything like it again.

With the New Year there were moves in other directions as well. The GOC, Sir Harry Tuzo, sometimes described as the 'last viceroy', left for a new appointment. Certainly there had been a suggestion of the 'viceroy' about his position, for during his tour he found himself having to act very much as a diplomat as well as a soldier before Direct Rule took that burden from him, and then he had become the security supremo for the whole province. He was a very good 'political' general though at times inclined to be ruled by his heart rather than his head.

He was being replaced by a rather different sort of man: Lieutenant-General Sir Frank King, a man who loved statistics and analysis — the original 'Shrivenham man'. A paratrooper who had fought and been wounded at Arnhem, he was a practical soldier and impatient of protocol. He was qualified as a pilot and flew himself around in a helicopter. He was, as someone put it, 'a soldier's soldier: more happy in a front line trench than a social function'. The very day he arrived to take up his appointment there was a bomb explosion in Belfast. He went down and spoke to a man who owned a shop which had been badly damaged. 'This is disastrous,' said the general sympathetically. 'It is disastrous,' agreed the shopowner, 'but it's not serious.'

This incident was in many ways to colour Sir Frank's view of his new job. It was a classic situation — in that it had all happened before — and to him the Irish had a splendid sense of humour and did not always take these matters too seriously. However, his first overall impression, as he looked at his soldiers spread across a damaged province, was that the military were paying too much attention to Londonderry and the border areas; they made good targets and were being caught in some terrible booby-traps. To him the key to the campaign was in Belfast. Here the IRA had to be removed from the streets, and it was from here that the military could dominate the countryside. He therefore made an early decision to strengthen the number of soldiers in the city at the expense of these other places. To make this possible he pushed forward in 1973 with the intelligence gathering operation, bringing in the use of computers, new weapons and more long-term surveillance.

One other matter that he dealt with quickly was the use of Interim Custody Orders. After Direct Rule had been established the previous year, Westminster decided that it was time to get rid of Detention without Trial under the Special Powers Act. Under this the Northern Ireland Minister for Home Affairs, and then the Secretary of State, could sign an order committing a person to indefinite detention — or internment. To make this process slightly less obnoxious, Westminster introduced a new quasi-judicial system in November 1973 under the Detention of Terrorists Order. This involved a initial Interim Custody Order (ICO), which would be signed by the Secretary of State if he felt that the case warranted further investigation. After twenty-eight days the person either had to be released or brought before a commissioner, who would then decide whether the detention should be continued. Later in the year this was to become part of the Emergency Provisions Act which had to be renewed every six months. Sir Frank felt that the great advantage of the ICO system was that the Army could lift suspected IRA leaders, and get them out of the way for at least twenty-eight days. No longer would they have to be content with those against whom they had hard evidence, like the boy caught with an armalite or laying a bomb.

So Lisburn got to work, thinning out soldiers on the border and in Londonderry and bringing them to Belfast. This policy also had the advantage of improving intelligence and within two months the Army once again had an ascendancy over the IRA and the violence. The MOD was able to withdraw two battalions, which meant that there could now be a ten-month gap between the four-month tours, changing the pattern very successfully. Part of the drive was also to bring down the casualty rate and de-escalate the situation. This was one of the guiding lines at the time. To do this the Army began to move more and more into the surveillance and information-gathering role which had started the previous year, and was now being substantially increased with more and more soldiers being trained by the SAS in their specialised techniques.

The new GOC was stamping his own particular mark on the province; and in particular he was making sure that the soldiers were being much more carefully tasked. He felt that far too many were out on patrols — one reason why eleven had died during his first month. So units started cutting down on patrols and building up the covert operations side. More and more Observation Posts were brought into use where soldiers could lie up for days at a time with binoculars, high-powered telescopes and night-sights. Linked by radio to patrols on the ground, they were able to dominate areas during the night as well as the day. For instance, they often found that getting into the attic space of one house gave them access to the whole row; they could bore holes in ceilings or move a roof tile or a brick fractionally and see what was going on in the house itself or outside in back gardens and side streets. Some soldiers might stay in the same spot for as long as three weeks. They would take up dry rations, water, a latrine bucket and chemicals, and use their radio very sparingly or in an emergency. Sometimes, if they felt that it was absolutely necessary, they would shoot from these positions.

These operations were always dangerous. An officer remembered one patrol being discovered when a pub owner noticed traces of urine coming down the wall and found three soldiers in his attic. Another operation the previous year ended in a soldier being killed. It was known as the Four Square Laundry operation and its discovery was a blow to Army intelligence. It was in fact a fake laundry which took in washing and returned it promptly. It had been able to do this by sub-contracting the work to a large laundry in Belfast which was completely unaware of the nature of the Four Square Laundry. The washing was returned in vans equipped with armour-plating and radios. The intelligence officers were able to examine clothes for tell-tale signs of blood or explosives, chat up locals and generally keep an eye on what was going on. They were given away, however, by one of the 'Freds', who had turned again and gone back to the IRA, and were ambushed on the Catholic Twinbrook estate. Despite Provisional claims, there were only two people working the van. The driver was shot dead. The woman with him, a member of the Woman's Royal Army Corps, was at that moment delivering laundry but, realising what had happened, she got herself out of the way, risking being shot rather than giving herself up. She scrambled through a series of back yards and gardens, badly shaken but otherwise undamaged. Two other undercover soldiers who were also identified by the same man were luckier. When the safe house in which they were living was attacked, they managed to fight it out with their revolvers and escape unhurt.

Basic gathering of information was another way to get intelligence. It was a laborious business and was done all the time by patrols who brought back details of everything they could from names to the colour of drawing-room walls. At the beginning of 1973 the numbers involved in collating and assembling this information were left to each unit but the numbers were comparatively small, around the normal wartime establishment of six men. It was decided that these units must be enlarged; which they were, until they became quite a large office organisation. Each unit built up a card-index system where every boy over the age of twelve and every girl over fourteen got a card. Everything about them would be on that card, including photographs. If any review of this information revealed a close involvement with the IRA, that person would then be put under personal surveillance which might well mean that he or she became a subject for an Interim Custody Order. Despite it being laborious, however, units used to compete with each other to improve their records.

The Army also had a computer. It was originally intended for all intelligence work but there was an outcry about it, particularly from Labour politicians. 'No doubt they thought that we would log them on our computers,' said a senior officer. 'Quite right, we would!' So the Army switched its main role to keeping vehicle information to help them catch the car bombers. Again, the basic idea for this system had been thought out by the civilian scientist, who, despite considerable pressure, was still in the province. He had considered that the prime value of Vehicle Check Points (VCPs) was to gather low-level information and to force the terrorist to change from casual movement — which was largely impervious to intelligence — to more systematic and sophisticated methods, which were far more vulnerable to intelligence.

Nearly all the bombs came up across the border from the south. The Army knew where they were being made and which roads were used, but the density of traffic made it impossible to check all cars. So the Army put a computer terminal down near the border to log all cars that came across, and the computer then told them which of these came all the way to Belfast. These could then be given a thorough search. 'That is,' an officer admitted ruefully, 'until a lorry-driver drove past our girl sitting typing in a ditch at the border terminal and put two fingers in the air and said "that" to our computer. That was four months after we got it going, so they knew about it.'

The best intelligence, however, often came from those within the IRA, or on the fringes, who were prepared to talk. One unit pulled in a suspect one day and as usual left him in the courtyard at the back of the police station to get cold. Then he was brought in and the intelligence officer soon realised that the man was morally disturbed by what was going on. The officer said later:

The floodgates opened. From what he told us we began raking in people we'd never heard of. Suddenly we could see the whole structure of this organisation. It was like the lights being turned on. Before we had just been fighting this amorphous mass, wondering who they were — with them hidden and us very vulnerable. Now the situation was reversed and we knew who we were looking for.

Early in May 1973 a deserter from the Army, Ranger Louis Hammond, was found in a Belfast alley shot through the head four times. He had been left there for dead. Previously he had been picked up by the Army who, when they discovered that he was a deserter, threatened him with a court martial. He had then begun to talk so much about the IRA that the intelligence officers decided that the Army could not have him back. They had to use him in intelligence and they did. When he outlived his usefulness he was packed off to England and found a job. He lost this and another four in quick succession, getting drunk and stealing. Then, against all advice, he insisted on coming back to Belfast where he was found, badly wounded, by the patrol. Another story had it, however, that he was an IRA double agent, who had been punished for giving away details of IRA embezzlements and frauds. When that information had come out in the *Sunday Times* it rocked the IRA, badly shaking confidence in its command structure.

It was often Army policy to give out that an arrest had come from a tip-off, from an informer, when it had not. It was done deliberately, according to one intelligence officer, to cause dissension in the ranks of the IRA. For the same reasons it was often put about that far more money had been stolen in some robbery than had actually been taken. Very often the Army found that soon afterwards, sometimes even the next day, there would be a number of knee-cappings. It was not good for IRA recruiting.

The Army was a heavy, brooding presence over the city at that time when their casualties were high. It was eyeball to eyeball with a resurgent Provisional IRA, and in the wings was an increasingly restless Protestant force. Sandbagged Army sangars guarded the police stations, and patrols were everywhere.

The Army ran everything in the Catholic areas. The RUC was still struggling to recover from the body blows of the past few years. It was subordinate to the Army, not in law but as a matter of fact. As far as the Army was concerned, to keep up the pretence that it was still 'acting in aid of the civil power' was merely a political whim. Not unnaturally, there was often a distinct lack of trust between the two forces. The Army felt that if it let the police know that it was about to engage in some delicate operation, the police would undoubtedly leak the details or try to frustrate the plan. One particular stamp, 'UK eyes only', annoyed the police very much indeed! So it often happened that the Army went off quite on its own to raid a house, to search premises, or to arrest people.

Still the Army suffered its casualties. In one incident that year a young soldier got separated from his patrol by a group of angry women. They took his rifle and twenty rounds of ammunition, calmed him down a bit by telling him that he would be all right, and kept him isolated until an IRA gunman was able to get there and shoot him. The *Belfast Telegraph* thought the incident reminiscent of tribal behaviour in more uncivilised parts of the world:

> Gary Barlow was a brave young man, he died honouring the orders of his superior officers, he played the rules of his Yellow Card right to the end. Even as he was being mauled he did not forget to uphold the name of the British Army, for considering the terrible circumstances, he still did not open fire.

A Royal Marine commander who served in Belfast at that time thought that although the Yellow Card had not been put in specifically to make life more difficult for soldiers, it did in fact do so. Discussing the Yellow Card with them, he found that they would accept that it was there to help, in the sense that it was a help to keep within the law, but it was also a symbol of the law, which was a restriction. That was how these men, who were out every night at personal risk of being shot, saw it. The officer thought that in terms of having to stay within the law, and maybe stand up in court and justify what they had done, they were indeed fighting with one hand tied behind their backs. But he did not think that this was wrong, and in fact felt that one of his main tasks as CO, in setting the tone of the tour, was to ensure that no soldier thought that it was wrong. He would keep emphasising that the rule of law was the all-important thing — that it was not acceptable to step beyond it. He argued that as a soldier had been given lethal weapons this imposed on him the responsibility of knowing how to use those weapons correctly — and of always using them responsibly. Young soldiers could easily understand the drive and the push to achieve the objective and to get there; it was part of their commando training to face the dangers and to be tough about things. But he had many, many times made the point that toughness was not synonymous with roughness; that indeed roughness was a sign of less toughness. In that sense he did not feel that soldiers were operating with their hands behind their backs. 'You are far more likely to get Alf Garnett in the safety of his home telling you that you have to be tougher,' he said, 'than you are to hear it from most of the young men you take with you.'

Bit by bit the Army made progress, whittling away at the IRA's freedom to operate when and where it chose, and therefore at its ability to claim its support from the vast majority of the Catholic community. It was trying to demonstrate the even-handedness of its operation, and disprove the lie that was put around about the soldiers and the way they behaved.

These stories were some of the bigger strains. Many COs were so anxious to be even-handed and to behave properly that sometimes they found themselves on the point of doubting their own soldiers. One commanding officer remembered an incident when a man with a bruised and battered face came in to say that he had met a patrol and asked them the way, and they swore at him and beat him up.

He was very, very clever at constructing everything. It all fitted and my chaps said, 'Yes, I did see him, yes I did speak to him at that time . . . but I didn't hit him.' Everything fitted with the patrol reports. I didn't think that they had beaten him up but I was beginning to wonder. The Special Investigation Branch (SIB) investigated it.

At the end one said to me, 'Like the last CO here, and the one before that, you will be worrying very much whether your blokes have been up to something they shouldn't. I can only assure you that — what I said yet again to the last CO and the one before that — it is the same guy we have investigated. We've done him eight times on this same complaint with different battalions. You are the third CO in this area he's tried it on. He probably went home and fell down his own stairs, or got beaten up by his wife!'

A paratrooper remembered operating in the Ardoyne and Shankill areas that year with rather different guidelines. It was a high-profile, high-intensity campaign by now and his company had just half a square mile to cover. Their job was to 'get in and prise open' the Ardoyne and ferret away in the Shankill to dig out the arms, ammunition and personalities that were wanted. It did not matter to them whether they were up against the IRA, UVF or anyone else.

> The methods we used were pretty rough and got rougher as the abuse we got became worse. We weren't surprised at getting abuse at three in the morning when we burst into someone's house. But it was the quality of that abuse! There is a great difference between someone abusing you in the heat of the moment and someone who actually means it . . . who really would love to see you dead. So why should we care?

When people complained that they were 'out of control' the paratroopers would retort that if they were, then many more people would have been lying round with bullet holes in them. There was no indiscriminate shooting — but they did admit rough treatment. One officer who was in Belfast when Gary Barlow was attacked by women and then shot by an imported gunman explained: 'Under those circumstances, even dealing with women and children, you can't afford to be nice. You know that they are after you. Look what happened to that young soldier — he died!' A senior commander remembered one of his young officers lying in the street, dying, with people spitting on him. 'His soldiers were there and they behaved in a very restrained way. Although this was an extreme case the provocation was, at times, enormous.'

The young civilian scientist was now working on how the Army could deal with terrorist organisations. He was also to examine further how the terrorist organisations worked, how they grouped themselves, how they trained and how their intelligence systems worked. It was to be a very practical analysis, not so much in uncovering vital new information, but in getting soldiers to think clearly about the enemy. He produced two papers on dealing with civil disturbances in the province but because of opposition from senior scientific civil servants and the antagonism he had raised in some quarters these papers were not distributed. However, some copies did 'leak out' and not only did the CLF take his stated policy on riots from one of them, but they were also straight away used as a basis for training soldiers going to Northern Ireland. 'In these various papers he identified the problems which faced us,' said one officer involved, 'I have no doubt that this allowed us to improve our tactics enormously, so that by the end of 1973 we had the Provisionals well and truly gripped.' NITAT was to rely heavily on these papers which were, according to one senior officer, 'probably the biggest single contribution to studying the campaign.' From them were produced the beginnings of an answer to the tactics of mob riots and large scale 'aggro' as well as the IRA gunman.

Soldiers attending a NITAT course would spend five days learning about the extremist organisations, and would be taught about their own areas and the sorts of incident which occurred in them, foot patrolling, reactions to an incident, the intelligence process and how to set it up, the Yellow Card, and all the other details they would need to know once they got to Northern Ireland. Then they would go down to Rype on the south coast, for practical training.

Now they could be taught the drills the Provisionals themselves used so that they would know what to expect. First: how to deal with crowds. Research showed that there were three ways to deal with this problem. The soldiers could 'be nice' and talk people out of it, or sometimes give them a 'bloody great whack', to teach them a lesson. The trouble was that people never knew where they were with this and it did not work. Then there was the so-called 'minimum force' approach. The necessary action would be taken to stop the crowd, but the weakness in this was that the trouble would always start again at the level it was stopped. The third way was to use enough force to stop the riot and prevent it starting again, which meant going in hard and patrolling firmly.

They were taught how the Provisionals set up an incident. The 'dicks', the young scouts, would come out first to inspect the area. Then the gunman would move into his position where he would wait for someone to bring him his weapon. When he had fired it he would leave it there and move away quickly, through a back door or a derelict house, and be two streets away or sitting down in a house having a meal in a matter of moments. Then someone else would pick up the weapon, maybe a girl with a long coat or pushing a pram, and take it back to the quartermaster's hide. If they were caught, all they could be charged with was possession of a weapon.

The classic procedure for soldiers under fire is to take cover and return the fire. They now had to be taught that the only way to succeed, if at all, was to move forward very fast and straight away start entering the surrounding houses. There were three reasons for this new drill. First, if they got in quickly they had a fair chance of picking up someone, or at least the weapon. Second, if the incident had been bloody, people inside would be in a state of shock and might say things that they would normally suppress. And, third, the more houses they visited the less chance there was that those who did talk would be identified. However, there were dangers in doing even this regularly, because it could set up a patrol for a devastating ambush.

They learned that the only way that the gunman could be stopped was to make sure that he was not confident about his escape route. Then he would not shoot. Initially the Army used single patrols but found that these were vulnerable. Pairs had the same problem. A gunman with well placed 'dicks' could keep track of their movements. More research showed that the patrols were also too big. If one soldier stopped to chat to someone, then the whole patrol had to stop, even if it were of platoon strength. So the patrols were broken down into a basic brick — a commander with his own radio, and three others. This gave them all-round defence and kept them small and very mobile. With three or five such bricks moving through an area a gunman would have a very hard job keeping track of them all. The uncertainty would put him off his aim.

Then there was the need to change the soldier's whole way of thinking from 'wanting to get a grip of the situation'. They were taught that it was vital to think before acting because unless they did so, they would keep falling into the 'come on' trap. It was hammered into them to think, 'If this is a come-on, what does he want me to do? If I do that, then what is he likely to do? So what should I do now to get him with *his* pants down?' Training officers were convinced that once soldiers started to think like this, more lives would be saved.

They were taught never to establish patterns: that the 'dicks' would notice where they would stop for a smoke on a particular bit of waste ground or where they might shelter in a particular shop entrance. They were taught that they were watched all the time. They were also taught to be courteous but firm. Slowly it was sinking in that the way a battalion behaved made a big difference to its overall success. Toughness was acceptable; roughness was not.

Gradually it began to be impressed on soldiers training for Northern Ireland that the tendency to react to each situation without a comprehensive plan or strategy was totally counter-productive. Most weaknesses, failures and shortcomings could be traced back to units and even individuals not having a clear aim. It was suggested that the aim should be 'to return Northern Ireland to normality within the United Kingdom, by destroying all terrorist organisations and by protecting individuals of both sects.' There was nothing new or controversial about this, but it was clear and simple and could be understood. There were three ways to achieve this — through intelligence, military tactics and contact with local people; and these should be engaged in with the sole purpose of achieving the aim. Moreover, each depended on the other. Patrolling was necessary to provide security for intelligence work and for local contact. Military operations depended on good intelligence. Unless military operations and intelligence were efficient and effective, the soldiers would be despised, and there would be no worthwhile local contact. Local contact meant precisely what it said: it was what soldiers said to local people, how they behaved towards them, and what they thought about them. It included community relations and public relations but, soldiers were told, it did not just mean building playgrounds, and it certainly did not mean 'appeasing local leaders by failing to carry out the Army's proper tasks.'

The success of all this depended largely on the judgement exercised by the individual soldier. It would be a corporal who had to decide whether a situation called for a rifle butt or a polite conversation; it would be a private who would spend two hours in a old woman's home chatting to her the day before she went in for an operation. It was this, the soldiers were told, which was the basis of warfare in Ulster, and the success of intelligence, tactics and contact depended on the individual soldiers' judgement — and understanding. One knowledgeable civilian observer put it to the soldiers quite bluntly:

If we leave Northern Ireland I have no doubt that most soldiers will say, as they do with Aden, that it was the fault of the politicians. However, I reckon that if we do leave, it will not be primarily because of the political decisions that have been taken — thus even releasing all the detainees is a setback that could be overcome. It will be because the Army has failed to adapt to the circumstances in Ulster. I am not saying it to be controversial; I am saying it because if you put all the blame onto other people, you learn nothing from your mistakes. The Army must develop and maintain the right approach in Northern Ireland — and it *must* have the right approach when it faces the next insurgency. I am not saying that local contact is going wrong, or that it will. What I am saying is that if things go sour in Ulster, it will be through local contact going wrong. Victory or defeat in an insurgency is very largely a matter of endurance

— of who gets tired first. We must be prepared for the campaign to last several more years — and work on this assumption.

So the training improved enormously and as the months went by was to become more and more sophisticated. On the ground the effects were noticeable as the Provisionals found it more and more difficult to operate effectively. In 1972 the Army had lost 103 soldiers and the UDR had lost 26; By the end of 1973, the Provisionals' success rate had slumped, with Army fatalities down to 58, and the UDR to just 8. But as Sir Frank King moved his campaign into high gear there developed the old 'Catch 22' situation. A great deal of the Army's success was due to better information and intelligence, and a lot of this was gathered by close contact, using intensive patrolling and searching. At the same time, these constant searches, both on the streets and in homes, were perhaps the biggest single bone of contention amongst the Catholics which contributed to their dislike of the Army. The Army was changing and improving but it still had not reached the stage where it had thought through all its policies to their proper conclusions.

Now the stage was set for the great turning point in the Ulster scene. The Army held the Provisionals, and new political structures were emerging. An Assembly had been voted in with the SDLP bringing in nearly all the Catholic votes and the Unionists irrevocably split. The idea — which had come out of the Darlington conference the year before — was to form a power-sharing executive to run the province, with the possibility of a Council of Ireland to strengthen links with the South. Months of delicate and painstaking negotiations had followed, and at the end of the year there was another conference, this time at Sunningdale, in Berkshire, in which the Irish Government was also involved. Here the details of the power-sharing executive were hammered out, but without the presence of Ian Paisley and his Democratic Unionists, who had not been invited. On 1 January 1974 the Northern Ireland Executive — consisting of six Protestants and five Catholics — took office. It was a historic moment and the high point of Westminster's political initiatives in the province. The needs and aspirations of all those who had been at Sunningdale had been carefully and delicately balanced. Provisions for a Council of Ireland gave Catholics reason to hope for a move towards a United Ireland and some measure of control over the RUC. The Protestant Unionists would normally have been appalled at the thought of such a link with Dublin. They drew comfort, however, from the fact that the Council had few powers but had brought with it Southern recognition as well as cooperation in the fight against the Provisional IRA. It was a brave attempt at getting a political settlement which would lead to the end of violence. Unfortunately it had in it the seeds of disaster. The majority of Protestants in Northern Ireland were firmly set against any such power-sharing executive and a Council of Ireland, and this had been clearly and accurately reflected in the composition of the new Assembly. That this had not affected the deliberations and conclusions at Sunningdale was because those opposing power sharing had not been invited.

As they took office in such high hopes that January there were already rumblings of discontent. Then in February there was a general election. Heath went to the country on the issue of 'Who governs Britain?', but in Northern Ireland it was very much an election for who was to govern the province. The Executive, born without the full quota of midwives, hardly had time to draw breath before it was assailed on all sides. Ian Paisley had not been there to welcome it into the world, nor had William Craig, Harry West or other Protestant representatives totally opposed to power-sharing and the Council of Ireland. In the province these were the only issues at stake in the general election, and those against both achieved a stunning victory, winning eleven out of the twelve Westminster seats.

Significant, too, was the gathering of their supporters; the Ulster Workers' Council and the Protestant paramilitary armies. For some months now both these groups had been considering what sort of action they should take, and industrial action had been in the forefront of their minds. Indeed, UWC officials had already been preparing for this. The UWC operated through a coordinating committee headed by Vanguard Assemblyman Glen Barr. It included three leading politicians: Ian Paisley (Democratic Unionist Party), Harry West (Official Unionist) and Bill Craig (Vanguard). Among the paramilitary representatives were leaders from the UDA, the Down Orange Welfare, the UVF, the Ulster Special Constabulary Association and the Orange Volunteers. The Army watched warily from the sidelines and a new Secretary of State, Merlyn Rees, brought in by Labour's victory, arrived to take charge.

The Army was now to be faced with a critical decision as the workers, and not the politicians, gathered to challenge the structure of the state. Should it act as 'breakers' of a civil strike, which was being threatened, or, by not acting, would it allow the delicately-built political initiative to collapse in the face of 'blatant threats'? The Army's decision was — and it made this quite plain all along — that dealing with a civil strike was the responsibility of the police. It was reluctant to take any action unless ordered to do so directly by the Secretary of State on two grounds. First, it had a profound belief that intervention would mean an immediate escalation of trouble. Second, its legal powers derived from the Terrorism Act. These powers did not cover civil confrontation unless a State of Emergency was declared. It might risk taking such action in Catholic areas, where there were no police, but not in Protestant areas where there were police. Moreover, the Army was heavily committed in the Catholic areas — where they were enjoying success against the Provisional IRA, and were reluctant to ease this pressure. The Chief Constable and the Secretary of State had been made aware of the Army's thinking right at the beginning and they had concurred with it. However a question mark was to remain over the Army's decision which was never removed.

New men were now appearing on the scene, and in a comprehensive account of that period Robert Fisk of *The Times* wrote that one of them — Billy Kelly — had never even been heard of before. He was a power station worker and a union conveyer but his influence was to grow 'phenomenally' over the next three years. His presence was a pointer to the most effective weapon that the UWC were to use in the weeks to follow.

> Kelly had been ready for six months. In that time he had travelled 15,000 miles round Ulster's six counties organising the UWC, talking to union shop stewards in coal and industry as well as to the power station workers whom he knew. He and Eric Montgomery, a Belfast station east shop steward, actually possessed written plans for the cutback of power and other supplies, the percentage of power that might be put on to the grid once the strike began, as well as the life expectancy of the telephone system if electricity were cut off altogether. Such documents might have been called subversive if the Army or police had seen them or realised their significance. They did not.

Another advantage the UWC were to have was the new Secretary of State, Merlyn Rees. He regarded Sunningdale as a typical example of the British Government's doing exactly as it pleased. He was somewhat bemused, however, when representatives of the UDA from all over the province came to see him, sat round the long table and demanded 'the end of Sunningdale and fresh elections'. He did ask Brian Faulkner about 'these people', but he was told not to worry about them. Nor was he fully aware of the significance of the political moves behind the scenes. Faulkner had told him that his people on the Executive would not be prepared to go any further on the matter of the Council of Ireland: they were already feeling the icy draught of Protestant disapproval. Moreover, two of the SDLP members had also decided to slow down on this matter, though they had problems with their party and could not announce it. By the time Rees realised the full significance of this it was too late to take advantage of it. For it was the 'threat' of this Council that was the spark which set off the strike.

The UWC had decided to go it alone; Paisley and Craig were not consulted and Paisley left it very late to jump on the band-wagon. The plan was that when the Assembly voted, on 14 May 1974, on an amendment expressing faith in the Executive, that would be the signal to call the strike and present everyone, including the politicians who supported them, with a *fait accompli*. The spokesman who announced it quietly to journalists in the Parliament buildings, after the vote had been taken, talked about backing for the strike which would come from power workers in the province. Electricity, he said, would be reduced from 725 to 400 megawatts. 'It is a grave responsibility,' he told the journalists and Government officials who were around at the time. 'But it is not ours. It is Brian Faulkner's. He and his friends are ignoring the wishes of 400,000 people who voted against them in the general election.' The technicalities and the figures did not make much impression on anyone.

The day before, the UWC had issued a statement warning 'If Westminster is not prepared to restore democracy . . . then the only way it can be restored is by a *coup d'état.*' That very morning they had placed a newspaper advertisement warning about the stoppage if the vote went ahead. It advised people to apply for supplementary benefits and announced that Advice Centres would be open in all areas.

So the strike started, slowly at first, with many people rather unsure of what they were doing. Nor did anyone know how the Army would react. The Protestant paramilitary armies, however, did back the strike and the momentum grew. Road blocks were established and manned by masked men; transport was disrupted and farmers blocked country roads; people were intimidated into returning home. The UWC controlled everything — milk, bread, petrol, and even passes for essential workers like doctors to get around. The Provisionals sat back and used their resources to get necessary goods and services into the Catholic enclaves.

It was a bitter time for the Executive, and particularly for the Catholic members, most of whom were convinced that if only the Army moved in, the strike could be broken. Indeed they saw it not as a strike but as a political *coup d'état*. Paddy Devlin complained bitterly that it was being carried out in front of an inert, combined security force of some 30,000 men. When not a single striker was arrested he saw it as giving the Loyalists the impression that the Army, police and Merlyn Rees all acquiesced in the 'illegal activity'. Another member, John Hume, urged a complete takeover of the oil supplies and the power stations. The generators there were of a conventional design and 300 technical people should have had no difficulty in doing this.

The row about the Army's involvement — or rather non-involvement — was to go on for a long time. The main accusation was that the soldiers were sympathetic to the Protestant strikers. There were accusations that the GOC, Sir Frank King, was making too much of his 'manpower' problems. If he had wanted to use his soldiers decisively, some said, he could have stopped the strike right at the beginning.

A senior civil servant, watching the politicians and the Army trying to work out how to deal with the crisis, thought that, while early and firm intervention might have stopped the strike, it would have been a short-lived victory. The basic Protestant opposition was too great for the Executive to have lasted more than another six to twelve months at the most. What interested him far more was whether the politicians, particularly a Labour government of the day, would have supported strong intervention by the Army in such a dispute.

Another observer had no such hesitations. 'The Stormont Government did absolutely nothing,' he said firmly. 'I felt that we were all a bit like the rabbit looking at the snake — paralysed!' He was certain that if the police had acted firmly and decisively, backed by the Army, roads would have been kept open and the gangs of arrogant and offensive teenagers dealt with summarily. It was not that everyone wanted to go to work, but he had seen for himself people who had set out and then turned back because roads were blocked by teenagers. What he was most desperate to see was some action by the Government which would show the Protestant leaders that it would not be intimidated. That firmness was never shown.

Lisburn had, of course, been giving the strike some considerable thought. One matter which touched on all their calculations was the experience of many other campaigns which told them that they could not do their job properly unless they had the broad support of at least one section of the community. Their prime job was to defeat IRA terrorists, and they did not have the support of the Catholic population; now they were being asked to go against the rest of the community.

this is precisely how they could have won it.

Lisburn was conscious that Faulkner did not have a following amongst the hard-line Protestants of East Belfast — or elsewhere, for that matter. It was obvious to them that the Government's policy must be to keep the Executive in power. It was equally obvious, especially to the soldiers on the street, that the Executive had no power, even before the strike started. When it did start, the position of the Executive became intolerable. Faulkner could not get petrol from his own garage to get in to work and had to be transported by the Army; Hume had to be air-lifted from his home in Londonderry.

For the first three days the Army left everything to the police because reports suggested that it was not too serious and more important, because 'no cries for help' came from the police. Lisburn had decided to wait either for an official request for help, or until there was an obvious failure on the part of the police. There were accusations of intimidation from all quarters but the police announced that they could do nothing about it unless the public cooperated. Buses were running normally and train and air services were not affected by the strike. Milk and bread deliveries were reported to be as normal but at the Belfast docks, dockers were refusing to unload fruit, vegetables and coal. A Government spokesman estimated that 30,000 people were not attending work, that £4m had already been lost in production and £2m in wages had been sacrificed. Postal and telephone services were being interrupted and petrol supplies were beginning to run low because of non-deliveries. When Sir Frank King did tour the UWC barricades, he suggested that the Secretary of State should ask for two more battalions in case the police in Protestant East Belfast needed help;

he was worried now about being sucked into a war on two fronts. Lisburn viewed the initial police handling of the strike with some misgivings. They did not think that the barricades would have gone up in Whitelaw's time. 'Merlyn was a nice chap to work with,' said one staff officer, 'but he didn't really terrify the chief constable.'

The Army, however, had done some considerable pre-planning. As they saw it, the key to the struggle lay in the power stations. They had already collected some 200 specialists from the combined services all round the world, some even from Hong Kong, although they drew the line at taking navy specialists without whom their ships could not sail. The specialists were all billeted at Aldergrove airport and from there went out to see what they could find. They went to all the power stations, covertly, at night — just one or two men to each place — and they went to study the plans rather than walk round the generators. One thing they quickly learned was that in a strike the management would also walk out.

Their reports indicated that although they could produce power without too much difficulty, they could only produce a fraction of the amount produced by the electricity workers, mainly because they lacked the manpower. This would also affect the distribution of supplies. Moreover, the strikers had barricaded themselves into their workplace across the causeway at Ballylumford, and it was clear that if the Army had to go in it would need considerable force. It seemed inconceivable to the Army that in these circumstances people would not commit at least minor acts of sabotage which would affect supplies probably for months to come.

These findings had been presented to the GOC, and they did not surprise him. He regarded his small force of skilled manpower as only to be used in a doomsday situation: in other words if the strikers all walked out and production dropped to zero. This would have an appalling effect on a province which relied on electricity. Bread and milk supplies would certainly be affected, but most dramatic of all, if production dropped below 20 per cent, the sewage in Belfast would rise up through the manhole covers and flood the streets. In this situation the Army would be quick to act, but while power was still flowing it believed that any involvement would have dire consequences.

To the Army, Rees seemed a very worried man, more concerned with placating Faulkner and keeping him in power than with letting him resign, which he kept threatening to do. Senior officers were on friendly terms with Faulkner and his brother was in the UDR, so they could keep in close touch. Since the Executive had taken office, they had watched Faulkner's popularity ebb away. From a different viewpoint, Rees could see that the police were not taking much notice of an Executive whose Catholic representatives were convinced that the strike could be put down. The noises from Dublin also irritated him because they suggested that all that was necessary was to call in the Army. 'They say use the Army! Put 'em down!' he exploded angrily to a colleague. 'They believe the Brits can solve Ireland — that all the Brits need to do is tell 'em what to do. But they never bother to talk to them themselves!'

Rees had little regard for the Executive himself. He felt that it had been created by Faulkner's group as 'jobs for the boys', despite the fact of the matter: that there had to be a balance between the parties and this was the only way to get it. In his view they would have been better off with four senior ministers and some junior ministers. 'They recreated departments!' he said scornfully some time later. 'Why, they even had a Minister for Information!'

The strike became more effective. On Thursday 23 May the gas supply was cut off in Londonderry; on farms across the province the cuts in electricity supplies meant that livestock in air-conditioned units were beginning to suffocate; thousands of chickens were being killed; 4,000 gallons of milk were being poured away, as it was every day now; there were cuts in water supplies; the telephone system was beginning to collapse, as was the postal system; fuel supplies were running very low. The UWC then announced that it would guarantee oil and petrol for doctors, nurses, vets and agricultural purposes, but warned that this would stop abruptly if the Government interfered. To emphasise this point it announced that its own pass system would be suspended because the Army had been discovered using some of them for its own purposes.

Each day the troops did deal with incidents, such as arresting the odd Protestant when he got 'too cheeky'. When they removed barricades, however, the locals would merely wait until they had gone before erecting them again. As many barricades consisted either of oil drums, or men with linked arms, this was not difficult for them. On this point the Protestants had always been careful not to confront the Army. At no time were Army vehicles impeded nor their right of way challenged. The Army insisted that its policy was consistent: they would not deal with a civil strike but would be quick to move in on terrorism. More troops were called in from the mainland but 'only to show willing and keep the roads open' as one somewhat cynical observer put it. Pressure grew, both to get the Army more involved and to keep it out altogether.

Lisburn was cagey about telling Rees the full reasons for the Army's non-involvement, particularly in the power stations. The Chief-of-Staff had been hammering the points in at Stormont meetings, saying that he was using information from an 'unimpeachable source' which had told him that the UWC strike committee would welcome the Army's moving in. The workers would merely remove critical bits of equipment and switches and leave. Production would run down to zero very quickly, and the Army would be left with 'egg all over its face' and unpopular with everyone. Lisburn reasoned that if they told Rees all this he would demand to know the sources of this information. That was something Lisburn dare not reveal.

The UWC strike committee was not the only place in which the Army had useful contacts. As the leaders of the Executive flew across to see the Prime Minister, Harold Wilson, about the crisis, the officers at Lisburn laid their contingency plans so they would know what was going on.

At Chequers, the three leading members of the threatened Executive pleaded with Harold Wilson to send in the Army to break the strike and arrest the leaders. Wilson refused, although a Whitehall mandarin had put a similar idea to Rees. 'Just because you are an MP,' he had argued, 'it doesn't mean to say that you are sacrosanct — or a goodie. There is a very, very strong case for interning Paisley and Craig, who are both undoubtedly in cahoots with the UDA.'

At a Cabinet meeting later that day in London, however, it was apparently agreed that troops could be used to go into the power stations and break the strike, if the Secretary of State decided that was what he wanted to do. Ministers had accepted that the Army could not maintain the totality of life in the province — and moreover could not shoot every Protestant on sight. Their feelings were that the Army could well 'have a go' at running the petrol stations and oil supplies; if this did not work they were not prepared to push the Army any further down this road. This decision was passed on unofficially and very quickly to Lisburn, where the GOC had already advised his staff that if he were ordered into the power stations he would require the order in writing so as to protect the reputation of the Army.

The next forty-eight hours were something of a mystery. According to Lisburn staff officers, the GOC sat down and wrote a letter directly to Rees. The message was succinct and contained the points the Army had been making all along as to why they should not become involved. It was then hand-delivered to Stormont, where Rees received it very late that night when he returned from the Cabinet meeting. Certainly if Rees had come back with any thoughts of using the Army in the power stations this letter must have helped to change his mind.

In London that night, Wilson followed up his decision to use the Army with a scathing attack on the strikers. The strike was being run by 'thugs and bullies'. Speaking on television he described all those taking part as 'people who spent their lives sponging on Westminster and British democracy and then systematically assaulting democratic methods. Who do these people think they are?'

The speech did not have quite the intended effect. For a start, whether right or wrong, it was a very damaging speech for the police and the Northern Ireland civil servants. Then, instead of being suitably cowed and crushed, the strikers saw this recognition as an award — and promptly pinned small sponges to their lapels. The Army maintained that it could have dealt with the strike in ten minutes by arresting all the ringleaders, had it been ordered to do so. It knew them all, and exactly where they were. However, the Army was well aware that such action would undoubtedly have already been considered by the strike committee, who would have laid contingency plans for a total escalation of the strike. They told Rees this and, acting cautiously and determined to look both ways, he contacted Wilson once again. Wilson was in his cottage on the Scilly Isles with no secure telephone, so Rees flew to RAF St Mawgan's in Cornwall, and Wilson had to fly there as well. Rees could still hear the GOC saying to him, 'Well now! You know it's all running into the sand. Once we are caught up in this, what do we do next?' The GOC, Sir Frank King, had kept telling him that the Army did not think that the situation was too bad, because people were still eating and there was no problem with water and sewage. Rees, however, thought that King was far too relaxed about it all even if there was an element of truth in what he said. He believed that the assessment was wrong and he knew by now that whatever he did the

Executive would collapse. The Protestants were already running for cover and Faulkner would resign. He passed this on quite bluntly to Wilson, who was phlegmatic about it. They discussed the technicalities of a return to Direct Rule and Wilson said 'Yes, of course. I'll get this side of the water teed up and ready.'

At Lisburn, staff officers waited for Rees's return and looked back over the past week. They thought it 'interesting': the week Merlyn Rees came of age. They knew he had been in a difficult position because there was great pressure on him to use the Army and the Cabinet had told him that he could. Then he had been persuaded against this, with King's letter playing a part by solid arguments. In a sympathetic way the Army officers contrasted the training of a politician to deal with a crisis with that of a soldier, who, from Staff College onward, was continuously involved in courses which thoroughly investigated such problems as this. Against this, the politician started life on the backbenches, and then, on promotion to ministerial rank, could be catapulted on to the front bench to deal with grave crises and would at once feel the loneliness of supreme command. 'It was just a lack of training,' one officer observed condescendingly. 'He improved a lot as time went on.'

So Merlyn Rees came back to Belfast to play out the final drama in the death of the Executive and the experiment of sharing power with the Catholic minority. He told the Army that they should move into the petrol stations and take over the distribution of fuel supplies. At dawn they moved in five helicopters to take over the Belfast refinery — but not before someone had thrown vital switch and brought one tank's output to a halt for forty-eight hours. Then they tackled the task of distributing petrol.

The plan was that civil servants would deal with the cash and issue the Green Shield stamps; but they never appeared. 'We found ourselves doing this,' recalled one bemused officer. 'We handled the cash and pumped the petrol. I don't expect they ever squared the books since then. But we did the chore they asked us to do!' As Lisburn had warned, within twelve hours everyone was on strike: the gas workers came out, and so did the grave diggers, saying, 'Let the Army bury the dead!'

Very shortly afterwards the Executive resigned, and that was the end of one political initiative, that had started eighteen months before at the Darlington Conference. Despite this, the Army was convinced that it had done the right thing, certain that it could not have broken the strike even if it had acted forcefully right at the beginning. The Army's argument was that people had come out on strike without barricades in the first place. Others had not gone to work because there was no power or because they were terrified, or both. 'It wasn't the barricades which stopped them', said an officer. 'They were just a symbol — a copy of the IRA barricades — to show that they had control of the town. Practically, they had no effect on the strike.' To the end the Army maintained there had never been any attempt to stop an Army vehicle, nor had there been any shooting or lawlessness in that sense. At all times, it emphasised, the soldiers had complete freedom of movement and access.

The decision to return to Direct Rule was inevitable, considering the way in which British politics work, and London's attitude towards Northern Ireland. This had always been that they wanted to keep things damped down as much as possible — neither taking high risks nor maintaining high profiles. In the end, however, it was accepted as a realistic decision — not least because this was what the British electorate wanted.

Now London had to get back to a situation where the profile of the Army would be kept right down — and that of the police pushed well up above the parapet. 'Police primacy' was to be the catch-word in future, although for the moment it was being kept under wraps.

Through all of this the Army still had its normal role to play, including dealing with explosives. As a cat has nine lives, so a pop-eyed, red and white Disney-like cat called Felix was the emblem rather naturally used by the Ammunition Technical Officers (ATOs) of the Royal Army Ordnance Corps, commissioned and non-commissioned, who were more generally known to the public as 'bomb disposal experts'. These were the men who were called out literally thousands of times to deal with unexploded devices ranging from hoaxes, through gas-pipes stuffed with nails, to sophisticated radio-controlled bombs of hundreds of pounds of high explosive. As the campaign went on the men who designed, made and planted these bombs became more experienced and it was more often than not a battle of wits in dealing with them. The ATOs were all brave men, and some of them knew that the terrorists were out to get them personally because of their success rate. Quite a number of them died, blown to pieces because of a tiny mistake or a slight misunderstanding of some new device. It was a risky business, requiring infinite care and patience.

One night in May 1974 a bomb was planted in Belfast which, had it gone off, would have enveloped the city in a ball of fire and destruction. When the ATO started to deal with it he did not know that it was a 1,000lb bomb — the biggest ever planted at that time. What he did know fairly soon after starting was that it was sitting on top of underground fuel storage tanks: one containing some 3,000 gallons of petrol. At that stage they thought the bomb might be as big as 200lb. If it went off it would take the top off the tanks like a knife through the top of an egg and the explosion would ignite the petrol vapour in the other tanks. A fireball with some 5,000 gallons of inflammable vapour was not out of the question.

The ATO in charge of this operation was Captain John Serle. At the back of his mind, throughout the long night, was the nagging suspicion that it might be a trap set specifically for him to avenge a success he had had a few days previously, and he said as much to his CO and his crew.

When the alarm bells rang Serle and his team were sitting watching television in their little mess in Albert Street. They all piled out and headed for the city centre, Serle leading in his 'pig' — a four-wheeled Humber armoured car. He was followed by a Saracen with an escort of a sergeant and eight riflemen, followed next by the 'special effects' radio 'pig', followed by a 'special support' four-ton lorry carrying sandbags, tow ropes, hooks, rollers, plate charges and all the rest of the gear. At the rear was an unmarked car.

They found the driver of a van who said that he had been hijacked and ordered to park his van next to the Government offices. However, he had not known where to find them so he had parked in the garage — right over the petrol storage tanks. The load of explosives inside was so heavy that the van was weighed down to its axles and Serle was very anxious to get foam pumped round it as quickly as possible to blanket the explosion should it go off.

I ordered the foam-laying kit out right away — a 'pig' with a generator, five hoses and two very brave soldiers inside. They drove to within thirty feet of the van, ran out the hoses which were to feed foam through the rollers — like toothpaste coming out of a tube in great gushing, never-ending blobs. The theory is great but this night we had a slight problem. The way in was narrow and had a four-foot wall running along each side. The 'pig' couldn't get into the garage and so had to park outside in Chichester Street, a big, wide street rather like Oxford Street in London. The foam crept along, filling the street, building up above even the four-foot walls, but it still did not reach the van. Those were two brave boys in that 'pig'. The armoured front was shut down in case the bomb went off, the generator was going full blast and it was very, very hot. They kept at it for three hours, until the foam in the street outside was up to a record twelve feet deep!

They had a break at this point, Serle was worried and very suspicious because the van driver had told him that the bomb had been set to explode after an hour and a half, and that time had long since passed. He knew, anyway, that the IRA never gave anything like such a long warning. After the break they went back and tried the foam from the other end of the street, with more success. Bit by bit the whole garage was filled up, covering the van, which produced another problem — it could not be seen properly any more. The next thing to do was to wash a way through to it using a robot, a miniature, tank-like, remote-controlled contraption, fitted with mechanical arms and television 'eyes'. The crew members were able to direct its progress forward from cover as they could watch its reflection in a shop window across the street.

The plan was to drop a small, plastic charge on the front seat and blow out the door. But then the robot broke down.

That really put the wind up me. The battery had failed for some obscure reason which meant it was helpless. The only way to get it out was for someone to walk up to it, hitch a rope round it and drag it clear. Perhaps that doesn't sound too difficult, but no one knew when the bomb might explode. I doubt if anyone's knees shook more than mine that night and I slipped and slid through the foam, trying frantically to get a shackle on that robot. It took a million years and then I still had to strain and struggle to man-handle it free.

The night was far from over. A replacement robot placed the charge in the van but then the foam which had been washed away to get at it had to be replaced. There was more sliding and slithering around, with Serle, up to his neck in foam, dragging huge plastic bags filled with the stuff to pack into the empty spaces. They all held their breath as the small charge was fired. There was a very small bang and some glass was broken. They felt like safe-breakers blasting their way into a strong-room. When Serle walked up to the van again to free the robot he could smell the explosives. It was a very,

very strong smell and it was then he realised that they had a monster bomb on their hands.

We still faced one last problem with the foam — how to wash away enough to get inside the van without losing any of the precious cushioning effect. In the end we managed it. I suppose it must have been getting on for five in the morning. Everything was now ready and I walked up to the van once again. It was an unbelievably long and lonely 100 yards. I kept my body pressed tight in against the wall of the foam, though much good that would have done to me if the balloon had gone up. I passed a rope through the front of the van and out through the back, then walked back and hitched it round a lamp post. I told the lads to give it a heave and that got the back doors open. I went back, looked inside, and saw a huge pile of sacks. I started to take them out, using a rope and hook, digging the hook into the neck of each sack in turn and then getting the lads to pull. The third time I went back I found the detonators — two little watches, both separated from the main explosive charge. Hallelujah! I was so relieved that without thinking I bent down and slipped them into my pocket. I went to the wall and sat down and suddenly realised what a bloody fool I was. I whipped them out of my pocket and cut away the detonator cord, once again realising much too late that I could have blown my fool hands off in the process.

The van was packed tight with explosives. As Serle got deeper in he found not only the sacks full of chemically-treated fertiliser — which makes a highly volatile mixture — but plenty of other interesting items, including sticks of commercial gelignite and a number of little cylinders measuring two feet by two inches in diameter — home-made IRA mortar bombs! With great care the team went on unpacking, inspecting, weighing, washing away water-soluble explosives, storing the others and slowly building up a mountain of death and destruction in the street. As he reached for the last sacks Serle suddenly spotted wires leading from them.

God Almighty! A booby trap right at the last knockings. The bastards really meant to have us this time. But we were lucky. They were just spare wires left over. What a let-off! I was just recovering from the shock when the garage phone started ringing. It sounded dreadfully impatient so I walked across and answered it, saying, 'Look, how many times have I told you not to ring me at work?' I suppose I must have been a little bit bomb-happy, but the man at the other end wasn't amused so I hung up. It was almost all over.

I walked into the street carrying the last two bags, gave a thumbs-up sign and a big cheer rang out. It seemed to echo right across Belfast from all the people who'd been following our night's work on the local radio network. It was only then I learned we'd topped the 1,000lb limit with our bomb. Chichester Street was returning to normal in the early morning light, the foam and plastic bags and debris being cleared away. I walked over to the 'pig' and lit a cigarette and sat down on my own — and cried. It had taken more than nine hours of solid, concentrated slog by some of the most loyal and wonderful soldiers in the world — Paddy, Terry, Miles, Gerry and all the rest of them. All of them knew that there would be a medal to come and I sat there and wept because although I might collect it, they had earned it too — every single one of them.

For defusing Ulster's first 1,000lb bomb, Serle was awarded the Queen's Gallantry Medal, and not long after he died — not from terrorist action, but painfully from cancer.

The uneasy stirrings of 'police primacy'
May 1974–April 1976

The downfall of the Executive was a blow not only for those who had created and formed it but also for the Army, which was now left wondering just who the Northern Irish were. It began to dawn on the Army that these people really were a different breed, that the 'bloody politicians' would never succeed in producing a solution, and that the main job of security might just as well be handed back to the police. The eagerness with which some senior officers had seized the Ulster situation as one in which they could train junior ranks in battle conditions began to fade. The whole affair was going on far too-long. They had been impressed with the way the Executive had tried to get down to business ('It produced men of character,' said one officer), and pleased with its broad political base.

The Army, however, was still very much in the driving seat. Each Thursday morning the GOC as Director of Operations would hold a security meeting at Lisburn. The Chief Constable, Sir Jamie Flanagan — the first Catholic ever appointed to this post — would drive over from Knock and it was, perhaps, rather humiliating for the police. Sir Frank King, however, was always pleasant, suggesting that 'Perhaps, Jamie, the police might . . .,' or 'Don't you think we should be doing . . .?' Sometimes he would give the Northern Ireland office representative a mild rocket about something, but always with a faint smile. They both knew what he was doing — putting on a bit of a show, a little bit of theatre. With Merlyn Rees now at Stormont, the security meetings there were always large. One officer commented, 'Every Tom, Dick and Harry used to come to them and they weren't terribly important as a result.' Other Army officers found Rees very easy to deal with, but were irritated that the politicians had to keep rushing back and forwards to Parliament. They always thought that a terrible weakness of the system — Whitelaw, for instance, was a bad traveller and was always feeling sick when he arrived on Monday mornings. They felt that Rees was continually looking over his shoulder, wondering what the attitude of his colleagues in Parliament might be to any action he took. No doubt, thought Lisburn, his position as a member of the Parliamentary Labour Party weighed heavily on his mind. There was also a strange kink in the chain of command that led from Stormont Castle to Thiepval Barracks at Lisburn. For the Army's position in Northern Ireland was protected by an important constitutional device: the fact of the matter was that the GOC was serving not the Secretary of State but the Defence Secretary. If he got an order which he thought detrimental to his soldiers he could always say, 'With respect, sir, this is something I must refer back to the MOD.' Then, if ministers could not come to an agreement the matter would be placed before the small Emergency Cabinet and the GOC would be asked to come and state his case. Staff officers recall that Frank King did this twice and that each time he won his argument.

The UWC strike and the way it was handled had produced much bitterness in many quarters. Some regarded the lack of performance by the RUC as a manifestation of their sectarian bias. Others felt strongly that the police could have coped had the leadership been better. Some police officers and civil servants, as well as a few Army officers, were perturbed about the lack of help from the Army, which had deliberately left the Protestant areas to the police. They felt that the Army just did not understand how police capabilities in these areas had been totally run down following the directives of Sir Arthur Young. This had meant the police were not trained to deal with public disorder, and this was a basic weakness which allowed the Army to dominate.

This all rather horrified the new Senior Deputy Chief Constable, Kenneth Newman. He was a policeman with an enquiring, businesslike mind and a solid background in troubled places such as Palestine. As an Englishman, and a Metropolitan policeman, he had astonished a number of people by applying for the job and even more by getting it. There had been a great number of applications, some from as far away as Hong Kong. At Lisburn officers gleefully recounted a rumour about Newman's interview for the job: 'He was asked why he wanted to do the job at all, and bearing in mind the state of the RUC at this time it was quite a loaded question,' recalled one officer. 'Newman, never a man to mince words, replied that the job he really wanted was that of Chief Constable, but that the Board would probably want to have a good look at him before giving it to him! This job would give them that opportunity.'

Newman always denied this story, but it was a fair reflection on his single-mindedness and professional expertise. It was also a sign both that the recruiting base for a very 'local' force was being broadened and of the fundamental changes that were to come which would transform the RUC and change the role of the Army. Newman, in fact, was interested in what he felt was a kind of laboratory, or experimental situation, in which many problems which had appeared — or might appear — on the mainland could be studied. The fundamental problem in Ulster for the police was of trying to operate in an almost alienated environment, and there was obviously a similar situation building up in the mainland in terms of ethnic minorities.

What had surprised him when he had arrived the previous year was the extent to which the Army had taken the lead. It seemed to him to be the wrong way round, and if the police were to start on any planned progression involving ultimate disengagement of the Army, then they really had to begin movement to reverse this situation. Newman wanted a robust and independent force running its own show on a professional basis. Only in this way did RUC officers feel that they could get off the psychological hook of being regarded as partisan — and in particular being regarded as second-rate to the Army.

While the police agonised over what they should do, the Army got on with running the campaign, and as ever was full of ideas. Now it was pressing hard for greater collaboration, including direct radio contact, with the South. The Army complained that if an incident occurred, and it was necessary to find an RUC policeman and then get him to contact his opposite number across the border, it was always too late to do anything. Hot pursuit across the border was another favourite demand. It was really an issue of principle, with the Army saying 'It must be we who deal directly with the South on security matters.' Their arguments fell on three basic counts.

First, there was no way the Dublin Government would ever agree to the Irish Army being in direct contact with the British Army. And they were absolutely right,' exclaimed a civil servant, somewhat horrified at the idea. 'It would have screwed up the whole of their internal politics as well. It would have been absolutely mad!' Second, if the Government was trying to get the police back into the lead, this was the wrong way to go about it. Third, and very practical, the RUC had much better relations with the Gardai than the Army could ever hope to achieve, and had been in close contact with them for years, despite all the talk to the contrary.

It seemed that there were two separate issues in this business of relations with the South. One was political, and it was just not possible to do much about it until the Labour Government of 1974 came in. Until then the overriding political need was to carry the Unionists along. A senior Cabinet minister said: 'What's more, the idea of Willie dashing down to Dublin just wasn't on! Anyway he was talking hard to the SDLP and they and Garret Fitzgerald were like brothers in those days!' The second issue was that the Army had a purely military attitude to the South. The Army pressed its case for overflying rights and hot pursuit across the border very hard, and there was considerable sympathy for it. But in the words of one man who was in the middle of all this, 'They were never within a hundred miles of getting such facilities.' Senior officers would continually say at Stormont that they knew where the explosives came from, they knew people were popping backwards and forwards, and while this was all perfectly legitimate it was a matter of what the officials could press for and get away with. Their main preoccupation was to talk and argue their way into getting better cooperation and something that would work in both the middle and the long term. They used newspaper leaks to gauge reaction, hoping that the British ambassador in Dublin would not get hauled on to the carpet too often for outrageous ideas in British newspapers.

Curiously enough, the Army never really expected to get hot pursuit, despite all the fuss it made. What it did hope was that if it made enough noise about enough matters then something would result — and something was better than nothing. It was the Army's basic attitude throughout this period, and it was coupled with its ever-recurring complaint that the Gardai and the RUC were twenty years behind the times with their technology and expertise. They wanted to get away from the situation where they had to go through a local Post Office exchange and wind handles on antiquated machines in order to reach an Irish minister outside Dublin. They wanted to get away from a situation where the RUC's top fingerprint expert was only a sergeant although the RUC led the world in interpreting bullet-print patterns. They could not get over the fact that in some places the RUC station sergeant would sign on at 10 a.m. and sign off at 4 p.m. to go home for his tea — and for the rest of the day. Lisburn kept saying that all this would have to change before the police would be ready to take over from them.

BELFAST 1974

'Well it could be
the Officials
firing at the Provos,
or the IRA
firing at the Prots,
or the UDA
firing at the Officials
or the UVF
firing at the Cats –
on the other hand
they could all be
firing at me?'

Still the soldiers patrolled and fought, and some died. They lived in squalor and worked endlessly, often drooping with fatique. Flitting across damp streets, flattening themselves against walls, eyes searching for tell-tale signs of snipers — the moved tile, a roof jacked up an inch. They listened to the warning sounds of banging dustbin lids and shrill whistles as they moved round, and had to hear as well the obscenities from women, young and old. They moved on foot along streets where the windows would be boarded up with grey corrugated iron or cement blocks; they moved in the small one-ton armoured 'pigs' or whined along in six-wheeled Saracens, rifles out the back, past the broken pavements where the grass struggled to grow. Often a burglar alarm would be ringing, unnoticed, on and on across the wide streets where the wind-blown debris of weeks would lie heaped in sheltered corners. At night, they crawled up back alleys, remembering where the lights would shine and where a wall would be painted white so that they would stand out as targets as they passed. They dealt with orders to 'go in hard' or 'tread softly' with equal stoicism. Sometimes they kicked against these restrictions. A soldier remembered being told that his patrols were not to go into two buildings on the Shankill Road — the UDA headquarters and the Orange Hall. He did not know the reason, but thought that maybe the authorities wanted to keep the Protestants happy and stop them shooting at soldiers. Perhaps, he thought, they wanted to make sure that if civil war broke out the Protestants would have the means to fight it.

I was in an attic next door to the Orange Hall one day and found a door that someone said led directly into the hall. 'To hell with it!' I said to my men, and opened the door. Well! It was all very embarrassing. Stacked neatly against the wall in this Orange Hall attic were nineteen super-duper ex-Army SLRs [self-loading rifles] and a great deal of ammunition.

In April 1974 the Government gave the first signs of its intention to bring back 'normal policing' to the province. It was a subject which had occupied a lot of minds and while the Army was for the idea in principle it had grave reservations about whether the police were ready for this role. The Army was even less enthusiastic about the plan for the phased release of detainees. There was particular derision over the plan to back this with a scheme whereby sponsors would be held responsible for their good behaviour. This idea quickly became known as 'taking a terrorist home for tea' and was later quietly dropped. The release of detainees, however, continued.

What Rees was trying to do was get rid of one obstacle which kept the warring political factions from coming together. There was obviously no known end to the problems of the province, but it was felt that if this were openly acknowledged there would be no real basis for doing anything at all. The policy had to be to maintain that the problem was temporary. One philosophy was 'to consider what goes on over here not always in terms of seeking a solution but in terms of managing a situation, a philosophy which probably prevented us from going completely round the bend!'

Now nearly five years into being 'in aid of the civil power', the Army was still concerned about the effect that the normal legal system was having on soldiers, particularly because in many areas they had virtually replaced the civil authority. Lisburn felt that because the Army had taken over much of the policing role of the RUC it needed a more sensible legal basis for what it was required to do, though not for criminal acts of violence. Legal advisers were aware that not many people drew the distinction between the theoretical basis for the Army's aiding the civil power and the practical basis on which its actions were judged.

At Lisburn serious discussion had been given to the introduction of martial law, for instance, but the civil advisers had pointed out that this would be politically unacceptable and the matter never went as far as ministers. More thought, however, was given to the method by which soldiers were tried. Lisburn was much more concerned with what some patrol in a city street or country field could or could not do on the basis of the instructions on the Yellow Cards and the ridiculous positions in which they might find themselves, which might bring them into the civil courts. So the proposition was put that soldiers should be tried by court martial with the argument that this would require a change in law only in relation to a situation in which someone had died. It was felt there was a distinct advantage in the Army's being seen to exercise its own discipline. One Army lawyer said:

> We had as great an interest as anyone in seeing unruly, licentious soldiery being punished. In order to keep discipline every Army has to keep that as an objective. But we couldn't do this because the job had been handed over to the DPP. I don't believe that these lawyers and the politicians should act as referees in this little fracas over here and apply the same rules to each side. The terrorist is deprived of his right to a trial by jury because potential witnesses are too terrified or biased . . . but why should a soldier be deprived of this right? Why should he come up in front of a Diplock no-jury court? In this sense I don't believe even-handedness requires the same rules to apply to each side.

It was pointed out that in previous campaigns outside the United Kingdom — in Aden, Borneo, Kenya, Malaya and elsewhere — civil court jurisdiction did not apply to the military because of the State of Emergency which was declared in each case. It seemed to the

Army that the only reason it did not apply within the United Kingdom was the unwillingness of politicians to accept that the Army was in a warlike, military situation. 'All this would have meant the authorities accepting that we were fighting a war, which was never accepted — never!', observed a Army lawyer. 'I distinctly remember this approach being the worst feature of serving in the Lisburn headquarters. Our situation was not appreciated sensibly — for political reasons.'

Not unnaturally, there was a different view, and a law officer at the MOD in London pointed out that if the soldier kept to the instructions on his Yellow Card, he would not end up in court. Allowing soldiers to be tried in civil courts for offences committed while on duty was a unique British position, but there was an awareness that while advantages might accrue from this practice, there were disadvantages which might not at first be obvious. One lawyer said:

> I wonder if anyone has ever worked out the statistics on the number of accurate shots fired by a unit while one of its members is up on a murder charge — and compared that with accurate shots fired before that? If Bloggins is up on a murder rap, aren't his mates likely to say, 'If I'm going to shoot, then I'm going to miss'? This is the soldier's dilemma. If he doesn't comply with orders to shoot when the situation requires it, then he's liable to put himself and his mates in danger. If he shoots and makes a mistake, he's liable to end up in the civil courts. As the law stands at the moment there is no alternative, but quite honestly I do not think there should be.

The GOC was worried about this, however, and had already taken up the matter personally with the Conservative Attorney-General, Sir Peter Rawlinson, and got nowhere, and again with his Labour replacement, Sam Silkin. He was particularly concerned about cases in which soldiers had been faced with sudden danger, such as in riots, or shooting incidents and quick follow-up operations. He told Silkin quite bluntly that he was worried that his soldiers might become disinclined to act aggressively when the situation required it simply because if anything went wrong they faced prosecution and imprisonment on the evidence of their ideological and actual opponents. He wanted a fresh look at the whole approach to the prosecution of soldiers: a bold, confident approach which would differentiate between the 'law-keepers' and the 'law-breakers'. He also argued that the principle of law which entitled a person to use force in self-defence was essentially a domestic or civilian concept. It implied an unwillingness to act aggressively, giving the initiative to the other side and producing a mentality of defence against an assailant rather than an attack on an enemy.

Sir Frank argued that all this went totally against accepted military tactics and operational planning. The state in its wisdom sent soldiers to Northern Ireland equipped with lethal weapons to catch terrorists and stop all sorts of law-breaking. It regularly sent soldiers to areas where they could be (and were) shot and blown to pieces or subjected to taunts and insults for eighteen hours a day. It was a warlike situation, and he did not think it right for soldiers to be judged by civilian standards which included the question: 'Did he do more than was necessary to defend himself and his comrades?'

What the Army really wanted was a general statement of policy that soldiers would not get thrown into the 'arena of the civil courts' except on the clearest evidence of gross brutality or crime. It was a fine intellectual exercise, it thought, to sit in Lisburn and tell the soldiers that equality before the law was important; that they had nothing to fear if they acted reasonably; that the top law officers of the land had all been in the Services and knew what it was like 'because they had all been at the sharp end'; that if the soldiers did go slightly beyond what was appropriate they would still be regarded sympathetically. One senior Army lawyer said:

> In my experience the soldiers never accepted this. For a long time the battalion commanders and more junior commanders felt that they were sending their men out with a question in the back of their minds that if they did their duty — as they saw it — would they get into trouble for doing that duty? You see, often when a soldier opened fire the impression was not so much, 'Let's see where those rounds went' but rather, 'Oh my God! We will now have to submit a report to the DPP. Someone will be asking questions in the House of Commons. We must get the right answers so that furious questioners can be told that the police are thoroughly investigating.' What a way to run a war!

Despite all the arguments, the Army did not get what it wanted. Perhaps it was time the police took back this unenviable role. Before that happened, however, there were going to have to be a great many more changes in both practices and attitudes.

The war for the minds of the people was not easy, and as far as the Army was concerned this was the first war in which it had fought where what happened at 3 p.m. could be on the television screen at 6 p.m. The officers found this very disconcerting. 'It was like being in a goldfish bowl,' commented one. They felt that it was impossible to conduct sensible operations from a military point of view if they were liable to have their actions picked over in public just a few hours later. They distrusted the immediate reporting of events, and found the tricks some of the media got up to rather distasteful. One general remembered inviting a French television crew into Army headquarters at Lisburn so that they could interview him. 'After we had finished,' he said disgustedly, 'they kept their camera rolling and recorded our private conversation. Now it was that sort of trick that made us loathe the media, although there were of course a number of highly responsible correspondents there.' They also resented the feeling that they were all the time being mocked and pilloried. 'I can remember one incident which absolutely infuriated me,' recalled a senior officer. 'It was when they described a soldier "standing like a tethered goat" having stones thrown at him! It was such a disgraceful way to describe a man doing what he had been told to do.'

The Army looked upon the campaign as a 'war situation', and found it very difficult to accept that reporters could 'hob-nob with the IRA who were out to kill us.' One general found that he got angry 'almost every day of my life' over something or other which had been broadcast, although he agreed that he was very prejudiced and had a fairly straitened view of things. He did, however, feel that the media had not been helpful to the Army cause, and that the press would have got more had they been more sympathetic in general policy, 'at least in treating the Army as "goodies" and the IRA as "baddies"'. In particular, he felt that there should be no interviews with terrorists.

> You have to lay down what your policy is going to be. If you are British then you ought to be pro-Government and pro-security forces, unless someone does something very wrong. In general the less publicity the terrorists get the better. It seems to me they were put in far too favourable a light. They were called freedom fighters rather than terrorists, but they had no political following of any kind. They never even tried to get it.

This was one complaint that came very early on in the campaign and which must have been put to every single journalist who worked in Northern Ireland during these years. It was one to which a great deal of thought was given. 'If a man holds a gun or a bomb,' said

[handwritten marginalia: on the contrary, the more exposed they are, the more they have to defend extremist positions.]

David Nicholas, Editor of ITN, 'whether to attack or uphold the law, then the society in which he operates has a right to know what is going on.'

Richard Francis, when Controller of the BBC in Northern Ireland, asked: 'Where does one draw the line when some of their community and welfare activities are encouraged and when officials of Her Majesty's Government meet them for political talks? It would be illogical and impracticable for the media not to cover their activities and, to do that responsibly, we believe it is necessary to interview and investigate the unpalatable side when the information to be gained outweighs the possible propaganda effect.'

By and large the printed press followed this line. 'I think it is newspapers' duty,' said the editor of one of the 'popular' papers, 'to talk to anyone — get an interview with the Devil, if he's prepared to let you down into Hell! Then we would decide whether to use it.' The editor of one 'quality' paper thought that it was no use pretending there was one section of the community with whom there should be no contact:

> One of the jobs of a newspaper is to report and analyse and try to help people find a solution . . . to suggest areas of political compromise. If no one is talking to the people causing the most up-front trouble, how is anyone going to produce meaningful initiatives in the sense that the Government has tried over the years — though without much success? They were all political and all depended on a calculation above all on what would work and what could be sold in the Catholic and Protestant communities.

Another editor commented:

> I think this throws back a certain responsibility on us here, because if the correspondent is going to be free to use his own discretion — which he must be — the newspaper must then always be on guard against that correspondent being used as part of propaganda.

Some officers felt so strongly about coverage given to terrorists that they advocated some form of censorship. They felt that the IRA had got to know how to stage events for maximum publicity and one officer pointed out that, during one tour he had made an analysis of sixty bomb explosions which showed that 80 per cent had been timed to obtain maximum coverage on television news bulletins. He went on to argue that editors should accept some form of responsibility.

'It would not be difficult to prove,' wrote I.D. Evans in a National Defence College thesis, 'that the media has affected and prolonged the situation in Northern Ireland. Fact sheets of individual incidents should be drawn up and examples of poor and purely sensational reporting catalogued.' He went on to suggest that most editors would not be averse to limited censorship, and if the approach was made at a high level, there could be agreement on such matters as forbidding contact with terrorists, minimum reporting of terrorist activities, and only accredited reporters being allowed in Northern Ireland. He added, for good measure: 'The key to success in achieving some form of control is that the principles should be accepted on a voluntary basis, and it must be made perfectly clear that it is not Government or Army censorship.'

However, another battalion commander who spent more than one tour in Northern Ireland was rather more sanguine about the press. He did not think that they had done a lot of damage, nor had he found them reluctant to check details with him, which he felt was the most that could be asked. 'Perhaps because the press was there,' he said, 'it made damn good sense never to be involved in a disgraceful incident! But I don't know if I would feel any differently if we had been pilloried or exposed by the press.'

It was in some ways a curious world where everyone was trying to learn how to cope with this new business of fighting a war on their own doorstep under the glare of television cameras and an interested world press. It produced one memorable observation from a Secretary of State:

> The information department of the Army was hopeless! It didn't know what was going on. Never in the picture . . . never briefed. On one occasion I said to the GOC, 'That bloody information department of yours! Always chattering away to the press but they know nothing!' And he said to me, 'Don't worry, Secretary of State, they don't know what is going on and I don't particularly care if they do get it wrong!'

Some Army officers were also fond of pointing out that television gave a very distorted view of the dangers of Northern Ireland while in fact it was much safer than most big American cities. At the worst of the 'troubles' the murder rate in Belfast was 18.8 per 100,000; that included the IRA members who were shot at by the security forces or who blew themselves up, and the soldiers and policemen who were killed by the IRA. At that time, one Army officer pointed out, the murder rate in Cleveland, Ohio, was 35.6 per 100,000 and that in twenty-five of America's major cities the murder rate was higher than in Belfast.

David Nicholas at ITN said:

> I suppose we could have done better showing country fairs and all that sort of thing. On the other hand I think that the nasty bits are infinitely worse than we have ever been able to show on film — the appalling aspects of some things, the inhumanity, the insensitivity, the squalor, the evil. You were rarely actually there when it happened. Most of the time what we captured were the consequences of violence on ordinary people.

Reporting a war on one's own doorstep is always more difficult than reporting someone else's war. First of all, events could be seen by so many so quickly. Then there was the immediate effect of what was said; for instance, would reporting a riot while it was going on, or even showing live pictures, inflame an already bad situation?

Neither the BBC nor ITN had previous experience of broadcasting inside its own transmission areas to a place where a civil insurrection was going on, although both organisations had seen and learned something of the experiences of the Americans during the riots and disturbances in Watts in August 1965. There was always a worry that by showing a riot 'live' this might have the effect of saying, 'If you catch a No.11 bus you might get there before it's all over!' However, both ITN and the BBC were aware of the dangers of rumours. 'As the Americans found,' said David Nicholas, 'rumours run rampant, and indeed rumour can be a much greater danger in triggering off second-strike riots with wild thoughts of retaliation when the original cause had been grossly amplified by rumour.'

Another officer, Brigadier Maurice Tugwell, who had had experience of public relations and the media in the early days in Northern Ireland, maintained that neither the Army nor the police were equipped in any way to cope with the sort of propaganda produced by the Provisional IRA:

> In the RUC 'PR' itself was a completely new idea. At first there was a tendency in the RUC to hostility towards a news media that seemed to many police officers as implacably biased against the Force and, in the Army, to disdainfulness about IRA methods so far removed from the military ethic. Pressure for change came from the troops and their officers who objected to having their every act misrepresented without apparent challenge and from journalists, who explained their need for frank, on-the-spot military accounts if their reports were to be accurate.

A television news editor was concerned enough about all this to take the matter up with the Director of Army Public Relations: 'I said to him, "Give it to me straight. Are we causing problems?" He was equally straightforward. "No," he replied, "you are not. As far as I am concerned we are perfectly happy. We would far rather you were interviewing our soldiers on the street than some bloody politician from Stormont! Anyway, our recruiting is up 27 per cent!"'

There was also a constant cry from some quarters that not enough 'good' stories were being told and not enough background information was being given. 'That argument for more background coverage does not impress me!' said David Nicholas firmly. 'More and more "background" explanation is the pious wish of journalists who want to be remedial therapists instead of holding up the mirror to nature.'

It seemed that the most anguished cries of pain about coverage in Northern Ireland came from those who felt the Republican and anti-establishment side was not getting a fair hearing. Peter Taylor, a reporter for Thames Television, complained more than once about the difficulty of getting his material on the air. He felt that the IBA had not encouraged investigative reporting and that this, combined with a general apathy towards the province, made it err on the side of caution when faced with controversy. He also felt that the IBA was not immune to political pressure, which he claimed was constant.

Another reporter with considerable experience in Northern Ireland was Simon Hoggart of the *Guardian*. He wrote:

Hardly a word is breathed against the Army in the popular papers or on radio and television in Britain. If criticism is made, it is invariably in the mouths of others, and always hedged with a full account of the Army's position — however sceptical the reporter himself might be. Most of this stems from Britain's traditional respect for its Army and the genuine fact that it is much more gentle than other countries' armies or police (one wonders how the Falls or Shankill Roads would react to the arrival of the French CRS). However, this goodwill would be quickly dissipated by an incompetent or else deliberately misleading PR operation.

The Army, of course, had its ups and downs in the field of public relations in Northern Ireland and came in for a fair amount of criticism itself, particularly in the earlier days — the days of the great 'Black Propaganda' scandal.

In 1971 it was decided that there should be an additional branch within the Army Press Office in Northern Ireland called Information Policy, which would be distinct and different from the Public Relations Department. Its formation was part of the attempt to look for some political solution, and its main task would be to issue facts on Government policy and describe what the Army was trying to achieve. 'What we ended up with,' said a senior officer some time later, 'was a press officer who dabbled in things he should not have. He acted in the most astonishing way and I think it fair to say he was pursuing a sort of dis-information policy all of his own without checking with anyone! It was most unfortunate! He was removed!'

It was at this period that Lisburn first realised that their press office was being referred to as the 'Lisburn Lying Machine', a name which first appeared in *Republican News*. However it seemed that this practice of disinformation continued for some time after that, even if in a more watered-down version. Robert Fisk, the *Times* correspondent, reported in March 1975 that it was only then that the Army had stopped the 'Black Propaganda' campaign against suspected extremists.

> During the past year several soldiers, with permission from their superiors, have been 'leaking' information . . . an officer attached to 39 Infantry Brigade at Lisburn last year toured newspaper offices in Belfast suggesting that a Protestant politician in Ulster had been involved in the disappearance of Mr Thomas Niedermayer, the West German Honorary Consul in Belfast, who was kidnapped from his home in Belfast just before Christmas 1973. The Army has also been responsible for forgeries in the past twelve months. One was a Sinn Fein poster in Newry and another a cleverly designed copy of a Provisional IRA poster which originally carried the silhouette of a gunman and the words 'Victory '74'. The Army's version, which was plastered round the streets in the Lower Falls, had the additional words 'but not through the barrel of a gun'.

Later, the *Irish Times* Northern Editor in Belfast, David McKittrick, regaled his readers with a story about a young Army captain from the Lisburn Press Office who became a frequent visitor to his office. It was explained that this was part of the Army policy of acquiring a more personal relationship, in which trust could be built up. He even introduced his colonel, and both assured McKitterick that the off-the-record conversations would be reported back only as 'a general chat.' During the visits that followed the captain gave nothing away, but was prepared to accept criticism that the press desk was not generally believed.

> Alas, the developing relationship was to be shattered — and rudely. I got my hands on a classified document. It was written by the captain and gave a precise account of our private talks. Copies of it had been sent to headquarters — even to some of the press officers about whose incompetence we had joked. When I handed it to the colonel — it was his copy, marked to the commanding officer — he blanched and murmured: 'This is a bit of a mess.' He was right. Where did I get the document? It was handed to me, accidentally, in a pile of papers, by the likeable young captain himself.

Slowly the Army worked on a public relations policy, bringing in unit Public Relations Officers who took the job seriously and were immediately accessible to journalists on the streets. They also started putting young soldiers up for interviews, on the basis that it would have far more effect for someone who had been engaged in an incident to talk about it than to use some senior headquarters officer. This new approach worked, and by and large the press was sympathetic towards the Army, despite the views of some officers who still thought its work was 'actively destructive of the military campaign.'

By August 1974 the *Republican News* was writing that 'the English Army has been defeated in its latest push for a military defeat of the Irish Republican Army'. In fact the Provisionals, now hard hit in the North, were to move their bombing campaign to mainland Britain. In October 5 people were killed and 54 wounded when a 'no-warning' bomb went off in a pub in Guildford, in Surrey. It was a pub often used by servicemen and in fact only one of the dead was a civilian. There was another attack on a pub at Woolwich, in London where two more people were killed, followed by an 'own goal' which killed James McDade in the Midlands. Then on 24 November two bombs were planted in pubs in Birmingham which were to have devastating results. The day was the anniversary of Dublin's Bloody Sunday of 1920, when the IRA ordered the murder of 14 British agents — most of them shot in their beds — and the authorities retaliated by opening fire at a football match and killing 13 people. In Birmingham a warning was given but it was far too late to have any effect, for the bombs went off just seven minutes later. Twenty-one people, mostly teenagers and young adults, were killed and many more terribly injured and scarred for life. One young girl's face looked, a few days later, as if it were covered with a red rash; in fact it was millions of minuscule splinters from wood pulverised by the explosion and blasted into her skin, never to come out. Others lost eyes, limbs and hearing.

A wave of anti-Irish revulsion swept the country, and a few hours later six men from Northern Ireland were arrested at Heysham, as they boarded the cross-channel ferry to Belfast, and charged with the offence. In prison they were beaten up and later said their confessions has been given under duress.

What this enabled the Labour Government to do was to rush through Parliament the Prevention of Terrorism (Temporary Provisions) Bill. With this they would be able to exclude anyone from either part of Ireland from entering England, Scotland or Wales if suspected of any terrorist connections. It also allowed the police to hold suspects without a charge for forty-eight hours and get this period extended to seven days on higher authority. Critics claimed it was a most repressive piece of legislation that created a system of banning not unlike that used by the South African Government.

The Provisionals lost a great deal of support because of these bombs, both immediately and in the long term. For years afterwards, the reason given by many on the Left for no longer supporting the IRA was, quite simply, 'Birmingham'.

Now the British wanted a cease-fire, and so did the Provisionals, who thought that the British might be war-weary enough to come to terms. Yet another truce was to be arranged and it started in a curious way, with top Provisionals meeting Protestant clergymen south of the border in the small town of Feakle, in County Clare. Unfortunately the Northern number plates of the clergymen's cars attracted the attention of the Gardai, and as they interrupted the meeting, the Provisional top brass left in rather a hurry.

It was, however, a start, and contact was maintained with Stormont becoming closely involved. But as officials explored the openings they came to realise that the Provisionals lived in a 'dream world' and did not understand the facts of political life, so they began to try to convince them that the way ahead was through the ballot box rather than the Armalite rifle. There were three main elements in this thinking. First, could they get a cease-fire which would actually work? Second, would such a cease-fire bring an end to the whole campaign? Both these elements were considered as unlikely, but the third element had more possibilities: that was, whether a cease-fire might not bring an end to internment and get the province back to proper law and order.

At Stormont senior officials would agonise and debate the issues for hours at a time. The most senior civil servant, Sir Frank Cooper, a man with a keen brain and a photographic memory, had the task of running these meetings with Sinn Fein representatives. To show willing, the Government announced compensation for some of those killed on Bloody Sunday, speeded up the release of detainees, sent the Price sisters back from gaol in England to serve their time in Northern Ireland and announced the opening of Sinn Fein incident centres in the hope that quick access to Government officials might lessen the chance of violent confrontations. It was all part of a deliberate policy of politicising the Provisionals, and aimed at the long-term stability of the province. The truce which was finally arranged with the Provisionals was therefore a boost towards this — and towards getting the Army off the streets and the police back on to them.

At Lisburn there was a certain amount of concern about the new policies and particularly the rapid release of detainees. Sir Frank King expressed his concern about this. 'I think it is fair to say,' commented a Stormont official, 'that had it been Sir Frank's decision he would not have followed this policy. However, he accepted it as Government policy and did not apply pressure to get it changed.'

There were still grave doubts at Lisburn about the reliability of the police. This was why the Army would still not always tell the police what it was doing. It knew that the Protestant paramilitary units, like the UDA and the UVF, actually felt they were helping the Army and had little doubt that many were ex-B Specials with friends in the RUC. After one major raid in which a large number of Protestants were lifted — and about which the police were not informed — relations between the GOC and the Chief Constable were very strained for some time. There were also problems of security closer to home. 'Our telephone was actually tapped by the Provisional IRA at one stage,' sighed a Lisburn staff officer. 'Really! You'd have thought you could trust your own phone in a headquarters like this, but we soon learned we couldn't trust anyone.'

As for the police, they thought that a GOC with a 'less amiable, less diplomatic' character might have made life very difficult. 'He smoothed away many tensions that might have arisen,' explained another policeman, and went on to say that while some of his colleagues thought the Army 'all boots and gaiters' he himself had a high regard for many commanders in West Belfast who were sensitive to local conditions. Often they would be the prime agitators in getting improvements, constantly lobbying for better conditions in the areas of deprivation in which they served.

The 'hearts and minds' campaign was also continued. The Army started summer holiday camps for both Protestant and Catholic children from deprived areas. 'It was really for selfish reasons,' explained an officer with surprising candour. 'We wanted them off the streets and out of our hair!' It was a sort of Army adventure training scheme with the children living on the coast in tents. The parents would have to pay £10 for each child, who would then spend a fortnight climbing rocks, sailing boats, doing physical training and watching films in the evening. They were all mixed in together and sometimes boys would be found hiding in the sand dunes to avoid being sent home. 'They all got on very well. They hero-worshipped some of the instructors. But once they got home they'd be fighting each other once again and stoning the soldiers as if they'd never been away.'

Now came 1975, the 'year of the cease-fire', which Lisburn felt had been brought about because by concentrating on Belfast it had, in one year, removed six whole Provisional IRA brigade headquarters. On 1 January the Provisional IRA announced an extension of their Christmas cease-fire on the understanding that the British would react to its 'peace proposals'. Two weeks later the Provisionals announced the cease-fire would end because there had been no reaction and because of a variety of other reasons, some big, some small and some outside the control of the British anyway. However both sides wanted a cease-fire which would allow them breathing space. The Provisionals wanted to regroup and retrain because they were in the process of losing the war; 150 of their men and women had been killed and their fund-raising efforts in America were faltering. Westminster wanted one in the hope that the Provisional IRA would abandon its shooting war which would then ease the atmosphere in the run up to the Convention elections. So secret talks went on, and on 9 February the Provisionals announced another, indefinite, cease-fire.

Deaths and injuries on both sides then dropped dramatically although there was a wave of sectarian killings. During this coming year Army deaths were to be cut once again by half from the 1974 figure — the total would be 28. The fatalities amongst the local security forces, however, would hardly alter at all; deaths in the UDR would go from 8 to 7, and in the RUC from 13 to 15. Civilian deaths, primarily from sectarian violence, would rise from 166 to 216.

So with fresh political initiatives on the horizon, the time had come once again for the Army to adopt a low profile, to stop hard targeting and to lessen patrols. Now it waited and watched to see what use would be made of yet another breathing space provided by it for the civil servants and the politicians. Some commanders were quite happy to do this, believing it would give a chance for the truce to work and some political settlement to be thrashed out. When, however, orders came down to battalion commanders that their men should carry their weapons slung, most thought that this was taking the low-profile policy too far and quite straightforwardly disobeyed. 'It was a very odd order indeed and I just said "no!" There were far too many dangerous men around who might not necessarily agree that they would not shoot at us, despite the cease-fire. We made a fuss and the order was modified a bit — the decision was left to the patrol commander. Quite right!'

It was, however, a time when some changes were possible, for the cease-fire saw soldiers actually attending mass at Corpus Christi Church in Ballymurphy. When the CO had first suggested this, the priest in charge had retorted, 'If you do, I shall preach a very anti-security force sermon.' The CO said he was quite happy with that provided that he got the right of reply. The first time his soldiers went, carrying concealed hand guns only, that priest did not take the service. After that there was a subtle change in attitude in that area. His men were not fired on again in Ballymurphy and people used to come up and give them odd bits of information. Then they started to take handicapped children regularly to the swimming baths, and although the Catholic families were not too keen to start with, they were soon saying, 'Why aren't you taking our children as well?' The way an area was dealt with was still very much up to the local Army commander. Each one had to judge what any particular section of his patch would accept at any given time.

During this long cease-fire, which was never officially broken, the Army was under quite tight control from Stormont. According to the police, who were watching with some interest, there was a constant stream of directives to Lisburn instructing the Army to 'go soft'. The police, however, felt that they themselves were able to carry on as usual with no undue, overt influence from Stormont. On the other hand Lisburn felt that it was not so bald as that, pointing out that once the cease-fire had started, then they had quite expected to hear noises from Stormont indicating that they should play it gently. As one officer put it, 'People were behaving and anyway we had most of their leaders locked up!' However, some Conservative MPs and most Unionists thought that the Army was going soft on the Provisionals and allowing those leaders who were at large to move freely around.

Almost inevitably stories began to circulate that the Army was allowing known gunmen to roam the streets freely and that they had been issued with 'safe conduct' passes. One was put about by Ian Paisley and referred specifically to Seamus Twoomey, one-time commander of the Provisional IRA Belfast brigade. It was said that

Rees himself had ordered that Twoomey should be left strictly alone. 'Nonsense! That was a mistaken idea on the part of a young officer,' Rees said briskly some time later. 'The Army could pick up Twoomey but they would have to have evidence against him, not just bring him in front of me on an ICO.' The reason, of course, was that Rees had decided to end detention without trial and his orders had been that the system of ICO was to stop. The Army knew that if they just lifted someone to get him off the streets for a while, as in the old days, the minister would not automatically sign the papers. 'That,' said an officer bleakly, 'was a much better form of "safe-conduct" pass than any bit of paper.'

Between January and June, in the first six months of that cease-fire, only one soldier was killed and even when the agreement started to fall apart during the second half of that year the attacks on the Army were far less than they had been. In September, for instance, 8 members of the security forces — none of them military — were killed, compared with a figure of 22 for the previous September. The sectarian violence, however, raged on and by the end of the same month 196 civilians had died — 37 more than for the same period in 1974.

Where the cease-fire did help was in setting the atmosphere for the Government's next political initiative — the Constitutional Convention. This was the elected conference of Northern Ireland parties to consider, as the White Paper put it, 'what provision for the government of Northern Ireland is likely to command the most widespread acceptance throughout the community there'. It consisted of seventy-eight members, on the same basis as the power-sharing Assembly which had collapsed; and forty-seven of these seats were held by Protestant Unionists of various persuasions but all united on one matter — there would be no power-sharing with Catholics. While it was sitting it was felt that the cease-fire — and the absence of bombs and bullets — would help the more militant Protestant leaders to be more reasonable. Not surprisingly, when the Convention did produce its majority report, the Westminster Government turned it down on the basis that it did not meet the criteria of the White Paper.

Sectarian killings continued. On 5 April, two months after the cease-fire started, came a tit-for-tat killing that was a clear example of this inter-sectarian bloodletting. Early in the evening two Catholics were killed in an attack on a pub in New Lodge Road,

Belfast and a great many more were injured. A few hours later a bomb went off in another pub, the Mountain View Tavern on the Shankill Road, where five Protestants were killed and many more injured. Even an experienced rescue worker was shocked at the carnage:

Now if you'd seen the inside of that place you'd have thought that all the wood had been put through a shredder. I went over to one chappie who was lying there and he literally had the head blown off him. I got all the bandages I had to try and compress his skull and his brains back in again. You hold on to that. You don't let go. You press it, trying to get the blood to coagulate. A nurse came and we got him onto a trolley but the first time I let go his head was in the casualty ward at the hospital. He was a beaten docket! It was just a matter of time and sure enough, he died the next day.

A week later six Catholics were murdered in a pub on the Short Strand and then this sectarian battle seemed to move south towards the border. It was here, too, that signs of involvement by some members of the security forces became evident — a complaint Catholics had been making for some time. In July the Miami Showband — an Irish dance band — was on its way back to Dublin when its van was stopped on the main road near the border. The singers and musicians had no cause for alarm — the seven men on the road block were wearing the uniforms of the Ulster Defence Regiment. Then three of these 'UDR' men began planting bombs which went off prematurely, killing not only three members of the group but two of their own gang as well. These men actually belonged to the banned Ulster Volunteer Force — a well-known Protestant murder gang — although one of them later turned out to be a sergeant in the UDR as well.

The Army had always believed that the cease-fire was a tenuous affair and by the middle of the year Lisburn was convinced that it would not last much beyond the autumn. Lisburn reasoned that, combined with the steady release of detainees, the cease-fire had allowed the Provisionals to collect weapons and explosives and above all replace their teenagers with mature and highly skilled men. There was, however, no thought of withdrawal. With thirteen battalions and some 14,000 troops, Lisburn was confident it could sustain operations indefinitely and without strain. Officers realised, rather wearily, that they were in a vicious circle; that military action would not solve the political problems, and political initiatives did little to solve the problem of violence. Some were more caustic, pointing out that if what ideological content there existed were removed, all that would be left were competing bands of criminal thugs who made a living by bank robbery, hi-jacking and running protection rackets. The wave of sectarian killings was, for them, a clear example of this.

That August the GOC, Sir Frank King, moved to a new post, leaving the province a much quieter place than when he arrived (his first month had been marked by 695 shooting incidents and 73 explosions). He had stirred controversy only twice: when his soldiers 'failed' to break the UWC strike of 1974, and when he had apparently attacked Government policy on the release of detainees. At a meeting in Nottingham, to which the press had not been invited, King expressed misgivings about the release of detainees. He was not too perturbed about this, however, because he felt that Army intelligence was now so good that if necessary those released could all be picked up again quite quickly. Unfortunately for the GOC, one reporter had got in, and what one person at that meeting described as 'a somewhat garbled account' appeared in the press and on television. There was a considerable indignation in some political circles that a general should leap into the political field in this way.

The GOC had no copy of his speech. In fact he had spoken from notes scribbled on the back of an envelope which had contained an income tax demand. Tongue in cheek, he sent this off to London to be examined. Then he discovered that a doctor at the meeting had made a tape-recording of the speech and when the uproar was at its height he had this delivered to London as well. Whoever was dealing with the matter obviously found nothing wrong, because no more was heard about it. Soon afterwards King's appointment as Commander in Chief of BAOR (British Army on the Rhine) was confirmed.

So Sir Frank went off to his new posting with a letter from the Secretary of State, Merlyn Rees, saying that he was sorry the general was going and adding: 'You have never played at politics and I have never played at being a soldier. That is why we got on so well.' But there were some at Stormont who thought that he was a hard-faced man and as much a political soldier as a soldier's soldier. 'King is the man I would have fighting for me,' said one official who worked in those corridors of power. 'He was as sharp as a razor and always looked as blunt as could be. Nice man! He would have cut my throat as quick as looking up — but he was a good soldier.'

The departure of King pointed up a curious and really rather unsatisfactory system with its roots deep in Army tradition and service jealousies. Every two years the GOC would be changed 'for career reasons'. If he had been a success, promotion and a new appointment was his; if not, he would go no further. In any commercial or industrial enterprise, it would be inconceivable to move the top man just as he was settling into the job; but to make matters worse, the Army insisted on choosing the new incumbent again 'for career reasons' and the Secretary of State would merely be asked to approve of — or perhaps even veto — the appointment. Two generals were now to be chosen in succession, each very different and both of whose expertise was probably better suited to other situations than the peculiar complications of Northern Ireland.

The first of these was Lieutenant-General David House, who had come from being Director of Infantry at Warminster. He found a situation in which the Army was enjoying considerable success, although there were some disturbing indications that all was not well. His intelligence officers told him that the phasing out of Detention without Trial, to which Rees was publicly committed, meant that the Provisional IRA was being re-strengthened and that their own intelligence was beginning to dry up. The 'wanted' lists, or 'Bingo Books' as the squaddies called them, kept by each unit and so carefully studied by every single soldier, were being cut down to only those names against whom evidence existed which would be admissible in court. At the same time units were being forbidden to enter houses either to check on those inside or to round up suspects for questioning.

The new GOC knew that it was an emotive subject and that detention was being represented as politically disreputable — particularly in terms of foreign opinion. However, he knew that it served a purpose on the streets and as violence began to rise he had to decide if the decision to end it was, in military terms, the right one. He decided it was, although he did have misgivings from time to time.

It was the decision that the politicians who had appointed Lieutenant-General House had wanted him to make. They had picked him in the hope that he would move away from a purely military approach, which had been the norm up to this time. House was an agreeable man, very cooperative with the police, and left no one in any doubt that he supported the new policy of police primacy. For the RUC this was a great help. They felt that the Army was always most responsive to the man at the top and under House they began to find the majority of Army commanders did genuinely try to implement the new policy.

At police headquarters at Knock, the man in the shadows was the Englishman Kenneth Newman, the senior deputy chief constable. The Army had noticed that he had been given a job which did not give him wide powers and which kept him well out of the way. However, he had strong views that the police should once again take over responsibility for security, because unless this happened the province would never even get started on the road back to normality. He was not the only person thinking along these lines. At the Northern Ireland Office Sir Frank Cooper approached a senior civil servant, John Bourne, and asked him to start thinking about what should be done. After the chaos of the past years, with political initiatives and power-sharing executives falling like autumn leaves, it was considered time to take stock. There was to be a basic philosophy behind any new ideas — that the existing structure of law and society must be maintained. This meant that the police would take back responsibility for security and for enforcing the law. The Army would have to revert to what it should have remained all along: 'the military in aid of the civil power'.

It was not an easy task, for the Army was naturally impatient with the restrictions of bureaucratic red tape. They asked many questions. Why could they not talk direct to the Irish Army? Why could the South not react more quickly? Why should soldiers not be tried in military courts? Why could the Secretary of State not use selective detention? Why could he not guarantee to sign Interim Custody Orders before they committed precious resources and time to finding suspects? The questions were usually countered by another: 'If we say "yes", can you guarantee 100 per cent results?

On John Bourne's committee sat Jack Hermon of the RUC; some senior Army officers including the Chief of Staff; various civil servants and a representative from MI5. It did not meet regularly like a normal committee, but all the members had their opinions canvassed, and finally its report appeared, under the title 'The Way Ahead'. It was never published, but it was mentioned by Merlyn Rees the following year when he announced the new policy of 'Ulsterisation' and police primacy. 'At the heart of the committee's conclusion,' he said, 'is the idea of securing police acceptance and effectiveness. By securing police effectiveness is meant the integration and acceptance of the police in the community to enable them to administer the law effectively. It does not mean a return to the past.'

By now Westminster had decided that a certain number of political options were 'dead ducks'. These were the Irish Dimension, full integration with Britain, a united Ireland, and independence. What was still alive and very much in the running was a system of devolved government with power-sharing. The 'Ulsterisation' policy was to be a major step in this direction. Then, in the middle of the wave of sectarian killings, Rees decided enough was enough and closed down the direct telephone lines between Stormont and the Sinn Fein incident centres, which was in effect saying that the cease-fire was over. Certainly the Provisionals took it as such, although there had been a number of incidents which could have been classified as breaking it, and in the border areas of South Armagh the cease-fire had never operated anyway.

One short winter's day, a four-man patrol of Royal Fusiliers lay in an observation post overlooking the border. Already, only halfway through the afternoon, the shadows were lengthening. The patrol commander, a lance-corporal, was slightly apart from the other men because they had set up a counter-trap to a bomb laid by the Provisionals and were waiting to see if anyone fell into it.

Their battalion base at Bessbrook lay just to the north of the Crossmaglen salient which sticks stubbornly into the Republic and was therefore surrounded on three sides by some forty miles of twisting border. The mass of Slieve Gullion lies on the horizon overlooking the wide sweep of the hills and the acres of bogland and small fields marked by tall hedges of hawthorn and wild rose. This was a most dangerous posting, and already some thirty soldiers had been killed here, over half in and around the market square at Crossmaglen itself — the largest village square in Europe, and known as the 'killing area'. On this Saturday afternoon, however, the Fusiliers were well out in the country; but unknown to them they had been spotted, and as the light faded away altogether, a large Provisional IRA unit opened fire from a stone wall just across the border. The first burst killed two of the Fusiliers, and shortly afterwards the other Fusilier was wounded. The Provisionals said later that they had then called out to the soldiers that if they laid down their weapons they would be given safe-conduct passes. If they did so call, the Fusiliers either ignored or refused the offer and the firing went on. Unable to dig in or build a sangar because of the nature of their operation, they were particularly vulnerable, and could not radio for help because the first burst had damaged the radio set. The firing was heard at the company base but no one reacted immediately. Bursts of firing like this were often heard as the Provisionals tried to lure patrols into an ambush. The duty officer wanted some more information before he sent out a patrol.

Despite his wounds, the remaining Fusilier still managed to get his rifle into action and return the fire, as did the patrol commander from his position a little to one side. Then the wounded soldier was hit again with a long, raking burst of machine-gun fire from across the border; this time he was killed. The attackers turned their attention on to the lance-corporal, seeking him out in the gorse and bushes which gave little cover from sight, let alone from high-velocity bullets. He, too, was hit — in the head, hand and back. He moved out, crawling and pulling himself slowly and painfully down the hill away from the border and towards the road.

Twenty minutes after it all started, reinforcements arrived. As the helicopter fluttered overhead in the dark with its searchlight probing down, the lance-corporal was found still alive and picked up. The attackers had vanished.

These shootings brought the number of soldiers killed in the province that year to twelve — nine of them in South Armagh. A sergeant had been killed by a booby-trapped bomb and four other Fusiliers had been blown up as they patrolled the border to Forkhill. At Lisburn, the GOC began to think more about the problems of the border; he re-deployed a battalion to the area and began to increase undercover work. Just before Christmas 500 men of the Ulster Defence Regiment were called up and also sent to the border area. Formed in 1970 to replace the B Special police reservists, the UDR was a unit under direct command of the GOC. This time they were to be used to seal off roads, patrol and generally allow the regular Army units to go on to the offensive and move into areas that had been more or less 'No Go' for months. Lisburn was well aware that this use of the UDR would be seen as provocative in some quarters and that the new Army offensive would be described as harassment. They were right on both counts.

By the end of 1975 some Army officers were seriously worried about South Armagh and what was known as the Murder Triangle. This name came about as a result of sectarian killings as well as those of soldiers and Provisionals in this area, which contained Armagh City itself and adjoining areas of County Tyrone. Some officers pointed out bitterly that they did not hold the initiative here; that since the cease-fire the Provisionals had killed twenty-six people in the area and were able to mount road blocks where they wanted. They also carried out long-range sniping from across the border and if they were caught on the other side — which seemed unlikely — all they would get would be six months for illegal possession of arms. Some Army officers thought it 'appalling' that no IRA patrol had been successfully ambushed and that the only 'kills' had come about more by good luck than astute planning. It was not a lack of military skills but rather a lack of numbers. There were only four companies to cover some 400 square miles. The Irish Army did patrol the other side and immediately to the south were 800 men of the 27th Infantry Regiment who patrolled 123 miles of border — which then stretched on for another 200 miles or so along the northern edges of Louth, Monaghan and Cavan. Unofficially it was estimated in the South that it would require two million men to seal the border effectively. The border with south Armagh, for instance, had 169 officially recognised crossing places and an unknown number of unofficial ones. The Southern Irish were well aware of terrorists who slipped back and forth, and were also aware that they had little chance of picking them up after incidents in the North. That was why they felt aggrieved at constant claims that the South was a 'haven' for terrorists from the North and the border wide open because of lack of cooperation. In 1975, this particular regiment had mounted 800 border patrols, set up 5,500 check points, dealt with 44 bomb-disposal calls and carried out 64 searches. During all this they had recovered 24 rockets and 3 rocket launchers.

North of the border the soldiers went at their work more intensely. The system in one unit working out of Crossmaglen was to give each platoon the names of some twenty people suspected of being involved in or on the fringes of the IRA. The platoon commander would then give two or three of his men a couple of names and tell them to contact them, make themselves known and learn everything about them. This was part of the 'buckets of information' so scorned by the police, who thought it amateur and a waste of time, but it allowed soldiers to check quickly whether people were lying —

although as one pointed out, it was amazing how many people really did not know the colour of their front hall carpets! The unit then improved on this by sending a few soldiers off to Newry to 'keep tabs on some of the ungodly on market days'. They found that it unnerved the opposition for a soldier to pop up in the market place and say, 'Hullo Michael! You live at such and such. How's your brother's farm doing . . .?' Then a small patrol would come down from Newry and do the same in Crossmaglen.

During 1975, the year of the so-called cease-fire, the Army and police had indeed enjoyed a brief rest from the killings as the paramilitary factions fought it out together. Then, for a while, the violence had moved across to the mainland. However, irate Loyalists were now demanding that what they called the 'real' counter-insurgency experts should be brought into south Armagh — the SAS. Rees was at this time juggling desperately with the demands and aspirations of Protestant and Catholic politicians involved in the constitutional Convention. In particular, Ian Paisley was making no secret of the fact that he would happily call and back another UWC-style strike if things did not go his way. Rees was a natural worrier about the politics of Ulster, but two events early in 1976 were to shock and horrify even that battle-hardened province, and led Harold Wilson to push Rees's 'careful, almost Byzantine' manoeuvrings to achieve political appeasement right off the stage.

It started with the killing of five Catholics from two separate families. In the first attack, three brothers were sitting watching television in their cottage home near Whitcross when at least three gunmen burst in and shot them. One brother died almost instantly. The second was killed as he made for the door. The third brother, only 18, threw himself under a bed and although a burst of automatic fire hit him several times in the leg and grazed his chest, he did not die.

In the second attack, masked men burst into another isolated Catholic farmhosue at Balldougan in the north of Armagh. Here the O'Dowd family — who had close links with the SDLP — were having a family reunion. In front of the women and children, two brothers were cut down by gunfire and their 61-year-old uncle also died in the hail of bullets. The boys' father was critically injured but survived.

Retaliation came a few days later. A group of eleven Protestant workmen were on their way home one evening from their factory in Glenanne when their minibus was ambushed on a lonely country road. They were ordered out, lined up and asked their names and religion. The minibus driver happened to be a Catholic and he was told to clear off. Then the gunmen opened up on the eleven men left standing on the roadside. Ten of them were killed and only one, badly wounded, survived. Part of the horror was that most of them came from the same small village of Bessbrook.

This attack was claimed by the hitherto unheard-of 'South Armagh Republican Action Force'. The Provisionals denied that any of their members had been involved, although there was little doubt anywhere that some Provisional unit had been involved — even if it was acting without orders.

Early the next morning the Defence Secretary, Roy Mason, called in his senior advisers. He told them bluntly that what had happened in south Armagh could not be allowed to happen again. More troops would be sent in, and he wanted more long-range, covert patrols merging into the countryside. A handful of SAS were already operating there, but their numbers would be increased and for the first time it would be officially announced that they were there. That very announcement would be worth dozens of troops, for the SAS by now had a fearsome reputation — even if it was based more on a lack than an abundance of knowledge about their methods. The meeting broke up and Mason went across to Harold Wilson with a *fait accompli*. Before that meeting ended the Army's Spearhead battalion — its emergency unit — had been ordered to fly direct to Northern Ireland with a troop of armoured personnel carriers as well as another two companies of reinforcements from Germany.

With all this activity Rees's careful, low-profile policy to keep tempers cool had gone out of the window. People began to wonder if the province was about to be swamped by a full-scale civil war with a million Protestants slogging it out eyeball to eyeball with 500,000 Catholics, and the Republican dragged willy-nilly into the fray as some small Catholic border community was wiped out. In the background, however, was the knowledge that Ulster had already gained quite a reputation for teetering on the brink like an undecided suicide.

The Provisionals now moved into the offensive and in the first two months of the year there were 129 explosives, 21 attacks on police stations, and 1 soldier, 2 UDR men and 6 policemen killed. Belfast airport came under mortar fire and in the Malone Road in Belfast, which graffiti had once immortalised in 'The Malone Road fiddles while the Falls burns', middle-class homes became the target for bombers. In April the first prison officers were murdered after the Provisionals had declared them a 'legitimate target' and the Europa Hotel, home for visiting journalists, was blown up for the twenty-sixth time.

There were some lighter incidents, though not many. One occurred during the Armagh Apple Blossom Festival. A patrol from the Royal Fusiliers stopped outside a building one evening and became very interested in what was being said inside. Crouched below an open window, they heard talk of bullets and bombs, informers and knee-cappings. The patrol commander placed his men carefully, and when people began to emerge they were promptly arrested. It took some time for the soldiers to be convinced that what they had been hearing were members of the Armagh Players rehearsing a play called *The Present*.

The police take a high-risk profile
May 1976–February 1978

In the spring of 1976 the Chief Constable of the RUC, Sir Jamie Flanagan, was told that he could not stay on — as he wished — for another tour of duty. The man who took his place was Kenneth Newman, who had spent the previous three years laying the groundwork for what he considered his most important task — restoring the primacy of the police. He faced a daunting, uphill struggle, not least because of Army scepticism about the ability of the police to carry out normal duties. Throughout the province there was now an appalling disrespect for law and order. For instance, there were still more than 600 unsolved murders arising from some 1,500 violent deaths since 1969. It seemed that psychopaths and homicidal maniacs could indulge in endless, motiveless and senseless murder. 'The price of human life is now so cheap in Belfast,' one policeman observed bitterly, 'that you can have old scores settled for the price of a few bottles of Guinness'. It took a special kind of courage to join the ranks of the RUC, for since 1969 seventy-seven members of the force had been shot down or blown up. Often, when Catholics tried to join, they would be turned away by a recruiting officer fearful for the safety of their families. 'One thing about being a police officer in Northern Ireland,' said another policeman, 'is that the funeral dirge gets into your soul.'

Incongruously, in the middle of all this carnage, fifty officers worked as community policemen and policewomen, tramping through the villages to talk to local people, acting like social workers and in the process running the biggest disco operation in the whole of the United Kingdom; each month some 30,000 youngsters now talked and danced through the rock and pop music of Blue Lamp Discos across the province. It had to be seen to be believed!

What Newman wanted was a hard but sensitive police force, and his aim was to beat the terrorists not just with community work and discos but with the best technical and scientific equipment. Gone were the days when the RUC could be taunted as a feudal force where 'the officers walked round in green cloaks and carried Irish blackthorn walking sticks'. The RUC was now organised like any other regional police force with directly comparable structure, pay, rank and promotion. The Provisional IRA saw all this as a sign that the Army wanted to minimise its own casualty rate by pushing the police back into the hard areas. The *Republican News* declared:

> It is obvious that the British Government has reached the end of the line regarding their hopes for military victory. They will now speed up the withdrawal of their troops and leave the Loyalist militia to carry the can. We are fully prepared to deal with the situation. The RUC face a long, hot summer.

The police made it clear, through their Federation, that they wished to remain a civilian force and did not want to be projected into a semi-military role. They might want to see the re-introduction of capital punishment, longer prison sentences and less remission — but they did not want to become soldiers. The new Chief Constable put it this way to a *Times* reporter:

> If you go on increasing the severity of the law, you upset the checks and balances of a free society and then find that you are no longer a democracy and that — of course — is the objective of the terrorist. The power of the law has already been increased to a degree that would be unusual in normal times. But you must nevertheless retain your options to protect society.

One of the first things Newman did was to have talks with the GOC. He had deliberately not sent any 'signals' to the Army about his intentions but now, in a series of hard negotiating sessions with Lieutenant-General House, they hammered out the details of a document known as the 'Joint Directive'. This was the effective instrument for reversing the roles of the Army and police. It stated the constitutional position quite plainly — that the military was in support of the police and was operating in aid of the civil power. It laid down a general regulator that all Army activity would be in response to police requirements. In more detailed and specific passages it laid down that all searches, arrests and even patrols would now be carried out with police agreement.

What the police were going to do, in fact, was adopt a high-risk profile. It had already been decided, quite coldly, that it was not possible for the police to take over responsibility for security gradually. A date had to be fixed on which they would take the lead whether or not they were properly prepared. In Protestant-dominated places like Carrickfergus and Bangor the Army would simply withdraw and the police would carry on. In hard areas it would mean putting the police up at the front in the certain knowledge that they would become targets for snipers and bombers and that there would be casualties. The date set coincided with Newman's appointment. Within weeks that phrase 'high-risk profile', which had been thought up by some Whitehall mandarin, had justified itself. The year was to see the death toll of regular and reserve police and members of the UDR more than doubled, while that of the Army remained the same.

Newman felt that the Army's high-profile periods of the past had been very counter-productive in a society with such a seriously alienated Catholic population. Moreover, he sensed that the Government had run out of political options and was about to start a phase of 'bush fire containment'. It was absolutely essential that the police concept of operations should dominate, and his strategy was to coordinate police and Army activity, selectively and accurately, on to the terrorist cells, leaving the host community as undisturbed as possible.

The Army's Spearhead battalion was withdrawn, but only two weeks after Newman took office there was a chilling reminder of how formidable the obstacles were on the path back to normality. In one week eleven people died violently, and in the following week there were vicious attacks on the police as they set about establishing themselves as the prime controllers of security. In the Fermanagh border village of Belcoo the Provisionals fired on two members of the UDR. They did not kill them but presumed — quite rightly — that there would be a security force follow-up. It was a classic 'come on', and it worked. A policeman stepped on a 15lb landmine and he and two colleagues were killed. A fourth policeman was blinded. It was the worst attack the RUC had suffered and led to a bloody spiral of reprisal killings between the UVF and the Provisionals.

The next attack was the following afternoon, when some twenty people in a pub watching football on television were injured by a bomb blast. That evening a car drove down the main street of the little village of Claremont in County Armagh. Most of the people there were Catholic, and there are just two pubs. Gunmen got out of the car and sprayed the first pub with automatic fire and then went to the next one where they planted a bomb. It exploded, killing three people. In another pub in Stewartstown a customer saw a smoking bomb and kicked it out of the door before it went off. Reprisals for this came with reports of an attempted bombing between Warrenpoint and Newry; a police patrol was ambushed and the sergeants died in a hail of bullets. The next to die was a civilian — a Protestant shot dead in a social club in north Belfast. The next day two Protestant brothers were singled out for murder and shot at their desks in an egg-packing factory in County Tyrone. These deaths in three days had left eighteen children fatherless. It all imposed a severe strain on the policy of shifting responsibility for security from the Army to the police, for five of the dead were policemen.

The Army also had some setbacks, though they were embarrassing rather than fatal. One evening two SAS men set off on a mission in a yellow Triumph 2000, in civilian clothes and armed with a Browning automatic pistol, a Sterling sub-machine gun and a large quantity of ammunition. They drove down one of the many winding, narrow roads along the border and somewhere they crossed into the South. They were somewhat surprised when they were stopped by a Gardai checkpoint, and one of them tried to cover the gun at his feet with the map he was using. They both denied that they were SAS, saying that they were paratroopers from Bessbrook, and had got lost. They had, they said, been road testing the car and had made a map-reading error. The Gardai took them both into custody.

Back at Bessbrook there was some concern when they failed to return. A search party of four more SAS men was sent after them, but this time two were in uniform with blackened faces — they had been in a secret Observation Post (OP) — and they travelled in two cars, well armed. They went down the same road and made the same mistake. Just after 2 a.m. they were stopped by the same road block.

'You are in the Republic,' a voice told them.

'It must be a map-reading error,' one SAS man replied hopefully. 'We are looking for two colleagues who have gone missing. Have you seen anyone like that?'

'We have indeed,' the policeman replied dryly. 'They are both in custody. Now you are here as well with illegally-held weapons. Please hand them over.'

'We've only made a map-reading error,' the SAS man said, a little desperate as the situation seemed to be getting out of control. No soldiers had ever been arrested before for straying across this meandering border. 'Let us go back. If the roles were reversed we'd do the same for you. After all, we are fighting the same bloody enemy, aren't we?'

The Gardai, however, were adamant, and not at all put out by being faced with a heavily-armed SAS unit. As they insisted that the weapons were handed over an Irish Army patrol came up in the darkness, and by now the SAS felt that they had to comply. The Gardai collected three Sterling sub-machine guns, two Browning pistols, a sawn-off, pump action shot gun and a good quantity of ammunition.

'Fuck me!' muttered one SAS man furiously as they were led off. 'Bang go my chances of promotion!'

They had been only some 500 metres inside the border, and were by no means the first to stray across. Only the year before the Irish Foreign Minister Garrett Fitzgerald had produced figures claiming some 300 incursions by British troops into the Republic. However, it was probably the reputation of the SAS which prompted the local Garda to stick to his decision, despite all sorts of pressures, and once the process had started there was no way to stop it. In due course the SAS men appeared in Dublin's Special Criminal Court, a setting more used to IRA men than British soldiers. Here they were acquitted of serious charges but found guilty of possessing illegal firearms, as it was considered that they had made a genuine mistake; although one astonished woman outside the court exclaimed: 'So they've got off — the murdering bastards!' It was a measure of the reputation they had acquired.

The Irish Government was pleased because it had shown that it was not to be pushed around, and the Army was pleased because it showed that its most controversial unit was not perhaps as evil as many supposed. Only a short time later there was yet another incursion into the South, this time near Emyvale, in County Monaghan. This is a particularly difficult border area where a salient sticks into the North and where roads continually run over the border and back again within a few miles with no signs at all. Seven soldiers crossed this time, and in a radio interview Garrett Fitzgerald remarked, rather wearily, 'For some reason your map-reading procedures in the British Army seem somewhat defective. How you find terrorists but can't find your way on a map I just don't know!'

'I think we've strayed across the border again, Sarge!'

In fact the training for Northern Ireland run by NITAT had now become very sophisticated. First, the unit going over would retrain in all the basic skills such as shooting, field-craft and patrolling. The second stage would be to go to a special training area at Smallcliff on the south coast, where the staff could reproduce almost any incident that had happened in Northern Ireland. Exact replicas of the areas where the unit was to go would be reproduced, down to the correct number of lamp-posts along the streets. Here the troops would operate with ordinary weapons but scaled down to fire .22 rounds — as much for range safety aspects as anything else. Bomb explosions, vehicle ambushes, hi-jacking of petrol tankers, hostage taking — all such incidents had been carefully analysed and the troops put through them again and again. It was very concentrated, with seven or eight incidents a day — far more than would ever really occur. It was also very hard work, and very varied. A patrol might be sent, for instance, to call on a certain house and a soldier would knock on the door.

'What do you want?' a voice would shout from inside.

'We want to talk to your son,' the patrol commander would reply.

'Well, he's not in. Just a wee minute while I come down to you . . .' Then the firing would start and the patrol be caught in whatever nasty situation the instructors had dreamt up for them.

The third stage would be more for the benefit of the officers, and particularly of the company commander, who would spend two whole days in the 'hot seat' handling a series of incidents and having everything recorded on to video. Some commanders were moved quietly aside after these sessions because they were found to panic, or react badly, or because they were found not to have the necessary skills. Sometimes they were replaced and did not go to Northern Ireland at all.

In July the IRA jolted the establishment in both London and Dublin with the murder of the British ambassador, Sir Christopher Ewart-Biggs. He had been in his post for only a couple of weeks, a striking-looking man who had lost an eye at the battle of Alamein and wore a tinted monocle. He was an urbane, polished operator who had served in Paris and the Middle East and had even written thrillers which had been banned by the Irish censors. By tradition, the job of the British ambassador in Dublin was a very social one, intended to keep everyone happy and the links with London open; but Ewart-Biggs did not seem to fit easily into this category. He seemed exceptionally well briefed on Irish affairs, and in the ever-suspicious minds of extreme Republicans there probably stirred a thought that his role was more that of a senior officer in MI6 than that of a diplomat. It was decided that he would be assassinated.

On a sunny summer morning, as Ewart-Biggs drove into Dublin with a young civil servant, Judith Cook, and the Permanent Under-Secretary from the Northern Ireland Office, Sir Brian Cubbon, he was blown up by a remote-controlled bomb. Both he and the young girl were killed. Two men with FN rifles were seen leaving the area, but no one was ever caught. Nor did anyone claim the murder until a few months later when an IRA source in Belfast claimed that the ambassador had been assassinated because he was in charge of intelligence operations aimed at Republicans in the South, and in revenge for SAS killings in south Armagh. This murder south of the border broke a long-standing IRA rule which had been made because they did not want to put their 'safe haven' at risk. Indeed, the pressure on them was increased. In Dublin the authorities rushed through a bill increasing the maximum sentence for membership of an illegal organisation from two to seven years. Both the Gardai and

Irish Army were also ordered to step up operations along the border.

A favourite ploy of the Provisionals was to plant a bomb in the North and set it off by wire or radio signal from the South. They knew that if a patrol found a bomb they would also look for the firing position and ambush it. This made life very difficult even for the toughest troops.

> You had no real control. All you could do was be as skilful as possible and anticipate where the bombs were. But even with special scanners in helicopters you couldn't always spot them. But you knew they were there! We found one once, 550lbs of Co-Op mix — and we found the firing position, on our side of the border. So I stood on this bloody thing as a lure while a patrol staked out the firing position to hit anyone who came along to fire it. Not very pleasant; in fact quite mad! But if the firing position was south of the border we couldn't even do that!

The time stretched on to August and the marking of seven years of the military 'in aid of the civil power'. A great deal had changed in that time, with corresponding shifts in the way that the politicians felt that the situation should be treated. On the ground this had meant a rapidly changing sequence of 'blow cold' and 'blow hot' directives, which the soldiers dealt with philosophically. At a higher level, though, pressure mounted to allow the Army to fight back. Airey Neave, shadow spokesman on Northern Ireland, said in the *News of the World*:

> There must be a change in security tactics. The Army and the local security forces must be released from their present low profile and go on the offensive. . . . Recent events have shown there is a massive support from both Catholics and Protestants for a determined anti-terrorist campaign. . . . The time is ripe to smash the Provisional IRA.

No doubt Neave had been influenced by Lisburn in his thinking; the previous week had seen an unprecedented number of rounds fired at the security forces. There had also been another incident which had caught people's imagination. An Army patrol had been in hot pursuit of an IRA gunman who, fatally wounded, lost control of his car and crashed, killing three young children. That night an aunt of the children, Mairead Corrigan, had broken down while being interviewed on television. One person watching was Betty Williams, who was so moved that she decided something must be done to stop the slaughter. She joined forces with Mairead Corrigan and together they started a Peace Movement which was to know no religious boundaries and which was to become something of a mass movement — if not long-lived. So there was a basis for the feeling that the moment was right to strike hard at the terrorist movement.

The GOC was on leave, but he flew back to Belfast and made his way to Stormont Castle. There, in the large room once used by the old Stormont Cabinet, he discussed the problems with Rees and Newman. House was a believer in the policy of police primacy and, as one observer noted, a 'fine tuner' of the Army's profile. Lisburn, however, was pressing hard for a number of changes in policy. They wanted to reintroduce internment and had a list of those they wanted to arrest. They wanted to change the rules of evidence so that Army intelligence could be used in the same way as it was in Dublin's Special Criminal Court, where a suspect could be convicted of membership of an illegal organisation on the word of a middle-ranking police officer. Rees also heard from the two men that his conditional release scheme for detainees was not working. More than 800 convicted terrorists had now been released and the police pointed out that this just about equalled their arrest rate — in other words, for every one they locked up Rees was releasing another. 'The terrorist doesn't fight under the Queensberry rules,' one adviser pointed out to him. 'Why should we?'

Rees, however, was not to be moved. His argument was that within the guidelines of the present policy there could be tougher security action, but not to the extent of forfeiting the growing support of the Irish Government. Dublin was becoming more stringent in its attitude towards the IRA and showing greater willingness to cooperate with the Army. This was not something to be cast lightly aside. An American journalist and author, Kevin Kelley, described the period in this way:

> The Peace people had no lasting effect on any of the key participants in the war. The IRA kept on attacking 'legitimate targets'; the Loyalist paramilitaries continued to murder Catholic civilians; the British Army, RUC and UDR adopted still more aggressive tactics during the second half of 1976. Devoid of political initiative and deprived of its 'peace' pawn, the British Government decided to launch a new military offensive against the Provisionals. Expanded SAS operations were part of this intensified counter-insurgency campaign . . . .

In September 1976 Rees left Northern Ireland to become Home Secretary. His time in Belfast had not been easy, starting as it did with the UWC strike and the hardening of Protestant antagonism to any form of power-sharing with the Catholic minority. He had read a great deal of Irish history and knew that the British Army had first been raised in 1689 to 'deal with the problem of Ireland'. One of his favourite books was J.L. Hammond's *Gladstone and the Irish Nation*, a huge volume which he kept on the desk in his office. Visitors remembered him on cold winter evenings, standing in front of a roaring fire, smoking a cheroot and 'chewing the fat' about Irish affairs. Every now and then he would dart over to consult the volume and then quote from it. Another book he often consulted was a collection of official papers about security matters in Ireland between 1916 and 1922, which had come from the Dublin Metropolitan Police, the Royal Irish Constabulary, the Irish Special Branch in London and the Viceroy's office. They showed the confusion, rivalry, and incompetence which existed between them, as well as their poor intelligence and endless worries about infiltration. 'When you see the Cabinet papers for the 1970s,' Rees would say, 'you'll see that nothing has changed!' These studies convinced him of one thing above all others — that the English did not understand Ireland, and that the problem had to be solved by the Irish. The Sunningdale conference which produced the power-sharing Executive was, he was fond of pointing out, an Anglo-Irish solution and it had failed.

The Army had found him fairly easy to get on with, although rather over-concerned about whether he was being too hard on the IRA. They also felt that he was low in the 'Cabinet pecking-order' and therefore rather too worried about what other people in the party thought of his actions. 'He was the sort of person who was always on the phone,' said one observer; although another Army officer felt that while Rees may have been ruled more by his heart than his head, he had been '. . . very perceptive. He had seen the propaganda value to the Provisionals of internment and had been determined to get rid of it. It was a bold step — but the right thing to do in the long term.'

As Merlyn Rees departed, the Army announced that there had been many successes but the toll had been heavy. Since January, 170 people had died, mainly victims of sectarian strife. 'The RUC and the UDR have,' it was pointed out, 'been specifically signalled out by the Provisionals. The death toll here is: RUC, 15; UDR, 7; Army, 6.'

In September Roy Mason, the bouncy, no-nonsense ex-miner

from Barnsley, arrived for his first visit as the new Secretary of State. He landed at Aldergrove Airport in mist and rain and was unable to take the usual helicopter ride into Belfast. Instead a convoy of Special Branch officers escorted him, coming down from the mountains through the mist to see the grey sprawl of Belfast lying below with the shipyards massed at one end. Far on the other side, set on the rolling green hills, was the white mass of Stormont and the quaintly-castellated Stormont Castle which was to be his headquarters. He had seen it all before as Defence Secretary, but now it would be his patch — or, as some thought, his political graveyard.

He spent just three hours looking round his new offices, meeting people and hearing about the rioting Protestants. Since early that morning the UDA had been carefully organising a controlled operation of hi-jackings, road blocks and at least twenty-six bomb hoaxes. The damage was estimated at £200,000 and the security forces were, as usual, clearing away the debris. The immediate cause of all this had been the alleged ill-treatment of UDA prisoners, but the trouble underlined the mounting tension between Loyalists and Republican extremists on plans to withdraw the coveted 'political status' from prisoners. It was not, however, a complaint that would strike a very sympathetic chord in the heart of the new Northern Ireland Secretary.

Mason's appointment had caught many people by surprise and some thought that it signalled a much tougher regime than that of the painstakingly thoughtful Merlyn Rees. In some ways they were right. Certainly the Army had no qualms about him at this stage. According to one Lisburn officer, he was 'a very tough little chap'. Perhaps his two years at the MOD had turned him more thoroughly into a general's man than anyone might have imagined an ex-miner might become. He seemed more relaxed than Rees and more inclined to let the professionals get on with their jobs. 'Less imaginative,' observed an officer, 'but much more direct.' However, he was soon to become known as 'Pitprop' Mason, a reference both to his time as a miner and to the ever constant possibility — in some eyes — that he would collapse under the weight of his own bombastic style. He was also a rather short man. Soon after his arrival he called four officials into his private office to brief him. As it happened, all four were well over six feet tall, and as they came in Mason, sitting at his desk, looked up and then jumped to his feet. The officials spent the session standing and got the distinct impression that Mason was making it clear who was the boss. 'He succeeded,' said the official briefly. 'Throughout his term of office there was never any doubt who was the boss. It was Roy Mason!'

His experience at the MOD gave him a flying start with the Army, and the lessening of Protestant violence allowed him to launch his ideas for the development of the province. Quite simply, there was to be no more nonsense about political progress: he would concentrate on boosting the economy and hitting the terrorist. This would allow the police to take the lead, put the Army firmly into a supporting role and bring the province back to normality. From this, political progress would flower in its own good time.

The police were inclined to agree with him. In particular, they realised that the amount of Protestant violence was regulated by the attrition rate against the Provisional IRA. When that was high, the Protestants were less worried about the situation and less likely to take action. The attrition rate affected other matters as well, the morale of the police themselves being just one. It was pointed out very strongly that they could not be seen to be getting into a reactive position. The only way to deal with the situation was to take the lead and hit the terrorist.

The implications of this strategy, which really began to take shape at the end of 1976, meant a steady lessening of Army activity and what the police felt were 'abrasive street contacts'. It also meant a tremendous effort by the police to improve their intelligence so that all operations could become more selective and accurate. Most important, it meant that the Army would no longer be taking the lead in the anti-terrorist campaign, but would from now on be asked to act in support of the police.

The second arm of this strategy, spearheaded by the police, was to work on the community with imaginative community relations programmes. The police reasoned that there was no point in talking to conventional leaders because as one police officer said, 'As the Americans say, they have their political ass to preserve!' So they would work away at sensitive areas, trying to get people to communicate. The police felt that this brought dividends; the broad-based Alliance party came out on the side of the police; and even the mainly Catholic SDLP, while never saying so formally in public, began privately to give help and encouragement.

Roy Mason thought little of the local politicians, and even less of what they were doing. He hit out at the Provisional IRA, scornfully describing them as 'reeling'. After a couple of accidents in which a 13-year-old boy was killed and a pregnant woman injured by a plastic bullet, he defended the Army: 'The Army has a duty to help the RUC maintain the rule of law within the law. This they will continue to do in the face of severe provocation from the Provisional IRA and their like, who are cynically trying to exploit a number of incidents in order to restore their waning fortunes.'

Mason would breeze around in a tweed safari suit made by a Belfast tailor to his own personal design, smoking his pipe, and establishing a style of Direct Rule rather different from the one imposed by his predecessor. He was personally convinced that his policy of keeping clear of the 'political whirlpools' helped to keep the crime level down and that this would come down even further if it were only ignored by the press. Lisburn watched his progress with interest and did not have much trouble serving him. 'He had a very tough image,' observed an officer, 'and he wasn't acting a part.'

There was no doubt that by the end of the year the RUC was beginning to get on top. In the first ten months the number of Provisionals charged with serious crime was up by some 75 per cent on the whole of the previous year. Newman's professionalism was boosting police morale and the increased efficiency of the police was to sting the Provisionals into some devastating attacks against the local security forces in the months to come. With financial aid from the United States beginning to drop (as one commentator put it, 'After all they are an achievement-oriented society and the Provisionals are not winning'), Republican supporters hit back to try to keep their image respectable. They particularly wanted the top political names in the States to continue to support their cause. Literature from the National Council of Irish Americans described Roy Mason as a military commissar — perhaps it was his tweed safari suit that got to them — and went on:

> The RUC is a private police force of three fragmented Unionist parties, legalised in Whitehall and financed with the US taxpayer's dollars through the International Monetary Fund. . . . The Army is not subject to civil process of the courts. . . . Judgeships in Northern Ireland are now filled by English politicians in London. . . . Since 1969 there have been no legislative reforms and civil rights remain suspended.

As the *Irish Times* correspondent David McKittrick pointed out, any 'lefty' jargon — such as the Provisionals occasionally used, especially to explain why they were murdering businessmen — was always carefully omitted from any propaganda intended for American consumption.

The United States was also a source of guns and ammunition which was rather more difficult to stop. The complexity of American administration was one drawback, and another was the variety of the gun laws, which were stringent in some states and very lax in others. It was possible, therefore, to buy rifles or hand guns without being traced. Intelligence officers estimated that 75 per cent of the weapons seized in Northern Ireland had come from the United States and that nearly half of these had been brought over specifically for use in Northern Ireland. The Armalite was still the favourite weapon as it was light and could easily be broken down. Fully automatic rifles could not be bought, but the Provisionals were delighted when they discovered a civilian version of the American Army's M16 assault rifle which could be bought as a hunting rifle! There were two types, and while it might say something about American hunting habits, the Provisionals had no qualms about using them. There was the Colt Ar-15 (semi-automatic) and the Ar-180 which had the virtue of a folding stock. With a high muzzle velocity and a flat trajectory the round could go through personal body armour and the sides of APCs, and by creating a tumble shock-wave cause terrible injuries. The Provisionals also got hold of some heavy M60 machine-guns which were stolen from an armoury in Massachusetts.

These advantages began to be offset by more cooperation across the border with the Republic. Now there were two infantry battalions south of the border, and contact between the police forces had improved. No one talked much about it — it was still an embarrassing subject in the South. Every evening, however, the telexes would clatter into life in various border police stations with details of cars that had been hi-jacked or stolen and other property that had gone missing. It was still an information-swapping exercise, but senior officers and specialists would also meet — especially those concerned with explosives — to discuss matters of mutual concern. Practically all border police stations now had scramblers fitted to their telephones to make cross-border talk more secure, although four-way radio links, for which successive GOCs had pressed, had been refused. 'Just as well, in some ways,' commented an Army officer. 'We often had difficulty in making out their southern accents!'

Whatever some people might have thought, and indeed on occasion voiced out loud, better cross-border cooperation did not just depend on the South's attitude and enthusiasm for it. There was often a reluctance on the part of British Army officers to cooperate. When an explosive device was found there could be a sense of foreboding and a marked reluctance to let the RUC know, let alone the Gardai. Somehow it was felt that the information would leak to the wrong place and any operation would be compromised. 'What surprised me,' said one company commander, 'was the amount of freedom of action we were given for our patrolling and our behaviour. How we did things was my decision.' He explained that he always wanted the RUC to let the Gardai know, certainly within twenty-four hours, that his men would be down on the border at a certain place and what they would be doing. 'I didn't personally talk to the Irish Army and the Gardai, but my men did. You see, if I knew I was covered from a particular side, then I could get on with my work without having extra troops there to secure it. I still believe this is the best way — to let people know what you are doing.'

So the degree of cooperation would often depend on the local commander, and while some kept everything to themselves, others wanted the RUC to know and to become involved. One described how a patrol had crossed the border accidentally, despite having four SAS troopers with them. It had been a misty evening and navigation was difficult. The patrol commander thought that he recognised the lie of the land and the helicopter put them down. Moments later a car roared past them and a soldier jumped into the road with his rifle, thinking it was a car trying to get away from them. He felt rather sheepish to find it full of Gardai. The patrol commander, however, had the presence of mind to keep his radio switched on. Back in his company OPs Room a somewhat startled Duty Officer heard him say, 'We have a little problem with the Gardai,' but quickly realised what had happened. He was particularly concerned about the SAS troopers who had hitched a ride and were going off on their own somewhere. 'Whatever we did,' he explained later, 'Those SAS boys were liable to gap it on their own and I didn't want a scene.'

Straight away he called in his RUC sergeant who was able to persuade his opposite number that a mistake had been made. Four minutes later the local Gardai sergeant arrived on the scene to find his man trying to take weapons from twelve heavily-armed British soldiers. He persuaded him that the intrusion was a mistake and the patrol was allowed to get themselves back into the North again.

Some of the Gardai, of course, thought the British soldiers quite mad to act as they did. 'We'd be here unarmed, with maybe an Army patrol to back us up,' said one, 'but not much! And there would be maybe a dozen fellows, black faces and armed to the teeth. I was amazed that they'd ever think of handing over their weapons. All they had to do was walk quietly into the darkness and there'd be damn all we could do about it — or want to!' In fact at least one company commander along the border gave his men specific instructions to do just that if it ever happened again. He reasoned that turning round and walking away might cause a fuss, but nothing like the fuss there would be if they were all taken into custody.

Early in 1977 the Provisionals began to hit hard at the local security forces. A length of twine under the car of a police reservist caused a full-scale alert one day, with the bomb disposal squad evacuating the area. All they found was a length of twine, but the reservist had been right to be cautious. Over the years the Provisionals had become expert at designing and manufacturing booby-traps. Only the week before, a bomb disposal sergeant had been killed by a bomb within a bomb in County Fermanagh. It had been packed into a milk churn, and when the sergeant had cleared the timing device and was lifting it out, a detonator underneath set off the second bomb, which exploded.

The bombs were often very simple and very deadly. The components were readily available — a few pounds of explosive, a detonator, a battery and a couple of feet of wire. The triggering device could be either a plate buried in the ground or, as in this case, a clothes peg. The jaws of the peg are held apart by a little wedge that is attached to a length of fishing line or gut. The line is stretched across a path or, as in a case a few days before, wrapped round the wheel of a car. Once the line tightens it pulls the wedge out, allowing the jaws to close and make contact. The electrical circuit is then complete. The bomb that killed the sergeant could just as easily have killed the milkman had he arrived early and started to move the bottles and churns.

The reservist who found the twine under his car — to which nothing had been attached — lived in Killea in a border area where the Provisionals planted a great number of bombs, three of them at the front doors of policemen's houses. The police were convinced that they were the work of the same group and, in these remote areas where everyone knew everyone else, there would be no mistake in picking the wrong house. That someone else might get blown up was, presumably, part of the risk that had to be taken. In fact during the first forty-eight hours of the year the Provisionals had, in so-called 'accidents', killed a 15-month-old baby, blown the legs off a 43-year-old woman and maimed an 18-year-old boy.

The Provisionals were also getting better with another weapon — the mortar. At the start of the campaign these had been very rough and ready affairs. In one incident a Provisional had burned his hands holding the tube while it was fired. In another a girl had been maimed when she looked down the barrel to see why the bomb had not gone off — and then it did. In the past year, though, the Provisionals had improved their techniques and mounted some mortar attacks firing their weapons electrically from the back of sand-filled lorries. Another firing position had been found within range of the GOC's house. In Dublin the Gardai raided a factory and found a whole pile of firing tubes made from lengths of metal pipe. In another raid they discovered a factory for making mortar bomb casings; these were being manufactured in a sophisticated way with lathes and being put together by an unofficial 'terrorist night-shift'. In the North more completed mortar and bombs were found. 'Quite simply a professional piece of plumbing,' as one officer put it. The bombs consisted of three pieces of drainage pipe welded together. The tail contained the propellant and was guided by fins made from heat-exchanger pipe. The centre section had between 8 and 16 ounces of explosives, which were set off by an impact fuse in the front section. No one had yet been killed in an attack with these, but they posed quite a threat.

> Crossmaglen is a happy place,
> Keep your head low and blacken your face.

A new company was arriving for its four-month posting — and in one month was to use up 2,336 tubes of camouflage cream. They came in by helicopter, fluttering in from their main base at Bessbrook, one of the busiest little airports in the world. As they came overhead it looked at first sight like any traditional Irish country scene — a peaceful village set in rolling hills and a patchwork of small fields bordered by mountain ranges. As they got closer they would be able to spot the difference. On the edge of the village they would see the

Army post, looking exactly as any schoolboy would expect a frontier post to look, surrounded by tall walls of corrugated iron sheeting with the gates closed and small slits from which to watch and fire. They would land on a muddy patch just outside a side gate and double quickly to get inside before a sniper might open up. Only three months before the fort had been mortared. The Provisionals had driven a truck right into the square and up to chalk markers for the front tyres. The windscreen had a marker on it to line up with one in the square. The bombs had destroyed a civilian garage outside the fort and some had fallen inside, penetrating the wire stretched across the top to catch them. Surprisingly, only one man was wounded.

Once inside the gate the men would tramp through the mud and across the catwalks to their living quarters — wooden huts with three-tier bunks. Here they would live for four months, cramped together in constant movement as they went on patrol, cleaned their weapons, got ready for patrols, ate, wrote home and slept. They got a Northern Ireland allowance of fifty pence a day for this, and the married men got another fifty pence on top of that as a separation allowance. One very small kitchen with two stoves fed 130 men, and if they were lucky they got a sack of potatoes to sit on as they ate. To wash themselves or their clothes they had to tramp through more mud, and around the washing machines the mud and water flowed back in as quickly as it was swept out. The officers were in much the same conditions, though not quite so cramped. In their tiny mess the regimental silver depicting the glories of the past was surrounded by the muddy boots of the present campaign.

The fort overlooked the large market square, (the killing ground on which seventeen soldiers had already died). From it the escape routes for the Provisional IRA ran out like the spokes of a bicycle wheel: four to the border only ninety seconds away and two north into the hostile territory of south Armagh. In the village flew the tricolour of the Irish Republic and the Starry Plough, and while the soldiers watched and checked the locals, the locals looked on them as an alien force. To stay alive a soldier had to be good, and alert. People had forgotten the days when policemen last walked the streets alone. Life was not made easier by the administrative problems of operating out of such an isolated place. For a long time the rubbish used to go out in a skip, by road. It was a pattern which had been noticed, and one day a skip which had been sitting in the middle of the fort for some ten hours exploded. After that as much rubbish as possible was burned, and flattened tins and everything else were made into underslung loads and airlifted out by helicopters. 'It was a lot of hard work, but it became a sense of pride that nothing those bastards did would stop us', recalled one junior officer. The main problem as the soldiers saw it was that if vehicles were used regularly they would be blown up. Sometimes, to the extreme annoyance of the local commander, headquarters staff would drive down to Crossmaglen, often unarmed, which seemed madness to those whose life was to move and fight in this dangerous area.

> Those idiots would want to inspect your weapons — or an armourer or some ass who just wanted to say he'd been to Crossmaglen. They'd try for two or three days to get a helicopter, fail, and then say, 'Stuff it!' and jump in a car. Quite mad!

It was a strange world, in which strict rules were not always obeyed. One was that no soldier could have a round in the breech of his rifle while he was on patrol in the village. The company commander disobeyed that and got caught out when a soldier accidentally shot himself in the foot. He was hauled over the carpet, but two months later, because he was then obeying the order, missed a terrorist who had fired on a patrol at the edge of the village. For months the machine-gunner had been able to push his safety catch forward and fire. This time he couldn't, and in the seconds it took him to cock and fire the gun, the target disappeared. The company commander went to his CO and told him what had happened. 'No bullshit, sir,' he said. 'That is what actually happened. Please reverse your orders.' The CO did so. He gave the company commander the freedom he wanted to operate as he thought best.

It was a rough, tough operational area, and the clear aim given to the soldiers was to kill and capture terrorists who operated there. Another aim some officers had was to see that their men survived. 'In my view,' said one, after a soldier had been killed, 'Ireland is just not worth dying for.'

One Sunday morning in January 1977, when most Crossmaglen villagers were in church, a four-man patrol of Royal Highland Fusiliers went down the road past the church towards the border. The patrol was supported by a Saracen which could give covering fire with its machine-gun. In the fort, the Duty Officer was in contact with the patrol by radio, and the company commander was in his office doing paperwork. Then, over the loud-speakers came the noise of firing, and the company commander heard his corporal report 'Contact. Dundalk Road. School. Wait out.' It was good procedure and he murmured, 'Well done, corporal,' under his breath. The contact with the patrol was lost and for two or three minutes he reviewed his options, well aware that it could be a classic 'come on' ambush. Five minutes later, however, he led a patrol of platoon strength out of three exits and down the road. He passed the Saracen with a rather frightened-looking soldier and asked him what had happened. 'I don't know sir. I went back to refuel. Then I heard the shooting and I've been returning fire.' Some distance down the road the company commander could see three bodies. Flashes were coming from just beyond them. It was some time before he found out exactly what had happened.

The patrol had been moving along the main road with the commander, Lance-Corporal Hind, on the left, Fusilier Reid ten yards behind him, and on the other side of the road were Fusilier Simpson and Fusilier Ferguson. It was just after midday and as they passed St Joseph's School they came under heavy fire, both automatic and single shots. The firing was coming from more than one position 300 to 400 yards away. At least one gunman was hidden in a van parked further up the road.

In the very first burst Lance-Corporal Hind was killed and his radio smashed. He had not made a contact report, despite the clear recollection of his company commander. As the rounds zipped up the road towards the school, Fusilier Simpson was also hit, and fell unconscious. The third member of the patrol, Fusilier Ferguson, had his arm smashed by a bullet, and the impact carried his rifle into the middle of the road. Only Fusilier Reid, at the back, had not been hit. From his position he could see perfectly well that his corporal had been hit and was probably dead, and that the other two had also been hit. His instinctive action should have been to hit the ground, crawl, observe, sight and fire. He was 20 years old and only fourteen months out of his basic training. Instead, he stood his ground and fired back. He knew that he had to make a noise, move about and fire in the direction of the enemy. As he did so Ferguson, despite his smashed arm, crawled to the middle of the road under fire, retrieved his rifle, and crawled back again. In pain and unable to hold his rifle normally, he rolled over on his back, rested his rifle against his foot and began to return fire.

By now Reid had fired one magazine and as the bullets whipped up past him, whining off the tarmac road, he doubled forward to check his patrol commander. Hind was dead. Reid fired another magazine and then grabbed his corporal's rifle and stood over his body, still firing. At this point a car drove up the road towards them. When the driver realised what was happening he tried to turn but before he could do so Reid, shouting to Ferguson to give him cover, ran forward and ordered him to drive on to Crossmaglen and raise the alarm. As he did so the gunmen stopped firing and left. The border was just two minutes drive away. For this action Reid was awarded the Military Medal, and Ferguson was Mentioned in Dispatches.

The mistake that day probably lay in the fact that the Saracen returned to refuel exactly as it had on a previous occasion. The Provisional unit may well have been lying in wait for two or three days for this to happen again, and when it did they struck. Despite noisy celebrations in the local pub that night, the soldiers were under strict orders not to be provoked. 'There's more than one way to skin a cat,' the company commander told his men, and proceeded to show them how. A week later one of the leading singers of that night set off to get married. He had to drive five hundred yards to the church and every hundred yards he was stopped by a very polite patrol who asked him to wait while his car was searched. A company officer recalled:

> It took him an hour and a half to get to church, and by the time he got there he knew exactly what was happening to him and why. It was something the locals had never encountered before. What they were used to were soldiers rushing into pubs, knocking glasses off the bar, grabbing people by the hair, rushing them into the fort, sometimes with bare feet across broken glass, shoving them into a chopper and without them having any idea what was going on or why they had been arrested. We tried a different approach.

This time the restraint worked. People came up to say they were sorry that the corporal had been shot, and finally information came that the lorry involved was in a certain deserted farmyard right on the border. The local SAS squadron commander was told and a flight over the area confirmed this. Just three days after the shooting, an SAS unit moved towards the border. Instead of getting into the comparative comfort of the empty farm buildings it moved into some scrub on the fourth side of the yard, only ten yards away, and settled down to wait. It was January, and cold and wet. Three days later, on the Saturday evening, a man arrived with two dogs, a collie and an Alsatian. The four SAS troopers watched motionless in the dusk. The man, a farmer from across the border, took the dogs into each building and methodically searched every room. The low scrub ten yards away was ignored completely.

The next morning, as two troopers were cleaning their weapons, they all heard a van drive up, stop for a moment and drive away. Moments later a man appeared, masked and carrying a sawn-off shotgun. He was very close and the troopers with their weapons broken for cleaning could not move without making a noise. One of the others decided that he would capture the masked man and began to worm his way round behind him. The idea was that when he got to a certain spot five yards away he would stand up and challenge the man, knowing that he was covered from two positions.

He moved to the spot, stood up and shouted, 'Stand still.' Unfortunately the masked man was not alone; there were two men covering him. By now the second trooper had also stood up, and the firing started. The masked man fell, hit as it turned out by fifteen rounds, seven of them from his own people. A running battle developed, but in ten minutes it was over and the other two unknowns had escaped across the border. There was no hot pursuit, and the SAS troopers had to let them go.

An officer said:

> Just two men killed during our tour. One was 22 years old, a Roman Catholic, a keen footballer, a nice young man engaged to be married. He was in Northern Ireland because that was his job and he walked into a bullet. The other was 21 years old, also a Roman Catholic, goalkeeper of the local football team and also engaged to be married. They were so alike — except that one was a soldier and the other a Provisional. Both killed within a week of each other. What for?

The Army built a concrete sangar to overlook the square at Crossmaglen and lessen the chance of surprise attack. An officer had spent a day and a half doing nothing but study the square. He decided on the best observation point and had a stand built on it in such a way that no one could guess what it was for. Then, in a single day,

9 'I told them to act firmly,' said the commanding officer.
'The men had clear orders: contain the riot for a while
and then go in hard and stop it.' 12 August 1976, Londonderry.

10a and **10b** An injured officer on the ground is the immediate target for rioters –

– and his men get him out in a hurry. The Queen's Jubilee visit, August 1979.

11 Police and army casualties are evacuated from the border area near Forkhill. This followed an IRA mortar attack on the police station, and the explosion of a booby trap in a hijacked lorry. January 1978.

12a A Provisional IRA Action Service Unit displays its weapons in the Falls Road, Belfast. August 1979.

12b Faces of violence: IRA gunmen show off their weapons. August 1980.

13 Girls scream abuse.
The 12-year-old brother of one has been killed by a plastic bullet.
November 1981, Belfast.

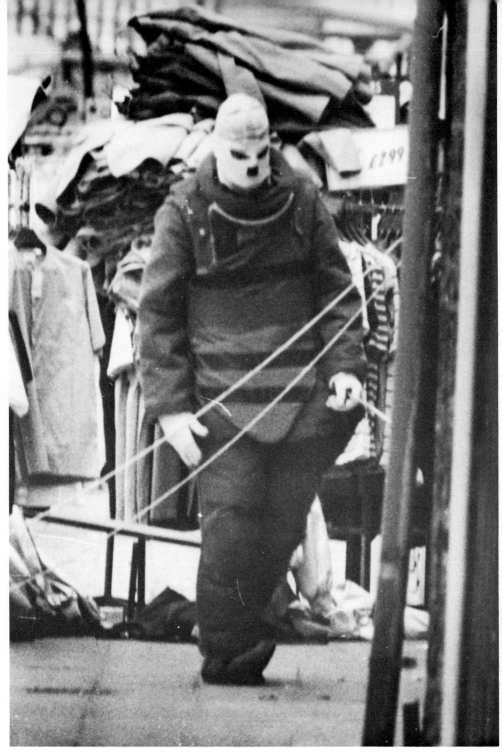

14 An anonymous bomb disposal expert (ATO) –
dressed in three stones of protective gear –
walks alone to defuse a fire bomb
planted in a Belfast city store. June 1983.

15 In Belfast city centre, a bomb disposal expert works to defuse a bomb
planted in a 2,000 gallon petrol tanker. It took him three hours.
The bomb had been suspended inside the tank on the end
of a fishing line. February 1977.

16 Fifteen years on. Sean Downes is fatally injured
by a baton round during disturbances in Belfast.
12 August 1984.

a stream of helicopters flew in a pre-fab concrete sangar and put it on the top. To the disgust of the local villagers it was up before anyone knew what was happening.

The sangar was named the Baruki sangar, after a paratrooper who had been killed in the square by a bicycle which blew up. His platoon commander remembered that when he came in from a six-day patrol that morning the bicycle had not been in the square. Then some military VIP had decided to practise helicopter approaches to Crossmaglen, so a patrol had to go out to secure the area. It returned to base two or three hours later, each man covered by his companions as they came into the square. Baruki was third in the patrol. As he turned to cover his mates, the bicycle exploded right beside him. 'So you began to realise that the IRA aren't mindless idiots,' observed an officer, 'that in fact they are quite sophisticated people, using sophisticated techniques and they think about what they are doing. They really do go into a lot of detail as to how they can get back at us.'

Sometimes they got back by mistake. In May an Army officer in plain clothes was abducted from a border pub, taken into the Republic, and shot dead. His body was never found but some of those who had taken and murdered him were found. From them, and from some of his colleagues, a curious story emerged of a brave and somewhat romantic character — a Grenadier Guards captain who had once served with the SAS. He was now a liaison officer between the Army, the police and the Special Forces in the area, notably the SAS who were there in squadron strength — about sixty. His name was Robert Nairac, and he had been around in Northern Ireland for some time, first in Belfast and later in south Armagh. 'My soldiers had great respect for him,' recalled a captain in the Parachute Regiment. 'He knew what he was talking about and he knew his way round. He wrote some excellent papers about young people in the Ardoyne. He was always up to date with intelligence and was very good tactically. If he had been in the Falklands campaign he would have won a VC without doubt. He was that sort of man.'

Nairac was also an intelligence officer, and his posting to south Armagh followed recommendations made two years previously by the young scientist who had also written a stream of reports on which the Army had based a great deal of its training. In late 1974, the young scientist put forward the proposition that Crossmaglen was an area in which terrorist activity was far ahead of anywhere else. He argued that there was a danger that this might create 'quality' in areas where it was poor. 'It is true that little of the Crossmaglen ideas or expertise have seeped through to the rest of the IRA,' he said. 'This is because of both the insularity of the unit and the thick-headedness of the rest of the IRA. However, it is extremely dangerous to assume that they won't take root in the future. Once this happens it is too late.'

He suggested that the problem was one of intelligence and not straight soldiering, for the IRA around Crossmaglen would not be beaten by the Army 'out-ambushing or out-shooting' them. 'We are up against a sophisticated enemy,' he said, 'and we must prepare accordingly.' He argued that only the cream of the Army's soldiers should go to Crossmaglen, and that all their energies should be directed towards local contacts and low-level intelligence. Complete dossiers should be built up on every man, woman and child in the area, and across the border, whether or not they were in any way involved with the IRA. This aim should be hammered home to soldiers, and those who would not accept it should be removed. 'It must be made quite clear to each soldier that the worse crime he can commit — worse than buggery, rape or shooting another soldier, is to compromise a source.'

What was needed was a good intelligence officer based in the area for at least a year. It would be a long-term intelligence operation, allowing him to build up little bits of information. South Armagh was recognised as a very, very hard target, and the intelligence officer must have imagination, determination, an ability to adapt and '. . . be reasonably brave. I would put his chances of surviving his tour of a year at less than 50 per cent.'

Nairac was posted to south Armagh about two years after that report was written, and when he arrived at Crossmaglen he asked for freedom to move around unrestricted. This was promptly refused by the local company commander. Nairac accepted this for the time being, although it was an indication of his unorthodox views. At Crossmaglen he was seen as someone with a personal crusade. Whenever any young people were brought into the base, he always made sure he talked to them. What he was hoping to do was to cut off the supply of young people into what he called 'the IRA drainpipe'; young people who were joining because of the way they were treated by the system or because they felt 'big' to have a gun. Nairac did not pretend to be a local: his English middle-class upbringing, with an education at Ampleforth and Oxford, would not have helped him there. He could, however, produce a passable Irish accent which gave him superficial cover. Sometimes alone, and sometimes with another officer he would visit pubs, mostly after hours, to sit and chat. It was not so much that he was trying to gain direct information as such — nobody was that open — but rather he was listening as locals expressed their feelings about events and the security forces in particular. On night back at base he sat up till three in the morning talking to a fellow officer. He had a premonition that he was going to be killed. 'I've got this feeling that I'm going to get the chop here,' he said. 'They are after me. They realise I am getting through to the young people and they know — or think they know — who I am. My only real worry is that someone looks after my dog.'

Worried or not he did not stop what he was doing. When a new unit arrived Nairac persuaded the commander to let him out without an escort or an adequate back-up unit. The commander presumed that with his long experience Nairac knew what he was doing. It was a fatal error by both of them. That Saturday night Nairac went alone to the Three Steps pub at Drumintree. It is a rather ugly, modern bungalow and it stands on a lonely crossroads in a high valley and is visible for miles around. It was crowded and noisy, with music playing and drink flowing. At some stage of the evening he was persuaded to go outside where six or eight men were waiting for him. They were Provisionals who had mistaken him for a 'Sticky' — an Official IRA man. Alone, and with no back-up patrol close by waiting for an emergency call from him, Nairac was overpowered after a furious struggle. The most obvious sign of this was the broken glass and a trail of blood found later in the pub car park.

The border is very close here and Nairac was immediately taken across it, away from any possible contact with Army or police patrols. According to the men who were later charged with his murder he kept trying to escape and was badly beaten up in the process. At one stage he actually managed to get a revolver off one of them which would have given him a chance of fighting his way out. Unfortunately it was not his own and it misfired. Bloodied but unbowed, he maintained his cover to the end, conduct which brought admiration, and death, from his captors who could not make up their minds whether he was a 'Sticky' or from the SAS. When they finally decided to kill him, one pretended to be a priest but this did not fool Nairac. They did, however, let him say his prayers before they shot him through the head. His body was never found.

Robert Nairac was eventually, and posthumously, awarded the George Cross. An officer involved in writing his citation explained that the rules were very strict. 'Before we made the award we just had to know whether he had given away any information when he was tortured. We found he had not.'

A long time later a friend recalled that Nairac had always been prepared to go into pubs in south Armàgh and join in a singing session. ' "Well, Danny, how about you giving us one?" someone would call out, and he would. He was always known as Danny. That's why it was so nostalgic when the choir at his memorial service sang the Londonderry Air. You know, some of my soldiers cried when they heard about his death.'

The manner of Nairac's death, however, pointed out the growing animosity between the Army and the police in this border area; an animosity which was to come to a climax two years later. 'There was no purpose his action could have served,' a senior police officer remarked tartly. 'He was a liaison officer and certainly he had not been tasked by the RUC Special Branch as all those operations were supposed to be. He was a bit of a cowboy!'

Undercover work and covert Observations Posts were becoming much more a pattern of military operations; and not just in the border areas. One commander in Belfast was convinced that the best and most effective way to dominate an area was to watch it from an unseen position. In one case hidden soldiers waited for six weeks before they shot a gunman and recovered his weapon. In another operation they lay up in a garage for three weeks and again shot and captured a gunman with his weapon. They had four intercepts during their tour and were successful in three. A company commander recalled:

> They said we couldn't get a covert OP into the Ardoyne. I said we could. We went round systematically unbricking and then bricking up again all the derelict houses.
>
> There were plenty of them! There was one opposite the Shamrock pub. When we bricked that one up we left two soldiers in there — for three weeks! When they came out they had almost lost the circulation in their legs, but the information they got was fantastic!

Bit by bit, the structure erected by Merlyn Rees to encourage political progress was removed by Roy Mason. Not for him the elaborate chain of communications which kept his office in touch with Republican and Protestant paramilitary groups. Even Laneside, the plush and heavily-guarded house on the shores of the Belfast Lough, scene of many secret meetings, was now up for sale.

In June 1977, Mason announced his new security policy. The Army was to be used more for undercover work, and the enforcement of conventional law and order was to be left to the police. Specialisation, rather than just numbers, would be the key to Army success. The first proper Army/police joint operations room was set up in North Queen Street in Belfast, with police on duty twenty-four hours a day. While the overall policy was not new, Mason freshened it up by adding greater weight to the no-jury, single-judge Diplock courts. Sentences were increased: for conspiracy to murder — life; for certain explosive offences — life; for membership of an illegal organisation — ten years.

It was also decided to increase the full-time establishment of the police and the UDR, an emphatic reminder that they were now expected to bear the brunt of the security operations. Indeed, examples of this had already been seen, notably in the successful way they dealt with another Protestant workers' strike attempt led by Ian Paisley, who hoped that it would have the same dramatic effect as the UWC strike in 1974 which brought down the Executive. Again this was a direct attack on the structure of the state. This time the reaction of the authorities was very different — almost a rebuff to an Army attitude expressed some time earlier by one officer, who had refused to allow his men to interfere to stop Protestant violence unless he was specifically asked to do so by the police. 'If they can't do it in the Orange areas,' he had declared to a *Times* reporter, 'then they cannot do it anywhere. It must be seen whether they have the capability.'

The RUC had, of course, been working towards this under Ken Newman. To raise the riot control capability of his men had been one priority. By the time of this attempted strike in 1977, they were not even 20 per cent of the way through that programme, but the little progress they had made helped enormously. Newman had been convinced back in 1974 that people had been outraged by the failure of the Army — then in control — and the police to deal with the barricades manned by teenage thugs. After a while the people had come to accept the situation. It was, he felt, a matter of public perception and he was determined that this attempt to repeat the success would not go the same way. He had sent down a very clear message to all his men along these lines. A sub-divisional commander recalled:

> He came round to see us. I told him that if we moved against the Protestants the whole place would go up in flames . . . that there would be the most fantastic backlash. He just said, 'You have no discretion in the matter. If there is a barricade it will be removed. If you feel you can't do it, I shall want to know why — personally.' My God! I was terrified — but it worked!

What was more, Newman made sure that his men were seen to be doing this. Knowing that they were about to remove a particularly large and well-known barricade in the Newtownards Road, he had that information passed directly to the newsrooms of the local television stations. He knew it would then also appear on the national news bulletins. What Newman was doing was banking on the professionalism of the police outweighing any sectarian bias they might have, and it was paying off. The police were on their way. The Army, too, was this time backing the police. One officer who had seen what had happened in 1974 was determined that as far as his patch was concerned the Army would make itself felt. He mobilised his battalion transport to give people lifts and made sure that every barricade erected was removed as quickly as possible. He recounted how he was in Tennant Street Police Station briefing Kenneth Newman on some crowds gathering in the Shankill Road. An officer up at the Ballylumford power station came through to say that the power workers were coming out. They were joining the strike, which meant real trouble. 'Newman didn't bat an eyelid,' he said. 'He went on talking about other matters. Ten minutes later the officer came on again. He said the men were not coming out on strike, but protesting for twenty minutes because they had been intimidated to strike. Again, Newman didn't bat an eyelid. Great! In disaster or triumph, just the same!'

Another example of the way in which the police were taking the lead was rather more violent — the death of three police officers in County Tyrone. A year earlier their presence in an unmarked saloon on that road would have been unthinkable; only the Army would have patrolled there. It showed how much the position had changed, and so did the shooting-up of a plain clothes police patrol in the heart of Republican Andersonstown, in Belfast. This was the sort of loss which caused officers at Lisburn to murmur, 'Very brave chaps, but they're just not ready for that sort of work.'

Despite these setbacks, the general number of bombings, shootings and killings had been reduced. Information was flowing better through the revitalised body of the RUC. Intelligence sources reckoned that the Provisionals were now some 20 to 25 per cent less effective than they had been the year before. However, they were still holding on. There was no call for a cease-fire and in their killing of members of the security forces they were maintaining their average rate, although the emphasis had switched to the local forces. Their changing organisation was allowing them to be flexible, and when they were badly hit they were more likely to say, 'Let's change our tactics.'

The police were also making inroads into the ranks of the Protestant paramilitary forces. Heavy sentences in the courts were acting as a deterrent, and there was less grassroots pressure for them to go out and kill people. A UVF man said, quite simply, 'The police are doing too well.' In fact it was only a shortage of staff that kept them from interrogating as many as they would have liked.

On the military side, pressure now began to grow from both the MOD and NATO for a sizeable force reduction. However, the stranglehold had to be kept tight for a while longer because this was Jubilee Year and the Queen was coming to visit the province. Any Provisional success would be not only embarrassing but also a severe setback to the new policy. For her to come was, of course, a political decision taken by Mason and one which could be appreciated by the Army. To them it was a measure of his directness. 'It was his neck in the hole,' said one senior officer. 'If he had any doubts about her coming, I certainly never heard of them.'

From the start, Newman made it quite clear that this was to be a police operation with the Army in support. Nothing was left to chance, and the Spearhead battalion — the Scots Guards — was flown over. The authorities were used to staging operations on a constant war footing, and they knew that the Queen was hardly likely to be walking up the Falls Road. 'But we even had a contingency plan for a maniac striking out of the blue,' emphasised a policeman. In fact the Queen came ashore only twice — both times by helicopter, which for her was a rare event. She visited the heavily guarded former governor's residence, Hillsborough, outside Belfast, and went further north to the New University of Ulster at Coleraine. There were none of the traditional walkabouts, no lines of cheering people, no posies thrust hopefully towards her. In more peaceful times she might have toured up through the Glens of Antrim, looking across to the Scottish coast only a few miles away. She might have gone the Giant's Causeway, one of the world's natural wonders, where an astonishing complex of thousands of basalt columns, many six-sided and twelve metres high, lead from the foot of the cliffs and disappear into the sea. She might also have cruised on Lough Erne, a huge, beautiful expanse of water studded with tiny islands. She missed all these as well as many of the ugly sights of a country ravaged by years of violence — the bombed buildings, the barbed wire, the concrete pillboxes outside the police stations and her own police and soldiers, heavily armed, warily patrolling the streets. Surrounded and guarded by them, however, she was at least able to come. 'Newman carried it off splendidly and with great personal determination,' commented a Lisburn officer admiringly. 'There were a lot of us Army around, but it was only to show willing.'

The attrition rate against the Provisional IRA and the Protestant thugs was now high. The police were beginning to find their feet and by the end of the year Roy Mason was jubilant. He told the *Daily Express:*

> We are squeezing the terrorists like rolling up a toothpaste tube. We are squeezing them out of their safe havens. We are squeezing them away from their money supplies. We are squeezing them out of society and into prison.

By the end of the year there was a new GOC, Lieutenant-General Timothy Creasey. He was very much an operational commander with extensive experience from campaigns in Burma, Iran, Iraq, Italy and Greece and more recently in Kenya, Aden and the Oman; he had just finished a period as Director of Infantry at Warminster. He arrived at a time the Army was trying to adjust to its new role in support of the police and finding that it was not easy. While Sir David House had supported the new policy, 'even if he was led to it by Merlyn', as someone remarked, Creasey had his reservations. This was not a role in which he felt comfortable. One reason why he had been picked for the job was that he was thought to be capable of improving the morale of soldiers at a time when many were leaving the Army because of poor pay and conditions. It was felt that in Northern Ireland of all places they needed a strong commander who could look after them.

After a very short time Creasey was making his views known. A guest at one reception he attended remembered him talking at length about the need to 'stop messing around and take out the terrorists'. Asked how he had dealt with the matter in Oman, he said they 'just disappeared'. He was told that this might be all right in Oman, with an endless desert in which to bury evidence, but that in Hooker Street, where he would have to dig through the tarmac, it would not be so easy.

This incident was a sign of problems to come between the Army and the police but for the moment it seemed as if some of the most deeply ingrained aspects of terrorism were yielding to the new policy. Civilian deaths, shootings and bombings had dropped. So too had deaths amongst the security forces, though not to the same degree. The police were pleased with the rate of attrition; the Army was cautious, readily admitting that they were not losing the war, but equally aware that in the past optimists had written off the Provisionals only to see them resurrected. Indeed, Roy Mason himself had to be taken on one side by a senior adviser and told quite bluntly to keep quiet about 'the Provisionals' being beaten. Too many times people had died after such announcements.

When reductions in troops were announced, Lisburn expressed reservations, feeling that their men were being spread too thinly on the ground. The police, however, were adamant that they could cope, pointing out that the Army no longer saturated an area after an incident but cordoned it off while the police and detectives went in. The police were quick to point out that this often resulted in much earlier arrests on hard evidence rather than a chance pick-up years later. Of eight men suspected of killing two soldiers in June, for instance, six were behind bars and awaiting trial only five months later.

At the end of the first full year of the new policy the Chief Constable, Kenneth Newman, said: '1977 will undoubtedly stand out as [a year] in which the police, with the support of the Army, made an enormous effort to reduce violence.'

For the Army, the year had been fraught with difficulty and strain. Moving from the leading role, which they had held for so long, was not something many officers found easy. It was not so much that they disagreed with the principle of police primacy, but rather that they felt the police were not ready for it. Lisburn had long accepted that there was no military solution to a problem which had its roots deep in the economic, social and political complexities of the past. However, they felt it was essential to have close civil and military cooperation so that there could be one central policy; a policy which would not underestimate the ability of small groups of armed men gaining support by threats, nor fail to realise that such a campaign was, on both sides, a 'war for the minds of the people'.

Some officers at Lisburn were keen to see a sort of system implemented which had been outlined by Frank Kitson in a book published that year called *Bunch of Five*. This did not refer specifically to Northern Ireland; with the campaign still going on this would have ruffled too many feathers. There seemed little doubt, however, that he had Northern Ireland firmly in mind when he put forward a 'sound framework' as the first requirement for a counter-insurgency campaign. Within this framework he suggested that there should be close coordination at every level; arrangements so that insurgents did not win the 'war for the minds of the people'; a suitable intelligence organisation; and a legal system adapted to the needs of the campaign. He wrote:

I have no doubt that a system can be devised in each of these four spheres which will be capable of achieving the aim, but I am equally sure that such systems can only be implemented with great difficulty on most occasions, and it may even happen that sometimes the best system can only be obtained by the payment of too high a price. It would then be safer for the government to accept a less good one and endure the prolongation of its troubles. This is naturally a political decision and providing it is made by the government in full knowledge of the likely consequences then it is up to all concerned to accept it.

Lisburn still felt uneasy with the police in control, and did not really feel that the Government had accepted the 'likely consequences'. Before long there was to be an incident which they felt only went to support their views. With the clampdown on explosives coming over the border, the Provisionals had now turned to using blast incendiary devices. These were produced by mixing crystallised ammonium nitrate with aluminium filings and fixing containers of this concoction to cans of petrol. The results were spectacular and devastating. The inexpensive and easily-concealed bomb would produce an ever-expanding fireball which would engulf a building long before any fireman could reach it, and then cause a fire which would be extremely difficult to control. A couple of pounds of this mixture would do the same amount of damage as a 400lb bomb of conventional explosives.

In February 1978 the Provisionals picked the La Mon House hotel near Comber in County Down in which to plant one of these bombs. It was about 10 miles from Belfast, and had a popular restaurant which on Fridays was always packed. The Provisional unit fixed the bomb to a window and gave a warning too late for anyone to act on it. Along with the blast that shattered and smashed objects and people alike came the terrible fireball, burning whatever was left and incinerating bodies out of all recognition. Twelve people died in this holocaust, and many more were badly injured. There was outrage from all quarters, and the Provisionals were forced to admit publicly that they had caused civilian deaths. However, they made no attempt to express remorse. The *Republican News* stated:

> There is nothing we can offer in mitigation bar that our enquiries have established that a nine-minute warning was given to the RUC. This was proved totally inadequate given the disastrous consequences. . . . All killings stem from British interference and from their denial of Irish sovereignty.

The Provisionals did not call off their fire-bomb campaign. The next day they hit the Ulster bus depot in Londonderry, burning sixteen buses and causing £500,000 worth of damage. This time no one was injured. The attacks were a chilling reminder that the high-risk policy of the RUC was indeed living up to its name.

Phase Eight
The Provisionals strike back — the Army wants control
March 1978–August 1979

. . . The food's gash . . .why can't we go and kick ten bells out of them?
. . . not another change! . . . this is the worst unit I've ever been in for
— tactics, patrol routine, sport, . . . change this, change that, boots on
. . . boots off, greasepits, films, fatigues . . . another lousy write-up in
Visor . . . rounds again . . . no prior warning . . . no eggs for banjos . . .
the goffa waller is expensive . . . why can't we hot pursuit this, that and
the other? . . . hand this in . . . sign for that . . . call that entertainment!
. . . not another visit . . . Groundhog's chewed the volleyball . . . E
company do it this way . . . F company get away with that . . . we used
to do it this way in 45 . . . SIB investigations . . . the info from Int is
rubbish . . . the search teams can't do their jobs . . . getting no sleep . . .
sanger duty . . . pongos . . . broken washing machines . . . get a hair cut
. . . Well, nobody asked you to join up!

So 41 Commando Royal Marines reported in *Spring in Springfield*
in March 1978, and the 'dripping' or moaning of soldiers was just the
same as it had always been and meant just about as little. They came
back, time and time again, wondering if things would have changed,
only to find that they were much the same. In four months one
company in West Belfast arrested over 100 people, searched 150
houses, 2,000 cars and twice as many people. They also provided a
football ground for the local boys' side, gave first aid to a child who
had drunk a bottle of Jeyes Fluid, ordered several ambulances and
fire engines, replaced an Alsatian dog they had run over by accident,
rebuilt two fences and visited Bushmills Irish Whiskey Distillery.
Behind the scenes there were changes, and many stemming from

a particular moment about two years before when detainees were being released from the Maze Prison. For two men it meant the chance to revamp and remodel the Provisional IRA along the lines of a modern terrorist movement. A great deal of research was done which led to new techniques and a much improved internal security system. The result of all this labour was just beginning to make itself felt, and was to be seen at its most bloody some eighteen months later.

'When Creasey arrived as GOC, he soon identified the nature and potential threat early on,' explained one of his officers, 'and he wanted a change of emphasis in the security policy.' In its simplest terms this would ensure that soldiers were employed as soldiers and policemen as policemen, for he had already found this distinction blurred and it worried him. He could see RUC patrols operating in a 'military but uncoordinated' manner which inevitably meant that they were identified as targets by an increasingly professional Provisional IRA and paying the penalty in casualties. Moreover, Lisburn felt that there were great difficulties to be faced in using a police force which had more than doubled in size within a decade to take over the role of the Army. The police was not a mobile force, able to deploy easily to areas where it was needed. It was pointed out, for instance, that stations like Coleraine and Ballymena were overmanned, while others like Newry, 'in the thick of the fight', were desperately short of policemen. It was the attempt to achieve a proper rationalisation of these problems — as Lisburn saw them — that caused the difficulties in overall command which were to touch on many events in the coming months.

The position was not greatly helped by the differing personalities of the two men at the top. Creasey was a tough, operational commander, used to the ultimate responsibility of running a war in a remote part of the Persian Gulf. Newman was a tough, intellectual policeman, with an external law degree from London University and a sound knowledge of social demography, which is an advanced, systematic method of getting to know a beat. He was determined to get his way and keep the dominant role in the security operation by running a police force in an increasingly modern, sophisticated manner.

As a chief constable, Newman was constitutionally independent and not under orders from Westminster or Stormont. This was not a position he chose to camouflage in any way, and some officers found it galling when the police made it obvious that they were 'answerable only to the law', even to the extent of sometimes resenting political direction from the Secretary of State or the Northern Ireland office. To some officers it seemed that, far from attempting to alleviate the friction between the police and the Army, the NIO sometimes, 'for their own reasons, played one off against the other — a sort of Divide and Rule.' But to others the silly thing seemed to be that on a personal and social level the two men, Creasey and Newman, got on rather well. Newman had always said that there were very few Army officers with whom he could not get on, on a personal level. Professionally, however, it was very different, and they did clash, and went on clashing, with Creasey bridling at the thought of Newman even suggesting that as chief constable he was in a position to control the Army, instead of having it in support.

These differences often arose because the classic position of the Army in support of the police was not always understood by policemen. The position was that the police detailed the task and the Army decided how it should be done. Occasionally the police would annoy the Army by telling soldiers what to do. The police might, for instance, ask for a route to be kept open, but then go on to say that two companies should do the job. That, however, was a military decision, and for the police to forget this division could mean difficulties, at any level, from the GOC down to the young platoon commander or the corporal on the ground.

The soldier did not so much want tougher physical freedom as a tougher mental approach. One border commander explained his feelings by describing an incident in which a petrol tanker had been hijacked and left 2,000 yards from his position. He decided to leave it where it was, despite pleadings from the RUC to get it moved.

> They said it was a danger to the village. I said that was the IRA's problem; they had put it there and they could move it. Then I went out and put six armour-piercing rounds through the engine block and the tyres — hoping to Christ my soldiers wouldn't shoot through the petrol tank on the back! It sat there for most of my tour and blocked off at least one IRA escape route. But the RUC weren't very happy about it!

The Provisionals were emerging as a much more professional force, as a secret Army intelligence report was to show the next year. They had reorganised their structure and rethought their strategy, coming up with what was described later as a policy of gaining political control 'with an Armalite in one hand and a ballot box in the other.' Their success rate grew, becoming the catalyst for the Protestant Loyalist backlash and putting additional pressures on the RUC and to a lesser extent the UDR. Again Lisburn argued that while police primacy was the right policy in principle, it was the timing of it that mattered. 'When terrorism is ebbing, then that is the time for the police to take over,' one officer explained. 'But if as you implement this policy the tide of terrorism starts to rise, this will bring all sorts of difficulties and you must think again.'

The police watched all this soul-searching by Lisburn with some interest. The new GOC was quite different from his predecessor, impatient with what was happening and looking for a good, strong, determined policy with clarity about its objectives. 'But it was a far more subtle and delicate operation we were engaged in,' observed a police officer. 'We began to wonder whether Creasey fully appreciated this.'

What Creasey realised was that the attrition rate had fallen and the Provisional success rate had risen. The La Mon bomb had reinforced his belief that the police were not ready to carry this new policy through, although the delay in warning had been caused by a faulty telephone kiosk. He felt that in the circumstances the new policy was potentially dangerous, in that it reduced the influence of his troops, but despite the MOD being happy to allow a GOC to pursue his own course, he was unable to halt this change, though he perhaps slowed it down a little.

Since control of security had passed to the police, the Army had slipped more into the background and was concentrating very much on covert operations. The result was a series of deaths starting in late 1977, a number of them innocent people. James Taylor, a 23-year-old wildfowler, was shot one Saturday night in November after he had been out shooting for the day. Billy Hanna, leader of an Orange band from North Belfast, was killed while walking home from a pub with a friend. A stake-out of soldiers fired on a group of bombers arriving to plant a bomb at Ballysillan Post Office. Hanna and his friend dived for the hedge but Hanna was fatally wounded. Three of the terrorist bombers were also killed and one escaped by car. Another terrorist was killed collecting bombs from a hideout staked out by soldiers. The police worried about these stake-outs, and particularly the fact that innocent people were being killed. Then came an incident which showed very clearly that a definite antagonism was growing between the Army and the police.

In July 1978, 16-year-old John Boyle went into the village graveyard at Dunloy, in County Antrim, hoping that on the headstones he might find some interesting information about his family. Unfortunately he found something very different. Hidden by one of the graves he came across a polythene package which contained an Armalite. He immediately told his father, who contacted the police, and a decision was made to stake out the graveyard in case someone came to collect the weapons.

That night four SAS troopers were briefed by the police. Three times a detective constable warned them that the boy's family might approach the site because they were working in adjacent fields, and that they should be very careful. He said later that he thought the soldiers did not pay much attention to what he was saying. Sergeant Bohan, who was to lead the SAS patrol, had already been to the graveyard with the detective constable, and his impression was that he had been told the boy's family would not return.

Early next morning the family was telephoned by the police and told not to go near the place. But it was too late. Young John Boyle was still curious about his find and went back to have another look. Well hidden round the grave was the four-man patrol waiting for a terrorist coming to retrieve his weapons. The soldiers knew that the rifle was one which had been used in three murders and eight murder attempts, including attacks on the police. When they saw the boy approach, two of them prepared to fire. 'I did not challenge him,' one of them explained later in court, 'because of the possibility of other terrorists surrounding him. He started to remove the rifle from the bag and turned — bringing it to bear on us. We fired and he fell.'

The boy's brother was haymaking in the next field. He raced across to see what had happened and was promptly arrested. The boy's father then arrived, having just been warned on the telephone about the stake-out. He was also arrested. Two hours later the Army announced that three terrorists had been stopped by a uniformed Army patrol and one had been shot dead. The other two were being held. The police did not deny this but warned reporters that it was not all as simple as it looked.

By mid-afternoon the police had announced that the Boyle family had no connection with any terrorist organisation. From that moment the full weight of the law was bound to fall on the troopers who had fired, and indeed they were brought to trial — for murder.

The trial was only the second in ten years in which a soldier had been charged with murder while on operations — and the first involving the SAS. The police investigation had been motivated, quite correctly, by a need to get at the truth and maybe by some guilt that the warning to the family had come too late to save the boy. There was no doubt, though, about police anger over the affair; anger both at yet another killing by soldiers in stake-out, and at the apparent immunity of the Army. The atmosphere of the courtroom changed noticeably so that the case became almost a trial not so much of murder but of the policy that had put the soldiers with their blackened faces and high velocity weapons there in the first place. The mutual suspicion of the police and the Army came through clearly. The detective constable bristled with indignation when it was suggested that he had told the Army the name of his informant — or given personal information about other Catholic families. Time and time again his answers started with the phrase 'I did not tell the Army. . . .' His superior, a chief inspector, was more forthcoming and said that he had offered to brief the four troopers who were going to the graveyard but the Army had declined. It appeared the police were anxious to protect their patch, and the Army to protect its tactics. To an observer it seemed that the Army really did feel above the law. When the soldiers were first questioned they were named to the detectives only by initial letters. When they first came to court they were named but not identified, five other men crowding into the dock with them. Only after strong protests were they properly identified on their second appearance in court.

The prosecution alleged that the boy had been shot in the back, but their expert witness had grave doubts cast on his evidence and the troopers were acquitted. Because of the importance of the case, the Chief Justice of Northern Ireland, Lord Lowry, was himself taking it. He told the court that he found the SAS sergeant an untrustworthy witness. He had been quite definite that the plan was to capture whoever came to the cache, but had been vague when questioned about the details of the plan. The soldiers must have seen the boy take up the rifle, and Lord Lowry felt it strange that they had done nothing about it at that stage. In fact the rifle was unloaded, but while the boy did not attack or consciously menace the soldiers, Lord Lowry concluded that, 'Unless they knew the rifle was unloaded, they may well have believed their lives to be in danger.'

Commenting on the case afterwards, the GOC, Lieutenant-General Creasey, said:

I have never doubted that the two NCOs who were on an operation properly mounted at the request of the RUC acted in good faith. The dilemma that these two NCOs faced making their split-second decision is one that can face every soldier in the province at any time. They know that any of their actions can be subjected to the full scrutiny of the law. But they have learned to live with the constraints made by the rules of *sub judice*, which have to be accepted, often in the face of wild allegations.

There was anger from some people at the acquittal and the Northern Ireland Civil Rights Association complained, as did the SDLP spokesman on law and order, Michael Canavon. For many months he had been campaigning against what he called the 'Kill, don't question' policy of the Army. 'John Boyle was a victim of a policy that continues to menace life in Northern Ireland,' he said. 'This is a nefarious policy that creates a new dimension in law — SAS law.' It was not a happy situation for anyone — the public, the police or the Army.

The Chiefs-of-Staff in London were now concerned about events in Northern Ireland for two reasons. First, by the command of control and second, the whole matter of the police having responsibility for security. It was very clear to them that the Army and the police were not working together as they should, particularly in the border areas of south Armagh, where there was great pressure on the security forces. 'They were difficult days,' observed a senior civil servant. 'The police and Army never seemed to compare notes. Things were at their very worst. A lot of people were being killed . . . a lot of bombs going off . . . it was a pretty nasty scene.'

A series of reports was ordered by the Chiefs-of-Staff to see how the Army's technological capabilities could be improved, to question whether it had the right posture and to examine ways in which it could improve its overall performance. It was emphasised that what was wanted in these reports were ideas for additional methods which would add considerable impact to the campaign: nothing that would conflict with the policy of police primacy, but rather something that would fit into it. There was a distinct irritation with what was felt to be the failure of the politicians and the NIO successfully to bridge the gap between policy and its implementation. The Army chiefs wanted clear direction on Government policy, not a number of different interpretations.

A stream of ideas came back to the MOD. Among them was one for a supremo-type figure who could coordinate police, civil and Army operations. The Chiefs-of-Staff liked this idea; what they had in mind was a supreme commander of the kind Templar had been in Malaysia — maybe not with such sweeping powers as a commander-in-chief would have over civil affairs, but certainly over the military and the police. Above all he would be the 'great decision-maker', and the man who would coordinate the intelligence operations. 'The advice going to the Secretary of State from the Army and the police,' explained a senior officer, 'was in some cases wildly different. I am not blaming Creasey necessarily, because the police were very jealous about asking for help, but it was a time when relations were at their very worst. Something had to be done!'

Another proposition put forward was hot pursuit across the border into the Republic. It was a constant plea from border commanders. A company commander explained why he felt it was so necessary:

> I chased one group down to the border. I was in a helicopter and we had two vehicles following on the ground. They made it across just ahead of us and then they got out of their vehicles, with their weapons, and waved. One of my men had just been shot and I was damn certain it was this lot who'd done it.

Another idea was for selective detention. The paper suggested twenty names as a priority for arrest. There was a second list of some forty names which the Army would consider a 'bonus' if they were allowed to pick them up. Yet another request was for direct communication across the border with both the Gardai and the Irish Army. These ideas were passed on to the politicians at Westminster, notably the Conservative spokesman on Northern Ireland, Airey Neave, but nothing came of any of them. To give such power to the Army would look far too much like waging total war, and it was not a scenario they wished to support.

It was not an easy situation for all the 'young Turks' under Creasey's command who were full of bright ideas and champing at the bit to get going. They resented being tied up in barracks when in their opinion they could be sorting out the situation so that they could then go home, or back to NATO or Germany, and do all the other things which they wanted to do. This sort of life was going too slowly for them, and many were aghast at the way the police seemed — to them — to be blundering bravely but foolishly into the most dangerous areas, not only in the strongly Republican areas of West Belfast and Londonderry but particularly in south Armagh — or Bandit Country, as it had become known.

The police, however, believed firmly that they should be in these areas and that the Army was wrong not to patrol in vehicles but only by helicopter and then on foot; it gave the Provisionals an undue advantage. They drew an imaginary line between Bessbrook and Newtownhamilton and below that, in what they considered dangerous country, they patrolled in unmarked police cars. They had no casualties in these patrols below this line, although they lost four policemen just to the north of it. A senior police officer observed:

> Understandably this sort of thing bugged Tim Creasey. He did not feel you could have two forces operating in one area and he regarded this area as black — in other words a military area only. Our analysis was different for we regarded this area as the key to our whole policy.

The police argued that, apart from anything else, cross-border communication was vital, and that this could not be achieved between the two Armies. The Gardai patrolling in the South would, understandably, feel rather annoyed if there were no RUC men immediately across the border to whom they could talk. The RUC therefore had to mount patrols and be seen in the area, and while they knew that this was not the way the Army would have managed matters, they went ahead.

The Army had now been around doing the same work for nine years, and in August the *Daily Mirror* ran an editorial which showed a definite switch in policy and put it out of step with every other leading national newspaper. It called for the Government to announce a decision to withdraw from Northern Ireland within a period of five years. Up to this time the paper had been hoping and supporting the idea that eventually the troubles would be cured; that there would be a political solution or that the Army would defeat the Provisional IRA. The paper felt that the situation had changed since the Army came in 'in aid of the civil power', and came to the conclusion that the English were part of the Irish problem and therefore not in a position to solve it. Only the Irish could do this, which necessarily entailed a British withdrawal. There was no criticism of the Army in this — indeed they felt the soldiers had 'behaved magnificiently'. It was more to do with a feeling round the world, and particularly in America, that while British troops were still in Northern Ireland a solution would mean their actual defeat. A senior editor explained:

> India is a parallel. Once again it is the old idea — Dr Johnson's argument — that nothing concentrates the mind so much as knowing you are to be hanged in the morning. It is brutal! But if Ireland had been up the coast of Africa we would have been out generations ago.

This did not strike a responsive chord with the Army. Although large parts of the province might seem peaceful, Lisburn was well aware that it was still confronted by a 'very effective, ruthless organisation' and that the Army was needed to back up the police efforts. One commander put it like this:

> I believe very strongly that if we just walk out and say 'Stuff it! Let the police carry on' they just could not operate. That is why we are here. It would be anarchy if we walked out, and a tremendous victory for an illegal organisation. The rule of law must win. We must work by it and obey it. The Army provides the back-up for this and it is, in my view, democracy working. If we walk out we are forsaking democracy. It is as simple as that!

The debate took hold for a while, but it was announced that the Army would be staying for the foreseeable future. Efforts would, however, be made to cut down on numbers while boosting police operations. Two battalions were removed from the streets as the Army went over to still more covert and surveillance operations, and a number of bases were knocked down. All that was needed now was a reserve which could go out and support the police when necessary to carry out essential tasks which the police could not do. That was the reasoning in some quarters. Others felt it was far too rosy a picture.

The Provisionals were now putting out feelers to other, similar organisations round the world, and for this they used the Sinn Fein Bureau for Foreign Affairs. They had contact with the West German-

Ireland Solidarity Committee; they had some contact with the PLO (two Irish names had been found in a PLO camp in the Lebanon); they tried contact with Cuba, but this was unsuccessful. They certainly had contact with Libya: arms seized on board the *Claudia* in 1973 had come from there, though supplies since then had been sparse. They had also welcomed Iranians as visiting pressmen attending IRA funerals. Possibly their best contacts were with the Basques, who had rather shocked them by being highly critical of their policy of shooting low-ranking soldiers. 'Kill the judges, generals and top ministers,' they were told. 'Go for the big personalities.' Contact with the Soviet bloc was slight, though for the first time AK47 rifles and Russian hand grenades were beginning to appear.

All this was part of the searching reappraisal that the Provisionals had been forced to make as the Army and police whittled away at their organisation. The two men who had been released from the Maze and who had started the reorganisation of the movement had convinced them that the 'one more heave' syndrome was unrealistic. The British were not just going to pull out. The armed struggle would go on, but there would now be new paths which could lead to the same end result for which they worked.

While security had been improved, the traditional battalion and brigade structure had gone to be replaced by small, four-man Active Service Units (ASUs). In these separate, tightly disciplined cells, only the leader would have access to one of nine operation officers, each responsible for a small number of ASUs. There were also specialised cells for sniping, executions, bombings and robberies. They would operate as often as possible outside their own areas in order to confuse British Intelligence. This was something the Provisional IRA had often talked about doing, but had yet to achieve. In the opinion of a number of intelligence officers, it was a system which did not fit easily with the gregarious nature of the Irish.

However, the idea was that by reorganising themselves along these lines, the Provisionals would become less dependent on public support, and less vulnerable to penetration by informers. These efforts did have an initial effect of improving security, and the number of arrests dropped by some 500-600 a year. The overall level of violence also dropped. 1977 and 1978 had been good years for attrition against the Provisional IRA. 1979, however, was a bad year and the falling attrition rate was largely the result of the increasing professionalism of the Provisionals combined with the after-effects of the Bennett Report on police interrogation methods.

The factors leading to the setting up of the Bennett committee had roots running back to 1976. Since becoming chief constable, Newman had made it clear that he wanted convictions, and he wanted them within the law. Between then and 1979, some 3,000 people had been charged with terrorist offences, most of them after making confessions while in custody. But complaints of ill-treatment also rose and in that first year, for instance, there were 384 complaints of assault during interviews. There was mounting public concern at this, and after Amnesty International had inquired into seventy-eight cases of alleged ill-treatment at Northern Ireland interrogation centres, Newman himself asked for an inquiry, convinced that on the whole the injuries had been self-inflicted as part of a propaganda campaign to discredit the police.

Judge Harry Bennett QC, an English Crown Court Judge, headed the committee to inquire into the matter. In reaching its conclusions the committee went outside its terms of reference to mention that there had been cases where medical evidence had been produced concerning injuries sustained in police custody which were not self-inflicted. Two of its main recommendations were that closed-circuit television should be installed in interview rooms and that suspects should have access to a solicitor after forty-eight hours.

The RUC detectives resented this. They felt that the report had been wrongly interpreted and that assumptions had been made on scant evidence. They maintained that this had been borne out later by the Police Authority in Northern Ireland when they issued a public statement that, after a thorough examination of all the doctors' reports, their conclusion was that the whole affair had been grossly exaggerated. The police pointed out that all the interview rooms had been fitted with spy-holes and that senior officers regularly inspected them; that prison service doctors were provided with a 'hot line' direct to the chief constable; that prisoners were given the right to be examined by their own doctors and that every allegation of ill-treatment was detailed in a report to the Northern Ireland Director of Public Prosecutions — without any action being taken.

The effect, whether from the tightening of procedures or the lowering of police morale, meant a drop in the rate of convictions, as well as repercussions elsewhere. The police were furious when, in America, the authorities reacted to the report with Congress placing an embargo on the sale of 6,000 .357 pistols to the RUC. All these events happened at a critical time, because just at this moment the Provisional IRA reorganisation was making itself felt.

One Army officer felt that while some people may have been 'roughed up' during interrogation, the pendulum had now swung much too far the other way. He was not surprised that under these new rules confessions were not forthcoming. The first principle in obtaining a confession, he explained, was to create a dependency by the individual on the interrogator which was done partly through disorientation and partly through exhaustion. Those were the facts of life, and no one was likely to volunteer, 'This is my confession and you can now lock me up for seven years!' It was applying a standard of justice in Northern Ireland which did not apply in the rest of the country. He felt that if ministers responsible were actually relying on the people of Northern Ireland for votes they would take a very different attitude.

The Provisionals had by now realised that they, too, needed the support of the people to survive and documents captured in the Republic showed that the movement was now trying to build a bridge back into the community. Proposals had been drafted for a People's Court, a People's Council and a People's Militia. These would be involved in such activities as Co-ops to ease the high cost of living, in housing and in policing. In particular the Councils would be controlled by Republicans — after suitable elections — and groups with other leanings would be excluded or undermined.

To mark these changes they had chosen the occasion of the annual pilgrimage to the grave of Wolfe Tone at Bodenstown in the Republic, where Provisional and Official IRA and INLA members all kept well apart from each other, the old men of the past with weatherbeaten skin and crumpled suits and the young men of the present with hard faces and hard eyes. They would gather in the shadow of a ruined, ivy-covered church to the wailing of the Irish pipes and then listen to the orations. Standing amongst the scattered gravestones they would listen to the messages of the past, steeped in the tradition of Patrick Pearse, who claimed, when he founded his Irish Volunteers to fight the British and before he was executed in 1916, that 'bloodshed is a cleansing and sanctifying thing, and the nation which regards it as the final horror has lost its manhood.' Each year at Bodenstown the Provisionals made the effort to make some big announcement. This year they had chosen Jimmy Drumm —

whose uncompromisingly Republican wife Maire had been murdered in a Belfast hospital — to give the speech. It marked a significant turning point for the Republican movement.

> The British government [said Drumm] is committed to stabilising the Six Counties and is pouring in vast sums of money . . . to assure Loyalists and to secure from Loyalists support for a long haul against the IRA. We find that a successful war of liberation cannot be fought on the backs of the oppressed in the Six Counties, nor around the physical presence of the British Army. Hatred and resentment of the Army cannot sustain the war.

It was felt in some circles — notably the RUC — that the Army had seized on this speech and, coupling it with other intelligence, had projected it in a very military manner. In other words, the Army had accepted that the basic policies of the Provisionals would be carried out in a military manner; that knowing about their reorganisation and tying this in with Drumm's remarks about a 'long haul', they now saw an extremely efficient and deadly Provisional movement facing them.

This assessment was still to come out, although intelligence officers were aware of the changes in the Provisional IRA structure. The Provisionals had yet to make this fully felt and indeed in the autumn of that year a leading hard-liner was trying to justify a dramatic fall in their activity. In an article in *The Times* he blamed infiltration by British Intelligence and the efficiency of the Army's undercover operations.

> The fact of the matter is it is increasingly difficult to operate with impunity. In Belfast there are three helicopters in the air all the time in touch with plain clothes units on the streets. There are soldiers staked out in hiding places. It makes operations much more difficult.

In the matter of confidential documents going astray the Provisionals got their own back by getting hold of a secret Army assessment on Future Terrorist Trends. It had been written by a senior Army intelligence officer, Brigadier James Glover, was dated 15 December 1978, and marked 'Secret'. Glover stated that it was designed 'to sketch as best we can the terrorist background' which would be useful to those having to 'develop the counter-measures we will need in Northern Ireland over the next five years.' The long and detailed report made chilling reading and showed a much higher assessment of PIRA (the Army term for the Provisional IRA) capability than anyone had thought possible.

According to this assessment, which became commonly known as the Glover Report, the Army could see no prospect of any political change over the next five years which would remove PIRA's *raison d'être* and expected its campaign of violence to continue as long as the British remained. PIRA had the dedication and the sinews of war to raise violence intermittently, and even if 'peace' were restored the motivation for politically-inspired violence would remain. Moreover, PIRA would continue to recruit the members it needed because its youth wing, Fianna na h-Eireann, provided a substantial pool of young aspirants, nurtured in violence and eager to carry guns. There were also steady streams of men coming from the prisons as embittered and dedicated terrorists. While there was no charismatic leader to pull them together, and most of the recruits came from the working classes, there was no evidence to support the contention that the rank and file were mindless hooligans. PIRA now trained and used its members with care and for the most part the Active Service Units (ASUs) were manned by men of up to ten years' operational experience. They constantly learned from their mistakes, developing their expertise and becoming more professional and better able to use modern technology for terrorist purposes.

The report found that armed robbery was almost certainly the greatest source of income for PIRA, running at around £550,000 a year, with another £250,000 coming in from racketeering. Overseas remittances were much less, estimated at £120,000 a year, mainly from NORAID in America and a subsidiary in Canada. Pay was the largest outgoing, normal terrorist pay being £20 a week to supplement the dole. The Army estimated that there were probably some 250 terrorists drawing this money with another 60 getting as much as £40 a week, all adding up to £400,000 each year.

The Army thought that PIRA would have to rely increasingly on armed robbery to finance the purchase of weapons although they might get hold of a prestige weapon — maybe as a gift — such as a surface-to-air guided missile. There were doubts about the quality of the middle ranks in the North, but it was thought that the ASUs would grow to become PIRA's most offensive arm. At the lowest level there would be a lunatic fringe of young hooligans who would sometimes be involved in terrorism and keep the old sectarian fears alive.

Examining the strategy of PIRA, the Army found that while there had been frequent 'cowboy' and sectarian attacks in the past, the trend now was towards hitting the security forces and moving away from politically damaging attacks on the economy. It was also possible that PIRA saw itself as an 'army' and clung to the remnants of what it believed to be a military code of ethics. That constraint was often blurred but there had, for example, been few attacks on the families of soldiers or policemen. However, in the interests of publicity PIRA might well stage a few spectacular attacks to show that their normal low posture stemmed from restraint rather than weakness. As they became more sophisticated and more perceptive they might also try to implement a more systematic campaign of assassination, imitating terrorism in West Germany, Spain and Italy. There would certainly be a general trend towards more precise targeting using greater expertise.

Looking at likely trends in the acquisition and use of weapons, the report pointed out that while PIRA might well acquire machine-pistols, the Armalite and Remington Goodmaster were both suitable for close-quarter work and sniping.

> We expect the main development in the next five years to be better sights, including possibly a laser sighting aid and night vision aids. Weapon handling and tactics used, particularly in rural areas, will probably improve. The Provisionals may well attempt to step up their use of mortars. They may readopt the Mk 6 or similar weapons for ranges up to 1,200 metres and the Mk 9 for ranges under 300 metres. Similarly PIRA will probably continue to attempt to obtain commercial mortars. The RPG-7 may well reappear for attacks on armoured vehicles and possibly security force bases or prisons. Although in general we expect the Provisionals to concentrate on simple weaponry, some anti-aircraft missiles may well be in their hands before the end of the period.

It was a gloomy document in view of the fact that many people thought the Provisionals were on the run. It certainly did nothing to back up Roy Mason's rather cocky claims that 'We are squeezing the terrorists like rolling up a toothpaste tube'. It showed an amazing and very disturbing gap between what the Government was saying in public and what they must obviously have been told by the Army in private, despite the disparaging view taken of it by the police. A senior police officer commented:

> Intelligence did suggest that the Provisionals would now be able to

maintain a sustained and protracted operation, but the whole report was much too pessimistic. You see, the intelligence officer who wrote it wasn't working in Ireland at the time and his report was written from the rather narrow standpoint of the future equipment and ordnance needs of the Army. Now, when people are addressing supply questions they do not take an optimistic view because that would hardly assist requisitions for new and better equipment. So that report was strictly slanted. It was not a general assessment but one to assist in the future equipping programme of the Army.

However, there was hardly a line in the report to give comfort to anyone but the Provisionals who rubbed their hands in glee at such a glowing write-up. Moreover, when they first leaked this stolen document, they left out a sensitive section on the Republic. Despite improvements in cross-border cooperation, there was still anger among many Army officers at what they thought was a scandalous lack of cooperation against a 'common enemy'. Not expecting the report ever to be read outside a specially selected group, the author had not minced his words on this subject.

Republican sentiment and the IRA tradition emanates from the South. Although the Fianna Fail Government is resolutely opposed to the use of force, its long-term aims are, as Mr Lynch himself admits, similar to those of the Provisionals. Any successor to Lynch in the ruling party will probably follow at least as Republican a line of policy. Fine Gael, though traditionally less Republican, is also now committed to a roughly similar line. We have no reason to suspect that PIRA obtains active support from Government sources, or that it will do so in the future, but the judiciary has often been lenient and that the Gardai, although cooperating with the RUC more than in the past, is still less than whole-hearted in its pursuit of terrorists. The headquarters of the Provisionals is in the Republic. The South also provides a safe mounting base for cross-border operations and secure training areas. PIRA's logistic support flows through the Republic where arms and ammunition are received from overseas. Improvised weapons, bombs and explosives are manufactured there. Terrorists can live there without fear of extradition for crimes committed in the North. In short, the Republic provides many of the facilities of the classic safe-haven so essential to any terrorist movement. And it will probably continue to do so for the foreseeable future.

One of the problems was that, as the security forces tightened their grip in the North, so the Provisionals were forced to make more use of the South. Earlier in the year, for instance, they had mounted a mortar attack on Newtownhamilton where, for the first time, they had succeeded in killing a soldier. The Army classified the weapon as a Mk 10 mortar ('That's just the Army name for it,' a policeman said condescendingly, 'they would call it that!'). The remarkable thing about this weapon was that it consisted of ten tubes, welded to the base of a truck which had been driven up from the South. They had been fired electrically in a ripple, hurling the mortar bombs on to the target where they had exploded ten seconds after impact. The truck had then driven off back to the South without being stopped on either side of the border. The Army point was that had there been close cooperation and willing, the chances of catching it somewhere would have increased enormously.

Early in 1979 a new CLF, Major-General James Glover, arrived in Belfast. It was his intelligence report which had fallen into the hands of the Provisionals, so he was well briefed on what was happening from the moment he landed. It was his opinion that the level of violence was now likely to rise and that this would demand a reappraisal of Army operations. The key — as always — was intelligence, but despite all efforts over the past ten years it was still an uncoordinated mess.

The sort of intelligence gathered by soldiers is usually different from police intelligence; what was needed, then, was for it all to be brought together and meshed into a constructive and useful pattern. This was not happening, and many operations were still being conducted on a broad basis of guesswork. The police, according to one Army officer, were 'swanning around risking their necks on operations based on nothing but stubborn pride and bravery. That was not a passport to success!' He explained that when the Army had been in the lead there had been close dovetailing of the police in support of the Army. Now that it was the other way round, the RUC was finding it very difficult to fit the Army into its scheme of things. At least, that was how Lisburn now saw it. 'They weren't even used to operating on a twenty-four hour basis,' complained a staff officer. 'At five o'clock they would shut up shop — like they did everywhere else in the UK. But of course it's at night that the terrorist strikes, and having no round-the-clock capability made it all a touch confusing.'

The Army felt uncomfortable without a clear chain of command,

and the police were less than enthusiastic about joint command. It was a situation that Newman would not tolerate, despite pressure from Lisburn. The police did not operate like the Army; they were not trained to do so, and they patently did not wish to do so. The educative process on both sides was going to be hard and long.

Creasey was now making his reservations generally known. He wanted the whole operation to go at a more measured pace and he wanted soldiers who were trained to fight to do just that, which would allow the police to get on with what they were trained to do — certainly not to fight. Because he was telling everybody that he was concerned, and because he was, after all, the commander on the spot, others were becoming concerned as well.

There now began to emerge an interesting difference between some of the Army commanders on the ground and Lisburn, both on the capability of the police and on what the Army should be doing about it. There were certainly problems in the border area of south Armagh where both the local commander and Lisburn were agreed that the police should take a back seat and let the Army do the fighting. According to the Army colour-code this was a 'black' area where the Army should play the dominant role because it was much too dangerous and difficult for the police. Other areas were designated either 'grey', where the police could operate but only with the back-up of the Army, or 'white', where the Army felt that it was safe enough for the police to operate entirely on their own. This understanding of the situation was not one shared by the police, and it caused a good deal of friction.

There was, however, a different atmosphere in other areas. In Belfast, for instance, the brigade commander's plan now was to get the soldiers off the streets and replace that type of patrolling with surveillance and terrorist recognition skills. One thing the brigade commander was determined to do was to stop the practice, by every battalion which arrived, of immediately lifting every suspect so that his photograph could be taken. 'You had to get to know the baddies pretty damn quickly but while a photograph was one aid, there was nothing like seeing them in the flesh and on location and it was less upsetting for everyone.' So NCOs from resident battalions who had been in the area for some time would act as guides, going round with the incoming soldiers and pointing out the 'baddies'. He also banned the use of the phrase 'police primacy' in his brigade area, insisting to his officers that they were involved in joint operations with the police, not under police command. So the Army and police worked easily together here, with the soldiers committed to the policy of police primacy—even though some of them disliked that phrase.

In Londonderry similar feelings prevailed. 'The Glover report,' said one officer, 'was written to show that matters were getting worse. Well I just do not believe they were! We had a positive, progressive, planned policy which everyone knew about and which allowed us to pre-empt events rather than just react to them.' Indeed, a senior officer returning to the MOD in London after a visit there commented that he was delighted that the 'police had their tails up' and were doing so well.

So profound were the differences, however, that on one occasion, when a Lisburn staff officer had asked the three area commanders along to explain to the police just how badly they — the police — were doing, those from Belfast and Londonderry had very little to say. According to one observer, one of them sat there 'white-faced and angry' at being asked to do such a thing.

These differences probably arose because, while some senior officers had never served in the province before, others had been working their way up from platoon commander level for the past ten years and they now had a real 'feel' for the place. This convinced them first of the absolute need to keep the police in the lead role and second, of the counter-productive results of operations that were 'over-aggressive'.

One commander with extensive experience in the province explained that the Army just had to 'think through' its policies. He pointed out that throughout the 1970s the Army had kept very full intelligence records on people, vehicles and houses where the IRA operated. These records were maintained by house visits and head checks and a comprehensive personal check system that operated twenty-four hours a day on the streets and in the pubs. This had led to many a success and often to arrests of people caught 'red-handed'. However, he went on to point out that despite these operational successes a very heavy price was paid in terms of relations with the community as a whole. To the police themselves, cause and effect became blurred and these counter-measures were seen as a cause of the troubles rather than a result of the IRA's actions. He argued, therefore, that it was right to reduce the level of 'preventive activity' and in turn accept a reduction in intelligence. There were three good reasons for this, he said. The first was that tension was lowered and people began to see that life could be good after all; secondly, violence and trouble initiated by the IRA became obvious for what it was and was rejected by many; thirdly, because of the reduction in street 'aggro' it was possible to cover areas with far fewer soldiers, who could then be allowed to stay for longer tours of duty which gave greater continuity to the whole campaign.

Despite the differences, and with the help of those who believed in it, the policy of having the police in the lead creaked along. The year 1979, however, was to see the strongest threat to its existence. The Republican terrorist organisations strengthened themselves and joined forces for a series of attacks which were to culminate in one bloody day in August.

Back in December 1974, the Official Sinn Fein — the political wing of the semi-comatose Official IRA — was split. A group of about eighty members left to form a new organisation which they called the Irish Republican Socialist Party (IRSP). They believed that, in the overall battle for an all-Ireland Republic, just as much emphasis should be placed on the working-class overthrow of the capitalist system. A number of them also took their weapons with them, and while the new organisation maintained that they had no military wing, they did become involved in a bloody feud with their old colleagues in the Official IRA. By the middle of the year a group calling itself the 'People's Liberation Army' had announced that it was to protect the IRSP from violent attacks by the Official IRA. It was later joined by Provisionals who were looking for action during the long cease-fire when the Army was not being attacked. It was an unpublicised military alliance which included mixed ASUs. In due course this group became the Irish National Liberation Army and with members such as these was responsible for some of the most bloody killings that followed.

By 1979 the Provisionals were reorganised, regrouped and ready for a renewed campaign against the security forces. They now had weapons which were more powerful than before, their security was better and they were planning their bomb attacks with great care and precision. They had two basic aims: to hit the security forces; and to hit the headlines.

At the beginning of March they showed their new organisation at work when they planted forty-nine bombs in twenty-two towns over a period of two days. This included the planting of incendiary bombs in five different hotels at the same time. Then they opened another front in Europe by murdering the British ambassador to the Netherlands, Sir Richard Sykes. They shot him, and his footman, as they stood by his Rolls Royce outside his house. The Provisionals did not actually claim this attack, but a spokesman in Belfast indicated that they were probably responsible. Sir Richard did, after all, have Irish connections, however tenuous. He had been given responsibility for overseeing a secret investigation into the assassination in Dublin of Sir Christopher Ewart-Biggs.

Then Colonel Mark Coe was murdered in Germany, and a plan to blow-up an entire British military band in Brussels failed only because of a last-minute change in schedule. In *Republican News* the Provisionals obligingly explained their reasons for these murders and attempted murders:

> Between tours all of them [British soldiers in the North] are either stationed in Britain or overseas and here they can rest from the dirty work they are doing . . . they think they can forget about Ireland until the next tour, but we intend to keep Ireland on their minds so that it haunts them and they want to do something about not wanting to go back. . . . Overseas attacks also have a prestige value and internationalise the war in Ireland. The British Government has been successful in repressing news about the struggle in the North, but we have kept Ireland in the world headlines. . . . Sooner or later an expression of discontent, possibly from the English people rather than the Army, will snowball and the British Government's ability to stay, which we are sapping, will snap completely.

Then, at the end of March, in the run-up to the British general election, the INLA hit right into the heart of London, murdering Airey Neave, one of Margaret Thatcher's closest political advisers and friends. She had, colleages said, always been able to rely on him for the truth, unvarnished by flattery or sycophancy. Moreover, he had master-minded her first great coup when she had ousted Edward Heath as Leader of the Conservative Party, as well as being behind the collapse of the Labour Government by bringing maverick Unionist MPs from Northern Ireland on to the Tory side. For her, his death was a particularly personal blow.

To kill him the terrorists had used a two-stage bomb. It contained a mercury tilt-switch which set off the main explosion. The bomb, with a small amount of nitro-glycerine, had been strapped under the driver's seat of Neave's car. It was set to reach zero, and therefore to set off stage two, after the car had been parked in the underground car park at the House of Commons. Neave had actually driven there with the bomb ticking away underneath him. When he left later that afternoon and drove up the ramp, the car jolted slightly and the bomb exploded. A policeman ran to him. He was lying in the driver's seat, both his legs gone, his face blackened, but still just alive. Half an hour later he was in hospital, but a few minutes after he got there, with his wife by his side, Airey Neave died. The INLA later announced that they had killed him because of his 'rabid militarist calls for more repression against the Irish people and for the strengthening of SAS murder gangs'.

Then the killings switched back to Northern Ireland. In April two soldiers were killed in Andersonstown and shortly afterwards another was killed and one wounded in an attack on an armoured car in Ballymurphy. The real targets, however, were to be local members of the security forces, for the Provisionals wanted to destroy the policy of pushing the police to the forefront in the battle against crime and terrorism. First, a prison officer was shot dead as he walked from a church wedding holding hands with his wife and six-year-old daughter. The next day, on an approach road to Bessbrook in south Armagh, a 1000lb lorry bomb was detonated as two police cars drove past, killing four policemen and injuring two more as well as eleven civilians. More incidents followed, with a woman warder being shot dead and three more injured outside Armagh jail; a Cadet Force officer was killed and one wounded in yet another shooting. In May, an Army sergeant and a police detective, both in plain clothes, were shot dead as they sat in an unmarked car.

Tragic though all these incidents were in themselves, they were overshadowed by two events which dealt cruel blows to the Army and the British establishment — if not the British people as well. They occurred on the same day during the month of August that marked a whole decade of the Army's involvement in 'aid of the civil power'.

On this calm summer morning on 27 August 1979, a party of holidaymakers got ready to go out on their final fishing expedition of the summer. They were to spend the morning just off the Irish coast at Mullaghmore, in County Sligo. They were all from England except for the boat-boy, a young lad from just across the border. No one took much notice of them as they scrambled happily aboard the thirty-foot boat which was moored in the small harbour. They were well known to the villagers, for the family owned the castle up the hill where some of them had been coming for holidays for thirty years and more.

As the boat chugged slowly out of the harbour, two Gardai watched it idly through a pair of binoculars. It was their job to inspect the boat from time to time, for the owner was a figure of some public importance. However, he had always insisted that he did not want any fuss, and they discreetly kept their distance. At least one other person was also watching the boat leave, but with far greater interest than anyone else. For there was a bomb on her, and he was going to set it off.

As the boat cleared the harbour, the two Gardai, to their horror, saw it explode and a column of smoke and flames lift slowly into the still air. The wooden boat, lifted clear of the water by the blast, was blown to shreds. Of the passengers, three died almost instantly: Earl Mountbatten of Burma, aged 79, last Viceroy of India and uncle of the Queen of England; his grandson Nicholas, 14; and the young boatman, Paul Maxwell, 17.

People round the bay and from the harbour rushed to help, some of them screaming with shock. Lifejackets, anoraks, shoes and fishing lines floated on the blue water as rescuers lifted the bodies of the dead, the living and the dying from the sea. Timothy, twin brother of Nicholas, lost an eye; Lord Brabourne injured a leg; Lady Brabourne and her mother-in-law, the Dowager Lady Brabourne, were more critically injured, and the Dowager died later in hospital.

The Provisional IRA claimed responsibility for the murders, rejoicing at the death of the man they called 'soldier Mountbatten', his grandson and the Dowager Lady Brabourne. They apologised for the death of the young boatman, saying that their latest intelligence had been that there would be other 'members of the royal family, not civilians, on the boat. It should have been a more mature man, serving as pilot, an older man who would have been able to weigh up the consequences of the political company he was keeping and the repercussions of it.' It was a fine distinction they drew, calling those who died 'non-civilians'. They were hoping by this act to shock the British into leaving the North. If it was fashionable to say that the English did not understand the Irish, on this occasion it was certainly the other way round.

This was not the last horror of this summer's day. Just a few hours later, eighteen soldiers were killed in a clever ambush along the border at Warrenpoint in the southern hills of County Down. The actual spot was known as Narrow Water, a stretch of limpid canal which formed the international boundary in a peaceful and lovely stretch of woodland. Violence, however, was no stranger to this area. Soldiers, civilians and terrorists had died here before in the turbulent troubles of the 1920s. Later, in 1972, a fugitive IRA gang from the North holed up in a disused farmhouse and poured some 3,000 rounds at British soldiers who were unable to close the battle because they could not cross the border.

This second tragedy of the day began just before five o'clock in the evening as a platoon of the 2nd Parachute Regiment was travelling along the road in convoy. It was a routine assignment and the soldiers, mostly teenagers, were relaxed but alert as they motored along in two four-ton trucks led by a Land Rover. The corporal sitting by the driver in the front truck noticed a trailer, parked by the road, carrying a load of hay. He thought nothing of it — after all, they were in the country — and then he heard a huge explosion. His truck swerved across the road and stopped, and he jumped out. As he sprinted back to the rear truck the air was full of burning straw floating and dropping all round him. The rear truck was a mass of tangled, blackened steel and out of it, on hands and knees, crawled a paratrooper, his uniform smouldering.

The platoon had six dead and two critically injured and they organised themselves into a defensive position in case there was another attack. Four hundred metres away was an old granite gateway, the gate lodge of Narrow Waters Castle, which would give shelter from any incoming fire. They took up positions here and soon reinforcements were arriving by air, men of the Queen's Own Highlanders with their CO, Lieutenant-Colonel David Blair, and more paratroopers.

A paratroop captain raced forward, a huge black cloud of smoke in front of him. Around him were bits of truck and bodies. To another paratrooper the place looked like a butcher's yard, except that here were the bodies of his friends. Ahead of them a Wessex helicopter fluttered down to evacuate the wounded who had been brought to shelter by the granite gateway. As it started to lift off, there was another huge explosion and a rushing wind hit the men still coming forward. The helicopter bucketed in the blast and the pilot fought to keep control and take it up away from danger.

As it went there was a great silence. The dead lay still and there was no sound from the wounded. The dust swirled thickly, choking the soldiers as they began to grope their way forward, searching for survivors. There was a quick chatter of small-arms fire. Battle was being joined at last, but the enemy was nowhere to be seen. Some firing seemed to be coming across the canal from the southern side of the border, and fire was returned in that direction. One man was killed on that far side. He was found later, wrapped in a white sheet, and turned out to be one of the Queen's coachmen whose parents lived in the Royal Mews. He had been on holiday.

In this second explosion at the Lodge Gate where the Provisionals had, quite rightly, expected the paratroopers to take cover, another twelve men died. They included a major, who was missing, as well as the CO of the Highlanders, David Blair, one of the most senior officers to be killed in Northern Ireland. It was by any standards a disaster — not only the single worst disaster suffered by the security forces but the worst the Parachute Regiment had suffered since it had dropped on Arnhem in the Second World War.

For the Provisionals, it was the biggest hit inflicted by the IRA in one incident since they had ambushed an Army column in 1921 and killed thirty-five soldiers. It was also revenge for Bloody Sunday and soon, on a building across the street from Sinn Fein headquarters in Belfast, there appeared a huge slogan:

13 GONE NOT FORGOTTEN — WE GOT 18 AND MOUNTBATTEN

Phase Nine
The Army steadies itself
— the withdrawal continues
September 1979–summer 1984

The new Conservative Government had hardly been in office six months, and Northern Ireland had not until now caught the attention of the Prime Minister, Margaret Thatcher. 'It threw London into the most terrible tizwaz and panic,' recalled a staff officer at the MOD. 'Suddenly everyone wanted to know what was going on over there and so did the Prime Minister. What's more, she wanted to know at first hand.'

Mrs Thatcher flew to Belfast, transferred to a helicopter and went on to Portadown, headquarters of 3 Brigade. She arrived about lunchtime and was met by the CLF, Major General Glover; he commented that he was surprised there had not been a similar incident to Warrenpoint before, because there had been a number of near misses.

They went into the headquarters where a buffet lunch had been laid out in a briefing room with maps and charts all round the wall. It all had a very military, operational atmosphere. The Prime Minister was 'very bossy and bustling' and eager to find out what was going on. The ritual of standing around clutching a drink and talking was not for her. Soon she said, 'Come along! Let's get on with this,' and sat down, her plate on her lap, and listened. All the officers there knew that time was short, and Major-General Glover briefed her first, using the maps and charts on the wall to illustrate what he was saying. He was followed by Brigadier David Thorne, in whose brigade area the eighteen soldiers had been killed. He was not happy about the state of affairs in the border area. He agreed with the other senior officers who had grave reservations about the capability of the police to manage on their own. As he talked, he pulled from his pocket a single lieutenant-colonel's epaulette and held it out in his hand in front of the Prime Minister. She looked at him and he said, 'Madam Prime Minister, this is all I have left of a very brave officer, David Blair.' There was a moment's silence. Mrs Thatcher's expression did not change but those around felt it had quite an impact on her. Then, one by one, with gathering momentum, the officers had their say.

The GOC, Lieutenant-General Creasey, spoke strongly about the changes he wanted to see. He argued that it was not good enough to leave cross-border communication to the RUC and the Gardai. What was needed was direct radio communication between the two Armies on each side of the border. Hot pursuit across the border was also an essential element in any counter-insurgency campaign. The Dublin Government must be made to see that they were all fighting a common enemy. Warming to his case, he then proposed that the way to deal the Provisionals a crippling blow would be to bring in selective detention. The Army knew whom it wanted to pick up and had a priority list of twenty names, and a second list of some forty people whom it would also like to see locked away as a bonus. Above all, however, there was the need for a supremo — a man who could pull the whole operation together, Army and police, and make it work properly. There were great difficulties in working with the police in control of security. The cooperation that was needed for an effective counter-insurgency operation was just not there. It was vital that a supremo be appointed, a Director of Operations who would be senior to both the GOC and the Chief Constable.

Mrs Thatcher had been taking a very keen interest in everything that was being said to her, and asking a string of pointed questions. Now she looked up at the GOC and said, 'Tell me, general, what sort of man this supremo is going to be?' The general looked a little nonplussed. 'Paint me a picture of this man you want,' she went on, 'Is he a bemedalled general? Is he a civil service mandarin? Is he a foreign office diplomat? Paint me a picture!'

The answer was lost to most people except Mrs Thatcher, but the officers standing around got the impression that their GOC painted a quick picture of a strong military figure and that this was not the right answer. 'I don't think that in any of this she was being critical of the Army,' one officer recalled, without understanding much about political realities, 'or saying "Don't be childish, why can't you get on with the police?" My whole sense of that occasion was that she was intensely sympathetic to the proposition.'

The working lunch lasted about an hour and a half, and the impression the officers got was that the reality of their problems had got through to the Prime Minister — that she had begun to appreciate the real capabilities of the RUC and what sort of terrorists they were up against. What they were asking for was to have complete control of security once again placed in their hands, something which would mean a total change in overall policy. As military men they had presented a military case, and they knew that the political balance would have to be added. Most of them were sure, however, that the Prime Minister had been convinced by their logic.

Nothing else had been laid on for her visit, but now someone asked if she would like to do anything else — perhaps visit an Army base? She said she would like to see Crossmaglen. An officer who was there remarked:

> It wasn't stage-managed — or even arranged. Then we suddenly thought, "What is she going to wear?" and someone grabbed a combat jacket from somewhere that would fit her and away we went. It was all very spontaneous and she picked it up which again I think was a measure of her interest and determination to see for herself what it was all about. She doesn't waste much time!

Mrs Thatcher flew down to Crossmaglen in a Wessex helicopter with the GOC and the brigade commander. Another helicopter followed. They crowded into the little Operations Room. Here, in the heart of an Army base considered the most dangerous place to which any soldier could be posted, she listened to the chatter on the radio and talked to the officers and NCOs who were in charge of operations that day. The large Operations Map on the wall in front of the Duty Officer showed clearly where some twenty soldiers had been killed within a few hundred yards of where she was standing. Then she went out and spoke to some of the soldiers. It was a personal touch, and it was appreciated.

In Gough Barracks, in Armagh, the Chief Constable, Kenneth Newman, and senior police officers were also waiting to brief the Prime Minister. Already they had had reports that the Army was keeping her away from the police who were, one police officer said, being 'humiliatingly excluded' from her presence. One senior policeman had been elbowed out of the Ops Room itself. It was yet another sign of the depths to which Army/police relations had sunk, in this area at any rate, in the past year or so. Newman and his staff officers had had very little warning of the Prime Minister's visit but they had a full brief ready, complete with maps and charts. Newman had been warned that Mrs Thatcher was likely to interrupt briefings with questions. However, when she arrived, taking off her Army combat jacket before coming in to see the policemen, she immediately sat down and listened to him for a full forty minutes without saying a word.

Newman knew the sort of briefing the Army had given her and the demands they had made because they had all been considered in the past and rejected for a variety of reasons. So he opened by telling her that unless she looked at the picture 'province-wide', the view would be distorted. South Armagh, admittedly a difficult area, should not be looked at in isolation because the policy of making the police more self-sufficient and allowing the Army to reduce its presence was having its successes, particularly in Belfast and Londonderry.

Newman was a very clear-headed policeman — some people thought without much emotion. He was fascinated by the sociology of policing, and would often express his views with the aid of complex flow charts, histograms, graphs and posters worthy of a polytechnic dissertation. He was a policeman who thought in terms of corporate management structure and a multi-agency approach to police problems. He was now to bring the full weight of his experience and skill to bear on the Prime Minister.

He explained that between 1976 and 1977 there had been a deep decline in the graph of various incidents and that on the plateau that followed while there had been peaks and troughs the mean level of success had risen slowly. He told her that although the previous year had produced some atrocious terrorist crimes it had also produced the lowest annual figure for such crimes since 1971. The number of deaths from terrorism had gone down, although attacks on soldiers and reserve policemen had remained about the same. One reason for the increase in police casualties, he pointed out, was the increased number of police in an expanding force. However, the level of intimidation, which was a good measure of terrorist activity, had also dropped, since 1974, to its lowest in a decade. The downward trend had only been broken momentarily by the abortive strike of 1977, when Protestant workers and politicians had attempted to repeat the success of the UWC strike of 1974.

Newman pointed out to Mrs Thatcher that while the Army had been in the lead role, little had been done to prepare the police to take over. This was being changed. He spelled out the successes of the Special Support Unit. This was a highly-trained, undercover surveillance unit which never broke cover and never gave evidence in court. It was central to his policy of watching the 'bomb tunnels' — the routes the Provisional bombers took out of the Republican areas. Teams from the unit would wait and watch, usually calling in the uniformed police to make arrests and raid arms caches. At times, however, they had themselves to engage in 'red-hot' pursuits. In this way they had been responsible for the capture of Bobby Sands, later to be elected to Parliament while in prison and to die on hunger strike. In another incident they had chased a Provisional IRA bomb team leaving Andersonstown. The Provisionals had crashed their car and then taken hostages in a house in a middle-class area of Belfast. So frightened was this gang of being shot that they insisted on having a priest from Andersonstown to oversee their surrender. On another occasion the unit had followed a load of bombs brought across the border and destined to blow up the oil refinery tanks in the Short Strand in Belfast. They had picked up the car at Newry, followed it to Belfast, watched the explosives being handed over to a Provisional Active Service Unit and then organised the Army to move in at 4 a.m. to lift the cache and arrest those about to use the explosives. In yet another incident members of the unit had painstakingly watched a weapons cache in West Belfast, followed the courier who had taken the rifle and then arrested the Provisional sniper as he was prepared to fire at a policeman.

Newman admitted that there were problems in the border areas but he was adamant that his men should continue to patrol there in vehicles, although it was official Army policy not to do so. He felt this Army strategy was not working because it gave the Provisional IRA too much licence. He knew, although he did not say as much, that the Army had constantly talked of pulling out of Crossmaglen altogether and consolidating their border base at Bessbrook. To the police, all this was a measure of the way the Army saw the border campaign, and it was one they were resolutely opposed to allowing.

Newman went on to point out that the whole climate in which they were now working needed a continuing law enforcement agency which could not only deal with terrorism but also relate sensibly to the community. He talked about the impracticality of the Army's suggestion for direct communication with the Irish Army. The South would never agree to the Army taking such a lead — it would distort their constitutional position. What was needed, he maintained, was an improved RUC presence in the border areas which could link to the Gardai patrols and then on each side of that link the Irish Army could be joined in the South and the British Army in the North. If the Westminster Government was serious about their policy of police primacy then a certain amount of time had to be allowed for all these changes to take effect.

There had to be a balanced strategy, Newman said, one which allowed a steady progress against terrorism to march side by side with improved relations between the police and the public. The police had put a lot of effort into their community relations programmes, which were having an appreciable effect. The police were involved in a variety of community projects, dealing not only with local matters such as tenants associations, but also summer holidays for children and a conference centre at Corrymela on the north Antrim coast. Here, people from difficult and deprived areas would be brought for a few days at a time to discuss problems with a variety of people, including a great many police officers. The police saw this as slow but discernible progress towards improving community relations and a very important strand in their strategy. Then, of course, there were the police Blue Lamp Discos, run by serving policemen and policewomen, which were now attracting over 200,000 youngsters each year.

One significant landmark illustrating this progress was, he felt, when the Alliance party, which had been formed to attract support from both communities, came out in public support of the police. No politician, he explained to Mrs Thatcher, who above all could be expected to take the point, could get so far out in front as to become cut off from constituency feelings. The Alliance party, with a lot of backing in the Catholic community, could not have done this unless they had sensed some appreciable warming of their political hinterland.

This sort of progress, Newman emphasised, could never be achieved by the measures advocated by the Army. For progress to be made the present policy had to be maintained even if it was slow and required patience. One matter of urgent concern, however, was the need to increase the force level of the RUC by 1,000 men. Once this was achieved the RUC would not only be better placed to deal with the situation, but the Army force level could be further reduced. His staff had been arguing for months with civil servants about the formula which could be applied to acquire these men.

Newman finished, and the first comment made by Mrs Thatcher was that the briefing had been rather different from the one she had had from the Army. She did not elaborate, other than to say that the Army's assessment had been much more pessimistic. She thought for a few moments and then looked up again.

'Did you say, Chief Constable, that you wanted an extra one thousand men?'

'Yes, Prime Minister.'

'Did you say that if you had them we could make further reductions in the Army?'

'Yes, Prime Minister, I did.'

'Right!' said Mrs Thatcher, 'You can have them.' She got up and left. It was rather a bald end to the briefing, but the police had won a major point — their extra men — and they felt they had impressed the Prime Minister with their case.

Margaret Thatcher knew, before she arrived, what sort of reception she would get from the Army and the police. Having just lost eighteen men in one day and the Mountbatten tragedy having had been heaped on to that, the GOC and the Army officers would, of course, be upset. The Army would be asking what had gone wrong with their tactics. Where did the blame lie? Was the Army itself to blame? Or the police, about whom some officers had such reservations? In the middle of all this heart-searching the GOC, with the morale of his troops to consider, would want to be seen in command, resolute, making an impact.

The police would not be so shocked, although they knew that they were in the firing line from the Army, and they were likely to give a more reasoned brief. Moreover, civil servants in the Northern Ireland Office and the MOD were naturally not unaware of the general's thinking. Their feeling was that the appointment of an overall security director with, no doubt, a tough military background would indeed set the present policy back a long way. So a few bright minds had been working on the problem long before the Prime Minister came over. They had reached the conclusion that while some appointment was necessary, it should be one which appeased the Army while not offending the police.

The Prime Minister had, according to one official involved, made up her mind on the matter before she had arrived. It seemed to him, and to others who were able to follow her progress closely that day, that she was in fact delivering a 'slap on the wrist' to the commanders of both Forces, and that in effect she was saying, 'For heaven's sake! Can you not get together and agree without this unseemly squabbling?'

So the Prime Minister left Northern Ireland, and returned to London where the next day she briefed the Cabinet on what she had discovered during her visit. There was a flurry of activity in Whitehall as papers passed to and fro with ideas from the Army, the police and other agencies involved in the province. The decisions were Mrs Thatcher's to make and there was no doubt that she had been moved by the Army's case. However, as a hard-headed politician she must have been thinking that it was never a good policy to make snap decisions and fundamental changes at moments of crisis — which is what the Army was asking her to do.

The decision in the end was that of the four major changes for which the Army had asked ('It was the last gasp of HQ Northern Ireland,' commented one civil servant unkindly) only one, watered down, would be allowed. There would be no hot pursuit across the border, no selective detention, and no direct cross-border communication with the Irish Army; but a supremo of sorts would be sent to the province. There was a long list of possible candidates. Some were ruled out because they had other important work to do, others declined the offer. In the end, Sir Maurice Oldfield, who had been head of the Secret Intelligence Service (MI6), between 1965 and 1977, agreed to go to 'oil the wheels and be a bit of a Solomon.' He would not, however, have the all-encompassing powers which the Army had wanted him to have. His title would be 'Coordinator', which indicated both his role and his function. The police were told privately that he would be 'more like a referee' than anything else. A close political adviser explained:

In the overall scale of Northern Ireland that day was not so totally shattering that it required huge changes. Of course it was horrific with so many deaths! But one incident concerned soldiers — with the Army admitting that they were expecting something like that to happen — and the other concerned Mountbatten across the border in the Republic. I think the Prime Minister's decision was based not so much on whether she thought the Army wrong and the police right — but on an intellectual assessment of the incidents in the overall context. You see, had she gone with the emotional approach of the Army, the 'Way Ahead' policy would have been in total ruins, and the whole forward movement of the province put drastically back to where it had been ten years before. We had enough problems without that happening!

Senior officers at the MOD, as well as Lisburn, had looked at this period immediately after Warrenpoint as a 'window of opportunity' to get some concrete things done which they felt would improve the situation. What they had done was to state their military requirements. They knew this was subject to the political factor, but they also knew that if soldiers did not state their military requirements then they were not doing their job. 'When we put forward proposals like these,' explained a senior officer, 'our expectation was never that we would get the whole package, and in this case we did not. And I would agree that with the possible exception of hot pursuit across the border, the decision not to give us what we asked for was right.'

What Lisburn had failed to realise was that once they had started asking for a 'supremo', the idea was effectively dead. That was the way the political antennae worked at Westminster and in the corridors of power in Whitehall, and they had not appreciated this subtlety. Whitehall had accepted that whoever they chose would have to be accountable to the Secretary of State. But it was also felt that he should be, in a typically British sort of way, someone 'rather floating'; that is, not someone seen as the absolute lackey of the Secretary of State, but someone who could go round and talk to everyone and set up a system which would be trusted by everyone. Sir Maurice Oldfield fitted well into this picture. One interested observer commented:

When he got there and started work, what he found was that the Army was fussed about the police moving faster. How the hell were the police going to do it? Had they got the right gear? They didn't understand about electronics and were miles behind the Army in all this sophisticated gadgetry which could be used for surveillance . . . and the worries went on and on. On the other hand the police were saying that the Army had nothing better to do than write papers. 'We don't have the people to do that,' they told Oldfield. 'We don't have that sort of staff system. We don't have people endlessly writing papers and thinking up new ideas —

not in the real world we have to live in!'

Oldfield was given three separate principal aides: a senior civil servant, a brigadier and a deputy chief superintendent. It was a unit that had to be trusted by everyone because it had to bring everybody together and it had two principal tasks. One was to take each of the geographic/commercial areas and examine them closely. It had to ask whether the Government was doing the right things in these places and bear in mind that they were all, to some extent, different. It had to examine not just the security situation, but everything — cultural, economic, commercial and so on. The other task was, as someone rather bluntly put it, 'to bang some Army and police heads together!'

What Creasey had done after Warrenpoint was to say, 'The police are bloody incompetent and I am not going to be run by them.' When Oldfield came to Belfast — determined to 'bang heads together' in the gentlest possible manner — and started to talk to the Army the first thing he said was, 'Quite frankly, I can't see what the problem is here.' This was because soldiers in Belfast had, for a long time, functioned in liaison with the police. The association of the brigade commander and the acting commissioner of police was very close. There was nothing new in that. The problem was really in changing the attitudes.

Sir Maurice spent very little time at his desk in Stormont and a great deal of time travelling round, moving from lunch at a police mess to dinner at an Army mess, moving around units talking to people and, more important, getting them to talk to him. He had by all accounts the classic approach, constantly asking people what their troubles were and then actually listening and taking it in. In this way he learned that the police felt that the Army was over-pessimistic at a time when they were making a number of adjustments and improvements and when there was a lot of work in the pipeline. Senior policemen felt that they could, for the time being, contain the situation on the plateau it had been on since 1976. They told him that there had been a steep decline in terrorism since then, and that it had remained steady. Moreover they knew what they had coming on stream. They felt buoyant and confident, certainly at the managerial level. The Army, for what many of them accepted were perfectly professional reasons, had chosen to raise doubts about the police capability to evolve to the point where they could handle matters in the border areas, Londonderry and West Belfast. 'They wanted to calm things down,' observed one police officer. 'They wanted to proceed more cautiously. We felt they were wrong.'

Lisburn admitted that they had not got what they wanted, but reappraised the matter after a short while and felt that Maurice Oldfield served the purpose. He was a man they respected; and, they found, so did the police and the NIO. He was able to bring people together. 'Having a supremo was the most stupid idea that ever came out of HQ Northern Ireland,' commented a civil service mandarin at the MOD. 'It was never supported by the general staff in London and it was never a starter, whatever they may have thought! So, when they didn't get what they wanted they switched their tack, saying, "Well! It ain't going well now . . . how can we do better?"'

The key was intelligence, although it was amazing that by now this vital matter had still to be sorted out satisfactorily. Lisburn was now going to try to turn from broad operations based on guesswork to the rapier thrusts of tightly controlled operations based on fine intelligence. It was something that some officers maintained had been happening very well until the events of August had stirred up an internal controversy.

In September, *Republican News* published a warning that there would be 'many more blows'. In an article headed 'What Next?' it said: 'Republicans will be striking at the British enemy again and again, sickening the English people of their six county colony and educating them through the only means that they appear to take to heart.'

The man whom the security forces named as being the driving force behind this Republican dedication to overthrowing the established order, north and south of the border, was Gerry Adams, a former Belfast barman. He had been interned in 1971 and released the next year to take part in secret cease-fire talks with William Whitelaw. He was interned once more but released in 1976 only to be charged again two years later with membership of the Provisional IRA. Seven months after this the Lord Chief Justice, Sir Robert Lowry, ruled that he had no case to answer and he was released again. In June 1979 he made the keynote speech at the annual pilgrimage to Wolfe Tone's grave at Bodenstown. This speech marked an important step forward in the Provisionals' plans to develop a radical, socialist policy so that, 'with an Armalite in one hand and a ballot box in the other' they could sweep the country in elections, declaring:

We stand opposed to all forms and manifestations of imperialism and capitalism. We stand for an Ireland free, united, socialist and Gaelic. . . . Our movement needs constructive and thoughtful self-criticism. We also require links with those oppressed by economic and social pressures. Today's circumstances and our objectives dictate the need for building an agitational struggle in the twenty-six countries, an economic resistance movement, linking up Republicans with other sections of the working class. It needs to be done now because to date our most glaring weakness lies in our failure to develop revolutionary politics and to build an alternative to so-called constitutional politics.

By the end of 1979 the two senior men involved in running security operations in Northern Ireland had left. Sir Kenneth Newman had become Commandant of the Police Staff Training College at Bramshill, in Hampshire. He was replaced by Sir John Hermon, who had risen through the ranks of the RUC and who had been Deputy Chief Constable in charge of operations in 1976. He had also sat on the Bourne Committee which produced 'The Way Ahead', the policy which had caused such misgivings in Lisburn.

Lieutenant-General Creasey left to go back to Oman and was replaced by Lieutenant-General Sir Richard Lawson, hand-picked as a 'political' general who would ensure that the Army toed the line on police primacy. Lawson had a DSO, and he had won a decoration from the Belgians for rescuing Belgian missionaries in the Congo. In a very tense situation he had out-faced 800 rebels who had already killed twenty-two priests and, armed with only a swagger stick, had persuaded them to release unharmed those who remained. In 1964, Pope John had made him a Commander of the Order of St Sylvester.

Lawson's tenure as GOC was in sharp contrast to that of his predecessor. He rarely came into public view but on one of the few occasions when he did, early on, he stamped his mark on the campaign in a carefully-worded speech to the Belfast Chamber of Commerce which was reported in the *Guardian*:

The primary role and purpose of any Army is to defend the frontiers of the State against external aggression. However, when paramilitaries or armed groups get within the gates and threaten the internal fabric of the State, the police may need the support of the armed forces. And let me stress the word 'support'. The Army do not stand in front of the police; nor do we stand behind them and certainly we do not stand in their place. . . . The question is not just what we should do but much more importantly how we should do it. There are a few who, out of sheer frustration and impatience, say to me: 'Go in hard, general! Flush out those terrorists whatever the cost. What we want are bodies and what we want are skulls and we do not care how you get them.' Well! Let my reply to those people ring out loud and clear: I am not in that business. I have not come here to destroy Ulster. For such a wild and totally impracticable course of action is not only a guaranteed recipe for disaster, it is also a sure-fire way to give the terrorist his victory on a plate.

A week later the same paper was quoting officers to whom the general had, presumably, been referring. 'You bring them in, hand them over to the police — and the buggers don't say a word for seven days. Then you have to let them go.' The report went on to say:

> . . . many would like the onus of proof to be on the accused in terrorist offences. Some want heavier sentences, less remission, or the right of British helicopters to pursue fleeing cars over the border so that the Gardai can be guided to them. . . . The young lieutenant in charge of a beleaguered post near the border said bluntly they ought to be allowed to go out and kill known terrorists. Further north, where the East Tyrone Provisionals are active (and they are among the most professional in the business) a world weary major said: 'Some people believe in selective internment. I believe in selective assassination.'

The other thing Lawson did was lower the public profile of the Army until it just about disappeared from sight. The national press, radio and television began to find that they were being denied facilities which in the past they had been given as a matter of course. When Yorkshire Television was filming 'Harry's Game', Gerald Seymour's best-selling novel of an Army undercover agent, the Army refused to help in any way at all. Indeed, when the general heard that the RAF had given permission for the unit to film on a disused airfield, he had the unit thrown off. Lawson believed that while the Army might be seen on the streets, their exploits should not be public knowledge. To some officers, this reaction to the more 'gung-ho' approach of the previous two years was, as one put it, 'a touch over-done!' However, as Lisburn saw it, there were good, practical reasons why the Army had moved from overt to covert operations in the context of Northern Ireland in the late 1970s. There were three reasons why the Army might show a high profile, and as each was considered it was set aside. One was straightforward attrition, but it was felt that soldiers were largely ineffective in this, other than as a framework for covert operations; another was deterrence, but this was unquantifiable; a third was reassurance of the uninvolved population, and in particular the Protestants, who were constantly worried about the loss of their sovereignty — but Lisburn knew this was a purely political tactic and that it should be recognised as such.

Lawson's approach was a subtle one, often behind the scenes where he engaged in a delicate juggling act with all of Ulster's various warring factions. To a newly arrived brigadier, his advice was straightforward.

'There are two things you must never do while you are here,' he said. 'You must never have a short conversation with an Irishman, and you must not have a plan.'

'No plan, sir? But I am a brigadier. I must have a plan!'

'No plan,' the general repeated firmly. 'It's the one thing against which all Ulstermen will unite.'

By the spring of 1980 more soldiers were being withdrawn as the Government followed its policy of reducing regular Army units and replacing them with local forces. Another 500 left because Lisburn was now making greater use of sophisticated technical equipment and had re-deployed units so that they covered larger areas. Moreover, outside the hard Republican areas both the police and the UDR were doing more regular patrolling.

There was still pressure, of course, to reduce the number even further as NATO commitments became more demanding, and in trying to strike a delicate balance between these competing requirements the Army was placing greater reliance on long term tours. There were now more resident battalions, with their families, which lessened the strain of separation on both sides. There were fewer short tours — now extended to four and a half months — which were always unaccompanied and during which the soldiers were on call twenty-four hours a day. It was a system which, the Army hoped, would allow soldiers to come over often enough to maintain their counter-insurgency experience and give junior ranks the chance to practise leadership and command in active conditions, and enable them to maintain their specialist skills within NATO.

The first real test for the new style RUC, with the Army in support, came with the hunger strike of 1981. Republican prisoners at the Maze prison outside Belfast decided that they would force

Westminster to grant them — at least unofficially — political status as prisoners, by allowing them privileges which included wearing their own clothes and organising their own working conditions. They, and women prisoners in Armagh jail, had been protesting about the withdrawal of their Special Category status for some four years now, first by 'going on the blanket' (which was all they wore) and then for the past two years by a 'dirty strike', which meant fouling their cells with faeces, urine, and in the case of the women, menstrual blood as well.

The first prisoner to refuse food was Bobby Sands, serving a 14-year sentence. Others joined him at regular intervals, each planning to die within two to seven days of each other in order to put maximum pressure on the Government and gain maximum publicity around the world. Tension and emotion mounted. Sands was nominated as an anti-H-Block/Armagh candidate in the by-election for the Fermanagh-South Tyrone seat at Westminster. Six weeks after he started his hunger strike he was duly elected as a member of Parliament for Westminster.

Sands died on 5 May just after 1 a.m. and within minutes rioting broke out in Belfast in which two people were killed. Through May, June, July and August a total of ten hunger strikers died, one after the other. With each death and each funeral there was rioting, and Lisburn was very concerned whether the police could bear the brunt of the violence. The Army was called out in support, and for the first time in a long period was involved in large-scale confrontations with rioters. But the new-style RUC passed the test with flying colours. They bore the brunt of the violence and at no time did they have to withdraw from set-piece riots and ask the Army to take over. It was the most serious security threat for a long time, but to the authorities the end result was a reaffirmation of the success and wisdom of the policy of police primacy.

By 1982, the Army force levels were coming down nearer to the 7,000 strong permanent garrison that the Government wanted as part of its long-term plan. The strength was now below 11,000, half the number it had been at the peak in 1972. The regular Army was supported by 7,500 full-time and part-time members of the UDR, who more and more were taking on the role as the RUC's first line of support when military assistance was needed. The regular Army was now concentrated in the hard Republican areas — West Belfast,

Londonderry and the border.

With the RUC now well in the forefront of the counter-insurgency campaign, they became targets not only for the Provisional IRA but also for regular criticism against security policy. Late in 1981 Ian Paisley had swung along the 'Carson trail' invoking memories of past glories and triumphs of extreme Protestant opinion against the Westminster Government. Along the way he encouraged Protestants to join his 'Third Force' which was supposed to take over and deal with terrorist violence where he thought the police and Army had failed. The atmosphere produced an unhappy and bitter feeling within the RUC itself which was still having growing pains. This immensely complicated problem showed for a moment when — by a very narrow margin — the Central Committee of the Police Federation passed a motion of no confidence in the Chief Constable, Sir John Hermon. The motion was later defeated at a more representative meeting but some damage had been done and it did not pass unnoticed outside Northern Ireland.

A short time afterwards, two members of the Tory backbench committee on defence visited the province and were entertained by the GOC, Sir Richard Lawson. One of the guests at the dinner was the Chief Constable. As the conversation warmed, one of the MPs leaned over to the chief constable. 'Now, Sir John,' he said, 'This motion of no confidence . . . very disturbing, isn't it?'

Hermon, unprepared for the question, was a bit flustered. He started to talk about the background to the affair, explaining that the vote had not been very representative and had anyway been overturned at the next meeting. Sir Richard was listening to all this, and then interrupted. 'Just a moment, gentlemen,' he said quietly but very clearly so that everyone could hear. 'I know you are my guest but I also know you well enough to be frank. Let me tell you that in this world there are three things which are of absolutely no value to anyone. The first are tits on a bull; the second are balls on a pope; the third is a vote of no confidence from a police federation.'

There was a shout of laughter, and the subject was dropped. Later, however, one of the visitors again went on the attack, saying that the propaganda of the Provisionals was very strong and the Northern Ireland Office should be countering it hard. A civil servant involved with this was brought into the conversation. He explained the importance of being truthful and the reasons behind the low profile policy, but still the criticism was maintained until once again Lawson stepped in and said firmly that, whether his visitors liked it or not, that was the policy and he supported it.

By the end of the year, however, more support had been poured into the RUC. The expenditure was increased by £34,500,000, bringing the total to £350,000,000. The force strength was also increased by 500 full-time members, 300 reserves and 336 supporting civilians, making a total of just over 8,000 regular police and 2,500 reserve police.

'Information is power,' said an intelligence officer who served in Londonderry in the early 1980s. 'So let's be quite clear about it — if you share it you lose some of that power.' He went on to explain that even at this stage, after ten years, the police still felt that the Army was some sort of enormous sieve, and that information given to any officer would automatically be passed up and up the line until it was common knowledge everywhere. He found that the police could not accept that he just wanted intelligence information so that he could make a military decision, not for its own sake. Sometimes he found that the police would only let information trickle out over a long period — maybe over twelve hours or more — which meant that operations failed when they might have succeeded. It was felt that one of the problems arising from the running of these sorts of operation by the police was that they did not like taking risks with people. If an operation produced bloodshed then it was, for the police, a failure, whereas to the Army it was a risk they would be prepared to take. 'The police are very loathe to task an operation where someone might get hurt,' explained a staff officer. 'But, while it is very nice of the police not to put you in that sort of position, it does mean you are not being your most effective. You see, if the other side takes risks — and they do — then you have to take them as well.'

It was still a learning process, but by now matters had largely settled down. 'You have a right to cooperation from the police,' said an officer, 'but you have to earn trust. Information is a raw product, and Special Branch have an apt phrase when they say a man is "all suck and no blow." You have to give something in order to get something back.'

Information was, of course, the key to success and if there was a tendency sometimes for a wily old Special Branch officer to hang on to his information, it was because he knew of enough examples where inexperienced young Army officers, anxious to gain kudos, had reacted to their information in an uncoordinated way. Informants could be — and indeed had been — discovered and killed because of this.

One of the Provisional IRA leaders acknowledged by many Army officers to have been most competent was Francis Hughes, who was to be the second hunger striker to die, in May 1981. When information came through about him, it was kept strictly within a small group of police and Special Forces, and a stake-out was mounted. The men in Hughes' ASU were in British Army uniform, and they were challenged — which they should not have been, because it was a restricted area and there should have been no other troops there. However, they were challenged, and this very probably led to the death of one of the soldiers and the wounding of another in the ambush party. Then, because of the lack of information, the follow-up with regular soldiers was slow. This meant that of the Provisionals, two got away, one was killed and Hughes was injured. Hughes, wounded, crawled a couple of hundred yards away to hide, but was found and arrested the next morning. 'Francis Hughes was a man for whom the police and the Army had the highest regard,' recalled an officer who had served for long periods in the border areas. 'He was a really professional terrorist. He used to have all his

boys doing runs every morning. There was none of this business of living softly. They lived rough and trained very hard, and when they came over the border at us they were really very, very effective.'

There were other ways to hit at soldiers, particularly those on the now more usual long, two-year tours. In the spring of 1982 the Cheshire Regiment moved to Shackleton Barracks at Ballykelly, an English-looking village on the road between Londonderry and Coleraine, a posting which had been a pleasant one for soldiers for some forty years. It was in a lovely part of the country, surrounded by rich farmland and plenty of space. During the summer some had been learning to glide and the unit hoped to get a glider before their next move to Hong Kong. The military married quarters housed a substantial number of the 3,500 people who lived there. Despite plenty of organised activity within the camp, soldiers and their families still wanted to get out and mix with the local community and live a life as near normal as possible. Some local hotels and pubs were listed as out of bounds because of the risk of an attack by the Provisionals or the INLA; others were not. One of those not out of bounds was the Droppin' Well at Ballykelly which had a regular Monday night Razzamataz disco, well frequented by soldiers from nearby Shackleton barracks. A couple of weeks before Christmas that year, as the disco was moving into its last thirty minutes, some of the 150 dancers heard a faint hissing sound. Then a huge explosion ripped through the single-storey room. The bomb had been placed with deadly precision by someone who knew how the room had been built. It blew out one wall, which brought the pre-stressed concrete slab of a roof crashing down on those underneath. It took rescue workers all night, under arc lights in a cold and biting wind, to free the living and the dead. As the night wore on and the wind tugged at the tape which sealed off the area, the crushed bodies were brought out. The next day another young victim died of her injuries, bringing the casualties among the soldiers and civilians to seventy injured and seventeen dead. It was the worst pub bomb disaster the province had ever experienced.

After this, security precautions for off-duty Army personnel were tightened, but not drastically. There would now be closer vetting of places which might be used by soldiers and their families, and a more elaborate screening operation was introduced. It was recognised, however, that soldiers on a long tour of duty, even in a dangerous area, could not be confined to barracks in the same way as a soldier on a four-month tour. So life went on, with hundreds of soldiers and their families leaving their barracks for the pre-Christmas shopping spree. They drank at their locals, danced at their discos and their children queued to meet the store Father Christmas, refusing to be cowed by IRA threats. At the same time the Army resisted any temptation to increase its profile by putting more men onto the streets. This was, again, in line with Government policy to keep the police in the lead, and it reflected the scaled down activity of both the Provisionals and the INLA. Now there were only some 10,000 soldiers in the province, and all the time the emphasis was on getting that number down even further.

The INLA claimed the Droppin' Well bomb. Eight days later two of its leading members, Seamus Grew and Roddy Carroll, were shot dead after a car chase. The police maintained that the two men had crashed a road block, injured a policeman, and when chased by a police car with flashing blue lights, had tried to escape. It had then reversed at high speed and stopped. The driver had jumped out and a policeman, believing he was about to be fired at, shot and killed them both. Little of this, however, was true. There had been no check point; no flashing blue lights; no reversing of the car and no one had jumped out. Both men were shot eighteen times where they sat. The police officer who shot them was John Robinson, a constable specially trained in anti-terrorist duties. He was armed with a pump-action shotgun and a machine pistol. He fired fifteen bullets into a passenger door, killing Carroll, reloaded and fired four or five shots at Grew from a range of about three feet. He was later charged, and acquitted, of the murder of an unarmed terrorist suspect.

All this information came out later in court, where the RUC did not contest that their first story had been a fabrication, nor that Robinson had been told not to reveal the nature of the operation because he would contravene the Official Secrets Act. What also came out in court was that an informant in the Republic had warned that Dominic McGlinchey — who was then a wanted man and who was captured later — would be coming across the border in the car driven by Grew. This incident followed others in which IRA and INLA men had been killed in circumstances which the leader of the SDLP, John Hume, described as conferring a 'licence to kill' and 'legalised murder'. In Dublin, the *Irish Times* commented later:

There is abundant evidence that for a considerable time the RUC and the British Army have operated, officially, a 'shoot to kill' policy against suspected members of the Provisional IRA and the INLA. In Latin America the forces which carry out such operations have become known as 'death squads' and have incurred the odium of the civilised world.

There were official denials of a 'shoot to kill' policy: but it was incidents such as the shooting of Grew and Carroll that began to throw some light on the campaign now being fought in Northern Ireland, a campaign that had changed radically since the days when soldiers went out on the streets in full riot gear. Now the emphasis was on undercover work of such secrecy that the policemen involved never used police stations, never went into court, worked from dead-letter boxes and used radio scramblers which encoded their messages. When they wanted to make physical contact with the enemy, they would call up the police Special Support Unit and very probably the Army as well. These unique, deep undercover units were run by a Tactical Coordinating Group. The Special Support Units, however, were not unique to Northern Ireland. A joint directive from the Home Office and the Association of Police Officers had laid down that all British police forces should have a team of highly-trained and skilled men to handle incidents involving terrorists, hijackings and hostages. All this was part of an overall strategy to keep the Army out of internal security work not only in Northern Ireland but in Britain as well.

The new GOC was Lieutenant-General Sir Robert Richardson, and his appointment was a sign of both the length of time the Army had now been committed to aiding the civil power, and the depth of Army expertise. For Richardson was the first GOC to be appointed who had also been a battalion commander in the province. Back in 1969 he had commanded the Royal Scots on two emergency tours, and later he had commanded the brigade in Belfast. Now he was the top Army commander with this depth of experience behind him, knowing the reality of the situation and happy with the policy of police primacy.

By the middle of 1983, the number of troops was still steady at around 10,000 and these included eight infantry battalions of which six were on the long, two-year tours. In addition there was also the Ulster Defence Regiment, now 7,000 strong and with both regular and part-time soldiers.

Now came the time once again for reviewing what was happening in Northern Ireland. In the 1970s, John Bourne had been asked to produce a blue-print for the progress of Northern Ireland and he did this in a report called 'The Way Ahead'. Now he was asked to review that policy to analyse how it was working and to suggest whatever changes might be necessary, through to 1990. He started work on this in the spring of 1984 chairing a committee which included the GOC and the Chief Constable. At the same time, the Army and the police began to cast their attention forward to the years ahead.

Naturally, some of their subjects and areas of interest overlapped. But between them all, there was first to be a detailed look at the next five years, with plans of what should be done about manpower, buildings, the shape of the conflict and the composition of the security forces. Then there was to be a much longer look forward over the next twenty-five years, to take the province right into the twenty-first century.

Running through both these phases would be a number of threads. One would be the acknowledgement that the way forward was not — for the foreseeable future — through a United Ireland. This was despite agonised calls for at least a commitment to a United Ireland from the Labour party, and despite the report of the New Ireland Forum in Dublin. After a year of deliberation on the future of Ireland, it had produced a report which was highly critical of the British Government, and which effectively backed a United Ireland as the only solution to the Irish problem. Behind the scenes, however, Westminster had recognised that the Unionists could not be coerced into it; Dublin had concluded that it could not afford it, and both the Common Market and America had come to the same conclusions. Instead, they all saw the future lying in much closer links between North and South.

This closer cooperation would mean a consequent reduction in the terrorist type of violence, which would mean a lessening of the role of the Army. However, there would be an increase in 'normal' crime, brought on by both the vast amount of racketeering which had been fostered during the past fifteen years of violence, and by efforts of the Provisional IRA to inflict their own form of justice on the Catholic communities. In the first six months of 1984 the police identified fourteen cases of punishment shootings, and presumed there were many more which were not reported. Most of those the police knew about were knee-cappings, although there were also two murders and fifteen beatings. Sinn Fein claimed that the IRA was merely responding to calls from the local community in carrying out punishment shootings on those identified as criminals. The party's publicity director, Danny Morrison, said that while Sinn Fein would not get involved in condemning or condoning such shootings, the IRA 'had a moral responsibility towards the oppressed sections of the community.'

These would be the real problems which lay ahead and would mean concentrating even more on improving the resources of the police, and increasing its full-time strength. At the beginning of 1984 the strength stood at around 8,000, with 4,405 part-time members. The Chief Constable, Sir John Hermon, was keen to see a significant increase for a force he described as 'extraordinary men doing an extraordinary job.' The RUC would not be unhappy to see its members increased to some 12,000 full-time policemen and women.

This, of course, would mean a reduction of the Army as soon as possible to the required level of around 4,000 to 5,000. It would also mean a reduction in the UDR, the part-time soldiers under command of the Army. There are some 7,000 of them, full-time and part-time, and the regiment is in fact the largest in the Army. Since its formation in 1970, it had gained a controversial image and the Catholic membership had dropped from a peak of 17 per cent down to 2 per cent. Its image took another battering in 1983 when eight members were charged with the murder of two Catholics in County Armagh. But in the fight against terrorism it had, by the summer of 1984, lost over 140 members. In the emotionally touchy atmosphere of Northern Ireland suggestions to alter its role and strength would spark off more than lively argument. The Protestants were particularly concerned about what they felt were lapses in security policy which had led to such incidents as the murder of the Rev Robert Bradford, MP, in November 1981; the mass breakout by 38 Republicans from the Maze prison in September 1983, (19 were still free in 1984); and the particularly dreadful massacre at the Mountain Hall Gospel Lodge in Darkley, in November 1983, when INLA gunmen sprayed the hall with bullets, leaving three dead and seven seriously injured.

However, apart from sectarian interests, the police view was that there would be less and less need for a military force such as the UDR, and the numbers would be better absorbed and made use of in a greatly expanded RUC Reserve. On the other hand, there was the current Army view that if the level of patrolling were to be maintained, the UDR would have to be around for some time to come to ensure that the force strengths were available for such work. There was also a strong, realistic streak running through the Army thinking: that there were many men of extreme views within the UDR who might be better kept under observation in a uniformed unit, where they could be kept under some form of control. These, of course, were all long-term considerations, but there was by this stage a definite question mark hanging over the future of the Ulster Defence Regiment.

The summer of 1984 saw the fifteenth anniversary of the Army being called out in aid of the civil power. August was also the month when the two tribes of the province remembered their moments of glory and suffering, and ensured that everyone else remembered them as well. The efforts made for peace were conveniently forgotten; no one marched to commemorate the short-lived peace movement which had grown from the deaths of the Maguire children in August 1976. Rather, the Protestants went back to 1689 to commemorate the day when the Apprentice Boys of Derry stopped the traitor Lundy from opening the city gates and handing them all over to the besieging Catholic army of King James II; it was the violence after this anniversary in 1969 which had first brought the troops out on to the streets. The Catholics had only to go back thirteen years to find an event to commemorate — the introduction of internment in 1971.

In 1984 the Protestant march in Londonderry passed off without incident. In Belfast, however, the march organised by Provisional Sinn Fein on Sunday 12 August ended with a police baton charge, and the death of one man — Sean Downes — hit by a plastic baton. The Army, as usual, was in a close supporting role, but played no direct path in the proceedings. It was, of course, not an ordinary march, for in prospect at the rally which followed was the appearance of an American lawyer called Martin Galvin, who had been banned from entering the United Kingdom. He worked for the New York sanitation department, and in his spare time was a publicist for NORAID. Westminster and Belfast had no doubts about his support for the Provisional IRA. The administration in Washington felt the same, and the Justice Department had attempted to make NORAID register officially as an agent for the IRA. Only by claiming the constitutional right against self-incrimination had NORAID managed to avoid doing this.

Having been banned, Galvin was duly smuggled in and appeared on a makeshift platform outside the Sinn Fein headquarters in Andersonstown. Before he could even open his mouth the police charged, showing a tough image which had not been seen for years, and indeed it was an old image which many police had been trying hard to change. Moreover, the police failed to arrest Galvin, who was spirited away, and the scenes of women and children cowering under policemen wielding batons and firing plastic bullets was a severe setback for the police, and a major propaganda boost for the Provisional IRA. 'It was the sort of stupid mistake we made fifteen years ago,' muttered one military observer. 'You'd think they would have learned by now!'

In fact it was the inevitable result of a new approach by top Ulster policemen who were trying to dampen down Protestant rage at the way in which the Provisionals were flaunting themselves in public. Funeral processions of suspected Provisional terrorists would be broken up by police charges when 'guards of honour' attempted to fire the traditional shots over the coffin. More seriously, in what a wide range of Catholics thought of as an official 'shoot to kill' policy, a number of suspected high-ranking terrorists, such as Grew and Carroll, had been shot dead in circumstances which gave rise to great concern.

It was a situation which highlighted the lack of political control of the police, on the basis that politicians had no influence over 'operational matters'. Some policemen were furious that the Home Office and the Northern Ireland Office had banned Galvin and then left them to sort out the inevitable trouble which would follow. To those at Lisburn who had served throughout the years in Northern Ireland, it all had a desperately familiar ring. For a civil servant in the same position, it produced an anguished cry of, 'What we need are three Englishmen at the top of the RUC. But they won't come. For a high-flyer, this place offers them a no-win situation!' A priest in Andersonstown felt that what little progress the police had been making towards becoming more acceptable in his community had been set back by years. 'Before Sunday,' he said, 'they were almost in a position to start one of their Blue Light Discos here for the children. That won't happen now!' In Dublin, a Government minister, also in some despair, commented, 'After all we've been through in fifteen years, how could they be so stupid as to hand it all to the IRA on a plate!'

But four days after that march, the police were able to show just how impartially rough they could be. During a trial in the Crumlin Road court in Belfast, fighting broke out when an Ulster Volunteer Force supergrass, 'Budgie' Allen, began to give evidence. It began as he started to sign depositions indicting defendants in a case where forty-seven people faced charges ranging from murder to the possession of firearms. The police drew their batons and dealt with it on the spot, although in the melée eight policemen and some of the defendants were injured. That night, they waded in again on the Protestant Shankill road, as the protesting spread there.

It was then that there occurred a small incident which illustrated the permanence of the policy of police primacy. The watchkeeper of the local Army unit heard a BBC news broadcast on his radio which spoke of trouble on the Shankill. He immediately rang the brigade watchkeeper at Lisburn to point out that no-one had called out his soldiers, or even asked them to go on stand-by. 'Don't you worry about all that!' came the laconic reply. 'The police can handle any trouble there. Go back to bed!' It was back full circle to the view of fifteen years before, only now the police were able to control the trouble, nipping it in the bud before it could spread and flare up into full-scale sectarian rioting. On this occasion, rioting did flare again during the following two nights, but it stayed in the Shankill district.

Two days later, the Rev. Martin Smythe, Official Unionist MP for South Belfast, suggested that the Northern Ireland Office may have been behind these riots in the Shankill district. He admitted that he had no evidence to back his allegations, but said that a situation could have been 'manipulated', in which the police could demonstrate its willingness to deal equally harshly with Loyalist and Republican rioters. 'My God!' groaned an officer, who had been around a long time. 'Does anything ever change in this place?'

The fifteen-year period had been an extraordinary one, particulary for the Army which had first been forced to define its role and then shape it. In those early days, the legal responsibilities, duties and obligations of the soldier had been set out in the *Manual of Military Law (1968)*, which had been published after changes in the law authorised 'any person to use such force as is necessary in the circumstances in the prevention of crime'. At that time, military doctrine for dealing with riots was based on the use of CS gas, followed by a clear warning for the crowd to disperse. After that, aimed rifle fire could be used to kill the ringleaders if this was thought necessary. In the circumstances the Army was prevented from taking even these steps in the early days by the arguably unlawful intervention of ministers who forbade them either to open fire or even to fix bayonets. Fifteen years later some officers felt that the Army had been very naïve: that the men had been trained to use force but were being prevented from doing so. As they now saw it an officer had two responsibilities under British law: that of responding to the request for aid from the civil authority, but also of doing more on his own initiative if he felt this was necessary. *The Manual of Military Law* clearly stated that once the military were called in, their commander, while he might be advised by others, was personally responsible for judging the degree of force to be used and whether or not it was necessary to open fire. On this basis some felt that there was an argument that early on the Army should have decided what force was needed, used it, handed back control to the civil power and got itself off the streets. Fifteen years later a senior commander explained:

> But we could not do that, because of the special circumstances which meant that British politicians did not wish to see themselves as setting up a renewed but discredited Stormont. Even with hindsight I don't think there was ever a military solution, but perhaps we should have thought through what we were attempting to do politically, before we started to unscramble the structure that was there.

So what position should the Army now take in regard to being called out 'in aid of the civil power'? Drawing on the experience of the past fifteen years, a number of principles with which any public order force must comply have emerged within Army thinking.

First, it must work under the rule of law and be responsible to the law and Parliament. Second, it must be compatible with the existing military/police organisation and command structures. Third, it must be both publicly acceptable and effective, which means professional, responsible, disciplined and skilled.

With those principles firmly established, however, the Army is still firmly of the opinion that it would not welcome any involvement, except as a last resort, in maintaining public order. Years of experience have shown Army commanders that it was far easier to become involved than to disengage, and Northern Ireland was a prime example. It laid the Army open to the sort of definition Enoch

Powell gave it when he wrote, in 1977:

> The role of the Army in aid of the civil power is perfectly clear and
> definite: it is a role which has been a hundred times proved and
> demonstrated in experience, and the disastrous consequences of
> departing from it are a military truism. It is not to replace the police. It
> is not to supplement the police. It is not to deploy armament which the
> police do not possess. It is to act as what it is: a killing machine, at the
> moment when authority in the state judges that order can no longer be
> maintained or restored by any other means. The Army is then brought
> in to represent the imminent threat, and if necessary to perform the act
> of killing, albeit minimal, controlled and selective killing. Having
> performed this role, it is instantly withdrawn and the police and civil
> powers resume their functions.

Powell, of course, failed here to take into account the non-lethal
measures which should be used before soldiers opened fire, but to
some senior officers his interpretation of the Army's role was precise
and accurate. In every way they felt it would be most unsatisfactory
to use soldiers as armed policemen, when their temperament,
organisation, training and command structure were geared to a
military purpose.

Other Army officers argued that Powell was dangerously wrong,
and that the Army was not an instrument purely for killing, even in
a conventional war. 'This was the mistake of 1914–1919,' said one,
'when both sides tried to find a key point, and then get through in
a trial of strength. That's why we had Paschendale, Loos and other
battles with such horrendous losses.' It was argued that the Army was
in Northern Ireland to 'win', not to 'kill'; killing was merely a means
to an end and victory was better achieved by catching the enemy off
balance.

Others pointed out that the Army was originally called in to
Northern Ireland because of the failure of the police to contain the
riots, and had this been the only reason it would have been
withdrawn shortly afterwards. However, the Army had to stay on
because of more serious and fundamental failures in that society: a
failure that meant that the police were not able properly to police the
Catholic areas, but only make forays into them; a partial failure of
local government services; and the most serious failure of local
politicians who did not have the flexibility or strength to deal with

the situation. According to one observer in Lisburn:

> The various attempts to achieve a 'political' solution have been both futile and harmful — just stirring the pot. Politicians in Dublin, London, Belfast and Washington have been like small boys eager to pick the scabs of slow healing wounds . . . and then show surprise at the blood which immediately flows. Our aim is to stay in the middle and keep them all apart, until they can do this less painfully.

In the early days the Army was welcomed by the Catholics, soldiers were given cups of tea, and spoke to assorted 'representatives'; they started discos, meals-on-wheels, adventure holidays and other 'good works'. They were then bemused to see all this crashing down on them in riots, shootings, killings and the alienation of the very people they had come to protect from mob violence. It was a long time before soldiers realised that one of the fundamental problems was that people's views of what behaviour is acceptable is governed, very largely, by what they are used to. The 'respectability' of killing in the Republican cause goes back a long way, and as for stoning, the local view was often, 'Well, the lad's doing no harm, he's just stoning the military.'

The Protestants were, by and large, dealt with by the police, and it was the Catholic communities which were of most concern to the Army. These communities were predominantly Republican, which meant that they had the same aspirations as the IRA, and the degree of involvement of sympathisers and active terrorists varied from time to time. One long-term planner at the MOD said:

> Put in a nutshell, the role of the Army is to identify which category a person is in, and try to persuade him into a 'better' category. This is *not* the same as the prevention, detection and prosecution of crime, and it has got bugger-all, directly, to do with killing people.

In 1969, when the Army moved onto the streets, the common military, and political, view was that the crisis would be resolved by the deterrence of the threat of force; by the use of force, particularly lethal force; and by the reassurance which the presence of the Army would give. Placed in such a situation, however, the soldier was under extreme pressure. He was continually reacting to events, to natural pressure from the people, or from terrorists. There was no clear guidance, and he soon saw that all his activities were ineffective other than in a very local sense. This applied to all ranks, from the GOC down to the section corporal. One observer of the scene said:

> I don't think many people who were not soldiers in Ulster in the early days realise the nightmare pressure and the difficulties. It wasn't just a fear of death or injury, although that had its effect. It was the feeling of uncertainty, frustration and helplessness; of not understanding what was involved, or what ought to be done, or what was going to happen next. Among well trained, disciplined and moral troops this leads to an involvement in activity for its own sake, which gives the illusion of achievement, while the situation gradually slips away. It leads to demands for will-o'-the-wisp solutions — like internment, cross-border cooperation, hot pursuit across the border, direct liaison with the Irish Army. But none of these would make any decisive difference. That's with good troops! With bad ones the results are terrifying! The casual killing by Americans of Vietnamese, and the murder squads in South and Central America, are a direct result of these feeling. In the last fifteen years in Northern Ireland the Army has been faced with terrorists embedded in a population sympathetic to the terrorists' ultimate aims. But it did *not* fall into the trap of spiralling alienation — which by all the classic theory is what should have happened. This is truly remarkable!

So senior Army officers studying the problems came to the conclusion that the best course for the future, within the United Kingdom, was to rely on the ordinary police to maintain order, and preferably without the use of specialist anti-riot units. One officer who studied this was Major-General Colin Shortis, who by 1984 was Director of Infantry at Warminster, and he was of the same opinion. After extensive experience in Northern Ireland he wrote in a paper published in 1982 that if the Army *were* to be used, then the potentially contentious issue of command and control had to be sorted out. There should be no question that either the Army or the police would 'come under control of the other'. Moreover, he also ruled out the use of 'elite' forces. Military experience in Northern Ireland had shown that 'highly trained, motivated and elite assault units can sometimes cause as many problems as they solve unless commanded by exceptional leaders of intelligence and morale stature.'

What Shortis did find was that the most complex and crucial factor to the whole problem of public order in the eighties was the adjustment of police attitudes and methods to the demands of a plural society. It was absolutely vital that there should, for instance, be more coloured policemen as well as an improved trust and relationship between the minority communities and the police. This, he felt, should be brought about even if it meant removing officers, often at intermediate level, 'who had failed to respond to the reality of a multi-racial Britain, whose minority members in time will be absorbed into our culture, as have the Romans, the Danes, the Normans, the Huguenots and many others'. These were not the opinions one would have ordinarily expected from an Army officer fifteen years previously. It was all a long way on from the first, shambling steps the Army had taken 'in aid of the civil power' back in 1969. The wheel had turned full circle, as the Army had learned its lessons and now counted the cost.

By the summer of 1984 it had lost 377 killed, the UDR had lost 146, the police — regular and reserve — had lost 198, and 1,668 civilians had died. It was a campaign which had totally changed the Army's anti-riot and counter-insurgency tactics, from the time when they had been put in to tackle the symptoms and 'be seen to be there', to understanding and tackling the fundamental nature of the problem, which was the terrorist embedded in the local population. This had involved local contact, intelligence and military action. To a large extent the Army did come to understand both the people and the enemy, a process which produced tough and experienced junior leaders of the kind who were to be so effective in the Falklands.

Any future involvement by the Army 'in aid of the civil power' is likely to give rise to much acrimonious discussion on the precise roles for the Army and the police. There is a great deal of talk even now about the 'correct' or 'ideal' role of the Army. But the point is that in a 'correct' or 'ideal' situation, the Army will not be needed. It is precisely because the situation is incorrect and not ideal that the Army will be required.

So, if the Army is to be considered in any future internal conflict, what will be its role? There must be as many answers to that as there are regimental commanding officers, which shows that this Army does go through the process of thinking about its problems. What emerges from this is that at least three, fundamental questions should be asked. First, what is the threat? Second, what has failed within the civil administration? Third, how is the local population involved or affected? 'Only when these questions are fully answered,' said one officer, 'can the role of the Army, and the intricate business of relations with the police, be decided. Until then, any discussion on all this is rather like the Zen Bhuddist process of "meditating about the sound of one hand clapping." '

Even so, only the general principles can be decided. What it does mean, however, is that flexibility, at all levels of command and control, is vital, and that individual imagination and effort will always have an effect. An officer who had once commanded a company at Crossmaglen said:

> One day I would like to go back to Loch Ross, just outside Crossmaglen. I would take a rod, or perhaps a gun, and walk across the local estates. Then at the end of a good day in the country call in at a couple of pubs and sit and chat . . . you know . . . 'Do you remember so and so?' I suppose that sounds almost traitorous, but I would love to go back in civilian clothes and wander around and meet people I knew there before — find out how it's changed — see what the attitudes are. Maybe in five or six years from now I'll be able to do that.
>
> Do you think I'm being a touch optimistic?

Another soldier with long experience in the province was probably rather more down-to-earth in feeling it would be a long time before anything like that would be possible.

> I think the solution will be triggered from the South, when the Government there finally decides it is not prepared to put up with this any longer, and we get the opportunity to coordinate our actions across the border. However, I am really convinced it will all trickle on until 2006, when there will be a Catholic voting majority in the North. Then, the democratic process will take the North into the South, and *Dublin* will have to deal with all the trouble that will undoubtedly come from the Protestant minority. And at that stage the British Army, thankfully, will be able to return to its other occupations.

Postscript

On 14 December 1984, Private Ian Thain, 19, was convicted of the murder of Thomas 'Kidso' Reilly, 27, and so became the first soldier to be convicted of murder while on duty in Northern Ireland. Thain was given a life sentence.

In a reserved judgement in Belfast Crown Court, Mr Justice Higgins said that in August 1983, Reilly had been drinking and acting in a disorderly manner. He had run away from an Army patrol, and the corporal had shouted: 'Get him!' Then Thain, whom the judge said was thinking intelligently, had shouted three times: 'Stop, Army, or I will fire!'

Mr Justice Higgins said that Thain, by his actions and decisions, had shown that he was not in a frightened or emotional state, for he had needed a steady hand to bring a rifle with a telescopic sight to his eye, aim and then fire through Reilly's heart. He went on to describe Thain as 'deliberately untruthful' when it suited him, for he had concocted a defence alleging that Reilly was pulling out a pistol to shoot him.

Several other soldiers have been convicted of murder during this fifteen-year period since August 1969, but these were all for criminal acts unconnected with their official duties.

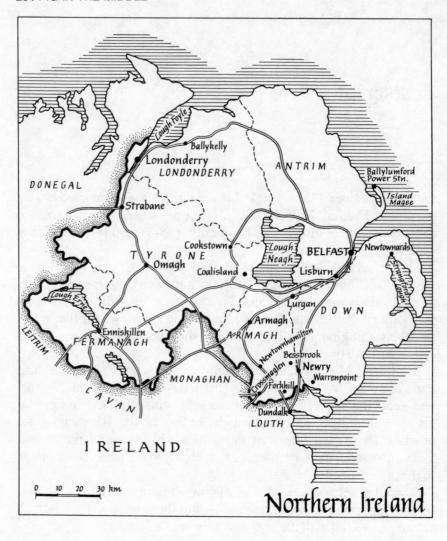

Northern Ireland

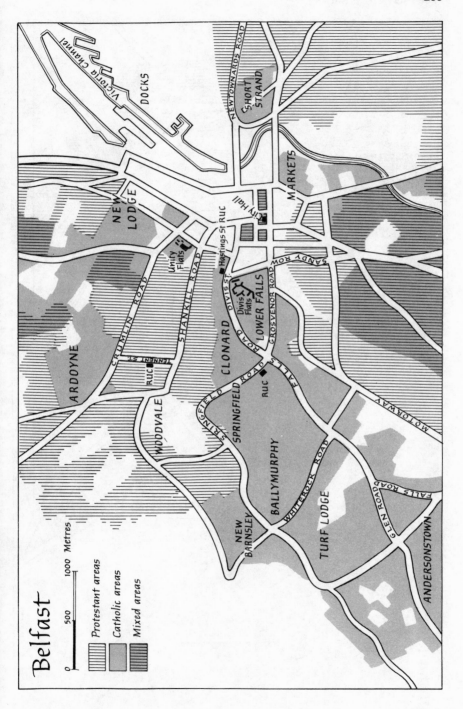

Belfast

Protestant areas
Catholic areas
Mixed areas

0 500 1000 Metres

Victoria Channel

DOCKS

NEWTOWNARDS ROAD

SHORT STRAND

MARKETS

NEW LODGE

City Hall

Hastings St RUC

Unity Flats

Divis St
Divis Flats

LOWER FALLS

SANDY ROW

GROSVENOR ROAD

CRUMLIN ROAD

SHANKILL ROAD

CLONARD

ARDOYNE

TENNENT ST

RUC

WOODVALE

SPRINGFIELD ROAD

RUC

FALLS ROAD

BALLYMURPHY

NEW BARNSLEY

WHITEROCK ROAD

TURF LODGE

GLEN ROAD

MOTORWAY

FALLS ROAD

ANDERSONSTOWN

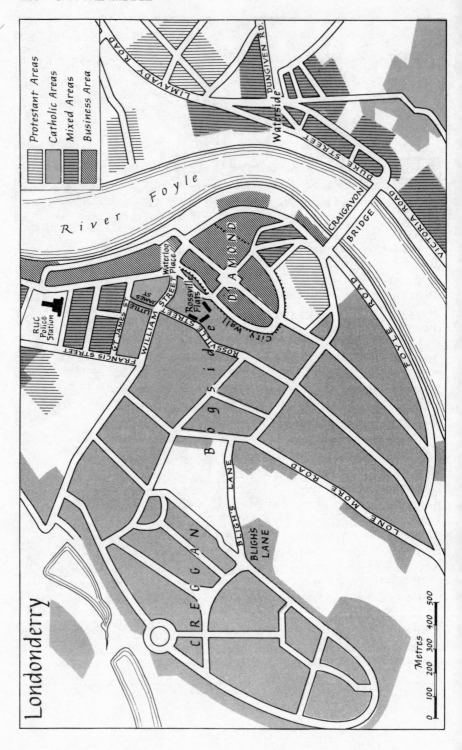

Londonderry

Protestant Areas
Catholic Areas
Mixed Areas
Business Area

River Foyle

LIMAVADY ROAD
DUNGIVEN RD.
Waterside
DUKE STREET
CRAIGAVON BRIDGE
VICTORIA ROAD
FOYLE ROAD
LONE MORE ROAD

RUC Police Station
St JAMES ST
LITTLE JAMES ST
FRANCIS STREET
WILLIAM STREET
ROSSVILLE STREET
Waterloo Place
Rossville Flats
City Wall
D I A M O N D

B o g s i d e
CREGGAN
BLIGHS LANE
BLIGHS LANE

Metres
0 100 200 300 400 500

Bibliography

Ackroyd, Carol; Margolis, Karen; Rosenhead, Jonathan; Shallice, Tim; *The Technology of Political Power* (Pelican Books, London, 1977).

Banks, M. (Major), *Brassey's Annual* (Brassey's Defence Publishers, 1972).

Barzilay, David, *The British Army in Ulster*, Vols 1-4 (Century Books, Belfast, 1973, 1975, 1978, 1981).

Barzilay, David; Murray, Michael, *Four Months in Winter* (Murray and Barzilay, Belfast, 1972).

Bell, Geoffrey, *The Protestants of Ulster* (Pluto Press, London, 1976).

Boulton, David, *The UVF 1966-1973* (Torc Books, Ireland 1973).

Bowyer, Bell J.(Dr), *The Secret Army, the IRA* (The Academy Press, Dublin, revised version 1979).

Boyd, Andrew, *Brian Faulkner and the Crisis of Unionism* (Anvil, Ireland 1972).

Boyd, Andrew, *Holy War in Belfast* (Anvil, London 1969).

Callaghan, James, *A House Divided* (Collins, London, 1973).

Chatres, David, 'Intelligence and Psychological Warfare Operations in Northern Ireland', (*RUSI Defence Study Journal*, September 1977).

Clark, Wallace, *Guns in Ulster* (Constabulary Gazette, Belfast 1968).

Clutterbuck, Richard (Dr), *Protest and the Urban Guerilla* (Cassell, London, 1973).

Coogan, Tim Pat, *The IRA* (Fontana, London seventh impression 1981).

Cooper G.L.C. (Brigadier), 'Some Aspects of Conflict in Ulster' (*British Army Review*, Vol 43 April 1973).

Cronin Sean, *Ireland since the Treaty* (Irish Freedom Press, Ireland, 1971).

Curran Charles, 'Should We Televise Our Enemies?' (*The Listener*, 20 June 1974).

Curran Charles, 'The BBC's Policy on Northern Ireland' (*The Listener*, 18 November 1976).

Deutsch, Richard; Magowan, Vivien, *Northern Ireland, a Chronology of Events* (Vols 1-3, 1968-1974), (Blackstaff Press, Belfast, 1973, 1974, 1975).

Devlin, Bernadette, *The Price of My Soul* (Andre Deutsch, London, 1969).

Devlin, Paddy, *The Fall of the N.I. Executive* (Delvin, Ireland, 1975).

Dillion, Martin; Lehane, Dennis, *Political Murder in Northern Ireland* (Penguin Books, London, 1973).

Downing, Taylor (ed), *The Troubles* (Thames MacDonald, London, 1980).

Edmonds K.R. (Wing Commander), 'The Military and the Media' (National Defence College, March 1975).

Evans E.D. (Major), 'Public Relations Practice within the Army' (National Defence College, 1976).

Faligot, Roger, *The Kitson Experiment* (Zed Press, United Kingdom, 1983).

Farrell, Michael, *Northern Ireland: The Orange State* (Pluto Press, London, 1976).

Faul, Dennis (Father); Murray, Raymond (Father), *Brutalities* (Abbey Printers, Ireland).

Faulkner, Brian, *Memoirs of a Statesman* (Weidenfeld and Nicolson, London, 1978).

Fisk, Robert, *The Point of No Return* (Andre Deutsch, London, 1975).

Flackes, W.D., *Northern Ireland, a Political Directory, 1968-1979* (Gill and Macmillan, Dublin, 1980).

Ford, G.H. (Air Commodore), 'Protest, Violence and Conflict' (Seaforde House Papers, 1974).

Francis, Richard, *Broadcasting to a Community in Conflict* (RIIA Chatham House, 1977).

Fraser, Morris, *Children in Conflict* (Secker & Warburg, London, 1973).

Geraghty, Tony, *Who Dares Wins* (Fontana, London, 1981).

Graham, P.W. (Lt-Colonel), 'Low-Level Civil-Military Co-ordination, Belfast, 1970-1973' (RUSI, September 1974).

Hastings, Max, *Ulster 1969* (Gollancz, London, 1970).

Hoggart, Simon, 'The Army PR Men in Ulster' (*The Listener*, 11 October, 1973).

Hooper, Alan (Major), *The Military and the Media* (Gower, London, 1982).

Kee, Robert, *The Green Flag* (Weidenfeld and Nicolson, London, 1973).

Kelly, Henry, *How Stormont Fell* (Gill and Macmillan, Dublin, 1972).

Kelly, Kevin, *The Longest War* (Brandon, Ireland, 1982).

Kitson, Frank (General), *Low Intensity Operations* (Faber, London, 1971).

Kitson, Frank (General), *Bunch of Five* (Faber, London, 1977).

Limpkin, Clive, *The Battle of Bogside* (Penguin Books, London, 1972).

McCann, Eamonn, *What Happened in Derry* (A Socialist Worker pamphlet, London, 1972).

McCann, Eamonn, *War and an Irish Town* (Penguin Books, London 1974).

McGuffin, John, *Internment* (Anvil, Ireland, 1973).

McGuffin John, *The Guineapigs* (Penguin Books, London 1974).

McCreary, Alf, *Survivors* (Century Books, Belfast, 1976).

MacStiofain, Sean, *Memoirs of a Revolutionary* (Gordon Cremonesi, 1975).

Mulligan, Martin (ed), *Ireland Unfree* (Pathfinder Press, Sydney, Australia, 1981).

Newman, Kenneth, 'Terrorism and Democracy – the Policing Dilemma' (Messina Conference, 1980).

Palmer C.P.R. (Colonel), 'Public Opinion and the Armed Services' (Seaforde House Papers, 1977).

Powell, Enoch, 'Misapplication of the Army in the "aid to the civil power" (4 October, 1977).

Rose, Richard, *Governing without Consensus* (Faber, London, 1971).

Scott-Barrett D.W. (Brigadier), 'The Media, Conflict and the Armed Services' (Seaforde House Papers, 1970).

Serle, John, (Major), unpublished manuscript.

Shortis, Colin, (Major-General), 'Public order in the '80s' (Royal College of Defence Studies, 1981).

The *Sunday Times* Insight Team, *Ulster* (Penguin Books, London, 1972).

Taylor, Peter, *Beating the Terrorists?* (Penguin Books, London, 1980).

Tone, T.W. *Autobiography*, (Vol 1) (Washington, 1826).

Tugwell, Maurice, (Major-General), 'Revolutionary Propaganda and Possible Counter-measures' (National Defence College 1976/77).

Tugwell, Maurice, (Major-General), 'Politics and Propaganda of the Provisional IRA' (New Brunswick University, 1976/1977).

Wain, C., 'Television Reporting of Military Operations' (RUSI, March, 1974).

Wallace, Martin, *Drums and Guns, Revolution in Ulster* (Geoffrey Chapman, London, 1970).

Wallace, Martin, *Northern Ireland: Fifty Years of Self-Government* (David and Charles, Newton Abbot, 1971).

Watt, David (ed), *The Constitution of Northern Ireland* (Heinemann, London, 1981).

Wilkinson, Paul, *Terrorism and the Liberal State* (Macmillan Press, London, 1977).

Defence Year Book (RUSI and Brassey's, Oxford, 1984).

The Northern Teacher (Belfast, 1973).

OFFICIAL PUBLICATIONS

(The Cameron Report)
Disturbances in Northern Ireland: Report of the Cameron Commission (Cmd 532, September 1969, Belfast).
A Commentary by the Government of Northern Ireland to accompany the Cameron Report (Cmd 534, September 1969, Belfast).
(The Hunt Report)
Report of the Advisory Committee on Police in Northern Ireland (Cmd 535, October 1969, Belfast).
A Record of Constructive Change (Cmd 558), August 1971, Belfast.
(The Compton Report)
Report of the Enquiry into the Allegations against the Security Forces of Physical Brutality in Northern Ireland, Arising out of Events on 9th August, 1971 (Cmd 4823, November 1971, London).
(The Widgery Report)
Report of the Tribunal appointed to inquire into the events on Sunday 30th January 1972, which led to loss of life in connection with the procession in Londonderry on that day (H.L. 101/H.C.220) (April 1972, London).
(The Scarman Report)
Violence and Disturbance in Northern Ireland in 1969 (Cmd 566, April, 1972, two volumes, Belfast).
(The Green Paper)
The Future for Northern Ireland: a paper for discussion (October 1972, London).
(The Diplock Report)
Report of the Commission to consider legal procedures to deal with terrorist activities in Northern Ireland (Cmd 5185, December 1972, London).
(The White Paper)
Northern Ireland constitutional proposals (Cmd 5259, March 1973, London).
(The Gardiner Report)
Report of a Committee to consider, in the context of civil liberties and human rights, measures to deal with terrorism in Northern Ireland (Cmd 5847, January 1975, London).
(The Parker Report)
Report of the Committee of Privy Councillors appointed to consider authorised procedures for the interrogation of persons suspected of terrorism (Cmd 4901, March 1972).

Glossary

Alliance Party   Launched in 1970, it aims to attract people from both sides of the community.

APC   Armoured Personel Carrier. In particular the one-ton Humber APC, used for years as a general purpose vehicle for soldiers and stores, and commonly known as a Pig.

Apprentice Boys of Derry   One of the many Protestant loyal orders. Named after thirteen apprentice boys who, in 1689, closed the gates of Londonderry to avoid it falling to the advancing army of King James II.

Ardoyne   A predominantly Catholic area of North Belfast where there was heavy rioting in 1969, and where the Provisional IRA was very active.

Armalite   The IRA's favourite rifle – a light-weight, high-velocity automatic single-shot rifle, much used by the American forces in Vietnam. It fires a small-calibre .233mm round, which allows large quantities to be carried. A great number of those recovered in Northern Ireland have been traced back to the arms dealers in the United States of America.

ATO   Ammunition Technical Officer. Commonly known as a bomb disposal expert.

AVRE   Armoured Vehicle Royal Engineers. Tanks with various pieces of specialist equipment, originally designed to deal with heavy concrete replacements on the Atlantic Wall in 1944.

Banjo   Sandwich (slang). Egg banjo is a fried egg sandwich with a great deal of salt and pepper.

Baton Round   Commonly known as a rubber bullet. Introduced in June 1970 as a weapon which would cover the 50-yard gap between rioters and soldiers, but would not cause bodily harm. Made originally of rubber – and later of hard plastic – it was about 6 inches long and weighed about 5 ozs. 55,000 were fired before the change to plastic in 1975. 44,000 have been fired since then to mid-1984. 15 people have been killed and a number injured or blinded. In July 1984 the European Commission of Human Rights ruled that they were 'less dangerous than alleged' and that their use did not amount to torture or degrading treatment.

Battalion   The major operational unit of an infantry regiment, commanded by a Lieutenant-Colonel. Strength about 650.

Bennett Report   The report produced in 1979 by a three-man committee headed by an English judge, Harry Bennett QC, on police interrogation procedures and the machinery for dealing with complaints against the police. It recommended close circuit television in interview rooms, and access to solicitors by terrorist suspects after forty-eight hours. It also went outside its terms of reference to say that medical evidence showed that some injuries sustained by suspects in police custody had not been self-inflicted.

Bloody Friday   21 July 1972. Eleven people were killed and 130 injured after 26 bombs, planted in Belfast by PIRA, exploded during a busy shopping afternoon.

Bloody Sunday   30 January 1972. Thirteen people shot dead by 1st Parachute Regiment after rioting by a mob of breakaway 'hooligans' which followed an illegal (but otherwise peaceful) march organised by the Derry Civil Rights Association).

Brick   A unit peculiar to Northern Ireland. It was the basic patrolling unit and contained just four men, commanded by a Corporal or Lance-Corporal. Different tasks would be met by using a variable number of bricks.

Brigade   A military formation consisting of three batallions, and commanded by a Brigadier. Strength between 1,800 and 1,900.

B Specials   The name commonly used for the Ulster Special Constabulary, set up in 1920 to combat the IRA, and exclusively Protestant. It was disbanded in 1970.

Cameron Commission   A three-man Commission of Inquiry under Lord Cameron set up in 1969 to inquire into the causes of violence since 5 October 1968. It found there had been a failure of leadership on all sides, and that on occasions that RUC had been inept.

Catholics   Members of the Roman Catholic Church. The 1971 census showed there were 447,919 in Northern Ireland – about a third of the total population of 1,519,640. But nothing is simple in Northern Ireland, and the term Catholics is often used in a political manner to denote those of Nationalist and Republican persuasions.

CLF   Commander Land Forces. In Northern Ireland this is a military officer with the rank of major-general who is responsible to the GOC for day-to-day military operations.

CO   Commanding Officer. A lieutenant-colonel who commands a Battalion.

Company   A unit within a battalion, commanded by a major. There would be a headquarter Company, a Support Weapons company and three rifle companies, with a strength of around 120 soldiers.

Compton Report   A three-man commission under Sir Edmund Compton which inquired into allegations that men arrested on the day internment was introduced on 9 August 1971, had been subjected to brutal treatment. In November 1971 it dismissed charges of brutality, but upheld those of ill-treatment because of interrogation in depth, which involved the five techniques of hooding, exposure to continuous noise, standing against a wall leaning on fingertips and deprivation of food and sleep.

CS gas   Used in riot control, it is contained in a cartridge fired from a hand gun, or in a grenade which is thrown. Sometimes known as tear gas, it has a choking effect and makes eyes water copiously.

Detainee   Someone held without trial for an indefinite period under Emergency Provisions legislation.

Diplock Courts   Following proposals by Lord Diplock, provisions were made in the Emergency Powers Act 1973 for 'no jury' courts for cases involving terrorist offences. One reason given for this was that witnesses were being intimidated by having to appear in front of a jury.

Direct Rule   Imposed by the central Government at Westminster in March 1972. The Northern Ireland Parliament at Stormont was suspended, which meant direct rule of the province from London.

Democratic Unionist Party (DUP)
Led by the Reverend Ian Paisley it was founded in 1971 on an uncompromising Unionist basis.

Falls Road   The main Catholic area of Belfast, running from the city centre largely parallel to the Protestant Shankill Road. It has seen endless confrontation between PIRA and the security forces, and sometimes between PIRA and the OIRA, and between the OIRA and the IRSP.

Fianna Fail   One of the two major political parties in the Irish Republic. It carries on the Republican traditions of Sinn Fein, which in 1921 was bitterly opposed to the Anglo-Irish Treaty which led to partition and the setting up of Northern Ireland.

Fianna na h-Eireann   PIRA's youth wing, whose members are often used as message carriers and decoys.

Fine Gael   One of two major political parties in the Irish Republic. It grew from the pro-Treaty faction of Sinn Fein. It formed the first Government of the Irish Free State. It is often regarded as taking a softer line of the issues of Northern Ireland, and on a United Ireland.

Gardai   Police force for the Republic of Ireland. (Garda – a policeman.)

Gardiner Report   A committee of inquiry headed by Lord Gardiner into measures to deal with terrorism in Northern Ireland in the context of civil liberties and human rights. It found, in January 1975, that detention without trial was a short-term necessity, that the Special Category status for prisoners should be ended and that the normal conventions of majority rule would not work in the province.

Gash   Rubbish (slang).

Goffa waller   Civilian who sells light refreshments to troops (slang).

Greasepits   Area for greasing vehicles. Very tedious form of work (slang).

Groundhog   Tracker dog (slang).

GOC   General Officer Commanding. The senior military officer in Northern Ireland who commands all services, Army, Royal Navy and Royal Air Force. He is a lieutenant-general.

H-Block   The name (based on the shape of the buildings) given by Republicans to the Maze prison outside Belfast for those convicted of terrorist offences. The prison was first officially known as Long Kesh, and later as the Maze Prison. It was here that Republican prisoners went 'on the blanket' in protest at the ending of the Special Category status. They stepped this up by refusing to leave their cells, wash or use toilet facilities. The protest culminated in the hunger strike of 1981 in which ten prisoners died. The first was Bobby Sands, on 5 May, and the last Mickey Devine, on 20 August.

Hunt Report   A committee headed by Lord Hunt proposed, in 1969, comprehensive changes in the security forces. In particular he recommended the disbandment of the B Specials. The announcement of this led to serious rioting by Protestants in Belfast, and the death of the first policeman to die in these troubles, Constable Arbuckle, shot by Protestant gunmen.

ICO   Interim Custody Order. A quasi-judical system brought in by the Detention of Terrorists Order 1973. It was an order signed by the Secretary of State if he felt a case warranted further investigation. It allowed a suspect to be held for twenty-eight days before being brought before a commissioner, who would decide if the detention should be continued.

Info   Information.

Int   Intelligence.

Internment   Internment without Trial was introduced on 9 August 1971 under the Special Powers Act. In an initial dawn swoop code-named 'Operation Demetrius', the security forces arrested 346 IRA suspects out of a total of 520 on their lists. One hundred and four were released within forty-eight hours, but in the same period widespread rioting claimed the lives of twenty-three people.

INLA   Irish National Liberation Army. This is the military wing of the IRSP. It is a small and particularly ruthless para-military group, which gained some disgruntled recruits during the PIRA ceasefire of 1975. It claimed to have planted the car bomb which killed Conservative MP Airey Neave in 1979.

IRSP   Irish Republican Socialist Party. An OIRA splinter group formed in 1974 by members who disagreed with the OIRA ceasefire. The feud between the two sides became very bitter with a large number of inter-factional shootings and assassinations.

Joint Security Committee   The Committee which meets each Monday at Stormont to discuss security policy. The Chief Constable attends and the GOC became a key member on being appointed Director of Operations when the Army was called in 'in aid of the civil power' in 1969. It was chaired by the Northern Ireland Prime Minister (with his Cabinet ministers as members) until Direct Rule was imposed in 1972, when the Sectetary of State for Northern Ireland took over the chair. A second security committee met at Lisburn each Thursday to decide operational policy. This was chaired by the GOC and attended by the Chief Constable. In 1977, when the Chief Constable was appointed Director of Operations, the meetings moved to police headquarters at Knock, with the Chief Constable in the chair.

Lisburn   Shorthand used for the headquarters of the Army in Northern Ireland, which is based in the market town of that name ten miles from Belfast.

Londonderry/Derry   Londonderry is the official name of the city and denotes the British connection. It is used by Protestants, for whom the city symbolises the ultimate in loyalty to the crown, after the apprentice boys barred the gate to King James II in 1689. Catholics and Republicans prefer the old Irish name of Derry.

Loyalist   A term used to denote Protestants who above all wish to maintain the constitutional link with Britain (though not necessarily accepting the authority of Westminster), and who oppose closer links with the Irish Republic.

Motorman   The military operation of 31 July 1972 which cleared the 'No Go' area barricades in Belfast and Londonderry. It was the biggest British military operation since the Suez campaign.

Nationalist Party   Strongly anti-partition in outlook, it faded after the rise of the civil rights movement in 1969.

New Lodge Road   A Catholic area of North Belfast and a centre of PIRA activity.

'No Go' areas   The phrase used to describe areas behind barricades set up between 1969-1972, to keep out the Army, the police and other sectarian groups. They were mainly in Catholic areas of West Belfast, and the Bogside and Creggan in Londonderry, and dominated by PIRA. Sometimes the Protestants set up their own 'No Go' areas, but usually in order to pressurise the security forces to act against those in Catholic areas.

NICRA   Northern Ireland Civil Rights Association. It was established in 1967 to campaign for civil rights, aiming particularly for one-man one-vote in council elections, the repeal of the Special Powers Act and the disbandment of the B Specials. It was often attacked by Unionists as a front for the IRA.

OIRA (The Officials)   Official Irish Republican Army, commonly known as the Official IRA (as opposed to the Provisional IRA). It came into being in 1970, when the IRA split over the proposal to recognise and use the political institutions in Belfast, Dublin and London. The Officials backed this proposal; those who did not walked out to form the Provisional IRA, taunting the Officials with being physically unprepared to fight back against the violence of 1969.

OP   Observation Post. These could be obvious ones, such as those around military positions, or covert ones, for secret surveillance.

Orangemen   Members of the Orange Order, the largest Protestant Organisation in the province. It was first formed in 1795 and took its name from King William of Orange who, during the religious wars of the late seventeenth century, beat King James at the Battle of the Boyne in 1690. This victory is celebrated each year on 12 July with huge Orange Lodge parades across the province. There are close links, and overlapping membership, with the Apprentice Boys of Derry, and Unionist politicians have nearly always felt it necessary to be members of the Orange Order.

Parker Committee   Headed by Lord Parker, it reported in 1972 on methods used to interrogate detainees, particularly the five techniques of interrogation in depth. Lord Parker and John Boyd-Carpenter held that these techniques, subject to certain safeguards, could be justified in exceptional circumstances. Lord Gardiner dissented. The Prime Minister then announced that these techniques would not be used again.

Peace Line   A physical barrier erected in 1969 between the Protestant Shankill and Catholic Falls Road areas of Belfast, to keep the two sides apart.

Peace People   Members of a movement started in 1976 after the three Maguire children were killed by an uncontrolled gunman's car (the driver had been shot by the Army). Two founder members, Mairead Corrigan and Betty Williams, were awarded the 1976 Nobel Peace Prize. It wanted a 'non-violent movement towards a just and peaceful society'. For a period it generated great emotion and huge combined rallies of both Catholic and Protestants, but it was broadly ignored by traditional politicians, and did not sustain its early promise.

People's Democracy (PD)   Established by students in 1968 to fight against what was considered to be repressive legislation. A radical, left-wing group, it proposed a secular, all-Ireland Republic, with the disbandment of the RUC and, later, the UDR. It often campaigned closely with Provisional Sinn Fein – although the relationship was not always comfortable.

Pig   The name commonly used for one of the Army's Armoured Personnel Carriers – the one-ton Humber, powered by a Rolls Royce six cylinder petrol engine. It was ugly in appearance and difficult to drive – hence the name.

PIRA (The Provisionals)   Provisional Irish Republican Army. Formed in 1969 because of opposition within the IRA movement to recognition of the political institutions in Belfast, Dublin and London. It supported the traditional IRA policy of abstentionism, and the use of force to achieve its aims. It was known as PIRA to the security forces, and as the Provies – or Provos – by the local Catholic community. It is the main organisation engaging in violence towards the security forces.

Platoon   A small infantry unit, strength about thirty-three soldiers. There were three to each rifle company and were commanded by a lieutenant.

Pongo   A soldier (Royal Marine slang).

Protestants   Members of the various Protestant churches. The 1971 census showed there were 892,210 Protestants in Northern Ireland, about two thirds of the total population of 1,519,640. The term Protestant is often used in a political manner to denote those who want to maintain links with British and who oppose closer links with the Irish Republic.

RPG Rocket Propelled Grenade. A hand-held anti-tank rocket which was Russian-made.

Rubber Bullet *See* Baton Round.

RUC Royal Ulster Constabulary. The police force of Northern Ireland which contains only a small proportion of Catholic officers.

Sandy Row A Protestant area close to the city centre with a very strong loyalist atmosphere.

Sangar A construction to give cover to a firing position – traditionally a small wall of stones or rocks but more recently can refer to a sophisticated, permanent structure of concrete and corrugated iron.

Saracen A lightly armoured six-wheel vehicle. Often used as an APC, it weighs ten tons and is armed with a turret-mounted Browning machine gun.

SAS 22 Special Air Service, the modern counterpart of the SAS Regiment raised in 1941 to operate behind enemy lines. Particularly trained for long-term surveillance and covert operations, each four-man operational patrol contains a signals, medical, demolition and linguistic capability to provide maximum flexibility. Its organisation and operations are shrouded in secrecy, to the extent that in some circles it is considered an assassination unit, whose reputation strikes more terror than its deeds.

Section The smallest formal infantry unit consisting of ten soldiers. There were three to each platoon, and were commanded by a corporal.

Scarman Tribunal The tribunal under Lord Scarman which investigated the violence of the summer of 1969. Its findings were published in April 1972. It found the disturbances arose from a complex social, economic and political mixture; that the RUC had been seriously at fault on six occasions, but was not a partisan force which had cooperated with Protestants to attack Catholics, and that both communities had shown the same fears, self-help and distrust of lawful authority.

Shankill Road Considered as the major Protestant area of Belfast, and the very core of loyalist strength.

SIB Special Investigation Branch of the military.

SLR Self-Loading Rifle. The standard Army high-velocity 7.62mm rifle.

Special Category The status given in 1972 to convicted prisoners of para-military organisations sentenced to more than nine months imprisonment. They were housed in compounds – in a prisoner-of-war type of regime – allowed to wear their own clothes and were not required to work. The phasing out of this system in 1976 led to the 'blanket' and 'dirty' protests (see H-Block) and ultimately to the hunger strike of 1981 in which ten prisoners died.

Special Powers Act An Act passed in 1922 (and since extended and amended) primarily to repress the IRA and other Republican organisations. It gave wide powers to the authorities, including the power to intern for years without trial or relief of habeas corpus. In law, it also removed any grounds for dispute about the exercise of discretionary powers, authorising the Minister of Home Affairs 'to take all such steps and issue all such orders as may be necessary for preserving peace and order'. It is arguably the most controversial piece of legislation ever introduced in Northern Ireland.

Squaddie A non-military term to describe any junior soldiers – usually corporals, lance-corporals and those of no rank such as private, marine, bombardier, sapper, trooper, guardsman, gunner.

Sterling Sterling sub machine gun. A light 9mm machine gun, with a range of around 150 yards.

Stormont Shorthand for the Parliament (and Government) of Northern Ireland, set up in 1921 and suspended in 1972 (see Direct Rule).

Sunningdale The name given to the conference held in December 1973 at Sunningdale, Berkshire, England, between the British and Irish Governments and the three major Northern Ireland political parties. It lead to the power-sharing executive. However, loyalist opposition to it led to a province-wide strike – organised by the UWC – and under this pressure the executive collapsed.

Tout Informer.

Ulster The old, nine-county province before partition in 1921. Three of these countries are now in the Irish Republic, but Ulster is still a name commonly used (by Protestants rather than Catholics) for Northern Ireland.

UDA Ulster Defence Association. Formed in 1971 as an umbrella organisation for a wide variety of Protestant para-military and vigilante groups in and around Belfast. It had a working-class image, a motto of 'Law before Violence' (though many members seemed to ignore this) and was the largest Protestant para-military organisation in the province.

UDR   Ulster Defence Regiment. Formed in 1970 when the B Specials were disbanded. It was a locally raised and mainly part-time regiment under the control of the Army. Catholics were encouraged to join and in the initial strength of 1,800 in April 1970, 20 per cent were Catholics. This percentage was not maintained. For instance, as early as November 1972, only 4 per cent of the 9,000 odd members were Catholic.

Unionist   A member of one of the various Unionist parties. The original Ulster Unionist Party provided the Government of Northern Ireland from 1921, until Direct Rule in 1972. It began to split up in the early seventies in the face of demands for liberal reforms. Until then, such was its power base that many of its MPs were able to fight unopposed election campaigns for both the Westminster and Stormont parliaments. It stood for maintaining the link with Britain, keeping its own parliament (Stormont) and fighting off attempts to link the North more closely with the Irish Republic.

UVF   Ulster Volunteer Force. An illegal Protestant para-military force. Originally formed by Lord Carson in 1912 to run guns to Ulster to prepare to fight against Home Rule. Many members joined the 36th (Ulster) Division of the British Army which was decimated during the battle of the Somme in 1916. The modern day UVF opposes any liberal reforms in Northern Ireland, and became heavily involved in the assassination of Catholics.

UWC   Ulster Workers Council. The organisation which orchestrated the successful loyalist strike of May 1974 against the power-sharing executive. It had extensive backing from the more extreme loyalist politicians as well as from Protestant para-military groups.

Vanguard (Ulster Vanguard)   Formed in 1972 by William Craig, it was a pressure-group which tried to paper over the cracks in the Unionist movement. It held a number of huge, fascist-type parades.

VCP   Vehicle Check Point.

Visor   The Army magazine in Northern Ireland.

Widgery Report   The inquiry into the shooting of thirteen people on Bloody Sunday, in Londonderry. Lord Widgery's findings were complex, on the one hand saying that there would have been no deaths if the illegal march had not taken place, and on the other that it might have been better for the Army to maintain its low profile approach, and not engage in a big arrest operation. He found that while the Army had been fired on first, some of the Army return fire 'bordered on the reckless', and that none of those killed were proved to have been shot while handling weapons.

Westminster   Shorthand for the Palace of Westminster, which contains Britain's Houses of Parliament – the Commons and the Lords.

Whitehall   Shorthand for the centre of Britain's civil administration system.

Index

Abercorn restaurant explosion, 100-1
Active Service Units (ASUs), 235, 239, 255, 268
Adams, Gerry, 261-2
Ainsworth Avenue, Belfast, 109
Aldergrove Airport, 149, 201
Aldershot bomb explosion (1972), 95
Allen, 'Budgie', supergrass, 276
Alliance Party, 202, 256, 291
ambulance service, 79-80, 82
Ammunition Technical Officers (ATOs), 154-8, 291
Amnesty International, 236
Andersonstown, 110-11, 219, 247, 255, 275
Andrews, Senator John, 102-3
Antrim Road, 50
Apprentice Boys of Derry, 1, 12, 274, 291; March (August 1971), 55-7, 58
Arbuckle, Constable, 28
Ardoyne, Belfast, 17, 35, 47, 138, 213, 216, 291
Armagh, 6, 60, 213; Gough Barracks, 253; women's jail, 265; *see also* South Armagh
Armagh Apple Blossom Festival, 190
armed robbery (by PIRA), 239
Armoured Personnel Carriers (APCs), 114, 116, 291
Aughrim, battle of, 9-10
AVRE (Armoured Vehicle Royal Engineer), 114-15, 116, 291

Baker, Gen Sir Geoffrey, CGS, 45-6, 51, 55, 66, 68
Balkan Street riots (1971), 36-7
Balldougan, murder of O'Dowd family at, 188
Ballendon, Lt-Col, 18
Ballykelly: Droppin Well bomb explosion, 269, 270
Ballykinlar, 15, 60
Ballylumford, 149, 218
Ballymacarret, 81, 129
Ballymena police station, 226
Ballymurphy, 41, 61, 247; rioting (1971), 44; Corpus Christi Church, 179

Ballysillan Post Office, 228
Bankier, Corporal William, 47
Barlow, Gary, 137, 139
Barr, Glen, 144
Baruki, paratrooper, 213
Basques, 235
Baton rounds *see* rubber bullets
BBC reporting, 169, 172
Beattie, Desmond, 54
Belcoo, Fermanagh, 193
Belfast, 14, 63, 73-83, 84-5, 132, 189, 224, 243-4; barricades, 6, 19, 24-5, 30, 31-2; sectarian riots/killings, 10, 14-19, 35, 54, 180-1; 'Murder Gang', 11; troops deployed for first time, 15-21, 24-5; Orange-Green Line, 15; and Peace Line, 24-5, 27; movement of population 36; Balkan Street riots, 36-7; Lower Falls curfew, 22, 37-9; McGurk's Bar explosion, 81-3; Christmas 1971 march, 85; Abercorn restaurant explosion, 100-1 UDA barricades and confrontation with Army, 108-10; Bloody Friday, 111-12, 113; local Catholic community in, 125-6; Protestant areas, 129; 1000lb bomb defused by ATOs, 154-8; Army covert operations, 216; and Army/police joint operations room, 217; police operations, 217-18, 219; 1981 hunger strike, 264-5; Provisional Sinn Fein march (1984), 274-5
Belfast Telegraph, 56, 84, 137
Bennett Report (on police interrogation), 236, 292
Bessbrook, 189, 247; army base, 185, 194, 207, 255
Best, Ranger, 108
Birmingham pub bombings, 175, 176
'Black Propaganda' campaign, Army's, 173, 174
black taxis, Provisionals', 68
Blair, Lt-Col David, 249, 250, 252
Bloody Friday (1972), 111-12, 113, 292

Bloody Sunday (1972), 71, 85-94, 175, 176, 250, 292
Blue Lamp Discos, 192, 256
Bodenstown, annual pilgrimage to Wolfe Tone's grave, 237, 261-2
Bogside (Derry), 24, 62, 71, 72, 73, 85, 86, 87, 112, 114; seige of (1969), 1-7; Operation Motorman, 116-17
Bogside News, 117
Bohan, Sergeant, 229
Bombay Street, Belfast, 17, 18
booby-traps, 206
border areas, 100, 132, 185-9, 193, 204, 207-16, 243, 255; cross-border cooperation, 161-2, 204-6, 241-2, 252, 258; Army patrols, 185-8, 209-12; and British soldiers' incursions into Republic, 194-6; Crossmaglen, 207-16; hot pursuit across, 232, 252; Warrenpoint murders, 248-50, 251
Boswell, Brig, 109
Bourne Report ('The Way Ahead'), 184-5, 262; review of (1984), 272
Boyd, Andrew, *Holy War in Belfast*, 10
Boyd-Carpenter, John, 104
Boyle, John, murder of, 229-31
Boyne, battle of the, 9-10
Brabourne, Dowager Lady, 248
Brabourne, Lord and Lady, 248
Bradford, Rev. Robert, murder of, 273
Bradley, Sam, 15
British Army; first development of, 6-7, 12-21, 24-5; Lt-Gen Freeland's appointment as GOC, 8, 11-12; counter-insurgency campaigns, 33-4, 41-4, 52-3; allegations of brutality and torture by, 38, 60, 65, 66, 79, 95-6, 104, 124, 138-9; Lower Falls curfew, 37-9; combined Army/police study day, 39-40; appointment of Farrar-Hockley as first CLF, 40; 'Some Facts about Northern

Ireland', 41; Kitson's theories, 41-4; IRA secret talks with, 45; Tuzo appointed GOC, 45-6; legal problems/powers, 47-9, 62-3, 96-8, 130-1, 165-7; Yellow Cards, 49-50, 137, 140, 165, 166; Intelligence, 51-2, 60, 69, 105, 119, 121, 132, 133-6, 141-2, 199, 242, 244, 267-8; internment, 53-4, 55-67; and interrogation in depth, 22, 65, 66-7, 104-5; in Derry, 70-3, 85-94, 244; in Belfast, 73-83, 84-5, 87, 132, 133, 224, 243-4; living conditions, 74-5, 81, 163, 208-9; four-month tours, 80-1, 133; McGurk's Bar explosion, 81-3; Bloody Sunday, 85-94; Direct Rule, 103-7; IRA cease-fires, 107-8, 110-11, 178-81, 185, 188; UDA confrontation with, 108-10; Bloody Friday, 111-12, 113; Operation Motorman, 112, 113-17; NITAT training, 121, 139-41, 196-7; information-gathering, 122-8, 133, 134-6, 139-40; and Protestants, 126-30; 'soldier's arrests', 131; Sir Frank King appointed GOC, 132; Interim Custody Orders, 132-3; covert operations, 133-4, 216-17, 228, 234, 238, 263, 264; computers used by, 135; and informers, 135-6; and UWC strike, 144-54; bomb-disposal experts, 154-8; relations with the South, 161-2, 184, 194-6, 204-6, 232, 241-2, 252; prosecution of soldiers, 165-7; media's reporting of events, 167-73; and public relations, 173-5, 263, 266-7; children's holiday camps run by, 177-8; Sir Frank King leaves Ulster, 182-3; and House appointed GOC, 183-4; border areas, 185-9, 194-6, 204-6, 209-16, 241-2, 255; Spearhead battalion, 189, 193; Provos 1976 bombing campaign, 189-90; Joint Directive with police, 192-3; in Crossmaglen, 207-16; murder of Robert Nairac, 213-16; joint operations room in Belfast, 217; Lt-Gen Creasey appointed GOC, 220; reduction in troops, 221, 257, 264, 265, 273; murder of John Boyle by SAS, 229-31; Chief of Staff reports, 231-2; Glover Report, 238-41, 244; and Glover's appointment as CLF, 242; Warrenpoint

ambush, 248-50, 251, 259; Mrs Thatcher's visit to Ulster, 251-9; Sir Maurice Oldfield's appointment as Coordinator, 258-61; and Sir Richard Lawson appointed GOC, 262-4; low profile policy of, 263, 266-7; Ballykelly bomb explosion, 269, 270; 'shoot to kill' policy, 271; Sir Robert Richardson appointed GOC, 271; rule of, 276-82
Brockway, Lord Fenner, 85
Brooke, Captain, 37
Brookeborough, Lord, 10-11, 37
B Specials (police auxiliaries), 5, 11, 13, 14, 18, 23, 27, 34, 98, 177, 186, 292; disbandment of, 28-9
Buncrana, Co Donegal, 117
Burntollet, 128

Cahill, Joe, 61-2, 78
Callaghan, James, as Home Secretary, 7, 25, 29, 35
Cameron Report, 27-8, 292
Canavon, Michael, 231
Card, Frank, 45
Carrickfergus, 193
Carrington, Lord, as Defence Secretary, 47, 50, 51, 56, 59, 115
cease-fires, 101, 107-8, 110-11, 176-7, 178-81, 181, 185, 188
Carroll, Roddy, 270, 271, 275
Carver, Sir Michael, CGS, 54-5, 57, 102-3, 112, 115
Channon, Paul, 111
Chates, David, 105
Cheshire Regiment, 269
Chichester-Clark, Maj James, 5, 16, 19-20, 24, 45, 46, 50, 51
Chief Constable see Flanagan; Hermon; Newman; Shillington, Young
Chief of General Staff (CGS) see Baker; Carver
Chief of Staff see Tickell
Citizen Press, 22-3
Clare, John, 5
Claremont, Co Armagh, 194
Claudia, 235
Clonard, 84; monastery, 17
Coalisland, 6
Coe, Colonel Mark, murder of, 246
Coleraine; New University of Ulster, 220; police station, 226
Commander Land Forces (CLF) see Farrar-Hockley; Ford; Glover
'the Committee', Catholic, 19
'Committee of Twenty', Catholic, 70, 72
Common Market (EEC), 55, 83, 272

'community spokesmen' (IRA leaders), 45
Compton Report, 66, 104, 293
Connolly, James, 2
Conservative Government, 35, 38; 1974 General Election lost by, 144; Mrs Thatcher's visit to Ulster, 251-9
Constitutional Convention (1975), 180, 188
Coogan, Tim Pat, *The IRA*, 11
Cook, Judith, 197
Cooper, Sir Frank, 176, 184
Cooper, Ivan, 62
Corrigan, Mairead, 198, 199, 297·
Corrymela conference centre,
Council of Ireland, 143-4, 146
Craig, William, 27, 99, 130, 144, 146, 151
Creasey, Lt-Gen Sir Timothy, GOC, 220-1, 226-7, 228, 231, 232, 243, 252, 253, 257, 260, 262
Creggan (Derry), 71, 72, 73, 85, 86, 87, 89, 112, 114, 116-17
Criminal Law Act (1967), Section 3, 49
Crossmaglen, 185, 187, 188, 255, 282; British Army in, 207-16; Mrs Thatcher's visit to, 253
Crumlin Jail, Belfast, 61
Crumlin Road, Belfast, 18, 276
CS gas (tear gas), 4-5, 13, 23, 37, 72, 85, 276, 293
Cuba, 235
Cubbon, Sir Brian, 197
Cunningham, Cyril, 105
curfews, 22, 37-9, 40, 50, 52-3, 77
Curtis, Gunner, 45
Cusack, Seamus, 54

Daily Express, 220
Daily Mirror, 233; printing plant blown up, 55; calls for Army's withdrawal, 233-4
Darlington conference (1972), 130, 143, 153
Democratic Unionist Party, 130, 143, 144, 293
Derry see Londonderry
detainees, 293; release of, 164, 176, 177, 182, 199, 226
Detention of Terrorists Order (1973), 133
detention, selective, 232, 258
detention without trial, 120, 132-3, 180, 183, 294; see also internment
Devlin, Bernadette, 1-2, 13, 35
Devlin, Paddy, 17, 60, 147
'dicks' (young Provo scouts), 140, 141
Dillon, Martin and Lehane, Denis, *Political Murder in Northern Ireland*, 128
Diplock ('no jury') courts, 131, 217, 293

Diplock Report, 130-1
Direct Rule, 43, 64, 83, 84, 94, 97, 102-6, 112, 126, 132, 152, 154, 203, 293
Donegall Pass police station, 15
Down Orange Welfare, 144
Downes, Sean, 274
Droppin Well bombing, 269, 270
Drumintree, 215
Drumm, Jimmy, 237-8
Drumm, Maire, 238
Dublin, 47; Easter Rising (1916), 10; march in protest at Bloody Sunday, 93-4; Special Criminal Court, 195, 199; murder of British Ambassador, 197; IRA mortar factories, 207
Dungiven, 6
Dunloy graveyard shooting, 229
Dyball, Brig, COS, 12

Easter Rising (1916), 10
Elizabeth I, Queen, 8
Elizabeth II, Queen, visit to Ulster (1977), 219-20
Emergency Provisions Act (1973), 131
Enniskillen, 101
Erskine-Crum, Lt-Gen, 45
Evans, I.D., 170
Ewart-Biggs, Sir Christopher, murder of, 197, 246

Faligot, Roger, 43-4
Falls Road, Belfast, 6, 15, 17, 24, 25, 73, 75, 101, 293; Lower Falls curfew (1971), 22, 37-9, 40, 79
Farrar-Hockley, Maj-Gen Anthony, CLF, 40, 45, 52, 66
Farrell, Michael, 40, 60, 77; *The Orange State*, 47
Faul, Father, of Dungannon, 95-6
Faulkner, Brian, 23, 53, 56, 57, 58, 59, 61, 77, 100, 102-3, 108, 110, 111, 130, 152; becomes Ulster Prime Minister, 51; and resigns, 103; and Northern Ireland Executive, 145-6, 148, 149, 150
Feakle, County Clare, 176
Ferguson, Fusilier, 210, 211
Fianna Fail, 241, 293
Fianna na h-Eireann (PIRA's youth wing), 239, 294
Fine Gael, 241, 294
Fisk, Robert, 145, 174
Fitt, Gerry, 6
Fitzgerald, Garrett, 162, 195, 196
Fitzpatrick, Father, of Ballymurphy, 111
Flanagan, Sir James, Chief Constable, 159, 191

Ford, Maj-Gen Robert, CLF, 58, 59, 65, 69, 86, 87-8, 89, 90, 102, 106, 109-10, 139; and Op Motorman, 114, 115, 116-17
Forkhill, 186
Fortnight, 38
Four Square Laundry operation, 134
Francis, Richard, 169
Fraser, Morris, 107
'Freds', 69, 134
Free Citizen, 23
Freeland, Lt-Gen Sir Ian, GOC, 8, 11-12, 21, 24, 25, 26-7, 28, 32, 35, 36, 49, 45; appointed Director of Operations, 26; Lower Falls curfew imposed by, 37; combined Army/police study day held by, 39-40
Free Presbyterian Church, 16

Galvin, Martin, 274-5
Gardai (Republic of Ireland's police force), 162, 176, 194-5, 197-8, 205-6, 207, 232, 233, 241, 248, 252, 256, 263, 294
Gardiner, Lord, 104
Gardiner Report (1975), 294
General Election, British (1974), 144
General Officer Commanding (GOC), role of, 8, 26-7, 28, 295; *see also* Creasey; Freeland; House; King; Lawson; Richardson; Tuzo
Geraghty, Tony, 79
Girdwood, 60
Glenshane Pass, 108
Glover, Maj-Gen, James CLF, 238, 242, 251
Glover, Report, 238-41, 242, 244
Government of Ireland Act (1920), 6, 10, 96, 99
Green Paper (1972), 130
Grenadier Guards, 25, 30
Grew, Seamus, 270, 271, 275
Grovefield Loyalist Centre, Willowfield, 35
Guardian, 173, 262-3
Guildford pub bombing (1974), 175

Hailsham, Lord, 97
Hammond, J.L. *Gladstone and the Irish Nation*, 200
Hammond, Ranger Louis, 136
Hanna, Billy, 228
Hannaway, Kevin, 45
Hannaway, Liam, 45
Hanson, Maj, 14
'Harry's Game' (Yorkshire TV), 263
Hastings Street police station, seige of, 14
H-Block, 294

Healey, Dennis, 66
Heath, Edward, 50, 57, 59, 102, 104, 246; and Op Motorman, 115; defeated in 1974 General Election, 144
Henry Taggart Memorial Hall, army disco, 41
Hermon, Sir John, Chief Constable, 184, 262, 266, 273
Highland Fusiliers, 46-7
Hind, Lnce-Cpl, 210, 211
Hitchcock, Maj, 23
Hoggart, Simon, 173
Holland, Mary, 25
hot pursuit, 104, 162, 198, 212, 232, 252, 255, 258
House, Lt-Gen Sir David, GOC, 183-4, 186, 192, 199, 220
Hudson, Brig, 15
Hughes, Francis, 268-9
Hume, John, 5, 62, 96, 147, 148, 270
hunger strike (1981) 264-5, 268
Hunt Report, 28-9, 294

IBA, 173
incendiary bombs, 222-3, 245
Information Policy (Army Press Office), 173
INLA (Irish National Liberation Army), 237, 245, 295; murder of Airey Neave by, 246-7; 'Droppin Well' bombing, 269, 270; and shooting of Seamus Grew and Roddy Carroll, 270, 271; Mountain Hall Gospel Lodge massacre, 273
Intelligence, 51-2, 60, 65, 66, 69-70, 105, 119, 121, 132, 133, 141-2, 143, 199, 214, 238, 242, 244, 261, 267-8
Interim Custody Orders (ICOs), 120, 132, 133, 135, 180, 184, 294-5
internment, 22, 53-4, 55-67, 68, 69, 77, 104, 117, 130, 131, 199, 295; Op Demetrius, 57-61, 98, 295; *see also* detainees; detention
interrogation (in depth), 22, 65, 66-7, 104-5, 236, 292
The Investigator, 35-6
IRA (Irish Republican Army), 10, 11, 20, 23, 29, 34, 35, 37, 61, 63, 72, 73, 101; split into Official and Provisional, 22, 30-1; Army Council, 31; Lower Falls curfew, 37-8; and Kitson counter-terrorist theories, 43-4; Army's secret talks with, 45; internment, 55-67, 68; Bloody Sunday, 85-94; cease-fire (June 1972), 107-8, 110-11; and Operation Motorman, 114-17; informers, 135-6; media's

reporting of events, 168-73; *see also* Official IRA; Provos

Iranians, 235

Irish Army, 161-2, 184, 187, 198, 232, 256, 258

Irish Republican Publicity Bureau, Dublin, 107

Irish Republican Socialist Party (IRSP), 245, 295

Irish Times, 174, 203, 270-1

Irish Volunteers, 237

ITN reporting of events, 168-9, 171, 172

Jacobs, Eric, 41

James I, King, 8

James II, King, 9-10

John, Pope, 262

Joint Directive (1976: Army/police), 192-3

Joint Security Committee, 46, 295

Joint Services Intelligence School, Maresfield, 66

Kelley, Kevin, 199

Kelly, Billy, 145

Kennedy, Paddy, 61

Killea, 206

King, Lt-Gen Sir Frank, GOC, 132, 133, 143, 147, 148, 149, 151, 152, 159-160, 177; and prosecution of soldiers, 166-7; appointed C-in-C BAOR, 182-3

Kitson, Brig Frank, 64, 121; *Low Intensity Operations*, 41, 43; counter-insurgency theories, 41-4; *Bunch of Five*, 222

knee-capping, 36, 68, 136, 272

Knock police headquarters, 6, 159, 184, 295

Labour Party/Government, 34, 38, 162, 175, 246; 1974 General Election won by, 144; calls for United Ireland by, 272; *see also* Mason, Roy; Rees, Merlyn

Lagan, Chief Superintendent Frank, 86, 87, 89, 90, 92, 93

La Mon House hotel fire bombing, 223, 228

Laneside, Belfast Loch, 217

Lawson, Lt-Gen Sir Richard, GOC, 262-4, 266-7

Lehane, Denis *see* Dillon and Lehane

Lenadoon housing estate, 110-11

Letterkenny Hospital, 54

Libération, 43-4

Libya, 235

Light Infantry, 2nd Bn, 30

Light Infantry, 3rd Bn, 14, 18

Ligoniel, 46-7

Lisburn Army headquarters, 8,

22, 28-9, 31, 34, 159, 160, 295; *see also* British Army

Londonderry/Derry, 23, 30, 38, 45, 70-3, 101, 111, 132, 244, 295; sectarian rioting, 1-6, 35, 54; troops deployed for first time in, 6-7, 12-14; 'No Go' areas, 24, 70, 85, 112; Apprentice Boys' March (1971), 55-7; barricades, 70, 114; 'Committee of Twenty', 70, 72; unemployment and religious mix, 70-1; YDHs in, 71-2, 85, 88; Bloody Sunday, 85-94; and Operation Motorman, 113-17; local Catholic community, 126; IRA fire-bombing of bus depot, 223; 1984 Protestant march, 274

Long, Captain William, 50

Long Kesh airfield, 24

Long Kesh prison, 54, 55, 77, 120, 124; *see also* Maze

Lower Donegall Street (Belfast), 101

Lower Falls area, 40; Balkan Street riots (1971), 36-7; curfew (1971), 22, 37-9, 40, 79; *see also* Falls Road

Lowry, Sir Robert (later Lord), Lord Chief Justice of Northern Ireland, 96, 230, 261

Lurgan, 6

Lynch, Jack, 47, 55, 241

McAteer, Eddie, 13

McCann, Eamonn, 13

McCorley, Col Roger, 11

McDade, James, 175

McGlinchey, Dominic, 270

Maguire children, death of, 274

McGurk's Bar explosion, 81-3

McKee, Billy, 45

McKittrick, David, 174, 203-4

MacLellan, Brig Pat, 86, 89-90

McVeigh, Patrick, 128

Magilligan, 60, 91

Maidstone prison-ship, Provisionals' escape from (1972), 95

Malone Road, Belfast, 189-90

Manual of Military Law, 276, 277

marches and processions, 129; banning of, 55, 58, 85, 86; Apprentice Boys' (Londonderry 1971), 55-7; Bloody Sunday (1972), 85-94; Burntollet People's Democracy (1969), 128; Protestant (Londonderry 1984), 274; and Provisional Sinn Fein (Belfast 1984), 274-5

Martin, Leo, 45

Mason, Roy: as Defence

Secretary, 189; as Secretary of State for N. Ireland, 200-3, 217, 219, 220, 221, 240

Mater Hospital, 59

Maudling, Reginald, as Home Secretary, 35, 36, 38, 84, 96-97

Maxwell, Paul, 248

Maze Prison, 226, 235, 294; hunger strike (1981), 264-5, 268; mass breakout of Republicans from (1983), 273: H-Block, 294; *see also* Long Kesh

media reporting of events, 167-75

MI5, 69, 184

MI6, 69, 197, 258

Miami Showband, 181

Military Police, 30

Military Reconnaissance Force units, 69

Montgomery, Eric, 145

Morrison, Danny, 273

Mountain Hall Gospel Lodge massacre, 273

Mountain View Tavern, 181

Mountbatten of Burma, Earl, murder of, 248, 257, 258

Mountpottinger police station, Belfast, 2

Mullaghmore, Co Sligo, Mountbatten's murder at, 247-8

Mullen, Father, 61

'Murder Gang', 11

Murder Triangle, 187

Murphy, Canon, 40

Murray, Father, of Armagh, 95-96

nail-bombs, 54, 84, 119

Nairac, Capt Robert, murder of, 213-16

Napier, Lt-Gen, 17

Narrow Water, murder of soldiers at, 249-50

National Council of Irish Americans, 203

National Democratic Party, 54

Nationalist Party, 296

NATO, 264

Neave, Airey, 198, 232; murder of, 246-7

New Barnsley, 42; Orange Order parade, 31

New Ireland Forum, Dublin, 272

New Lodge Road, Belfast, 82, 83, 180-1, 296

Newman, Sir Kenneth: as Senior Deputy Chief Constable, 160-1, 184; as Chief Constable, 191, 192, 193, 199, 203, 217-18, 221, 226-7, 236, 243; Queen's visit, 219-20; Mrs Thatcher briefed by, 253-7; appointed Commandant of

Police Staff Training College, Bramshill, 262

Newry, 6, 188, 194, 255; police station, 226

Newsletter, 47

News of the World, 198

Newtownhamilton, 242

Nicholas, David, 168-9, 171, 172

Niedermayer, Thomas, 174

94th Locating Regiment, Royal Artillery, 45

NITAT training, 121-2, 139-41, 196-7

'No Go' areas, 19, 24, 25, 34, 70, 73, 85, 94, 104, 108, 112-13, 127, 186, 296; Operation Motorman, 112, 113-17

NORAID, 239, 274

Northern Ireland Civil Rights Association (NICRA), 20, 22-3, 231, 296; Bloody Sunday, 85-94

Northern Ireland Committee of Cabinet (London), 56-7

Northern Ireland Executive, 143, 144, 145-7, 148, 149-50, 151-2, 159

Northern Ireland Parliament *see* Stormont

Observation Posts (OPs), Army, 133-4, 216, 296

O'Dowd family, murder of, 188

Official IRA (OIRA), 38, 47, 75, 78, 215, 237, 245, 295, 296; IRA split into Provisionals and, 22, 30-1; Aldershot bombing, 95; *see also* IRA; Provos

Oldfield, Sir Maurice, Northern Ireland Coordinator, 258-61

O'Neill, Hubert, coroner, 93

Operation Demetrius, 57-61, 65, 295

Operation Motorman, 112, 113-17, 118, 127, 296

Orange Hall, Shankill Road, 164

Orange Order, Orangemen, 31, 35-6, 296

Orange Volunteers, 144

Osborne, Private Maurice, 30

Paisley, Rev. Ian, 16, 18, 27, 56, 130, 143, 144, 146, 151, 179, 188, 217, 266

Parachute Regiment, 213; 1 Para, 87-8, 89, 90, 91, 93; IRA bombing of HQ mess, Aldershot, 95; 2 Para, 249-50

Parker Committee (1972), 104, 297

patrols, British Army, 73-4, 75-6, 88, 103, 119, 133, 134, 140-1, 185-8, 209-12

Peace Line, 24-5, 27, 297

Peace Movement, 199, 297

Peacocke, Sir Anthony, Inspector General, 6, 12

Pearse, Patrick, 237

People's Democracy (PD), 23, 40, 60, 71, 77, 297; Burntollet march, 129

PIRA *see* Provisional IRA

PLO, 235

police *see* RUC; Special Branch; SPG

police primary policy, 154, 184-5, 199, 217-19, 221-2, 228, 243-4, 245, 246, 266, 270, 276

Porter, Robert, 6-7

Pounder, Lnce-Cpl John, 30

Powell, Enoch, 277-8

power-sharing executive, 130, 143-4, 153, 159, 184

press coverage *see* media

Prevention of Terrorism (Temporary Provisions) Act (1974), 175-6

Price sisters, 176

Prince of Wales Own Regiment, 3, 13

prison officers, Provos' murder of, 190

protection money, 68

Provisional IRA (Provos: PIRA), 22, 30-2, 35, 39, 40, 45, 52, 53, 55, 68, 76, 78, 79, 98, 220, 297; Lower Falls curfew, 37-9; terror campaigns, 40, 45, 46-7, 55, 76-7, 78, 95, 108, 111-12, 118; internment, 53-4, 55-67, 68; 'justice' dealt out by, 68; recruitment to, 77, 104, 113, 239; escape from *Maidstone* prison-ship, 95; Abercorn restaurant explosion, 100-1; cease-fires, 101, 107-8, 110-11, 176-7, 178-81, 185, 188; and Direct Rule, 104; Bloody Friday, 112-13; strength of, 113, 118; Army research into, 123-4; intelligence officer, 124; 'dicks', 140, 141; propaganda, 172, 266; mainland Britain bombing campaigns, 175-6, 246; border areas, 185-9, 206, 208-16; 1976 bombing offensive, 189-90; murder of prison officers by, 190; reprisal killings, 193-4; murder of Ewart-Biggs, 197; US support for, 203-4, 239, 274; booby traps devised by, 206; and mortar attacks, 207; in Crossmaglen, 208-16; murder of Robert Nairac, 213-16; attrition rate against, 220, 221, 228, 235-6; fire-bomb campaign, 222-3; reorganisation of, 226, 227-8, 235-6, 237, 238, 245; foreign contracts, 234-5; and Active Service Units (ASUs), 235,

239, 256; Jimmy Drumm speech at Bodenstown, 237-8; Glover Repport, 238-41; sources of income, 239; and terrorist pay, 239; and weapons, 239, 240, 242, 245; and Southern Ireland, 241-2; 1979 campaign, 245-50; murder of Earl Mountbatten, 247-8; and Warrenpoint ambush, 248-50, 251; bomb tunnels (escape routes), 255; Gerry Adams at Bodenstown, 261-2; hunger strike at Maze, 264-5, 268; punishment shootings by, 272-3; and Belfast march (1984), 274-5; *see also* IRA; Official IRA

Queen's Own Highlanders, 249

Queen's Regiment, 2nd Battalion, 16-17, 30

Rawlinson, Sir Peter, Attorney-General, 166

Red Hand Commandos, 128

Rees, Merlyn, Secretary of State for Northern Ireland, 144, 145-6, 147, 148, 149-50, 151-3, 159-60, 164, 180, 182, 183, 188, 199, 201, 216; Ulsterisation and police primacy policy, 184-5; leaves Ulster and appointed Home Secretary, 200

Reid, Fus, 210-11

remote-controlled bombs, 197, 198

Republic of Ireland (formerly Irish Free State): British Army's relations with, 161-2, 184, 194-6, 204-6, 232, 241-2, 252, 258; hot pursuit across border into, 232, 252; Provos' activities in, 241-2; murder of Earl Mountbatten, 247-8; calls for closer links between Northern Ireland and, 272; *see also* border areas; Dublin; Gardai

Republican Labour Party, 54

Republican News, 173, 175, 192, 223, 246, 261

Richardson, Lt-Gen Sir Robert, GOC, 271, 272

Robinson, John 270

Rooney, Daniel, 128

Rosemount police station, 5

Royal Anglians, 41

Royal Green Jackets, 47, 89

Royal Highland Fusiliers, 209-11

Royal Irish Rangers, 108

Royal Marine Commandos, 27, 91; 45 Commando, 62-3; 41 Commando, 224

Royal Regiment of Fusiliers, 81-83, 190; IRA shooting of, 185-86

Royal Regiment of Wales, 16-17
Royal Scots, 271
Royal Victoria Hospital, Belfast, 55
RTE (Irish TV), 99
rubber bullets (Baton rounds), 47, 62, 72, 85, 291-2
RUC (Royal Ulster Constabulary), 11-12, 13, 20, 21, 23, 77, 136, 160, 161-3, 177, 178, 184, 192-4, 199, 200, 203, 205, 217, 226, 238, 298; seige of Bogside (1969), 1-6; Sir Arthur Young's Force Order, 29, 30; combined Army/police study day, 39-40; Sir Graham Shillington appointed Chief Constable, 45; interrogation by, 66-7, 236-7, 292; and intelligence, 51, 69, 242, 267; alleged torture and brutality, 27, 95-6, 236, 275; relations with Gardai, 162, 233, 252, 256; and public relations, 172, 218; Kenneth Newman appointed Chief Constable, 191, 192; Blue Lamp Discos, 191-2, 256; Joint Directive with Army, 192-3; community relations, 202, 256; control of security by, 217-19, 222, 226, 228, 231; and joint operations room, 217; Queen's visit, 219-20; murder of John Boyle, 229-31; US Congress embargo on arms sale to, 236-7; Provisionals' attacks on, 246; Mrs Thatcher's visit, 253-8; force strength increased, 256-7, 267, 273; Sir Maurice Oldfield's appointment as Coordinator, 258-61; Sir John Hermon appointed Chief Constable, 262, 266; hunger strike (1981), 264-5; shooting of Seamus Grew and Roddy Carroll, 270, 271; 'shoot to kill' policy, 270-1, 275; covert operations, 271; Belfast march (1984), 274-5
RUC Reserve, 2, 5, 273

Sands, Bobby, 255, 265
SAS (Special Air Service), 66, 69, 128, 133, 188, 189, 197, 199, 211-12, 229, 247, 298; incursions into Republic, 194-5, 205; murder of John Boyle, 229-31
Scarman Report (1972), 298
Scots Guards, 219
Scottish settlers, 8-9
SDLP (Social Democratic Labour Party), 54, 78, 113, 130, 131, 143, 146, 162, 188, 202, 231, 270

Sea Eagle, HMS, 5, 30
Serle, Capt John, 155-8
Seymour, Gerald, *Harry's Game*, 263
Shankill Road, Belfast, 15, 17, 23, 24, 27, 28, 108, 110, 130, 138, 164, 181, 218, 276, 298
Shillington, Sir Graham, Chief Constable, 3, 4, 6, 45
'shoot to kill' policy, 270-1, 275
Shorlands, Belfast, 14, 15
Short Strand, Belfast, 35, 181, 255
Shortis, Maj-Gen Colin, 280-1
Silkin, Sam, Attorney-General, 166
Simpson, Fus, 210
Sinn Fein, 31, 176, 245, 250, 272-3; incident centres, 176, 185; Bureau for Foreign Affairs, 234-5; IRSP splits away from, 245; Belfast March (1984), 274-5
Smallcliff army training area, 196
Smith, Howard, 70
Smythe, Rev. Martin, 276
Snow, Major, 82
South Armagh, 185-9, 197, 214, 231, 232, 243, 246, 253; Murder Triangle, 187; *see also* Crossmaglen
South Armagh Republican Action Force, 189
Soviet Union, 235
Spearhead battalion, 189, 193
Special Branch, 42, 51, 52, 53, 58, 60, 66, 105, 201, 216, 267
Special Category, 299
Special Investigation Branch (SIB), 138, 298
Special Patrol Group (SPG), 39
Special Powers Act, 49, 60, 96, 97, 132-3, 295, 299
Special Support Units (police), 255, 271
Spring in Springfield, 224
Springfield Road, Belfast, 35, 108; police station, 36, 59, 60, 106
Stewartstown, 194
'Sticky' (OIRA), 215
Stormont Government (Northern Ireland Parliament), 5, 6, 10, 11, 16, 20, 21, 22, 23, 24, 27, 28, 36, 37, 41, 46, 54, 64, 77, 78, 95, 159, 160, 199, 201, 299; Faulkner becomes Prime Minister, 51; intelligence system, 51-2; internment, 58-9, 60-1; Derry march banned by (1972), 85-6; legal powers, 96, 97, 98; suspension of (1972), 102-3, 118; *see also* Direct Rule: Northern Ireland Executive
Stout, William, 53-4

Strabane, 6
Strand Road Traders' Association, 88
strikes, Protestant workers': UWC (1974), 144-54, 160, 182, 217; (1977): 217, 218
Sullivan, Jimmy, 29
Sunday Independent, 112
Sunday Times, 41, 79, 136
Sunningdale conference (1973), 143, 145, 200, 299
Sykes, Sir Richard, murder of, 246

Tactical Coordinating Group, 271
Tara, 128
tarring and feathering, 36, 68
Taylor, James, 228
Taylor, John, 54
Taylor, Peter, 173
Tennant Street police station, Belfast, 18-19, 218
Thaine, Private Ian, 283
Thames Television, 173
Thatcher, Margaret, 246; visit to Ulster, 251-9
Thiepval Barracks, Lisburn, 8, 160
Thompson, Brig W.F.K., 77-8
Thorne, Brig David, 251-2
Tickell, Brig Marston, COS, 65-6, 150-1
The Times, 5, 30, 32, 145, 174, 238
Todd, Lt-Col W.A.E., 3, 4
Tone, Wolfe, annual pilgrimage to grave in Bodenstown, 237, 261
Tugwell, Brig Maurice, 78-9, 172
Tuzo, Lt-Gen Sir Harry, GOC, 45-6, 50, 51, 54, 55, 56, 58, 62, 70, 96, 103, 113, 115; Sir Frank King takes over from, 132
27th Infantry Regiment, 187
Twomey, Seamus, 179-80

Ulster Defence Association (UDA), 108-10, 111, 126-7, 128, 144, 145, 151, 164, 177, 299
Ulster Defence Regiment (UDR), 28, 50, 142-3, 149, 178, 181, 186, 193, 217, 265, 271, 273-4, 281, 300
Ulster Freedom Fighters, 128
Ulster Loyalist Association, 27
Ulster Special Constabulary Association, 144
Ulster Volunteer Force (UVF), 32, 124, 125, 127, 144, 177, 181, 194, 219, 276, 300
Ulster Workers' Council (UWC), 188, 300; 1974 strike, 144-54, 160, 182, 200, 217
Ulsterisation policy, 184-5

unemployment, 70, 126
Unionists, 6, 30, 36, 37, 41, 50-1, 103, 143, 144, 246, 300; *see also* Northern Ireland Executive; Stormont
United States: support for IRA from, 203-4, 239; and embargo on arms sales to RUC; NORAID, 239, 274
Unity Flats, Belfast, 28
Upper Falls, 119

Vanguard (Ulster Vanguard), 99, 130, 144, 300
Vehicle Check Points (VCPs), 135
Victoria Barracks, 4
Victoria Police Station, 92
Vietnam War, 22, 26, 34

'wanted' lists ('Bingo Books'), 183
Warrenpoint, 194; murder of British soldiers at, 248-50, 251, 259
'The Way Ahead' *see* Bourne Report
West, Harry, 144
West German-Ireland Solidarity Campaign, 234-5
White, Dick, 66
Whitelaw, William, 102; as first Secretary of State for Northern Ireland, 103, 105; 106-7, 112, 130, 160, 261; truce with IRA, 107-8, 110; talks in London with IRA leaders, 110, 111; Operation Motorman, 112, 114, 115, 117

Widgery Report, 91-2, 93, 300
William Street, Derry, 89, 116
Williams, Betty, 198-9, 297
Wilson, Harold, 34, 151, 152, 188, 189
Wolseley, Harold, 15
women, 76, 123, 125-6, 139, 265
Woodvale area, Belfast, 108
Woodvale Defence Association, 101
Woolwich pub bombing, 175

YDHs (Young Derry Hooligans), 71-2, 85, 88, 89, 91
Yellow Cards, 49-50, 137, 140, 165, 166
Young, Sir Arthur, Chief Constable, 29-30, 36, 39, 45